ROBERT E. LEE AT WAR:

The Mind and Method of a Great American Soldier

MH PRESS

MILITARY HISTORY PRESS

of Virginia.

Gen. Robt E Lee. Com.^r in Ch.^f C.S.A.

ROBERT E. LEE AT WAR:
The Mind and Method of a Great American Soldier

VOLUME ONE:
TRAGIC SECESSIONIST

BY
SCOTT BOWDEN

SENIOR EDITOR
MATTHEW DeLaMATER

EDITOR
ELIZABETH HARWOOD

EDITORIAL CONSULTANT
DOUGLAS DeLaMATER

SPECIAL CONTRIBUTIONS BY
SCOTT FARRAR, JULIA PUTNAM, MATTHEW SCOTT BOWDEN, JAZEN REUSS, KAREN SPICER AND HILL COLLEGE RESEARCH CENTER, HILLSBORO, TEXAS

BOOK AND DUST JACKET DESIGN
SCOTT FARRAR

SERIES SENIOR GRAPHICS CONSULTANT
SCOTT FARRAR

TACTICAL BATTLE DIAGRAMS BY
ARNE LIMNER

PRINT MANAGEMENT & PRODUCTION BY
INNERWORKINGS
GRAND RAPIDS, MICHIGAN U.S.A.

DESIGN, LAYOUT & IMAGE EDITING BY
ELIZABETH HARWOOD

FIRST NORTH AMERICAN EDITION 2012
ISBN 978-0-9853572-2-1

MH PRESS
MILITARY HISTORY PRESS

TABLE OF CONTENTS

List of Maps..vii

List of Illustrations..viii

Acknowledgements xi

Publisher's Preface xi

Publishers Acknowledgements xii

***

Chapter One—*"Look Upon Things as They Are"*—
The Curse of The Lost Cause

Author's Introduction 1

The Cause and The Lost Cause 7

The Lost Cause Becomes the Cause Lost..11

Chapter Two—*"I Do Not Know What My Position Will Be"*—
A Great Talent and A Year Wasted

"The Very Best Soldier I've Ever Seen" 21
    Lee's Early Years 22
    Lee and The Mexican War 24
    Lee's Study of the Great Captains and West Point Years 26
    Lee Goes to Texas 30
    Lee Returns to Virginia, and the John Brown Raid...........................36
    Lee Returns to Texas 38
    Lee's Recall to Washington City 40
    Lee and Secession Crisis 42
    The Coming of War and Lee's Decision to Resign His Commission 44
The New Washington..54
Politicians, Fantasies and Lee 57
    First Manassas and Its Impact 61

Rank Without Command 64
    Lee, Joe Johnston and Harpers Ferry..71
No Authority—No Results..78
    Lee and the Developing Western Virginia Crisis.........................80
Lee in Northwestern Virginia—The Cheat and
Sewell Mountain Campaigns 85
    Lee and His Dealings With Loring, Floyd and Wise 87
    Lee Pieces Together an Offensive Plan.......................................91
    Orders for The Cheat Mountain Offensive...................................96
    Cheat Mountain 100
    Sewell Mountain..104
    Lee's Return to Richmond...108
"Another Forlorn Expedition"—Lee is Sent to South Carolina...................109
    Lee Arrives in Charleston 111
    Lee's Defensive Initiatives...112
    Lee Buys His Most Famous Horse, "Traveller"...........................115
Real War Begins...117
    Lee is Recalled to Richmond..119
Lee's Wasted Year—Summary and Analysis of His Use
and Performance, April 1861 to April 1862..121

Chapter Three—*"The Enemy is Pushing Us Back in All Directions"*—
The Confederacy on the Cusp of Disaster

    The Impending Doom Brought On By a Flawed Strategy 137
Formula for Disaster—Jefferson Davis and the
"Strategy of Defense by Dispersal"...139
    The Politics Involving Lee's Recall from the Southeastern Coast..............142
Another New Position, But Still No Authority—Lee's New Role.................146
    Lee as Advisor to President Davis...147
    Lee is Called Upon to Author a Conscription Bill 150
"Strategy of Defense by Dispersal, Combined With Retreat,
Brings Nation to the Brink" 152
    Lee, Johnston and the Shaping of the Peninsula Campaign.......153
    The Value of Richmond and Lee's Efforts to Save the City.......157
"A phenomenally mismanaged battle"—Johnston's Abortive Offensive
at Seven Pines and its Aftermath...167
    The Battle of Seven Pines...170
    The Wounding of Joe Johnston and Lee's Ascension to Command 172

Appendices

Appendix A—Lee's Military Timeline..176

Appendix B— Selected, Notable Military and Political Relatives
of Robert E. Lee 179

Appendix C—Order of Battle: Confederate Forces in Northwest
Virginia, Late Summer and Fall, 1862...181

Appendix D—Order of Battle: Confederate Forces on the Southeastern
Coast under command of General Robert E. Lee Late 1861-Early 1862 185

Appendix E—Further Comments on Robert E. Lee, the 2nd Cavalry,
Camp Cooper and the 40-Day ReconnaissanceThrough West Texas.................189

Appendix F—J. K. F. Mansfield's Inspection Report of Camp Cooper,
Texas, July 31st through August 3rd, 1856...195

Appendix G—1860 Population Distribution of the Eleven Future
Confederate States..199

LIST OF MAPS

Camp Cooper, Texas 31

Charleston Harbor................................43

The Southern States 57

Richmond................................65

Kanawah Valley 91

Position of Opposing Forces
at Cheat Mountain................................94

Lee's Plan of Operations
at Cheat Mountain................................99

Rust Advances...100

Donelson's Move 101

Area Where Colonel Washington
Met His Fate...103

Kanawha Valley 104

The Confederate Heartland.....................118

New Orleans Gulf Coast 118

Albemarle Sound and
New Berne Area 148

Virginia Peninsula from
Old Point Comfort to Williamsburg........155

Detailed Map of the City of Richmond....157

Winfield Scott's Legendary
"Anaconda Plan"......................................159

The Virginia Peninsula
Looking From East to West 160

Richmond Battleground............................168

Johnston's Plan—Seven Pines 173

Savannah, Georgia 184

Lee's Forty Day
Reconnaisance Expedition 188

Map of Texas, 1857..................................190

Cheat Mountain: Initial Positions 201

Rust Captures Wagon Train 202

Rust Skirmishes with Brooks...................202

Anderson Manouvers Across Turnpike....203

Higgins Approaches Anderson.................203

Higgins Skirmishes with 1 Tn;
Coons Returns..204

Kimball Attacks Rust................................204

Donelson Moves on Camp Elkwater 205

Coons and Higgins Attack Anderson.......205

Anderson in Trouble 206

Anderson Withdraws.................................206

Area in Which Colonel Washington
Met His Fate...207

LIST OF IMAGES AND ILLUSTRATIONS

Chapter One—

General Robert Edward Lee .... Front

Lee's Equestrian Statue, Virginia
Monument, Gettysburg .... Opposite 1

Old Haynie Memorial
Methodist Church, Rice, Texas 2

Winfield Scott 3

Karl von Clausewitz 4

General Robert Edward Lee 5

Spotswood Hotel, Richmond 6

Ruins of Charleston 7

John C. Calhoun 9

Various post-war emblems 10

The Lost Cause Memories 11

Jubal Early 12

William Nelson Pendleton 12

James Longstreet 13

1913 Reunion photo of the 8th Texas
Cavalry, "Terry's Texas Rangers" 16

Intruder in the Dust Book Image 18

George Pickett and
James Longstreet, July 3, 1863 19

Old Fort Phantom Hill, Texas 20

Chapter Two—

"Light Horse Harry" Lee 22

Mary Randolph Custis 22

Lee Family Genealogy Tree 23

Storming of Chapultepec Castle 24

Photograph of Chapultepec Castle 25

Scott's Entry Into Mexico City 25

Lee's Photograph in the early 1850s 26

Antoine Henri de Jomini 26

Napoleon in His Study 26

Napoleon Crosing the Alps 27

Equestrian Portrait of Napoleon I 27

Hannibal Barca 28

Gustavus Adolphus II of Sweden 28

Eramus D. Keyes 29

Jefferson Davis in 1852 30

Photograph of the the Clear Fork
of the Brazos at Camp Cooper, Texas 31

Comanches 32

Old Fort Phantom Hill, Texas 32

Fort Chadbourne 33

Photograph of the ruins of
Fort Chadbourne 33

Photograph of the Double Mountain
Fork of the Brazos River, north of
modern-day Rotan, Texas 34

Photograph of Double Mountain,
Stonewall County, Texas 34

Albert Sidney Johnston 36

Mary Custis Lee 36

Arlington House 36

John Brown 37

Engine House, Harpers Ferry 37

The Marines Storming the
Engine House at Harpers Ferry 37

John Brown Hanging 38

Comanche with scalp 39

San Antonio Military Plaza 39

The Bonnie Blue Flag 40

The Alamo 41

Photograph of modern-day Fort Mason 41

Winfield Scott 42

Charleston, South Carolina 43

Francis W. Pickens 44

Robert Toombs 44

Bombardment of Fort Sumter 45

View of Sumter from the
Charleston Rooftops 45

Horace Greeley 45

Blair House, Washington City 46

Francis Preston Blair, Sr 46

War Department Building,
Washington City 47

Virginia State Flag 48

View of Wartime Alexandria, Virginia 48

Newspaper Image of Robert E. Lee..........50

Marshall House Hotel in Alexandria 50

Christ Church in Alexandria 51

John Letcher 51

The Capitol at Richmond......................52

Washington Crossing the
Delaware River 54

Garnet Wolseley..................................54

George Washington Statue in Richmond ..55

View of Richmond...............................55

Manassas Junction 58

Fighting on Henry House Hill, Battle of
Manassas...58

Confederate Troops
Leaving for Manassas...........................59

Battle of Manassas................................60

Infantry Charge at Manassas 61

Newspaper Advertisement for
Lecture about Old Dominion.................62

"On to Richmond!".............................63

Capitol Square, Richmond.....................64

Chief Justice Roger B. Taney 66

1855 Harpers Ferry Rifled Musket..........67

Confederate Troops Swearing In 68

Volunteers for The Cause........................69

Joseph E. Johnston................................71

Photograph of the Confluence
of the Potomac and Shenandoah rivers.....72

Harpers Ferry Vista...............................73

US Armory, Harpers Ferry....................73

Confederate recruits..............................74

Robert Patterson 75

The Burning of the
Harpers Ferry Armory/Arsenal................76

Destroying one of the bridges
at Harpers Ferry.................................76

Richmond, Virginia..............................77

Pierre G. T. Beauregard 78

Jefferson Davis Equestrian Portrait 79

Robert S. Garnett.................................80

Battle of Rich Mountain 80

George B. McClellan.............................81

Death of General Robert S. Garnett..........81

Mounted image of General Beauregard....82

William Wing Loring..............................86

Western Virginia Infantry 87

Henry A. Wise.....................................88

Arkansas Emblem..................................88

John B. Floyd.......................................89

Armistead Lindsay Long 90

Federal Camp on Cheat Mountain...........92

3rd Arkansas Volunteer Infantry..............93

Albert Rust...93

Tennessee Flag.....................................96

William Rosecrans.................................108

Richmond, Virginia..............................108

Judah P. Benjamin.................................109

Charleston, South Carolina.....................110

Charleston and Savannah Railroad
through the Swamp..............................111

One of the flags of the
3rd Florida Volunteer Infantry................112

South Carolina State-issued currency
and $2 rail ticket 113

Images of Fort Pulaski 114

Lee on Traveller 115

Flag of the so-called "Dallas Artillery"
and a Confederate Envelope...................120

Jefferson Davis......................................121

Zachary Taylor 122

Winfield Scott 123

Battle of Buena Vista 125

Inauguration of Jefferson Davis
in Montgomery, Alabama.......................128

Chapter Three—

Capitol Building, Richmond...................136

Attack on Fort Henry.............................138

Great Seal of the Confederacy...............138

George Washington Statue
in Richmond 139

Fighting on Roanoke Island...................141

George Wythe Randolph.......................142

Images of Cotton and the
Impact of Jefferson Davis' Policies........143

Jefferson Davis' Letter Refusing to Sign
the Congressional Bill Creating the
"Office of Commanding General
of the Armies".......................................144

The Bill as Passed by the
Confederate Congress..................... 144-145

The Confederate War Department..........146

Walter Taylor 147

Ambrose E. Burnside..............................149

Charles Marshall....................................151

Cartoon About the
Confederate Conscription Act 151

Fortress Monroe at Old Point Comfort...153

C.S.S. Virginia......................................154

The Battle Between the *U.S.S. Monitor*
and the *C.S.S. Virginia* 154

Fortress Monroe.....................................156

New Orleans Battle.................................156

Richmond Armory 158

Rockett's Wharf at Richmond 158

Abandoning of Norfolk 159

Jefferson Davis 161

Washington City 1861 162

View of the *U.S.S. Monitor* after its
battle with the *C.S.S. Virginia*.................163

Drewry's Bluff images............................164

Refugees 165

Bridge over the Chickahominy River.....166

George B. McClellan 166

Farm near the Chickahominy River........167

Image of the area near Fair Oaks............169

The Fighting at Seven Pines 170

Behind the Federal lines, the fighting
at Seven Pines near Fair Oaks 171

Joseph E. Johnston.................................172

Appendices—

Lee Family Genealogy Tree 178

Henry "Light Horse Harry" Lee 176

Lee's boyhood home in Alexandria........176

Marquis de Lafayette 176

Mary Randolph Custis 176

Winfield Scott 176

Confederate First National Flag 177

Jefferson Davis 177

Lee in 1861 177

Lee in 1865 177

Fort Pulaski..184

Grounds of Camp Cooper.......................191

Building at Camp Cooper 191

Camp Cooper Historical Marker 191

Post Returns from May, 1856......... 196-197

Camp Cooper Grounds 196

Robert E. Lee's "Conquer or Die"
Pincushion 208

AUTHOR'S ACKNOWLEDGMENTS

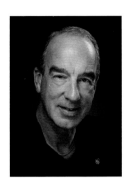

This project could have not been undertaken without the generous and kind assistance of many. I am greatly indebted to the staff of the Harold B. Simpson History Complex at Hill College, Hillsboro, Texas, and especially to Anita Tufts, who helped locate many documents for this project. In Washington, D. C., my thanks go to the helpful staff members who assisted at the Library of Congress and National Archives. I am deeply appreciative of the generosity and time extended by Julia Putnam of Albany, Texas, owner of the site of Camp Cooper that was described by Robert E. Lee as "my Texas home." My sincere thanks to Scott Farrar for his generosity, vision and expertise that was instrumental in developing "the look" for *Robert E. Lee at War*. I also appreciate the original maps prepared by Arne Limner. Special thanks go to my editors and to Matthew DeLaMater for reading and re-reading the manuscript many times, and for Matt's unswerving belief in this massive, eight-volume project.

Scott Bowden
Arlington, Texas

PUBLISHER'S PREFACE

When initially evaluating a project of this scope, both as an avid Civil War buff as well as a cautious publisher, one pressing question had to be answered: What new could be said about Robert E. Lee, some 150 years later, that justified an undertaking of this magnitude? No simple recapitulation of earlier work, such as Douglas Southall Freeman's classic biography, or a dry rehashing of Lee's battles, could truly merit the time and resources necessary to execute this project. I felt it incumbent that the author, Scott Bowden, had to prove a strong case that this sesquicentennial history represented a remarkable contribution to our understanding of Lee as a man and as a general. This standard, it seemed, given the quantity of work out there, seemed like a particularly stringent one to meet.

Thus, to my mind, *Robert E. Lee at War* would need to weave original analysis and new interpretation, for if many of the core facts had not been changed, the fresh contextualization would need to be persuasive and humanizing to a man often seen as an icon. Furthermore, the series had to be ambitious in scope, and strive to be a definitive work, and not merely timely, revisionist or controversial. As I waded further and further into the narrative, with all this in mind, I came away quite astonished. How was it possible that so many legions of writers had failed to ask so many of the questions I was now confronting in the text? How had so much been missed or avoided by noted Civil War scholars? I will leave it to the reader to answer these questions for themselves as they delve into the heart of this narrative, except to say that with each revelation, I became more determined that this series should come to light as a worthy piece of Civil War and Robert E. Lee scholarship.

Thumbing through these books, the reader may be struck by the large quantity of visual images and maps throughout the text. This is, more or less, what Military History Press has come to stand for as it grows. All too often, it seems, the economics of conventional publishing produce two kinds of books on the Civil War: one, the "pretty picture" books in which the written content is secondary to the photographs and layout, and two, the text heavy works which are maddeningly short on maps and additional contextual material. At MHP, we simply insist that our readers should have the best of both worlds; high quality text and beautiful, lavish illustration should not be mutually exclusive, but the standard for this day and age.

Publisher's Note:

We chose the more old-school footnoting style—that of having the information available at the bottom of the page—to facilitate the reading process. Personally, we don't enjoy thumbing back and forth, and certain new styles of footnoting are simply inhospitable to fellow scholars.

Also, given the length of the work, each book will not receive an index, but rather a multi-volume index will be produced in the future.

PUBLISHER'S ACKNOWLEDGMENTS

The publisher wishes to thank Robert Spicer, Dustin Traynor, Tricia DeLaMater, and our Long Lake NY support, including Alex Roalsvig and Cindy Black in the town office, Emily Farr and Pat Blodgett for their help at the library, and Justin and Jarod Quackenbush and the Longview Lodge staff for "logistical" contributions.

VOLUME ONE:
TRAGIC SECESSIONIST

VOLUME TWO:
HOPE ARISES FROM DESPAIR

VOLUME THREE:
ASCENDING STAR

VOLUME FOUR:
DECISION IN THE BALANCE

VOLUME FIVE:
MARS

VOLUME SIX:
PURSUIT OF VICTORY

VOLUME SEVEN:
VANISHING DREAMS

VOLUME EIGHT:
COLOSSUS

Volume One:

Tragic Secessionist

CHAPTER ONE

"Look Upon Things As They Are"— The Curse of The Lost Cause

"Live in the world you inhabit. Look upon things as they are. Take them as you find them. Make the best of them. Turn them to your advantage."
—Robert E. Lee[1]

Author's Introduction

When the disparate seeds of this project were firmly planted, I can only broadly construe. Growing up in 1950s and 1960s Texas placed me at a fascinating vantage point in time—the Old South had not yet completely disappeared, and the New South had not yet fully arisen. The rapid pace of change and progress that my generation of white Southerners experienced left me with an attendant hunger to sort through and preserve a complex view of a past being all too rapidly simplified and redefined. For it is in the paradoxes of any culture that historical truth necessarily contends, ultimately defying easy narratives and cherished myths. This seems especially apt for American history in general, and Southern history in particular, for many Americans in our present debates echo past contentions that do no service by substituting simplification for that which is inherently complex. As Edward L. Ayers, a leading present-day historian of the South, stated succinctly: "Simple explanations that ignore complication in an impatient determination to get to a bottom line or root cause are worse than useless."[2]

My own personal narrative, as it pertains to this project, sorts out in memory thematically, and comes back in juxtaposition. I remember, for example, lying in bed as a boy, suffering from rheumatic fever, as my family patiently read stories to me from the *We Were There* and *The Story of* collections. These introductory tales of famous Americans and history's dramatic moments, forever launched my historical imagination. Only as I write this does another realization draw upon me: that my determination to place the narrative as near to the moment of historical decision almost certainly owes a small debt to the thrilling form of these books. Then too I recall my first "job," working in the black soil of Navarro County, Texas, close by the cooling, long afternoon shadows of the old Haynie Memorial Methodist Church, picking cotton by hand alongside sharecroppers. Sun-scorched, sweaty and exhausted, I could not imagine the fortitude necessary to confront a lifetime of such labor; this my grandfather had done. Certainly I came away with a strong taste of the incalculable sweat-labor involved in what was for a long time the South's dominant cash crop. Perhaps this limited exposure enhanced my appreciation for the benefits and opportunities of an education that featured some outstanding elementary and secondary school teachers. Later, in college, my frequent discussions with one of my professors at Texas Christian University still resonate, particularly what

---

[1] Robert E. Lee to his son, George Washington Custis Lee, while Custis was in his second year at West Point. Quoted in Emory Thomas, *Robert E. Lee: An Album* (New York, 2000), p. 47.
[2] Edward L. Ayers, *What Caused the Civil War? Reflections on the South and Southern History* (New York, 2005), p. 135.

he said about "remarkable claims" made by certain historians; I will never forget how he often reminded me that "remarkable claims demand remarkable evidence."

No doubt my numerous battlefield excursions during those school years set in motion questions about the intense forces impacting the moment and context of any decision. I tried to find where exactly certain generals stood, or where regiments and brigades once held firm or wavered, and, having reached the spot—amidst an ineffable sensation of historical awe—I would wonder what exactly could be seen through the smoke and din at an appointed hour so long ago. My thirst increased for more knowledge about specific command decisions on these battlefields, and soon there I was, checking and rechecking books out of local college and public libraries, my questions only increasing.

Author's collection

The Old Haynie Memorial Methodist Church, Rice, Texas.

Certainly there was much more to my fascination. In competing in sports at a high level—an experience my early health troubles would seem to have precluded—I was fortunate to gain some invaluable insight into dynamics of decision-making under stress. My college basketball coach—the fairest-minded man I ever knew—repeatedly emphasized that building character was of incalculable value. He also reminded me of Hemingway's great line about courage defined as "grace under pressure." In evaluating Robert E. Lee and his contemporaries, I confess that I have often held these examples and standards in mind.

And yet, all in all, perhaps more than any other influence, it was my remarkable great-grandmother, who, having lived more than a century, would spend numerous hours answering questions from an inquisitive teenager about life in the South. From the front room rocking chair in her white frame house that fronted the Shiner Highway on the east edge of Gonzales, Texas, she told stories spanning the time from Reconstruction to the late 1960s. In her Texas drawl, she made the past and present connect with an unforgettable immediacy. This indelible experience no doubt propelled me toward a quest to understand a richer history of a land and time that now only exists with the tales of my forefathers.[3]

* * *

Regardless of many seeds nurtured through my youth and young adult days, undertaking a new appraisal of Robert Edward Lee seemed unimaginable back then. Yet, undeniably, by my late 20s, the idea of pursuing this present project began to surface. Whenever a chance arose, I seized the opportunity—compulsively I must admit—to retrace the Virginian's steps, whether it was at Chapultepec Castle during the Mexican War (where I had first visited as a

---

[3] Some of the titles read to me from the Grosset & Dunlap Publishers *We Were There* series were: Felix Sutton, *We Were There at the Battle of Lexington and Concord* (New York, 1958); Earl Schenck Miers, *We Were There When Washington Won at Yorktown* (New York, 1958); Margaret Cousins, *We Were There at The Battle of the Alamo* (New York, 1958); and William O. Steele, *We Were There With The Pony Express* (New York, 1956). Some of the titles in the Grosset & Dunlap *The Story of* series with which I became acquainted were: Enid LaMonte Meadowcroft, *The Story of George Washington* (New York, 1952); William O. Steele, *The Story of Daniel Boone* (New York, 1953); Winthrop Neilson, *The Story of Theodore Roosevelt* (New York, 1953); Enid LaMonte Meadowcroft, *The Story of Crazy Horse* (New York, 1954); Margaet Leighton, *The Story of General Custer* (New York, 1954); Lorena A. Hickok, *The Story of Franklin D. Roosevelt* (New York, 1956); and Jim Kjelgaard, *The Story of Geronimo* (New York, 1958).

Courtesy Library of Congress

teenager), or more recently on the plains of Texas where he led the famed 2nd U. S. Cavalry in the late 1850s and in 1860. Naturally, the sites of our nation's most terrible war beckoned, and I went from the southern coasts of South Carolina and Georgia, to the fields of Virginia, Maryland and Pennsylvania. After two decades of intently studying and analyzing Robert E. Lee, I still found many questions to be answered. Even while undertaking and finishing works in the Napoleonic field, my mind was often on Lee. I noted with keen interest how he was being portrayed by the late 20th century historians. The crop of revisionist works seemed largely off-base, and devoid of any requisite military realism. Finally, my questioning process seemed to demand a resolution. Therefore, after finishing *Last Chance for Victory: Robert E. Lee and the Gettysburg Campaign*, followed by completing more Napoleonic titles, I took up this project. I wanted to present, as best I could, the facts and pressures confronting Lee in his most daunting hours.

A diligent student of the military arts, Lee built a strong foundation for his command decisions by pursuing a rigorous course of self-study involving history's Great Captains—generals such as Alexander the Great, Hannibal, Caesar, Gustavus Adolphus II, Frederick the Great and Napoleon. In this regard, I have become convinced that much can be gained by readings on the Great Captains (and their wars), particularly in the books Lee himself read. In fact I see it as essential archway leading into Lee's military thinking. Perhaps this reflects bias on my part, and it certainly strikes against the practices of many, if not most, who write about the "American Iliad." Typically, the best recent works contain lengthy blow-by-blow accounts of the war and its battles, and, in Homeric fashion, depict the heroism and sacrifice of numerous colonels, captains, regiments and common soldiers with impressive depths of scholarship, and numerous excerpts of gripping first-hand accounts. Yet, none delineate the staggering impact of Napoleon Bonaparte and the Napoleonic era, particularly as to its profound advances in such things as organization, command staff, logistics, tactics, grand tactics, operational theory, and training. If nothing else, I modestly hope that this study can help to raise awareness of what I see as a large void in our perspective on the war.

Among Lee's other historical influences, Frederick the Great, known for the words *"toujours l'audace,"* probably ranked foremost, followed by Alexander the Great, Hannibal, Julius Caesar, and, to a lesser extent, the Swedish warrior King Gustavus Adolphus II. Much closer to home, George Washington—the great grandfather-in-law to Lee—stood as much more than a military hero and father of the country; he represented the salient role model upon which Robert E. Lee formed himself. Few studied Washington's generalship with a keener interest.

As a historian, this matter of extolling influences presents a certain methodological problem. On one hand, it is impossible to document—to state with exactitude—the direct impact of a particular historical campaign battle or famous general upon a given moment in Lee's mind. However, the historical blueprints of the campaigns and battles fought by the generals who Lee had studied in-depth are undeniably present in the Confederate general's own science of war. And while there is no documentary evidence that Lee recalled Napoleon's *en échelon* attack at Austerlitz as he ordered forward Longstreet's attack at Second Manassas—the largest coordinated infantry assault ever witnessed on the North American continent— or remembered George Washington's daring flank march at Princeton as he planned the much-larger scale, audacious maneuver at Chancellorsville, or that he invoked Hannibal's legendary defense of Carthage as Lee strove to transfer the defense of Richmond to enemy soil. However, failing to draw the parallels of Lee's actions and those of the past generals he knew so very well would be a failure of omission, and would obscure rather than illuminate Lee's mind and method of war. Within these pages, I have drawn upon Lee's favorite readings, combined with his orders and his own actions, to offer up a fresh analysis of his generalship. Additionally, I have tried to explain how the chaotic nature of command and control during the 19th century period of warfare—which the great military theoretician Karl von Clausewitz described as fraught with "friction"—represented a unique environment to operate in, one which modern readers may not fully appreciate.

Courtesy Library of Congress

Karl von Clausewitz

Clausewitz's fame is largely due to the importance and influence of his magnum opus, *On War*, arguably the most important single work ever written on the theory of warfare and of strategy.

Conveying the subtleties of Southern culture and language presents a challenge to a historian, even to one who has the benefit of an intimate familiarity with the region. Perhaps such issues are generally best handled in literature, and left to writers like William Faulkner and Robert Penn Warren, but, in this matter of understanding Robert E. Lee, his soldier's mind and method, I have attempted to explain his point of view and the nuances of Southern interactions as best I can. Hopefully, readers will come to trust my interjections on Southern language and culture as a basis to understand Lee's interactions with others, and to context further his style of communication. In brief, Southern language of the period was usually polite and deferential. What was *understood* as part of the aristocratic culture of antebellum America—certain linguistic rituals— can appear to modern readers as something ambiguous. However, I hope to show it was nothing of the sort. Always keenly aware of the prickly nature of a Southern man's pride, Lee's courtesy and respect found expression within the context of his time and his patrician manners.

* * *

Lastly, no matter many times I may be on the ground over which Lee moved, no matter how many times I stand on Reel Ridge or Cemetery Hill at Sharpsburg, or on Seminary Ridge or other points at Gettysburg, or do the same on other fields that once blazed with a fire, there is, for me, one scene of Robert E. Lee that returns to my thoughts.

It was Monday, April 22, 1861. Three days earlier, Lee had learned that Virginia delegates had voted to withdraw Old Dominion from the Union. Fifteen hours after he heard that news, Lee tenured his resignation from the army he had loved so much and in whose uniform he had given more than three decades of honorable and distinguished service. Once word got back to Richmond that the antebellum army's leading soldier had resigned his commission, Virginia Governor John Letcher sent an invitation to Lee to come to the Confederate capital. Lee surmised what the invitation meant: he was about to be offered command of Virginia's military forces. Leaving his Arlington home for what was to be the last time, Lee rode into Alexandria under a sunny sky. Boarding his railroad car, the temperatures warmed into the mid-80s as Lee's train carried him to Gordonsville, then to Hanover Junction,

General Robert Edward Lee

This oil on canvas by Benjamin Franklin Reinhardt (1829-1885), was painted in 1861 and published in Paris in 1862. It is perhaps the best early-war image of Lee.

and finally towards Richmond. At stops along the way, vocal crowds of Virginians jammed the rail platforms, calling for a glimpse of the famous son of "Light Horse Harry" who they now looked upon as the heir to the revolutionary mantle once borne by George Washington. At Orange and again at Louisa, Lee yielded to the masses and stepped to the rear of the car to bow to the cheering crowds.

The face of Robert E. Lee that greeted the assembled citizens of the Commonwealth was not the "face" most commonly associated with him. That look comes from the mid-to-late war and post-conflict photographs of Matthew Brady, Julian Vannerson and Minnis & Cowell. These photographs do not come close to capturing the vitality of the man who stood at the back railing of that train, rather they testify to the extraordinary toll the war would take upon this soldier. The 54 year-old Robert E. Lee that rode the rails to Richmond that unseasonably warm April afternoon had a full head of black hair with a small sprinkle of gray; his face was clean shaven except for a short mustache that was entirely black; his brown eyes, healthy complexion, and athletic physique prompted Theodore Stanford Garnett, Jr., who was traveling with him into Richmond, to recall that Lee "was handsome beyond all the men I had ever seen." After all, Lee had long been considered the most striking man in the army. But far more importantly, he was quietly self-assured, possessing unfailing tact and without the slightest pretense of conceit, a man apparently born to lead and who unmistakably looked the part. Recalling the combination of looks, along with his personae and power of the Confederate chieftain, Erasmus Keyes—who served with Lee before the war and against Lee during the war—succinctly stated: "No man could stand in his presence and not recognize his capacity and acknowledge his moral force."[4]

As the train continued south, Lee sat quietly, looking out the window at the passing countryside, undoubtedly weighing in his mind the forthcoming consequences of a divided nation gone mad and his place in the unfolding drama. Against the ominous din of the country's greater disunion, and in stark contrast to the euphoric roars of the crowds that met him along the way, Garnett noticed how Lee's "countenance was serious and clouded with somber." Indeed, Lee knew that if war came to pass, it would be long and the cost immense. Events had consigned him to a tragic role, and Lee had been forced to make a choice of potentially sacrificing *everything*, except, as he said, "save that of honour."[5]

The train that arrived in Richmond that afternoon was nothing less than

[4] *Southern Historical Society Papers,* 52 volumes (Richmond, 1876-1957), "Glowing Tribute to General R. E. Lee," by Theodore Stanford Garnett, Jr., vol. 28, pp. 108-109; Erasmus D. Keyes, *Fifty Years' Observation of Men and Events, Civil and Military* (New York, 1884), please see assessments of Robert E. Lee on pp. 166, 204 and 205.

[5] *Southern Historical Society Papers,* "Glowing Tribute to General R. E. Lee," by Theodore Stanford Garnett, Jr., vol. 28, p. 109; Robert E. Lee, *To Markie: The Letters of Robert E. Lee to Martha Custis Williams,* edited by Avery O. Craven (Cambridge, 1933), letter of January 22, 1861, pp. 58-59.

an engine of fate, and Lee arrived proud but solemn amidst the jubilation. Stepping down at the Virginia Central depot at 17th and Broad streets, Lee took a carriage to the new and elegant Spotswood Hotel. After taking a room and eating an early supper, he hurriedly left the hotel. Walking through the noisy streets, past the equestrian statue of George Washington in Capitol Square on his way to see Governor Letcher, Lee heard in the distance the catchy air of a minstrel song named "Dixie" as well as the French Revolutionary "La Marseillaise." The lively music was carried on a breeze that stirred countless new flags, many of them the single-starred "Bonnie Blue Flag" that flew from windows and porches of numerous houses and buildings. Without calling attention to himself, Lee did not go in the front entrance, but instead slipped through a side door into the Capitol and climbed the stairs to the office once occupied by his father to confer with Governor Letcher.

After the meeting Lee returned to the Spotswood. No one recorded how Lee slept that night, but I imagine that it must have been fitful. For Lee's journey undertaken that day had barely begun. Four more Aprils remained unfurled. The blood to be shed still coursed in burning young hearts, and as Richmond glittered with a sweet gallant light, no one is remembered to have given voice to terrible premonitions of blazing fires and a dark capital city of ruins.

—*Scott Bowden*

The "new and elegant" Spotswood Hotel
Richmond, Virginia

Courtesy Library of Congress

Ruins seen from the Circular Church,
Charleston, South Carolina, 1865

The Cause and The Lost Cause

By the end of April, 1865, four grueling years of war had just ended. More than 665,000 soldiers, Americans all, lay dead from military operations; civilian losses stood at over 50,000, overwhelmingly in the South. Well over a million wounded and maimed had made the long trek homeward; thousands would succumb to the long-term effects of wounds, their lives cut short, their livelihoods diminished. Many ex-soldiers found the war's demons could not be shed. Some sought solace in the church, others in the barrooms, others "lit out for the territories" and headed west while still others decided to leave the blood-soaked continent altogether and sought to make a new start on foreign shores. No system of psychology had yet been developed to contend with the widespread affliction of trauma and grief. No sociology existed to measure the general effects of the bleak aftermath of war. No poet's art could express the staggering magnitude of the people's collective mourning. Victorian America stood upon the brink of Modernity shattered and united only in name, its institutions and beliefs shaken.

Naturally, the subjugated South fared the worst. Every third Southern household saw one of its members dead; the vast number of widows and orphans was uncounted. The South, invaded by Federal armies, lay in utter ruins. A $2 billion investment in land had been destroyed and millions of dollars of crops confiscated. Returning home, former Confederate soldiers could see virtually nothing other than the cruel trail of total war; chimneys stood without houses, rubble lay strewn where mills had been smashed and factories wrecked, charred timbers and stone foundations remained of sturdier structures. Barren farm fields and fenceless pastures—robbed of livestock, devoid of seed—yielded a canvas of wanton destruction. A destitute Southern population on the brink of starvation gave further agony to the conflict's devastating impact. From this land of destitution, something would need to take hold—some salve, some remedy—and in the ashes of the former Confederate States arose what would become labeled as The Lost Cause.[6]

Indeed, the South had been cast back in time, into subsistence living, into a violent, primitive, individualist and provincial life where a culture of poverty was now the norm. Under these trying circumstances, where almost everything, save dignity, had been stripped from them, most Southerners remained proud. Edward A. Pollard, the prolific Southern journalist, knew well the makeup and suffering of the former compatriots who had fought for "The Cause" for Southern independence, and he wasted little time in coining the phrase "The Lost Cause" in his 1866 book of the same name. Pollard, who had been an acting editor of *The Richmond Examiner* during part of the war, had several published works before, during and soon after the conflict. He had achieved notoriety before the war by publishing a sentimental portrayal of slavery as a largely benevolent institution, of which excerpts published in the North inflamed Abolitionist anger. However, his most famous work, *The Lost Cause*, would come out during the initial stages of Federal occupation, and its pages provide an immediate contemporary view into the soul of the post-war South. Pollard's 750 page history of the political conflict and subsequent War for Southern Independence found a receptive audience in the grieving and increasingly embittered former Confederacy. In its pages, Pollard provided for his readers a partisan history of their region. In presenting a Constitutional Jeffersonian argument in a way that could be understood, preserved and passed on to the younger generation, Pollard wished to emphasize that the sacrifices borne by Southerners during the war were legitimate and noble.

Pollard's book gained wide popularity, even though the work's animus against Jefferson Davis embroiled him in controversy with some. And while Pollard's grasp of the Federal principle and contract government missed the point of how it could be interpreted by those not favorably inclined towards the Jeffersonian view of democracy, his portrait of the state of the Union in his time must still be considered as essential reading for anyone wanting to understand the conventional wisdom in the South. Further, Pollard's work helped inspire many Southerners to labor vigorously to preserve many facts about the circumstances under which the Federal Union had been brought into existence, how the issue of secession was always believed to be legal

"There is but one conclusion that remains for the dispassionate student of history. Whatever may be the partial explanations of the downfall of the Southern Confederacy, and whatever may be the various excuses that passion and false pride, and flattery of demagogues, may offer, the great and melancholy fact remains that the Confederates, with an abler Government and more resolute spirit, might have accomplished their independence."

Edward A. Pollard
The Lost Cause

---

[6] *Encyclopedia of the Confederacy*, Richard N. Current, editor in chief, 4 volumes (New York, 1993), vol. 1, p. 127; according to contributor Donald S. Frazier, the staggering losses translated into nearly 30 percent of all Federal troops becoming casualties, while 48 percent of the Confederates who answered the call to serve were killed or wounded. James B. McPherson, *Battle Cry of Freedom* (New York, 1988), p. 619, footnote 53, estimates that Confederate non-military casualties alone amounted to 50,000.

Many Southerners' mid-19th century view of the Union is to a significant degree embodied within the Fort Hill address made by John C. Calhoun.

"The great and leading principle is, that the General Government emanated from the people of the several States, forming distance political communities, and acting in their separate and sovereign capacity, and not from all of the people forming one aggregate political community; that the Constitution of the United States is, in fact, a compact, to which each State is a party, in the character already described; and that the several States, or parties, have a right to judge of its infractions; and in case of a deliberate, palpable, and dangerous exercise of power not delegated, they have the right, in the last resort, to use [James Madison's] language of the Virginia Resolutions, "to interpose for arresting the progress of the evil, and for maintaining, within their respective limits, the authorities, rights, and liberties appertaining to them.

"This right of interposition, thus solemnly asserted by the State of Virginia, be it called what it may—State-right, veto, nullification, or by any other name—I conceive to be the fundamental principle of our system, resting on facts historically as certain as our revolution itself, and deductions as simple and demonstrative as that of any political or moral truth whatsoever; and I firmly believe that on its recognition depend the stability and safety of our political institutions...."

John C. Calhoun, Fort Hill, July 26, 1831

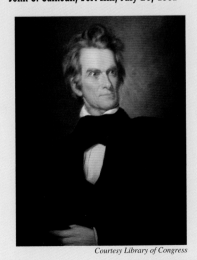

Courtesy Library of Congress

as noted during several state Constitutional ratification conventions,[7] and how the sacrifices born by Southerners during the war had to be kept fresh in the hearts and minds of their youth. *This is why,* that to the men and women of the defeated Confederacy, the conflict they knew as the War for Southern Independence was seen as a just struggle for sovereignty that was within their legal rights as citizens of their respective states, as well as a continuance of the legacy of their Anglo-Saxon ancestors. As such, The Cause for independence—which became The Lost Cause after the war— assumed a sacredness of the heart by those who had lived the experience.[8]

But The Lost Cause fed from better, deeper and more powerful wellsprings, including from Robert E. Lee himself, a man unsympathetic to the firebrands of Pollard's ilk. Once Lee offered his sword in defense of Virginia and family, however, he fully embraced his duty as a revolutionary. When the war had ended, Lee viewed The Lost Cause as a vehicle for preserving a true record of the sacrifices of his men, and as a means to articulate for posterity the difficulties under which his army labored. "I am desirous that the bravery and devotion of the Army of Northern Virginia be correctly transmitted to posterity," Robert E. Lee wrote to a great many of his former general officers soon following the war. "This is the only tribute that can now be paid to the worth of its noble officers and soldiers..." In a subsequent letter penned on March 16, 1866, to Jubal Anderson Early, Lee opined: "It will be difficult to get the world to understand the odds against which we fought."[9]

As the assembling of records and memoirs commenced, memorial organizations throughout the South began forming in the late 1860s. Initially, the most prominent Southern organizations comprised of veterans of the two great Confederate armies—the Association of the Army of Northern Virginia and the Association of the Army of Tennessee. Other organizations of the state and local variety included other veterans who had served the Confederacy in various military organizations. Confederate Memorial Day was established (the observance of which varied by state) and the many memorial organizations were very active in dedicating monuments—both funeral and battlefield— to those who had worn the gray. "Lest ye forget," appeared on countless monuments, and was a popular epithet. Stories of Confederate arms inspired and entertained distinctive regional rituals that included Sunday dinners on the church grounds, political campaign barbecues celebrating the Democratic party, and at spiritual camp meetings spurred by the war and post-war religious revivals. In this manner, the South's remaining traditional institutions sanctified Lost Cause venerations and helped restore regional pride in a public manner.

Throughout the harshness and exploitation that marked Reconstruction, more Southerners responded to the call of The Lost Cause, and additional

---

[7] Please see "Form of ratification, which was read and agreed to by the Convention of Virginia," *The Debate on the Constitution* 2 volumes (New York, 1993), vol. 2, p. 557; and "Ratification of the Constitution by the Convention of the State of New York" *The Debate on the Constitution,* vol. 2, p. 536. Also, the delegates from Rhode Island wrote: "That Congress shall guarantee to each State, its *Sovereignty* (emphasis in original), freedom, and independence, and every power, jurisdiction, and right, which is not by the Constitution expressly delegated to the United States."

[8] Edward A. Pollard, *The Lost Cause* (New York, 1988 facsimile of the Original 1866 edition). Pollard's 1858 work, *Black Diamonds Gathered in the Darkey Homes of the South*, was meant to be a satirical slap at the abolitionist Horace Greeley. Within its pages, Pollard had hoped to counter *Uncle Tom's Cabin* with pro-slavery anecdotes and homilies; however, events soon swept any attention away, and Pollard went on to cover the unfolding war as a newspaperman. At one point, he was captured at sea and spent time in a Federal prison.

[9] *Recollections and Letters [of Robert E. Lee],* edited and annotated by Robert E. Lee, Jr. (New York, 1904), pp. 194 and 196.

associations emerged. While the Lee Memorial Association (1870), Confederate Survivors' Association (1878) and the United Confederate Veterans (1889) limited memberships to veterans, more popular inclusivity would ensure a longer posterity. Family members followed in the steps of the veterans and got involved as well. Because the war had left so many widows and orphans, and because those of the war generation were growing increasingly elderly, the United Daughters of the Confederacy formed in 1895 and included any female relatives of men who had served. These ladies were and continue to be a powerful organization. "Generations of white Southern women," wrote notable social historian David Blight, "were to be the caretakers of The Lost Cause tradition." The Sons of Confederate Veterans organized shortly thereafter. Throughout the South, these groups kept The Lost Cause flourishing throughout the 20th century and into the 21st century. Hence, The Lost Cause—the veneration of those who had served the Confederacy in its attempt to gain independence—has been kept alive by Southerners who first lived the events and subsequently by their heirs. In so doing, Southerners achieved in defeat a unity of the heart and mind that they never fully realized during the war.[10]

* * *

Interestingly, a powerful catalyst for Lost Cause commemoration came from Northern interests that recognized in Southern sentiments significant commercial opportunity. Eager to capitalize on a reopening marketplace, Northern publishers realized profits in a region where the native print industry had virtually perished during the war. Engraving and lithographs of the Confederacy's leaders, and famous Southern military incidents poured forth from publishing houses all over the North. One such example is New Yorker Frederick Halpin's famous 1872 engraving of *The Last Meeting of Lee and Jackson,* which "won far greater acclaim and acceptance" than the 1869 "original E. B. D. Julio painting on which it was based."[11] The popularity of this image and other pieces became standard home art all over the South; innumerable homes had walls adorned with portraits of Lee, "Stonewall" Jackson and Jefferson Davis.

This confluence of mostly Northern publishing interests with the great popularity of Lost Cause subjects poses an interesting twist on the meaning of the cliché that history is written by the victors. In this case, certain Northern interests helped promulgate The Lost Cause message, and certainly this would not have happened if it was deemed subversive rather than, in a sense, a useful palliative for the South while at the same time promoting a conciliatory and unifying nation.

By the turn of the century, much of what The Lost Cause venerated had indeed been embraced by the North as well. In this, Robert E. Lee became a shared icon, embodying virtues of honor and military genius, rather than a divisive figure. President Theodore Roosevelt reflected this perception when he wrote that Robert E. Lee was "without any exception the very greatest of all the great captains that the English-speaking peoples have brought forth." Indeed, by the early 1900s, the stature of Robert E. Lee had grown from a regional icon to national hero.[12]

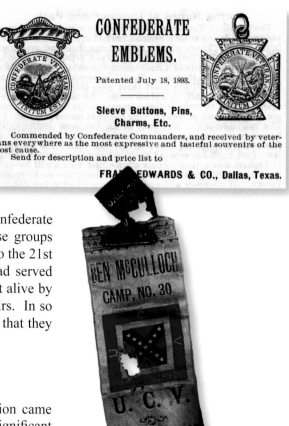

Top: an advertisement for Confederate Veteran medals. Above: reunion ribbon worn by a Texas Confederate veteran for various events. Below: United Daughters of the Confederacy logo.

---

[10] David W. Blight, *Race and Reunion: The Civil War in American Memory* (New York, 2002), p. 256.

[11] *Encyclopedia of the Confederacy*, vol. 3, p. 951.

[12] Clint Johnson, *The Politically Incorrect Guide to the South* (Washington, 2006), p. 139.

The Lost Cause was memorialized in song, prose and poetry. Well past the half way point of the 20th century, Sunday afternoon socials, Memorial Day gatherings and heritage organizations throughout the South would honor those who had been part of the conflict more than one hundred years earlier with recitations from popular poems, such as "The Stainless Banner."

Courtesy Library of Congress

The Lost Cause Becomes The Cause Lost

While the nation was making progress to heal the deep wounds caused by the war, other forces were at work creating the conditions by which the message of The Lost Cause would be called into question. One such force was the organization that evolved into arguably the most influential group of ex-Confederates— the Southern Historical Society, a group founded in New Orleans in 1869. Although the society never boasted large numbers, it included some of the most respected former Confederate officers and government officials. After the passing of Lee, the society relocated to Richmond in the 1870s under the leadership of Jubal Anderson Early. One of the more notable of former Confederate general officers, Jubal Early left a great impact through the *Southern History Society Papers*. The *Papers* preserved after-action reports (the *Official Records* as authorized by Congress did not begin publication until the 1880s), reminiscences, and other important historical material about the Confederacy. Equally important, the *Papers* were central in developing interpretations about battles and other events that still have a great impact on the historiography of the Civil War.

In his tireless enthusiasm to honor his fellow Confederate soldiers and The Cause for which they fought, and in his inexhaustible admiration for General Lee and the army in which he served, Jubal Early did much more. With unintentional irony, he created the conditions by which The Lost Cause message of the society as well as other advocates who promoted the accurate meaning and circumstances of The Lost Cause would become tainted. How did this happen?

Lee could not have foreseen that his words to have proper tribute to his former officers and soldiers would have the effect they did on one who was, at one point, one of his most trusted subordinates. In some ways, Jubal Early was a kindred spirit with his army commander, as he also opposed secession but took up the sword to defend his native state and fight for The Cause of Southern independence. Like Lee, Early also understood the soldiers he led. Like Lee, Early shared the men's long and arduous hardships. These are some of the reasons why, after the war, artillerist Edward Porter Alexander remembered Early as "a remarkable corps commander," who in 1864, "fought against all odds & discouragements."[13]

To be sure, Jubal Early differed significantly from Lee. While Lee was intellectual, polished and gracious, Early was crude, irascible and combative. Lee never wavered from his desire to always strike hard at the Federals whenever an opportunity arose, while Early sometimes hesitated—and the times he did seemed to be at the most inopportune. However, Jubal Early never hesitated in answering Lee's call to preserve the history of the Army of Northern Virginia. Embracing the challenge with all the energy and

"Lost Causers" Jubal Early (left) and William Nelson Pendleton (right) blamed James Longstreet for the defeat at Gettysburg and consequently the loss of the war.

Courtesy Museum of the Confederacy

devotion he had exhibited during the conflict, Early authored two books (*Autobiographical Sketch and Narrative of the War between the States and A Memoir of the Last Year of the War for Independence in the Confederate States of America, Containing an Account of His Command in the Years 1864-1865*), as well as penned voluminous articles that appeared in notable newspapers and periodicals. Seemingly tireless in his efforts, Early wrote countless letters and delivered numerous, fiery speeches that promoted the military aspects of Confederate history. Through these efforts, plus the position and prestige he held as an officer in the Association of the Army of Northern Virginia and the Southern Historical Society, "Old Jube" exerted enormous influence on the writing and remembrance of the late war. Indeed, his shadow was so great that whoever wrote something about the Southern war effort which Early did not agree knew that he would have to contend with Early's opposing—and often stinging—viewpoint. As artillerist Robert Stiles (who served under Early) related: "No man ever took up his pen to write a line about the great conflict without the fear of Jubal Early before his eyes."[14]

---

[13] Edward Porter Alexander, as quoted in Philip R. N. Katcher, *The Army of Northern Virginia: Lee's Army in the American Civil War* (New York, 2003), p. 241.

[14] Robert Stiles, *Four Years Under Marse Robert* (New York, 1903), p. 191.

Early's flowing ink and sharp tongue had been kept in check as long as Robert E. Lee was alive. All that changed when Lee passed away on October 12, 1870. Once the commanding general was gone, no single figure could keep in check all the clashing personalities once part of the Army of Northern Virginia, and no one alive in the South had enough stature to utterly demolish any blatant falsehoods that might surface about former compatriots. Therefore, Lee's death ignited a political fight over interpreting Gettysburg. Subverting Lee's charge that "the bravery and devotion of the Army of Northern Virginia be correctly transmitted to posterity," Jubal Early set about to affix his own interpretive stamp on Gettysburg and the reasons why the South lost the war.

What did Early do to influence the interpretation of Gettysburg as well as Lee's overall generalship? First, Early spread the contemptible groundwork for blaming James Longstreet (the former commander of the First Corps of the Army of Northern Virginia) for the Confederate loss at Gettysburg. Early did this in a speech at Washington and Lee College on the anniversary of Robert E. Lee's birthday, January 19, 1872. In that oration, delivered about 15 months after Lee's death, Early marked the beginning of what became an intensely personal feud between himself and the man Lee called "My Old Warhorse." In that speech, Early did not directly charge Longstreet with dereliction of duty, but the insinuation was clear; Longstreet's delay in attacking on July 2, 1863, robbed the Confederate cause of its best chance to win at Gettysburg, and hence, their best chance to win the war.

As faulty as this misrepresentation was, a positively slanderous one emerged exactly one year later. Early's theme was expanded upon in another speech at Washington and Lee, this time by William Nelson Pendleton, the former chief of artillery in the Army of Northern Virginia. In an outrageously malicious charge, Pendleton hatched one of the worst falsehoods ever perpetrated on the historiography of the Civil War. Pendleton falsely testified that Longstreet had been ordered by General Lee "to make an attack at daylight the next morning [meaning July 2]," and that Longstreet chose instead to sit "on his horse until about 4:00 P.M. of that day and could plainly see that reinforcements of the enemy arriving hour after hour…and thus Longstreet's "failure to assault at daylight was the cause of the loss of the Battle." Nothing could have been further from the truth and Pendleton knew it.[15]

Yet another occurrence took place in 1873 when Early headed a group of Virginians that took control of the Southern Historical Society. The new leaders moved the society's headquarters to Richmond, and in 1876, began promoting the fiction about Longstreet being to blame for the loss at Gettysburg within the pages of the *Southern Historical Society Papers*. Early's insinuation and Pendleton's accusation went unquestioned by most people, and the tale had the imprimatur of a prominent publication. Other officers were encouraged to submit reminisces, some portions of which were taken out of proper historical context in a way that seemed to corroborate the Longstreet delay myth. By the time the *Papers* had been published for several years, Longstreet was the most compromised of all ex-Confederate officers. His post-war politics (Longstreet joined the Republican party about two years after the war) combined with the spreading story about Longstreet costing the Confederates their chance to win at Gettysburg, turned public opinion decidedly against "Old Pete."

If the story hatched by Early and Pendleton was baseless, then why didn't significant numbers of other former Army of Northern Virginia officers come

"The truth will be known in time, and I leave that to show how much of the responsibility of Gettysburg rests on my shoulders."

James Longstreet

GEN. LONGSTREET, C. S. A.

Courtesy Museum of the Confederacy

---

[15] A summary of the Early speech at Washington and Lee, along with its impact, may be found in: Scott Bowden and Bill Ward, *Last Chance for Victory: Robert E. Lee and the Gettysburg Campaign* (Cambridge, 2001), pp. 367-375.

forward to vigorously defend Longstreet? How did the slander gain such traction when officers closest to Lee knew the whole thing to be false? In the simplest of terms, Early and his supporters used the Southern Historical Society to act out a political agenda. White Southerners were overwhelmingly conservative Democrats. White Southern Democrats suffered the most at the hands of Reconstruction agents. Therefore, when James Longstreet switched political allegiances from the Democratic to the Republican Party in the spring of 1867, the overwhelming majority of his fellow compatriots felt utterly betrayed. To most Southerners—and certainly to those closest to Jubal Early— Longstreet's shift in political affiliations was an act beneath contempt. In their eyes, Longstreet's alliance with the agents of radicalism represented the highest betrayal. Therefore, rather than being brutally honest about Gettysburg, Early, Pendleton and their sycophants made Longstreet the convenient scapegoat. Even those officers closest to Lee, who wrote to Early and others in response to Pendleton's speech, did not overexert themselves in trying to set the record straight. The political environment of the time meant that defending Longstreet would fall on deaf ears, and "Old Pete's" foolish critiques of Lee harmed his case immeasurably, particularly with Lee's former subordinates. Interestingly, Edward Porter Alexander, one of Longstreet's prominent artillery officers and the man who directed much of the bombardment prior to "Pickett's Charge," was one of the few who opposed Early's efforts.

Hanging the loss of Gettysburg—and by implication the loss of the war— directly on Longstreet for his performance on July 2, 1863, has widely affected the historiography of the Civil War. It shifted the focus of historians to a false controversy, and few have been able to refocus. Early especially would escape historians attention on his inactions that day.

Certainly, "Old Pete" did not help himself in defending these malicious charges. His various writings after the war often conflicted with the facts or contradicted his own after-action and wartime correspondence. Almost as bad was Longstreet's self-promotion, for he comes off as an opportunist who portrays himself to be smarter (especially at Gettysburg) than General Lee, who seems pathologically aggressive in Longstreet's portrait. One does not have to have much of an imagination to envision how such a stance played throughout the South.

Therefore, in an ironic twist that seems only possible in fiction, legions of historians continue to this day to ignore the facts and simply repeat variations of the Early-Pendleton fiction. Indeed, different versions of the Longstreet delay myth involving the fighting on July 2, 1863, are to be found within the pages of more accounts on Gettysburg than can seemingly be documented.

Another Lost Cause theme to emerge from the Southern Historical Society was that Robert E. Lee was a military genius whose failure was one of a colossus in command of an army that only succumbed due to the North's overwhelming numbers and resources. While, as Lee stated, "It will be difficult to get the world to understand the odds against which we fought," the main problem in advancing this theme absent its proper context was that it overlooked Jefferson Davis' complicity in badly mismanaging the resources that could have been made available to the Army of Northern Virginia. Indeed, Davis' insistence upon adhering to an illogical policy labeled as the "strategy of defense by dispersal" deprived Lee of valuable troops that could have dramatically tipped the scales in the South's favor on numerous battlefields, including the pivotal struggle so intently studied by the Southern Historical Society contributors— Gettysburg.

Therefore, Early's other main theme concerning Robert E. Lee as a military

Jubal Anderson Early

The man called "Old Jube" or "Old Jubilee" by his troops was a capable officer. Distinguished as a brigade commander at First Manassas, Williamsburg (where he was wounded in the shoulder), Cedar Mountain, Second Manassas and Harpers Ferry, Jubal Early's performance at Sharpsburg garnered praise from Lee. Proving himself capable of handling a division at Fredericksburg when he sealed a breach during a crucial moment during the Federal assault against the Confederate right, by the time the war had moved into its third spring, Early was a major general and permanent commander of Richard Ewell's former division. In the Chancellorsville campaign, as well as at Second Winchester in the opening phase of the Gettysburg campaign, Early handled is division well. However, at Gettysburg, Early's performance remains controversial, and represents one possible reason in his seeking to scapegoat Longstreet.

On July 1, 1863, Early led his division to Gettysburg, arriving on and behind the Federal's right flank just in time to help shatter Oliver O. Howard's Eleventh Corps and chase it through town. Despite very light casualties to his command in its devastating attack against the Eleventh Corps, Early's reluctance to pursue his defeated foe and seize the high ground south of town, coupled with his muddled interaction with his corps commander (Richard Ewell), represented one of the great lost opportunities of the war. The following day, Early arguably had his worse performance as a division commander. Despite having all day to prepare his division for action, he failed to properly deploy his brigades. As a result, the success achieved by his two leading brigades in their evening attack on East Cemetery Hill went unsupported.

The following spring, Early performed unevenly in the Overland Campaign. His failing at the Wilderness to launch a timely flank attack against the Federal right represented another missed opportunity. Nevertheless, Lee thought enough of Early to put him temporarily in command of Powell Hill's Third Corps when that commander fell ill. When Lee decided to replace the dismally-performing Richard Ewell with a new commander of the Second Corps, he

genius—a theme deserving examination by establishing valid criteria and proper contextualization—has come under increasing fire from Lee detractors. All of these detractors—all of them—misjudge Lee's military performance by either tying it to the emotional issues of Confederate politics, or employing with increasing frequency a growing list of invalid criteria (that sadly includes *ad hominem* attacks on opposing writers) in their attempts to call into question Lee's military judgment. Adding to the confusion, writers who defend Lee often fail to establish valid criteria of their own, and essentially conduct the battle on terrain selected by their foe.

Ultimately, the historical record of Lee's tenure as army commander has become increasingly modified and redefined by a growing number of defenders and critics. Both groups seem to miss the mark. Critics tend to label everything positive about Lee to come out of the post-war South as the product of the "cult of The Lost Cause." The falsehoods hatched by Early and Pendleton in the *Papers* continue to be perpetrated. Unfortunely, these are so deeply rooted in Gettysburg lore that they detract from Lee's real record at the crucial battle. Certainly, there exist many issues about Gettysburg or Lee's generalship in the *Papers* that do not square with the facts. However, rather than examine carefully and determine independently the validity of each of these viewpoints, revisionist and reductionist writers, due in part to the Early-Pendleton fiction, have dismissed all things that might relate favorably to Confederate issues. As a result, there exist today almost a countless number of distortions concerning treatment of Confederate subjects, and most notably, General Lee's performance as commander of the Army of Northern Virginia. Indeed, Lee's true impact and his status as the focal point of the Confederacy's war effort has today been saddled with so many invalid criticisms that many students of the Civil War have to face a daunting task to separate fact from fiction. All of this has been very bad for understanding American military history and Robert E. Lee's proper place within it.

* * *

President Rutherford B. Hayes ended Reconstruction in 1877 and withdrew the occupying Federal troops. Over 20 years passed before the Spanish-American War in 1898, when Southerners were given a chance to demonstrate their loyalty and honor under fire for the reunited nation. The South responded enthusiastically. One paper proclaimed, that "upon any battlefield of the war Confederate veterans and their sons will be seen upholding the national honor and guarding the country's safety with all the steadiness and resolution that characterized them in the early sixties." One of the unintended humorous moments of the war found prominent ex-Confederate general "Fighting Joe" Wheeler leading his men against Spanish troops in Cuba and shouting: "Go get those Yankees!" The war's aftermath seemed to make reconciliation between North and South easier.

Late that year in a much-publicized speech in Atlanta, President William McKinley announced to the South that the Confederate fallen would be officially honored alongside their Federal counterparts. "In the evolution of sentiment and feeling under Providence of God," McKinley told the Georgia legislature, "when in the spirit of fraternity we [the Federal government] should share with you in the care of the graves of Confederate soldiers." After the blood of the two sections was shed in common and following the President's lead, the Confederate Survivors' Association declared in their Charleston meeting of 1899, "These dead, at least, belong to us all." These and other reconciliations,

---

selected Early, and then gave him a daring mission: Early was to detach his command from the rest of the Army of Northern Virginia around Petersburg, move westward and clear the Federal forces out of the vital Shenandoah Valley before heading north to threaten Baltimore and Washington. If this audacious move proved successful, Lee hoped that Grant would divert troops from the Richmond-Petersburg area while also causing incalculable political damage to the Lincoln administration prior to the fall election.

From mid-June to November 1864, Early and his command (numbering from 8,000 to never more than 14,500) marched more than 1,600 miles, fought in 75 battles and skirmishes, threatened Washington and sent the city into panic. Grant diverted the Federal Sixth and Nineteenth corps from Petersburg to Washington. Eventually overwhelmed, Early was driven out of the Shenandoah, his inspired campaign rivaling in many respects Jackson's famous 1862 Valley exploits.[1]

Like his army commander, Jubal Early (1816–1894) hailed from a prominent Virginia family. He graduated from West Point in 1837, and he proved to be a man of forceful character who did not back down to anyone. At six-feet tall with piercing eyes, Early was considered a striking figure, despite the fact that he fought rheumatism that he contracted during the Mexican war. He rode into battle wearing a slouch hat topped by a black ostrich plume, and his stinging curse phrases impressed many with their originality. One such example occurred during the 1864 Valley campaign when Early arrived at Lynchburg, rose up in his saddle and yelled at the nearby Federal cavalry: "No buttermilk rangers after you now, you God-damned Blue-Butts!"[2] Following Lee's surrender, Early lived abroad until 1869, returning to Lynchburg, Virginia, to practice law and continue his writing pursuits.

---

[1] A concise and readable account of Early's 1864 Valley campaign is: Frank E. Vandiver, *Jubal's Raid: General Early's Famous Attack on Washington in 1864* (Lincoln, 1992 reprint of 1960 original).

[2] *Encyclopedia of the Confederacy*, vol. 2, pp. 501-502.

Photo taken at the 1913 reunion of Terry's Texas Rangers, San Marcos, Texas

reunions and declarations coincided with the swelling national remembrance of the honorable service by the Confederate soldier.[16]

The developing respect by many Northerners for the staggering price paid by Southerners in their bid for independence helped spark a great deal of excellent scholarship on the era known as Reconstruction. The magnitude of the corruption authorized by the Republican military rule of the South was indeed unprecedented in American history. What once passed between Southerners as stories by word of mouth became documented as numerous scholars chronicled in great detail the tragic tales of abuse and political racketeering that plagued the Reconstruction South. These studies began appearing shortly after the turn of the 20th century. For example, Columbia University historian William Archibald Dunning's *Reconstruction: Political and Economic* (1907), along with James Ford Rhodes' *History of the United States from the Compromise of 1850 to the Final Restoration of Home Rule at the South in 1877* (1900), and Claude Bowers' *The Tragic Era: The Revolution after Lincoln* (1929) chronicled vindictive stories of a corrupt governing body run amuck. Later in the 20th century, E. Merton Coulter's *The South During Reconstruction* (1947), James G. Randall's *The Civil War and Reconstruction* (1951), Bernard A. Weisberger's "The Dark and Bloody Ground of Reconstruction," in the *Journal of Southern History*, volume 25 (1959), as well as William

---

[16] *Richmond Times*, as quoted in Paul H. Buck, *The Road to Reunion 1865-1900* (Boston, 1937), p. 306; *Speeches and Addresses by William McKinley: From March 1, 1897 to May 30, 1900* (New York, 1900), p. 159.

Archibald Dunning's *Essays on the Civil War and Reconstruction* (1965) brought further light to Republican retribution inflicted upon the South.[17]

The Reconstruction scholarship—especially from authors who resided North of the Mason-Dixon line—gave legitimacy to Lost Cause sentiments. This new meaning helped galvanize many Southerners with a self-righteousness that they were indeed in the right in seeking independence, and that the post-war South had been unjustly and cruelly treated under the yoke of the conqueror. This mentality proved to be an important part of the belief system for the turn-of-the-century South—still dominated by former Confederates and their families—and this had the effect of strengthening the hold of The Lost Cause well afterwards.

As the United States became a world power during the 20th century, a more unified "Golden Age" of Civil War literature ensued, and followed in the "American Iliad" view of the conflict as a great national tragedy. Among this body of work stands Douglas Southall Freeman's Pulitzer Prize-winning four-volume *R. E. Lee*. Powerful in breadth and magisterial in its prose, Freeman's work unfortunately follows along with The Lost Cause myth involving Longstreet as perpetrated by the Early-Pendleton school. Freeman's work is influential—and so compelling in its canonization of Lee as Lost Cause icon and James Longstreet as Lost Cause scapegoat—that contending with its legacy poses a great challenge to Lee scholars. Freeman's subsequent work, the three-volume *Lee's Lieutenants*, is similarly powerful; but it has the same historiographical problems as *R. E. Lee*. Bruce Catton's *Army of the Potomac* series, another Pulitzer winner, is a beautifully written and often elegiac account of the war in the East; in it, Lee appears as an imposing genius through the eyes of his adversaries. Mississippi novelist Shelby Foote—a friend of William Faulkner, Walker Percy and Robert Penn Warren—also received the Pulitzer for his famous trilogy *The Civil War: A Narrative*; his work might be characterized as one novelist's Southern Renaissance take on the "American Illiad." An original, easy-to-read work, it reflects his Southern liberal view, wherein regional pride and a strong sense of place mixes uneasily with issues of slavery and race. Foote's trilogy was not without controversy. He labeled Nathan Bedford Forrest and Abraham Lincoln as *the* two great geniuses to emerge from the war, is praiseworthy of Jefferson Davis, and follows in the Longstreet reactionary school that portrays Lee as a "compulsively aggressive" army commander.

As these works gained wide readerships, they provided a portion of the salve that helped many 20th century Southerners hold sacred The Lost Cause; however, they also helped provide the political and social ammunition for a caustic critique. Published works favorably portraying Southern leaders, when combined with societal challenges of segregation and racism, along with small numbers of extremists who hijacked Confederate symbols, have been turned on Southerners in a way as to damage the higher Lost Cause message. For example, beginning in the 1930s, and with increasing frequency since the 1960s, different revisionist writers have challenged the interpretations of the

---

[17] William Archibald Dunning, *Reconstruction: Political and Economic* (New York, 1907); James Ford Rhodes, *History of the United States from the Compromise of 1850 to the Final Restoration of Home Rule at the South in 1877* (New York, 1900); Claude Bowers, *The Tragic Era: The Revolution after Lincoln* (New York, 1929), E. Merton Coulter, The South During Reconstruction (Baton Rouge, 1947), Bernard A. Weisberger, "The Dark and Bloody Ground of Reconstruction," *Journal of Southern History*, volume 25 (1959), James G. Randall, *The Civil War and Reconstruction* (Lexington, 1951); and William Archibald Dunning, *Essays on the Civil War and Reconstruction* (New York, 1965).

older Reconstruction school of history previously anchored by Dunning.[18] Bent on altering the historical perspective of the Old South by reinterpreting Reconstruction, the revisionist group of writers has been dominated by what one scholar describes as "Marxists of various degrees of orthodoxy."[19] Using Marxist-class analysis, revisionists paint the picture of Reconstruction as just revenge for secession. Therefore, the revisionists never deny the facts about Reconstruction: they simply offer radically different interpretations. After all, as one revisionist Reconstruction author wrote, ex-Confederate soldiers were indeed "lucky" that they were not executed *en masse* after the war.[20]

Revisionists gained significant headway in one respect: they framed their interpretations about the war and Reconstruction as an issue of good (the North) triumphing over evil (the South). This inaccurate, factually-challenged and emotion-based simplification, utilizing the fallacy known as "presentism" (filtering one's understanding of the past by that person's standards of today), has been repeated with an ever-increasing frequency since the 1960s, and has contributed to the atmosphere by which the various themes of The Lost Cause have become obfuscated. The Cause is now often incorrectly equated as an attempt to destroy the Union solely to preserve slavery, whereby independence was only a necessary by-product. Even worse, the phrase Lost Cause, or the name-calling of "Lost Causer," or "neo-Confederate" are now bandied about in increasingly regularity as a disparaging term deliberately meant to invoke emotions by implying racists and racism, largely in order to silence other viewpoints or to dismiss Confederate legacies. Such characterizations have, in turn, encouraged the cynical notion that anything or anyone connected to the former Confederacy was fundamentally immoral, and *any* defense connected to Confederates or the Confederacy is tantamount to being anti-intellectual. This inaccurate and gross simplification has also had a tragic impact on the military historiography of the American Civil War.

With regards to Robert E. Lee, this "presentism" mentality not only mischaracterizes Lee's decision to resign his commission, but anyone who wishes to place his generalship in a favorable light. There is no question that being delegitimized from the outset by the forces of reductionism is a hazard in this undertaking. By having to contend with those who wrongly invoke name-calling, or attach extremist motives to all Southern scholarship and to all issues Confederate, the well seems poisoned from the outset.

Writers must therefore face a compelling irony. Will Civil War historiography continue to assume the same path as pre-war history? Will extremists drive the narrative, frame the debate, and drown out the voices of reasoned scholarship? Or, can the middle hold, and will a complex view embracing multiple causation, valid criteria and in-depth analysis prevail over modern reductionism and mythmaking?

One method embraced by this lengthy study of Robert E. Lee is to return to contextualization, to focus on the historical moment. Nobel prize-winner William Faulkner does this in literature with his famous stream of consciousness passage of Pickett's Charge in his epic, *Intruder in the Dust*:

---

[18] For one such example, see W. E. Burghardt DuBois, *Black Reconstruction in America* (New York, 1935).

[19] Kenneth M. Stampp, *The Era of Reconstruction: 1865-1877* (New York, 1966), p. 9.

[20] Stampp, *The Era of Reconstruction: 1865-1877*, pp. 9 and 218.

George Pickett taking the order to charge from James Longstreet, Gettysburg, July 3, 1863.

For every Southern boy fourteen years old, not once but whenever he wants it, there is an instant when it's still not yet two o'clock on that July afternoon in 1863, the brigades are in position behind the rail fence, the guns are laid and ready in the woods and the furled flags are already loosened to break out and Pickett himself with his long oiled ringlets and his hat in one hand probably and his sword in the other looking up the hill waiting for Longstreet to give the word and it's all in the balance, it hasn't happened yet, it hasn't even begun yet, it not only hasn't begun yet but there is still time for it not to begin against that position and those circumstances which made more men than Garnett and Kemper and Armistead and Wilcox look grave yet it's going to begin, we all know that, we have come too far with too much at stake and that moment doesn't need even a fourteen year-old boy to think: This time. Maybe this time with all this much to lose and all this much to gain: Pennsylvania, Maryland, the world, the golden dome of Washington itself to crown with desperate and unbelievable victory the desperate gamble, the cast made two years ago...[21]

What Faulkner creates in literary terms is something historians should also emulate. By working to bring to life all the stakes confronting every decision, and by not starting with the end result, historians can breathe new insight and appreciation into subjects that have been wrongly considered closed. This school of "outcome-based" history is an easy trap to fall into, and produces books that justify the end result as the only probable one. This line of thinking leads to foolish themes such as the Confederacy lost the Civil War when it fired on Fort Sumter, or the spurious idea, ignited by Early and Pendleton, that Gettysburg, and hence the war, was lost by the South on July 2, 1863, when Longstreet delayed his attack. Yet another Pulitzer Prize-winner, James McPherson, handily dismisses such an approach when he penned: "Most attempts to explain Southern defeat or Northern victory lack the dimensions of *contingency*—the recognition that at numerous critical points during the war things might have gone altogether differently;" and "Northern victory and Southern defeat in the war cannot be understood apart from the contingency that hung over every campaign, every battle, every election, every decision during the war."[22]

This Sesquicentennial project seeks to be an account of Robert E. Lee that is richly contextualized, objective, and told within the fullness of understanding contingency as the key to historical analysis. It seeks, as Lee once put it, to "Look upon things as they are."[23]

---

[21] William Faulkner, *Intruder In The Dust* (New York, 1991 reprint of 1948 original), pp. 190-191.

[22] McPherson, *Battle Cry of Freedom*, pp. 857-858.

[23] Robert E. Lee to George Washington Custis Lee, quoted in Emory Thomas, *Robert E. Lee*, p. 47.

Phantom Hill
0-1212

"I Do Not Know
What My Position Will Be"—
A Great Talent and a Year Wasted

"You may win salvation under my command, but hardly riches."
"The first duty of the soldier is to pray hard; the second is to fight hard."
—Gustavus Adolphus II, King of Sweden[1]

"The Very Best Soldier I've Ever Seen"

Long before the storm clouds of war burst in the spring of 1861, Robert E. Lee's reputation marked him as one of the most prominent officers in the United States Army. Graduating second in his Class of 1829 from West Point (placing first in tactics and artillery and garnering the most coveted and important rank open to a cadet, that of Corps Adjutant), Lee served with the greatest distinction on General Winfield Scott's staff during the Mexican War, during which time Lee won three brevet promotions for bravery. On that stage of conflict, Lee repeatedly displayed remarkable endurance, courage, and a superb eye for terrain. The rare combination of admirable qualities and war-time accomplishments, combined with Lee's long years of superior service with the army's *élite* Corps of Engineers, resulted in him being held in high esteem by his fellow officers and his superiors.

General Winfield Scott, the highest ranked American soldier of the first half of the 19th century and the only general officer of that time to have served in three major wars, credited Lee for much of the success of the Mexican campaign.[2] Years after the conflict in an official letter dated in 1858, Scott described Lee as "the very best soldier that I ever saw in the field."[3] Scott expressed his appreciation numerous times. In a conversation with Kentucky Congressman William Preston, Scott declared Robert E. Lee to be "the greatest living soldier in America."[4] "I tell you that if I were on my death bed to-morrow," the aging General in Chief of the Army eloquently informed Preston, "and the President of the United States should tell me that a great battle was to be fought for the liberty or slavery of the country, and asked my judgment as to the ability of a commander, I would say with my dying breath,

---

[1] Gustavus Adolphus II, King of Sweden, quoted in Peter G. Tsouras, *Warrior's Words: A Quotation Book* (London, 1992), p. 328 and Theodore Ayrault Dodge, *Gustavus Adolphus* (New York, 1998 reprint of the 1895 original), p. 400.

[2] Reverend J. William Jones recalled a specific tribute paid by General Scott to Lee: "When, soon after Scott's return from Mexico, a committee from Richmond waited on him to tender a public reception in the Capitol of his native State, [Scott] said: 'You seek to honor the wrong man. Captain R. E. Lee is the Virginian who deserves the credit for that brilliant campaign.'" *Southern Historical Society Papers*, Rev. J. William Jones, "The Friendship Between Lee and Scott," vol. 11, p. 424.

[3] Southern Historical Society Papers, Rev. J. William Jones, "The Friendship Between Lee and Scott," vol. 11, p. 424.

[4] General Winfield Scott, as quoted in Douglas Southall Freeman, *R. E. Lee*, 4 volumes (New York, 1934-1935), vol. 1, p. 294.

let it be Robert E. Lee."[5] Just before the Civil War, Scott told a close friend: "I tell you, sir, that Robert E. Lee is the greatest soldier now living, and if he ever gets the opportunity, he will prove himself the greatest captain of history."[6]

Robert Edward Lee certainly had the lineage of a military man. Born on January 19th, 1807, the son of Revolutionary War hero and Virginia Governor Henry "Light Horse Harry" Lee, Robert was only six years old when his father ignominiously fled from his creditors and left the country. In the absence of his father, Robert was raised by his mother, who deeply impressed upon the youth her devout Episcopalian faith and characteristics of duty, honor, courage and self-discipline.[7] These traits were certainly prominent throughout Lee's life.

From his days as a student at West Point, and as opportunity presented itself during his career as an army officer, Lee studiously read military history and theory. Lee's interest in military history was certainly reinforced when, in 1831, he married Mary Anne Randolph Custis, the only child of George Washington Parke Custis, the step-grandson of the nation's first President, George Washington. Also, Lee's new wife was the daughter of Mary Lee Fitzhugh Custis, a cousin of Robert's mother. The marriage to Mary Custis made Lee a great-grandson-in-law to George Washington, and provided Robert with an unlimited access to the extensive collection of the young country's most revered man—and Lee took full advantage of the opportunity as he meticulously studied the campaigns of Washington the general. In addition, the marriage greatly expanded Lee's notable relatives, as he was now a member of one of the most extensive, influential, and well-to-do families of Virginia.[8]

In 1852, Lee returned to West Point as superintendent, having previously served as an engineer and as a member of Scott's staff during the Mexican War. Even though he fought the appointment, Lee approached the new duty assignment with his usual professionalism and drive for excellence. As superintendent (not to be confused with the post of Commandant of Cadets, who at the time was William J. Hardee), Lee demanded strict discipline at the academy, and he won the respect of the cadets. Furthermore, he not only oversaw the strengthening of scholarship at the academy, Lee also revealed his unique talent of understanding and working through inadequacies of his comrades and cadets without letting such tolerance undermine his authority– something that famous biographer Clifford Dowdey characterized as adding "the dimension of humanity to his standards as a disciplinarian."[9]

Courtesy Library of Congress

"Light Horse Harry" Lee

Courtesy Library of Congress

Mary Randolph Custis

---

[5] *Southern Historical Society Papers*, Rev. J. William Jones, "The Friendship Between Lee and Scott," vol. 11, p. 424.

[6] *Southern Historical Society Papers*, Rev. J. William Jones, "The Friendship Between Lee and Scott," vol. 11, p. 425.

[7] Freeman, *R. E. Lee*, vol. 1, pp. 2-10 and pp. 30-32; Alfred J. Mapp, Jr., *Frock Coats and Epaulets: Psychological Portraits of Confederate Military and Political Leaders* (Landham, 1990), p. 136.

[8] For a brief overview of Lee during this stage in his life, please see: David J. Eicher, *Robert E. Lee: A Life Portrait* (Dallas, 1997), pp. 2 and 15.

[9] Clifford Dowdey, *Lee* (New York, 1965), p. 102.

Opposite: Lee Geneaology Tree

Courtesy Library of Congress

GENEALOGY of the
LEE FAMILY
OF VIRGINIA AND MARYLAND.

Lee & The Mexican War

ATTACK ON CHAPULTEPEC, SEP? 13? 1847.

MEXICANS ROUTED WITH GREAT LOSS.

Storming of Chapultepec Castle

Courtesy Library of Congress

In early May of 1846, as word reached the public of the opening clashes in what would become the Mexican War, Lee, as an engineer, found himself languishing in the fifth year of work on the fortifications of New York Harbor. Supervising this underfunded and painstakingly slow construction, Lee, as with many career officers throughout the army, desperately hoped instead to be sent to the fight. Failure to draw that assignment would mean forever being held in lower regard than the engineering officers who would distinguish themselves under fire. As each day passed, his career chances seemed to be diminishing beyond recovery, but Lee's anxious wait ended at last in mid-August, when he was sent to serve in San Antonio de Bexar, home of the Alamo, under General Wool. Lee wasted no time, making an impressively rapid journey via New Orleans, before reporting for duty by the end of August.

Lee's Mexican War odyssey would include serving in tight quarters and ultimately under fire, alongside many future Civil War general officers, an experience which would, years later, add to his ability to gauge the capabilities and command tendencies of his foes and subordinates alike. At the time, Wool's staff included Irwin McDowell, Union Commander at Manassas, and William B. Franklin, who would later command a corps facing Lee's Army of Northern Virginia at South Mountain and Antietam in 1862. The 39 year-old Lee's initial assignment was to find a road for Wool's men as they advanced to join Taylor in a supporting column to the north of his advance on Monterey; Lee helped perform the role of trailblazer, making numerous reconnaissance missions in planning for a fairly rapid and lengthy march. Wool's ultimate objective, Chihuahua, Mexico, deep inside enemy territory, would ultimately prove impractical, and instead Wool ended up joining Taylor's forces. While this phase

of the war would lead to no combat, Lee carried his duties out with zeal and notable efficiency—and Wool's largely volunteer force benefitted by executing marches that matched professional standards. However, Lee's practical education in the realities of war had hardly begun.

Captain Lee's great opportunity came in mid-January, 1847, when he was transferred to General Winfield Scott's command. There he joined Scott's Vera Cruz invasion expedition, becoming a member of Scott's immediate general staff. Tucked away onboard Scott's steamer Massachusetts, Lee bunked with former West Point classmate Joe Johnston, reestablishing a bond of wartime camaraderie which Lee took as true friendship, but which, years later, seemed sadly to sour under Johnston's sense of rivalry and envy. The other members of the staff included PGT Beauregard, Gordon Meade, and George B. McClellan. Together, they would spend long hours working intimately

Lee & The Mexican War

with the architect of one of the most audacious military campaigns in 19th century military history. The experience could not have been better designed to produce a superior general officer; working side by side with Scott, Lee and his fellow staff members were given a veritable finishing school in the art of war.

Chapultepec Castle   *Courtesy Library of Congress*

Ironically, Lee's baptism of fire took place at sea, in a rather remarkable risk that Scott undertook to reconnoiter the landing sites and defenses. Freeman writes: "Lee went with the rest [Scott and staff] aboard the steamer Petrita and they ventured so close to the castle fort off Vera Cruz...that the men on the other ships expected to see them blown out of the water. The castle opened on the Petrita when it was a mile and a half distant, but the fire went wild." Lee would soon experience even closer calls; serving on Scott's staff required just the sangfroid Lee would prove to possess in abundance.

Lee's adventures in Mexico provided a record of daring escapades, close calls, and remarkable feats of military achievement; he never spared himself from taking personal risks in the line of duty. At Vera Cruz, March, 24, 1847, Lee directed the crucial emplacement of artillery, 700 yards from the Mexican fortifications before unmasking the battery to decisive effect in a dangerous artillery duel. Lee wrote of the affair to his son Fitzhugh that "the shells thrown from our battery were constant and regular discharges, so beautiful in their flight and so destructive in their fall. It was awful! My heart bled for the inhabitants. The soldiers I did not care so much for, but it was terrible to think of the women and children." These telling remarks reveal, as other letters home do, how the war marked Lee's psyche in a way that would profoundly influence his conduct of the Civil War, and how, years later, he violently objected to Johnston's strategy of allowing the citizens of Richmond to fall under siege. Lee would always be haunted by the images of civilian suffering he encountered on the road to Mexico City, and his words reveal a man of sensitivity and honor that harken more to the "civilized" wars of the past rather than to the modern war that would ultimately engulf the South.

To single out Lee's finest hour, perhaps no battle revealed his attributes more than the Battle of Cerro Gordo (April 11-18, 1847). Charged with finding a way to outflank and attack Santa Anna's formidable position blocking the road from Vera Cruz to Jalapa, Lee characteristically embarked on a daring personal scouting mission that nearly resulted in his capture. In preparing and leading the flanking assault that turned the position while avoiding a bloody frontal assault, Lee played a critical role in arguing for the plan that Scott adopted; it was essentially Lee's plan that led to the victory. Even McClellan, in western Virginia, cited Cerro Gordo as a masterpiece in making his operational plans.

Scott's march on Mexico City, untethering himself from the traditional logistical tail of an army and heading overland in a move of Napoleonic boldness, not only reinforced Lee's own propensity for audacity, but demonstrated that such risks should only be undertaken after clear-sighted assessments of the situation, and evaluations of whether time is pressing or in favor of a cause. For Scott and his army, advancing and retaining the initiative more than justified the gamble.

Lee covered himself in glory in battle after battle. At Cherubusco, on the approach to Mexico City, he pushed himself beyond the point of exhaustion to find a means to cross the "impassable" terrain of the Pedregal to find a practical route of attack that once again would saves lives and maximize the chance of success. General PF Smith wrote of Lee (Freeman, p 271) that "I wish to record particularly my admiration of the conduct of Captain Lee of the engineers. His reconnaissances, though pushed far beyond the limits of prudence, were conducted with so much skill, that their fruits were of the utmost value—the soundness of his judgment and personal daring being equally commendable."

In the seizure of Mexico City or the battle of Chapultepec, Lee, as at Vera Cruz, oversaw the placement of the American batteries charged with blasting a breach into the city. On Lee's advice, Scott postponed the culminating assault from the afternoon of the 12th until dawn of the 13th; no other staff officer apparently had the audacity to confront Scott with a cautionary note when his blood lust was up. Scott demurred, and the wisdom of Lee's advice bore out the next day when the Americans achieved their signal victory. Lee, after directing the preliminary bombardment, further exposed himself in leading an attack party through difficult terrain, before assisting the wounded General Pillow to safety. Appropriately enough, Lee's superhuman energy at last broke in the war's culminating engagement, and Lee actually passed out at one point while in the saddle.

Scott's Entry into Mexico City   *Courtesy United States Army Art Collection*

Those familiar with the academy praised Lee's accomplishments, but the sedentary routine chafed the physically active Lee. He particularly excelled in horsemanship, and riding was his preferred method of exercise. He got little satisfaction in being confined to an office, preferring instead the freedom of activity. While many officers may have found it socially fulfilling to entertain the constant parade of politicians and dignitaries who called on the academy, Lee tolerated the intrusions with grace and humility as his self-effacing sense of duty required. What he could never get used to, nor ever like, was the weather along the Hudson. "The climate is as harsh to me as my duties," Lee wrote Anna Fitzhugh on 23 April 1854, "& neither brings any pleasure." Given his temperament, Lee knew of "the impossibility of either giving or receiving satisfaction" while he was in charge. It was "as little as a year into his assignment at West Point," wrote biographer Paul Nagel, that Lee "admitted: 'I have less heart for the work.'"[10]

Courtesy Library of Congress

Matthew Brady's portrait of Lee during the time he was superintendent at West Point

Lee's demanding administrative duties at the academy left fewer hours for self-study than Lee would have liked. However, he became a member of the "Napoleon Club" that existed among the officers at the academy, chaired by the renowned professor of military history, Dennis Hart Mahan. Mahan taught from the works of the already famous military theoretician, Baron Antoine Henri de Jomini, that emphasized Napoleon's art of war that was, in substantial part, derived from Frederick the Great, the Great Captain greatly admired by George Washington. Richard McCaslin, another Lee biographer, noted that "Lee probably enjoyed the link to Washington's hero."[11]

Lee's personal book collection, along with the works drawn from the library at West Point, formed the basis of his reading while superintendent. Among the 48 titles (some containing multiple volumes) he drew from the shelves of the academy's library during his tenure were six on geography and fifteen on military history, biography and the art of war. Of the fifteen titles specifically war-related, seven dealt with Napoleon and his campaigns. Lee evidently found Napoleon's early Italian campaigns of 1796-97 and his expedition to Egypt to be especially fascinating as the volumes covering those extraordinary maneuvers and resulting battles of Napoleon were the ones Lee most frequently procured. Lee principally studied Baron Gourgaud's and the Marquis of Montholon's *Mémoires pour server à l' histoire de France sous Napoléon, écrits à Sainte-Hélène* as well as General Savary's *Mémoirs du duc de Rovigo* and Barry Edward O'Meara's *Napoleon at St. Helena*.

Courtesy Library of Congress

Baron Antoine Henri de Jomini

Lee combined his reading of these books with his own copies of notable histories about the French Revolution and Napoleonic wars. He used Baron de Jomini's *Traité des Grands Opérations Militaires* published in 1804-05, which contained Napoleon's insightful notes on the author's observations and conclusions. In addition, Lee had in his personal library many volumes on the art of war and military fortifications. Also, Lee owned an 1838 edition

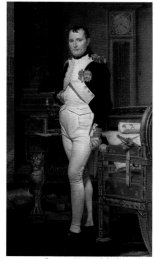

Courtesy National Gallery of Art, Washington, D.C.

Napoleon In His Study

---

[10] *Maryland Historical Magazine*, vol. 51, no. 3 (September, 1956), Robert E. Lee to P. G. T. Beauregard, June 25, 1862, pp. 249-251; *Virginia Historical Society*, Robert E. Lee to Anna Fitzhugh, 23 April 1854; Paul C. Nagel, *The Lee's of Virginia: Seven Generations of an American Family* (New York, 1990), p. 253.

[11] Richard B. McCaslin, *Lee in the Shadow of Washington* (Baton Rouge, 2001), p. 55.

Napoleon Crossing the Alps

Equestrian Portrait of Napoleon I

of Jomini's most mature work, *Précis de l'art de la guerre*, and General Rogniat's *Considérations sur l'Art de la Guerre* published in 1816 that contained a lengthy dissertation written by Napoleon. Importantly, Lee did not limit himself to reading military subjects. He possessed copies of various classical histories, including those by the famous Roman historian, Publius (or Gaius) Cornelius Tacitus, who authored the *Annals and Histories of Rome*, as well as *Germania*, the latter work written in the ethnographic traditions established from the time of Herodotus to Julius Caesar.

In reading the books that Lee studied, many parallels are obvious in hindsight; Napoleon's insightful observations on defensive warfare certainly struck a chord with Lee. For example:

But must a capital be defended by covering it directly, or by the defending army's barring itself up in an entrenched camp in the rear of the invader? The first method is the safest: it allows of disputing the passage of rivers, and defiles, even of creating field positions; of receiving all the troops in the interior as reinforcements, whilst the enemy's forces would be insensibly decreasing. The second method is a very bad measure because it lets oneself be shut up in an entrenched camp; if that happens, one runs the strong risk of being cut off, or at least blockaded, and of being reduced to cut one's way, sword in hand, to procure bread and forage. Four or five hundred wagons a day are required for provisioning an army of 100,000 men. The invading army, being superior in infantry, cavalry, and artillery, by one-third, would prevent the convoys from arriving; and, without blockading them hermetically, as fortresses are blockaded, it would render all access to them so difficult, so that famine would set in.

There remains a third way: to maneuver incessantly, without submitting to being driven back on the capital which it is meant to defend, or shut up in an entrenched camp in the rear. For this purpose it is necessary to have a good army, good generals, and a good commander-in-chief. In general, the idea of covering a capital, or any point whatsoever, by flank marches, carries with it the necessity of detaching troops, and the inconveniences attached to all division of force, in the face of a numerically superior army.[12]

Napoleon further commented:

Military men are strongly divided on the question of whether there are greater advantages in attacking or in defending; but there is no doubt at all about this question, when, on one side, there are smaller numbers of battle-hardened troops, skilled in maneuver, having inferiority in

12 Napoleon as quoted in Baron Gaspard Gourgaud and Comte de Charles-Tristan Montholon, *Mémoires pour server à l' histoire de France sous Napoléon, écrits à Sainte-Hélène*, 4 volumes (London, 1823), vol. 4, pp. 304-305. There were four editions of this work listed in the West Point library catalog of 1853, and Lee appears to have used two editions.

artillery, and on the other there is a much larger army, having in its train a great deal of artillery, but whose officers and soldiers are not as hardened to battle. The smaller force must augment its numbers through maneuver and then profit from that initiative by striking hard blows that makes possible the defeat of the larger force.[13]

Baron de Jomini summarized his reading of Napoleon and the operational value of the offensive in the following passage:

Courtesy Library of Congress

Hannibal Barca

There is another [principle], still more manifest, that has been demonstrated by the greatest events in history. Every army that maintains a strictly defensive attitude must, if attacked, be finally driven from its defensive position; whilst by profiting by all the advantages of the defensive system, and holding itself ready to take the offensive when the occasion offers, it may hope for the greatest success. However, a general who stands motionless to receive his enemy, keeping strictly on the defensive, may fight ever so bravely, but he must give way when properly attacked....

A general will find indispensable that 1) far from limiting himself to a passive defense, he should know how to take the offensive at favorable moments; 2) that his *coup d'oeil* must be certain and his coolness never in doubt; 3) that he be able to rely with certainty on his troops; 4) that in taking the offensive, he should by no means neglect to apply the general principle that dictates his battle deployments; and 5) that he strike his blows upon decisive points. These truths are demonstrated by Napoleon's conduct at Rivoli and Austerlitz.[14]

"After his study of Napoleon," wrote Douglas Southall Freeman, "Lee's major military reading at West Point seems to have been of the American Revolution."[15] Lee not only continued his studies of Washington's campaigns and battles, but also those of Nathaniel Greene and Daniel Morgan in the Southern campaigns.

Lee also devoted time to earlier Great Captains. Through Charles Rollin's multi-volume *Ancient History*, Lee not only revisited the victorious campaigns and battle tactics of Alexander the Great, but also absorbed the strategic concepts introduced by legendary Carthaginian general, Hannibal Barca, the "Father of Strategy." Hannibal's audacious transfer of the strategic defense of Carthage onto the Italian peninsula, along with his brilliant tactics at numerous battles, especially Cannae, no doubt represented an apogee of battlefield command that inspired Lee to seek decisive victory through bold planning. To learn about Caesar's exploits, Lee absorbed Jacob Abbott's *History of Julius Caesar*. Although there were no apparent books either owned privately, or checked out of the West Point library by Lee devoted exclusively to the campaigns of Gustavus Adolphus II of Sweden, Lee did use at least two atlases that included the great Swedish king who brought to

Courtesy Library of Congress

Gustavus Adolphus II of Sweden

---

[13] Napoleon's notes on General Rogniat's, *Considérations sur l'Art de la Guerre* (Paris, 1816).

[14] Baron de Jomini, *Traité des Grands Opérations Militaires, ou Histoire Critique des Guerres de Frédéric le Grand, Comparées ay Système Moderne, avec un Recueil des Principes les plus Importants de l'Art de la Guerre*, 4th edition, 8 volumes (Paris, 1851), vol. 3, p. 122-123.

[15] Freeman, *R. E. Lee*, vol. 1, p. 355.

the operational realm for the first time "a persistence in seeking and fighting battles." The best known of these atlases was the 1831 publication of Franz G. F. von Kausler's two-volume study, *Atlas des plus mémorables batailles, combats et sieges des temps anciens, du moyen âge et de lâge moderne en 200 feuilles*, and Samuel Augustus Mitchell's 1846 release, *A New Universal Atlas* that included George Washington's campaigns in North America. Lee owned many French titles on military theory and history, like *Essai sur l'art de la guerre* by Lancelot, Comte Turpin de Crissé. Lee's taste for these historical works was what "Napoleon considered as the necessary substratum of a strong military background."[16]

Beyond books, Lee also utilized his tenure as superintendent getting to know many more officers and cadets. Among the corps of cadets, some 24 Northern men who attended West Point while Lee was superintendent became general officers in the Federal forces directly opposed to him while he was in command of the Army of Northern Virginia. Fourteen Southern cadets, including his son Custis and his nephew Fitzhugh, rose to become general officers in Lee's famous army.[17]

Among the officers Lee came to know well while at West Point was Massachusetts-born Erasmus D. Keyes. Keyes was well known to General Winfield Scott, although Keyes had not served on Scott's staff when Lee won so much fame during the war with Mexico. Nevertheless, Keyes had gained a sterling military record that garnered Scott's recommendation for him to become an instructor at West Point during the time that Lee was superintendent. Keyes had already known Lee before they were stationed at West Point, as both previously served alongside General Scott on West Point's Board of Visitors. Through his association with Lee before and during Lee's superintendency at West Point, Keyes was certainly impressed with the soldierly and socially refined Lee, remembering that Lee was one of the fairest-minded men he ever met and "exempt from every form and degree of snobbery" even though "his sense of superiority and fitness to command" were undeniable. "No man," admitted Keyes, "could stand in his presence and not recognize his capacity and acknowledge his moral force." Keyes later wrote: "I will not deny that the presence of Lee, and the multiform graces that clustered around him, oftentimes [intimidated] me, though I never envied him, and I doubt if he ever excited envy in any man. All his accomplishments and alluring virtues

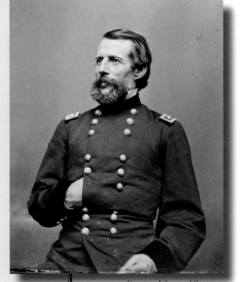

Courtesy Library of Congress

Erasmus D. Keyes

---

[16] Mitchell, Samuel Augustus, *A New Universal Atlas Containing Maps of the various Empires, Kingdoms, States and Republics of the World* (Philadelphia, 1846); Scott Bowden, translator and annotator, *Napoleon's Apogee: Pascal Bressonnet's Tactical Studies 1806* (New York, 2009), "Original 1909 Foreword;" Russell F. Weigley, *The Age of Battles: The Quest for Decisive Warfare from Breitenfeld to Waterloo* (Bloomington, 1991), p. 18; Lancelot, Comte Turpin de Crissé, *Essai sur l'art de la guerre*, 2 volumes (Paris, 1754). The list of books checked out by Robert E. Lee is on record at West Point. For a complete list of books in the West Point Library at the time that Lee was superintendent, consult: *Catalogue of the Library of the U. S. Military Academy, West Point, Exhibiting Its Condition at the Close of the Year 1852* (New York, 1853). Please see the January 10, 1853, "Remarks" by Librarian Henry Coppée for a summary of the library's holdings.

[17] Fitzhugh Lee came close to being expelled from West Point. For a brief summary of the incident, see Emory M. Thomas, *Robert E. Lee: A Biography* (New York, 1995), p. 156.

---

[1] Jefferson Davis, "Report of the Secretary of War, December, 1856," Library of Congress.

appeared natural in him, and he was free from the anxiety, distrust and awkwardness that attend a sense of inferiority, unfriendly discipline and censure."[18]

During his time as superintendent, Lee found himself working with former West Pointer Jefferson Davis. The latter had been a United States Senator from Mississippi and then afterwards named as Secretary of War for newly-elected President Franklin Pierce, and the two men worked to further strengthen the curriculum at the academy. Over the course of the next two years, Davis and Lee built a relationship based largely on Lee's professionalism and consummate courtesy towards his civilian chief.

By the winter of 1854, President Pierce and Jefferson Davis had become very concerned about the United States' lack of military strength on the frontier. The entire army of the United States, per Secretary Davis' report of December, 1854, consisted of only 10,745 personnel to protect America's long seacoast, borders and frontiers. With few available troops offering protection, the migrating population and newly-established towns from Kansas to Texas became inviting targets for 40,000 potentially hostile Plains Indians. As war parties raided with increasing frequency and seeming impunity, the cries for protection finally reached Washington City.

Jefferson Davis in 1853

At the urging of War Secretary Davis, the President moved Congress to act, and two new regiments each of cavalry and infantry for frontier duty were authorized.[19] These were to be crack outfits, officered by the finest men in uniform. In keeping with that goal, Robert E. Lee was assigned as lieutenant colonel and second in command of the 2nd Cavalry (Jefferson Davis named his favorite officer and Mexican War comrade, Albert Sidney Johnston, to command the regiment). For the 48 year-old Lee, "the change from my present confined and sedentary life, to one more free and active, will certainly be more agreeable to my feelings and serviceable to my health."[20]

* * *

The summer of 1855 found Sidney Johnston, Robert E. Lee and the newly-formed regiment assembled in Saint Louis, Missouri, where years before Lee had engineered a remarkable course change of the Mississippi River widely credited with saving the vital river port. By the time Lee made his way to Texas, it was April, 1856. Some 1,800 miles from his Virginia estate, Lee called his new post "my Texas home." Named Camp Cooper after the army's adjutant general and Robert E. Lee's brother-in-law, Samuel Cooper, the site had been selected in early January of that year when Colonel Sidney Johnston and Major William J. Hardee led the regiment southward and across the Red River into Texas until arriving at Camp Cooper. Located in modern-day, south central Throckmorton County—approximately the extreme northeastern edge of what is widely known as West Texas, and situated on the north side of the Clear Fork of the Brazos River—Camp Cooper is about seven miles north of

---

[18] Erasmus D. Keyes, *Fifty Years' Observation of Men and Events, Civil and Military* (New York, 1884), pp. 166, 204 and 205.

[19] *Documents, 1st Session, 34th Congress,* vol. 1, part 2, p. 3, as cited in Freeman, *R. E. Lee,* vol. 1, p. 349.

[20] Dowdey, *Lee,* p. 103. Like many Southerners, Albert Sidney Johnston went by his middle name, Sidney.

present-day Fort Griffin State Historical Site. The post provided a staging area from which the army could adequately protect the expanding population of settlers in the region. Four companies from the 2nd Cavalry were initially stationed at Camp Cooper, joined later by two companies from the 1st United States Infantry. The remainder of the cavalry regiment was initially stationed at Fort Mason (in present day Mason County) about 170 miles south of Camp Cooper and about 100 miles north-northwest of San Antonio de Bexar (that place was later designated as another garrison post for the regiment). The establishment of frontier forts made possible many famous Texas settlements.

Author's collection

Clear Fork of the Brazos

Unusually positioned on several acres of low-lying, fairly level ground, Camp Cooper sheltered behind a high, steeply sloping bank that protected the area during the winter months from the piercing northerly winds. Locals believed that whoever selected the site could not have picked a worse place for the camp. While sources differ on whether Johnston or Hardee selected the site, in his notes of Camp Cooper from his inspection of that site from July 31st through August 3rd, 1856, Inspector General Joseph K. F. Mansfield (who would later be killed in the fighting at Sharpsburg) stated that it was Major Hardee who established the camp on January 2nd, 1856, and that Lee took command on April 15th of that year. Located on the northern bank next to the river with higher terrain almost immediately across the river to the south, the camp, blocked by the higher bank and the trees lining the river, sat too low to consistently catch the predominant southwesterly breeze. As a result, the place was still and sultry during a significant portion of the year. Scarce rainfall exacerbated the misery of the hotter months, and the water in the Clear Fork, although sometimes marginally clear, typically became brackish and barely palatable for human use. Scorching summer temperatures, when combined with inadequate protection from the Texas sun, punished men and horses alike. When, during these months, Lee would ride from Camp Cooper to exercise and to catch a breeze, he would write his wife that the wind seemed to come off the Texas prairie "like the blast off a hot-air furnace." One summer day in 1857, Lee recorded that the temperature was 112 degrees "in the Hospital Tent, the coolest place we have."

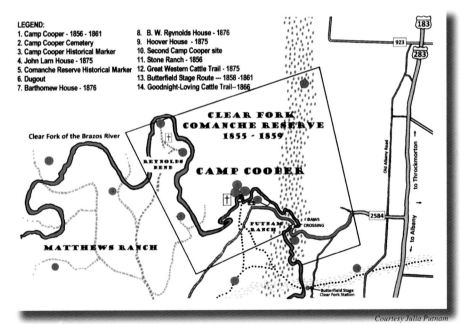

LEGEND:
1. Camp Cooper - 1856 - 1861
2. Camp Cooper Cemetery
3. Camp Cooper Historical Marker
4. John Lam House - 1875
5. Comanche Reserve Historical Marker
6. Dugout
7. Barthomew House - 1876
8. B. W. Reynolds House - 1876
9. Hoover House - 1875
10. Second Camp Cooper site
11. Stone Ranch - 1856
12. Great Western Cattle Trail - 1875
13. Butterfield Stage Route --- 1858 -1861
14. Goodnight-Loving Cattle Trail--1866

CLEAR FORK COMANCHE RESERVE 1855 - 1859

CAMP COOPER

Clear Fork of the Brazos River

REYNOLDS BEND

MATTHEWS RANCH

PUTNAM RANCH

DAWS CROSSING

Butterfield Stage Clear Fork Station

Old Albany Road

to Throckmorton

to Albany

183

923

283

2584

Courtesy Julia Putnam

Map of Camp Cooper

The most frequent visitors to Camp Cooper were the 577 "settled" Comanche Indians from the reservation immediately across the narrow river, along with western diamondback rattlesnakes, chaparrals (the rattlesnakes' most feared predator) and tarantulas. Beyond the immediate reaches of the garrison roamed "wild" Comanche and Kiowa Indians. Lee and the four companies of the 2nd Cavalry at Camp Cooper spent various periods of time on the vast Texas prairies trying to survive the parching summer heat, inhospitable arachnids, pit vipers and fierce, wild Comanche and Kiowas.

Lee recognized that the "marauding Indians" were a formidable adversary, for they "were well armed with guns, revolvers and bows, and fought with desperation" while being "mounted on fleet American horses." The desolate terrain, the weather and the reality of living continuously under threat of attack by Indians made life on the plains of Texas difficult. Lee wrote of the challenges at Camp Cooper in his letters home, in which he held fast to discipline and order, to ideals and honor, and to patriotism and purpose.

To deter and intercept Indian raiders, Lee either led or ordered expeditions (also called reconnaissance) out of Camp Cooper. One of the better-documented expeditions led by Lee into Comanche country in West Texas began on June 12th, 1856. Lee knew the expedition would tax both men and beasts, and he decided to take his best units, companies A (from Alabama) and F (from Kentucky) with him, while leaving

Courtesy Library of Congress

Lee considered the Comanche (shown here) to be a formidable adversary

companies E (from Missouri) and K (from Ohio) at Camp Cooper. According to orders, Lee was to rendezvous with companies B (from Virginia) and G (recruited nation-wide) at or near Fort Chadbourne.

Departing Camp Cooper, Lee led his column initially southwest across rolling prairies of parched grass and mesquite trees, past the blackened ruins of Old Fort Phantom Hill that had been abandoned and burned two years earlier. From Phantom Hill, continuing southwest another three dozen miles, Lee saw the landscape change to the classic West Texas desert terrain of sand-swept broken flats and tumbleweeds. Moving west of modern day Abilene, across the low, dry hills that offered frequent sightings of chaparrals running over the wide mesquite flats, the column made its way towards the 2,400-foot landmark of Castle Peak, about seven miles south of present day Merkel. In the van of the column rode Lee with his celebrated Delaware Indian scout, Jim Shaw, and his Delaware Indian trackers. As the column moved deeper into the desert, Lee peered across the hot plains, the heat came off the Texas sand, rippling the horizon with its optical illusions. Two companies of the blue-clad troopers of the 2nd Cavalry, their accoutrements shining and with the wagons and teamsters, brought up the rear of the column.

Author's collection

Old Fort Phantom Hill

Pushing further southwestward, Lee directed the column to Mountain Pass, a conspicuous mountain rimming the plain several days march south of Old Fort Phantom Hill. Beyond the rock-strewn gap of Mountain Pass, lined with cedar brush and mesquite trees, Lee ascended to the tableland and continued to Fort Chadbourne, a short distance north of present-day Bronte, in Coke County. When Lee brought the column within sight of the fort on June 17th, two companies of troopers dispatched from Fort Mason were waiting, along with a freight wagon bound for Camp Cooper loaded with ammunition and supplies. Lee re-supplied his column, and headed south the next day.

Two days out of Fort Chadbourne and crossing the Colorado River, Lee received word from his scouts that widespread flames and dense columns of smoke could be seen coming off the Texas prairie to the south and west.

Texas State Archives

FORT CHADBOURNE, TEXAS

Middleton, Wallace & Co. Cincinnati, O.

Courtesy Texas Historical Society

Fort Chadbourne

Lee reasoned that the fires could only have been set by the Indians as some sort of signal to other warring Indians. To shorten the time that any hostiles might have to gather against him, Lee continued to push his 210 troopers southward. Shaw's Delaware scouts brought news that all the prairie south of the Colorado River was afire, which meant that there would be no grasses on which Lee's horses could graze. Lee was contemplating his next move when the Delaware returned with reports that there were no signs of recent Comanche activity to the south and west. Lee therefore turned the command to the northwest, and again striking "the red-clay breaks of the Colorado," moved upriver in order to keep his command watered.

Since the Comanches had long controlled the region of the upper Colorado, Lee decided to continue northwest in search of the Indians. For several days the column moved along the Colorado in the searing heat. Near one of the campsites where Lee and his troopers spent one night, the town of Robert Lee was founded, which is the county seat of Coke County, Texas. The northwestward march continued until the column reached the area of "seven wells" before turning northeastward, then northward, Lee leading the four companies of the 2nd Cavalry west of present-day Sweetwater, Roby and Rotan. The country blazed heat and the ground had baked rock-hard from the drought of that year. The prairies over which coveys of blue quail would run before the sounds of men and horses were instead vacant. Creek beds that usually held refreshing water for the prairie chicken and occasional desert traveler were almost dry. Instead, briny pools of stagnant water "occasionally covered with green scum" represented all the water that could be found. As might be expected, these water sources were teeming with bacteria that afflicted the troopers with dysentery and diarrhea. Suffering but led by a determined commanding officer, the troopers of the column continued northeastward to the Double Mountain Fork of the Brazos, and then to the flat-topped buttes of Double Mountain in Stonewall County. Reaching the

Author's collection

Ruins of old Fort Chadbourne

Double Mountain Fork of the Brazos on June 28th, Lee called a halt in order to rest his men and horses from the punishing effects of the Texas sun and heat. As the column made camp at the southern base of Double Mountain, the men and their horses enjoyed the shallow waters of the river. Lee, meanwhile, studied the area and plotted his next movements.

All around, Lee saw evidence of prior Indian camps amidst the desolation. Eroded gullies and hills of this part of West Texas went in all directions, with more prickly pear cacti to the west and more low-profiled mesquite scrub brush to the east. In the middle of this inhospitable land, and needing to find a way to discover the whereabouts of the hostile Indians and to bring them to bay, Lee decided to strengthen his command through elimination. The heat and

the effects of a continued bad diet and worse water had weakened men and horses alike. Lee therefore selected the sickest troopers, mounted them on the feebler of horses and sent them southward to where they would come across the Clear Fork of the Brazos River, and follow it home to Camp Cooper.

For three nights, Lee maintained a temporary camp at Double Mountain while the command scouted in different directions during the day. After the second night, Lee decided to lead two companies northward until reaching the Little Wichita River, then retraced his steps back to the Double Mountain camp. Two other companies led by Earl Van Dorn moved in the opposite direction towards the Clear Fork of the Brazos, then doubled back to Double Mountain camp.

Finding no large war parties in the Double Mountain region, Lee then headed the reunited companies back toward Big Spring. Now headed southward, Lee again split his command, sending the two companies from Fort Mason further southward to the headwaters of the Concho River before having them head home. While this movement was underway, Lee led the Camp Cooper companies southeastward along the Colorado, with one company moving down the left bank while the other moved down the right bank. With no sightings of large war parties, it became evident that most of the "warring" Indians had vacated the Texas plains, probably moving northward for the summer. Lee then turned his two companies homeward. Crossing the Colorado below Valley Creek, Lee then headed northward past a point that was east of Fort Chadbourne to the headwaters of Pecan Bayou, and then northward to Camp Cooper. When the column arrived back at Camp Cooper, the members had been gone for 40 days and had traversed 32 present Texas counties while riding over 1,100 miles.[21]

Author's collection

Top: Double Mountain Fork of the Brazos
Bottom: Double Mountain

---

[21] Camp Cooper, Lee's expedition against the Comanche and his courts-martial duties details

Following the expedition, Lee's orders sent him to attend court-martial activities. In connection with those duties, Lee traveled extensively throughout Texas, as far west as the Rio Grande and Brownsville to the southwest, to Fredericksburg and San Antonio in the Hill Country, to Indianola on the Gulf Coast in the southeast. While Lee was involved in those activities and travels, the 2nd Cavalry under the command of Sidney Johnston—including other notable officers John Bell Hood, George H. Thomas, Earl Van Dorn, Edmund Kirby Smith, George Stoneman, Jr. and Fitzhugh Lee—patrolled the Texas plains. By December, 1856, Johnston had been convinced of the need for a new site for Camp Cooper, and the regimental commander gave Lee a new mission to find a suitable place to relocate the camp. After considerable scouting, Lee found a desirable spot five miles upriver to the west that held a "magnificent" view from the bluffs overlooking this part of the river. However, Lee remained

---

may be found in several sources, including: Freeman, *R. E. Lee*, vol. 1, pp. 363-364; Thomas, *Robert E. Lee: A Biography*, pp. 165-166; Dowdey, *Lee*, p. 107; Maurine Whorton Redway, *Marks of Lee on Our Land* (San Antonio, 1972), p. 54; Carl Coke Rister, *Robert E. Lee in Texas* (Norman, 1946), pp. 19-52; James R. Arnold, *Jeff Davis' Own: Cavalry, Comanches, and the Battle for the Texas Frontier* (New York, 2000) pp. 78-91; Colonel M. L. Crimmins, "Colonel Robert E. Lee's Report on Indian Combat in Texas," *Southwestern Historical Quarterly*, vol. 39, no. 1 (July 1935), pp. 23-24 and 54-55; Colonel M. L. Crimmins, "Colonel J. K. F. Mansfield's Report of the Inspection of the Department of Texas in 1856," *Southwestern Historical Quarterly*, vol. 42, no. 4 (April, 1939), pp. 351-388; Harold B. Simpson, *Simpson Speaks on History* (Hillsboro, 1986), "Lee West of the River," and "Thunder on the Frontier: The 2nd U. S. Cavalry in Texas, 1855-1861," pp. 94 and 104; Frances Mayhugh Holden, *Lambshead Before Interwoven: A Texas Range Chronicle 1848-1878* (College Station, 1982), pp. 50-54; Joan Farmer and Lawrence Clayton, *Tracks Along the Clear Fork: Stories from Shackelford and Throckmorton Counties* (Abilene, 2000), pp. 82-90; Herbert M. Hart, *Old Forts of the Southwest* (Ann Arbor, 1964), pp. 41-44; Texas State Historical Plaque at the Camp Cooper site, Throckmorton County, Texas; unpublished article titled "Camp Cooper: 1856-1861," by Martha Doty Freeman; unpublished manuscript titled "A History of Camp Cooper, Throckmorton County, Texas," by Martha Doty Freeman, for Aztec of Albany Foundation, Inc., Albany, Texas, October, 1996; personal commentary from Julia Putnam, owner of the land on which Camp Cooper is located and current Chair of the Shackelford County Historical Commission, made during the visit to Camp Cooper by the author and publisher, September 6, 2010; Texas State Historical Plaque at the Comanche Reservation, across the river from the Camp Cooper site, Throckmorton County, Texas. There were both "settled" Comanche Indians as well as "wild" Comanche and Kiowas in the region.

Each company of the 2nd Cavalry was raised from a specific geographic area and rode specific colored horses. The four companies under Lee's command at Camp Cooper were: Company A, consisting of troopers from the state of Alabama and rode grays; Company E, made up of troopers raised from Missouri and rode sorrels; Company F, comprised of troopers raised from Kentucky and rode bays; and Company K, consisting of troopers raised from Ohio, and rode roans. The two companies from Fort Mason that joined Lee for the 40-day reconnaissance mission were Company B, consisting of troopers from Virginia and rode sorrels, along with Company G, recruited nation-wide and rode browns.

In the Comanche country expedition that began on June 12th, 1856, Lee pushed his command an average of more than 27 miles a day—a total of 1,100 miles, which was a remarkable achievement given the barren nature of the Texas terrain combined with the weather. Some accounts state that all the columns comprising this expedition collectively traveled an astounding 1,600 miles during this grueling 40-day expedition, and all done under conditions described by Robert E. Lee as: "The weather was intensely hot, and as we had no tents we had the full benefit of the sun…the water was scarce and bad, salt, bitter and brackish."

The horses of the 2nd Cavalry were known to have been superior animals, selectively purchased by a special team of officers "authorized to buy the best blooded stock available" from Kentucky, Indiana and Ohio. During the six years that the 2nd Cavalry was on the Texas frontier, "most of these horses were still serviceable" when the regiment was ordered to the East for the beginning of the Civil War. Even with this impressive service record by the four-legged warriors of the regiment, the claim by some that Lee pushed his men and horses during the Comanche country expedition across West Texas a total of 1,600 miles over a consecutive 40-day period of time during the summer where "the water was scarce and bad," can only be described as a feat bordering on the near-unbelievable.

very concerned about the lack of water supply at the new location, a drawback when compared to the water availability at the present site. His troopers only had enough time to build a bake oven on this site before Lee was summoned to South Texas for another assignment.[22]

In late July, 1857, Lee got a reprieve from his other duties when Colonel Johnston received orders to report to Washington City. Lee had already departed Camp Cooper to attend courts-martial duties, having left Captain George Stoneman in command. From Fort Mason, Lee took a stage to San Antonio where he spent three months as acting commander of the regiment. However, the command stint in San Antonio was short lived. In October, Lee was called home to Arlington; his father-in-law, George Washington Parke Custis, had died.

Two years had passed since Lee had been with his family. As he rode up the tree-lined approach to the majestic neo-classically styled Arlington house—one that resembled the Temple of Theseus in Athens and overlooked the Potomac River and Washington City—Lee knew from the letters he had received in Texas that of his seven children, only two—"Rob" age 14 and Mildred age 11—remained at home with his wife.[23] Dismounting in front of the columns of the mansion, walking across the wide portico and into the entry way of the family sitting room, Robert E. Lee had to have been shocked by what he saw: his wife was all but an invalid.

The same age as her husband, Mary Custis Lee made a stark contrast in physical appearance to her soldier-husband. As Robert stood in the doorway, with his toned frame and straight soldierly posture, Mary remained seated looking extremely pale and fatigued. Her weakened frame appeared frail and boney, her sharp-featured, thin, patrician face—and always careless hair and appearance—made her resemble a woman that could more likely pass for Robert's mother. Partially crippled by rheumatoid arthritis, Mary's right arm hung almost uselessly. Her face looked drawn from the effects of the sharp pain that constantly racked her body. So painful was her semi-invalidism that her moans of agony broke her sleep at night and would awake Robert. Lee saw to care for his crippled wife with all his energy, while also tackling another

MAJ. GEN! A. S. JOHNSTON.
Published by E. Anthony 501 Broadway N.Y.
Entered according to Act of Congress in the year 1862, by E. Anthony, in the Clerk's office of the District Court of the U.S. for the So. District of New York.

Courtesy Library of Congress

Albert Sidney Johnston

Mary Custis Lee

Courtesy National Park Service

Arlington House

[22] Holden, *Lambshead Before Interwoven*, pp. 57-58; Robert E. Lee to Mrs. Lee, Camp Cooper, June 29, 1857. Robert E. Lee Papers, DeButts-Ely Collection, *Library of Congress*.

[23] Lee's two oldest boys, George Washington Custis Lee ("Boo") and William Henry Fitzhugh Lee ("Rooney") were in the army, while the oldest daughter Mary Custis Lee ("Daughter") was living away from home and the two middle daughters, Anne Carter Lee ("Annie") and Eleanor Agnes Lee ("Wigs") were away at school; "Rob's" real name was Robert Edward Lee, Jr.; Mildred Childe Lee's nickname was "Precious Life."

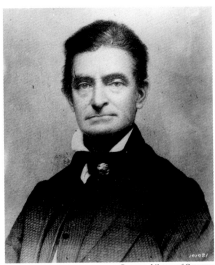

John Brown

Courtesy Library of Congress

formidable task—acting as executor of his father-in-law's disorganized and heavily debt-laden estate. To get George Washington Parke Custis' numerous debts paid off and to bring the property back to a profitable basis, Lee was forced to ask for a year's leave from the army: the break ultimately lasted for more than two years.[24]

Lee's leave of absence abruptly ended on Monday, October 17th, 1859, in a peculiar twist of destiny. A first lieutenant of cavalry by the name of James Ewell Brown ("Jeb") Stuart—one of Lee's favorite cadets while superintendent at West Point—arrived at Arlington with a summons from the War Office. Stuart was a Virginian, had served in the cavalry on the plains (he was with the 1st Cavalry in the Kansas territory) and was on leave from the army. Stuart and his wife had brought back to Virginia their first child to see the grandparents, and while there, the young officer had come to Washington City in the hopes of gaining an audience with War Secretary John B. Floyd. Stuart wanted to sell him on the new device that he had invented for attaching a cavalryman's saber to his belt. Instead of getting to make his pitch, Stuart found himself on a mission to hurry across the Potomac and deliver an urgent message for Lee to come to the War Department without delay.[25]

Without a moment to waste, Lee did not pause to put on his uniform when he received the summons, but immediately rode with Stuart into Washington. Once there, Lee was informed by Secretary Floyd and President Buchanan that the government's arsenal at Harpers Ferry, Virginia had been seized by a group of "ruffians" out of Kansas hoping to stir up a slave insurrection. Taking Stuart as a volunteer aide, Lee went to Harpers Ferry to head the government's response to John Brown's raid. Arriving at the ferry, Lee took command of a detachment of 90 United States Marines that had arrived via rail from Fortress Monroe, and quickly assessed the situation. Brown and his group had indeed taken arms and equipment from the government's arsenal, murdered two townspeople and held another 13 as hostages; they were holed up in a small engine house on the northeast side of town.[26] In the early morning light of October 18th, Lee swiftly executed an attack. The marines stormed the engine house at the point of the bayonet (Lee had ordered them not to fire, so as to try and prevent harm to any of the hostages), killed two of the raiders, wounded Brown and captured him along with the rest of his followers—all without harm to the hostages.[27]

Engine House, Harpers Ferry

Courtesy National Park Service

Although there had been no slave insurrection (there were hardly any slaves in this area of Virginia that later became part of West Virginia), what John Brown failed to achieve through his ineptly executed raid, he achieved at his trial that followed. His calculated martyrdom inflamed the extremists on both sides to new rhetorical absolutes. The praise of the abolitionists and many newspapers in the North—embracing the "higher law" argument—met indignation and rage in the South: how could one section of the country ignore the

THE STORMING OF THE ENGINE-HOUSE

Courtesy Harpers Weekly

The Marines Storming the Engine House

---

[24] Dowdey, *Lee*, pp. 111-112.

[25] Thomas, *Robert E. Lee: A Biography*, pp. 179-180. Stuart later secured the patent for his saber hook, and sold the rights to the government for $5,000.

[26] Some sources list the number of hostages at nine, with another five defined as "non-participants." In any event, Brown and his men held a total of 13 people who had not chosen to be there.

[27] For details on John Brown's raid, please consult: David M. Potter, *The Impending Crisis 1848-1861* (New York, 1977).

Courtesy Harpers Weekly

John Brown Hanging

rule of law and advocate servile insurrection against the other? Regardless of rhetoric, Brown's raid made it a practical impossibility to disassociate slavery from the growing sectional crisis, or to rationally discuss the possibility of gradual emancipation. When John Brown was hanged on December 2nd, 1859, a flood of emotion and recrimination widened the growing national schism that had previously and primarily revolved around tariffs and related issues of two very different economic systems. A collision of American cultures—what historian Clifford Dowdey describes as "the fundamental division in the nature of the republic as it was conceived"—had picked up steam at an alarming rate. Meanwhile, Lee, having played a thoroughly professional role in this bizarre tragedy, was making his way back to Texas; in keeping with his character, he had little to say about the entire disturbing episode.[28]

* * * *

Shortly after his 53rd birthday (January 19, 1860), Lieutenant Colonel Lee returned to Texas as acting commander of the Department for the then-absent 69 year-old Brevet Major-General David E. Twiggs. The department stretched over the most desolate area of Texas from around Lee's old Camp Cooper in the north, extending southwestward to the Rio Grande River and continuing to Brownsville. There was trouble in Texas, and Governor Sam Houston wanted the Federal government to help do something about it. The Penatekas, Tanimas and Naconies Indian tribes, as well as Mexican banditos led by Juan Cortinas, were terrorizing south Texas along the Rio Grande.

Cortinas represented the biggest problem. He and his band of irregulars had been pillaging and murdering for years. Although badly beaten and scattered

---

[28] Dowdey, *Lee*, p. 121. Also see: Charles Adams, *When in the Course of Human Events: Arguing the Case for Southern Secession* (Lanham, 2000).

Courtesy Texas Historical Society

Comanche with scalp

at a fight near Rio Grande City, on December 27th, 1859, by a combined force of U. S. Cavalry and Texas Rangers led by Major Samuel P. Heintzelman and John S. "Rip" Ford, respectively, Cortinas remained undeterred. He recruited many new banditos within the friendly borders of Mexico, and arrived back in force in less than six weeks. Again crossing the Rio Grande near Brownsville, Cortinas and about 500 of his men "laid waste the Rio Grande Valley from Brownsville to Rio Grande City, a distance of 120 miles." The army lacked enough troopers to cover all the territory that Sidney Johnston described "as open as an ocean," but Lee did not let the lack of adequate resources affect his efforts to deal with Cortinas. With orders in hand from Secretary of War John B. Floyd "to stop Mexican depredations, and, if necessary pursue the Mexicans beyond the limits of the United States," Lee prepared the 2nd Cavalry for an expedition. Leaving San Antonio on March 15th, Lee led his troopers across the vast, south Texas plains towards Edinburg and the Rio Grande. During the days in the saddle, Lee scouted the terrain, directed the reconnaissance and organized the patrols, drawing on his experience leading elements of the 2nd Cavalry on prior, extended expeditions.[29]

By the time Lee arrived at the Rio Grande on April 7th, Cortinas had fled before the combined force of a company of U. S. Cavalry led by George Stoneman, Jr., and "Rip" Ford's Rangers. Lee found that the Mexican border town of Reynosa had been supporting Cortinas, and admonished the officials not to support Cortinas, lest they invite a war. The Rio Grande campaign had already cost Cortinas' banditos heavily, losing 151 in one engagement and more than 300 in another. Casualties among Federal troops and Texas Rangers amounted to one ranger killed and 16 troopers wounded. With efforts at trapping and capturing Cortinas unsuccessful, and with the bandito leader and the surviving members of his band having withdrawn to the Burgos Mountains some 100 miles in the interior of Mexico, Lee left 40-percent of the 2nd Cavalry along the Lower Rio Grande as a deterrent. Meanwhile, to the north and west, other companies of the 2nd Cavalry that included a young nephew, Lieutenant Fitzhugh Lee, dispersed a group of marauding Indians.[30]

The frontier fighting with the 2nd Cavalry served to further enhance Lee's physical stamina, eye for terrain, horsemanship and command abilities. Yet, in the barracks and around the campfires, the growing topic of discussion concerned the possible secession by the states of the Lower South. Lee clearly and frequently

Courtesy Harpers Weekly

San Antonio Military Plaza

[29] In addition to the 40-day expedition Lee led in the summer of 1856, he led another lasting 27 consecutive days. Neither had resulted in combat.

[30] Freeman, *R. E. Lee*, vol. 1, pp. 405-409; Rister, *Robert E. Lee in Texas*, pp. 40, 115-128; William Preston Johnston, *The Life of Gen. Albert Sidney Johnston* (New York, 1997 reprint), p. 191; Crimmins, "Colonel Robert E. Lee's Report on Indian Combat in Texas," *Southwestern Historical Quarterly*, vol. 39, no. 1, pp. 21-33; Redway, *Marks of Lee on Our Land*, p. 56; Arnold, *Jeff Davis' Own*, pp. 267-296; Harold B. Simpson, *Cry Comanche: The 2nd U. S. Cavalry in Texas, 1855-1861* (Hillsboro, 1988), pp. 140-144; Simpson, "Lee West of the River," *Simpson Speaks on History*, pp. 94 and 104; Emily Virginia Mason, *Popular Life of General Robert Edward Lee* (Baltimore [Second Revised Edition], 1872), pp. 68-69. For a detailed account of the Rio Grande campaign against Juan Cortinas, please see: Richard B. McCaslin, *Fighting Stock: John S. "Rip" Ford of Texas* (Fort Worth, 2011), pp. 85-98, and Arnold, Jeff Davis' Own, pp. 267-280.

voiced his opinions over the growing sectional crisis. "I am not pleased with the course of the 'Cotton States,' as they called themselves," Lee wrote in a letter home. He hoped that "wisdom and patriotism" and "the dictates of reason" would eventually prevail in order to avert secession. Yet, Lee believed that if the secession movement came to be, and if it were opposed by force, "a Union that can only be maintained by swords and bayonets, and in which strife and civil war are to take the place of brotherly love and kindness, has no charm for me." The soldier who had apprehended John Brown, the engineer who had once helped change the course of the Mississippi, the officer Winfield Scott believed deserving of honors involving the victory over Mexico, Lee none the less felt a fatalistic resignation as he watched the nation continue on its tragic collision course.[31]

The results of the election of November 6th, 1860, finally set into motion what had been simmering for three decades. Within four days of the news that Abraham Lincoln had won, South Carolina lawmakers issued a call for a convention to withdraw their state from the Union; they voted to secede on December 20th. Other states followed South Carolina's lead, and by the middle of January, 1861, six "Cotton States" had passed ordinances of secession. In San Antonio, there was hardly any talk other than what was happening across the South; sentiment for secession was on an emotional overload, and throughout most places in Texas, people raised versions of the "Bonnie Blue Flag"—a field of deep blue with a single white star, representing the sovereignty of their state and advocating secession. Writing on January 23rd, 1861, Lee thought the secession movement to be nothing short of "folly, selfishness and short-sightedness" that would result in a "fearful calamity." While Lee believed that the South "has been aggrieved by the acts of the North . . . [he] would defend any State if her rights were invaded." Lee also declared that "if the Union is dissolved," he would "go back in sorrow to my people and share the misery of my native state . . . and save in defense will draw my sword on none."[32]

Bonnie Blue Flag and Song Lyrics Title Page

A little more than one week after Lee penned these thoughts, Texas delegates passed an ordinance of secession, becoming the seventh state to withdraw from the Federal compact. Three days later, on Monday, February 4th, Lee was ordered to Washington; he was to report to his old commander, General-in-Chief Winfield Scott. On the 13th, Lee relinquished his command and departed Fort Mason for San Antonio where he planned on seeing the department commander, General Twiggs, before traveling to the coast and taking ship to Virginia. On the road to San Antonio, Lee stopped at a well-known spring, where he came upon 1st Lieutenant George Blake Cosby of his regiment. When Cosby found out where Lee was heading, he "told [Lee] that General Scott wanted to consult with him as to a campaign against the seceding states. He feared so, too [and] if he found my surmises correct he would tender his resignation and offer his services to his native State."[33]

When Lee arrived in San Antonio, he found the secessionists in control: General Twiggs, the department commander, had already surrendered his 160-man garrison. In the chaos of the moment, three secessionist commissioners

---

[31] For a concise collection of these, and other related letters on this topic, consult: Freeman, *R. E. Lee*, vol. 1, pp. 417-424.

[32] Freeman, *R. E. Lee*, vol. 1, pp.420-421; Kevin R. Young, *To The Tyrants Never Yield: A Texas Civil War Sampler* (Plano, 1992) p. 44.

[33] Rister, *Robert E. Lee in Texas*, p. 158.

representing the Jacobin-sounding "Committee of Public Safety" demanded that Lee resign his commission on the spot and join the Confederacy; refusal to do so would result in him being denied transportation for his effects. Indignant at such impudence, Lee told the commissioners that he held no allegiance to any revolutionary Texas government and that they had no authority—moral or otherwise—to cause him any delay or deny transportation of his belongings.[34]

THE ALAMO, SAN ANTONIO, TEXAS, LATE HEAD-QUARTERS OF EX-GENERAL TWIGGS.—FROM A SKETCH BY A GOVERNMENT DRAUGHTSMAN.—[SEE PAGE 182.]

Courtesy Harpers Weekly

The Alamo

With the situation chaotic, Lee strode angrily from the commissioners to seek out an old acquaintance. Lee went to see staunch Unionist Charles Anderson, who later became Governor of Ohio, and was the brother of Robert Anderson, later known to the nation as the commander of the garrison at Fort Sumter. Lee relayed the story of the Texans' impudence with such a wrath that Anderson never forgot. After assuring Lee that he would forward his belongings, Anderson remembered what Lee then said: "I shall so report myself at Washington. If Virginia stands by the Old Union, so will I. But if she secedes, then I will still follow my native state with my sword, and if need be with my life. I know you think and feel very differently, but I can't help that. These are my principles, and I must follow them."[35]

To get home expeditiously while avoiding as many confrontations as possible with secessionist commissioners like he had encountered in San Antonio, Lee decided to take the stage to Indianola on the Texas coast. From there he could procure water-born transportation for New Orleans and then Virginia. Lee arrived in Indianola on Friday, February 22nd, the 129th anniversary of the birth of his hero, George Washington. Taking a steamer from the port on Matagorda Bay, Lee reached New Orleans three days later, where he took another ship home. Before that boat docked in Alexandria, Virginia on March 1st, Lee had read enough newspapers to know that the Provisional Congress of the newly-formed Confederate States of America had already met in Montgomery, Alabama, and that an old acquaintance had been installed as President. Jefferson Davis was a logical choice for chief executive, because for years he had expounded on what Clifford Dowdey described as "his theories of the rule of the plantocracy—in or out of the Union." By the time Lee joined his family at Arlington, the course of the Federal government marked a pressing issue. Furthermore, if Virginia seceded, how would he fit into the equation, given the fact that he was still an officer in the United States army?[36]

Author's collection

**Modern-day image of
Fort Mason**

---

[34] The three members of the "Committee for Public Safety" were Sam Maverick, Judge Thomas Devine and Philip Luckett. See: Young, *To The Tyrants Never Yield*, pp. 40 and 49-52.

[35] *Southern Historical Society Papers*, Charles Anderson, "Lee and Scott," vol. 11, p. 443-449, and *Texas Before and on the Eve of the Rebellion* (Cincinnati, 1884), p. 32; Rister, *Robert E. Lee in Texas*, pp. 160-161. Lee never recovered his belongings. Anderson sent the bags, but the ship on which Lee's trunks were loaded passed by way of New York, where the cargo was seized.

[36] Rister, *Robert E. Lee in Texas*, pp. 160-161; Clifford Dowdey, *Experiment in Rebellion* (New

The denouement in Lee's bewildering situation began taking shape shortly thereafter.[37] Per his orders, Lee reported to General Scott. Arriving at General Scott's outer office, Lee was greeted by his acquaintance, Erasmus Keyes, who now held the rank of lieutenant colonel and was serving as General Scott's military secretary. Showing Lee in to see the general, Keyes left the two men behind closed doors for the next three hours. When the meeting broke up and Lee departed, Keyes observed that the usually talkative Scott had nothing to say. Keyes believed that for a man who liked to gab about what had been discussed "after having had a private interview with an important person," Scott's conversation with Lee must have been so deeply solemn that Scott not only kept a tight lip immediately after the meeting, he never made "reference to the subject of his conversation with Lee."[38]

What passed between Scott and Lee during those three hours is evidently only reported second-hand, but from those sources, the substance of at least a part of what was said can be reasonably reconstructed. Lee asked Scott what was going to be done concerning his orders, and told Scott how he felt. An anxious Lee wanted to know if he "was to be placed on duty against the South" because he had "to know so that he might at once resign." The aging Scott, still a physically imposing figure at six-feet five-inches tall and weighing at least 230 pounds, tried to convince Lee of what Scott described as the folly of tying himself to his native state if it chose secession. Scott also believed the sectional turmoil would soon be resolved peacefully. According to a conversation with William Allen, Scott showed Lee "a mass of correspondence between himself, Lincoln and others, which made Scott think there would be no war. . . One of Seward's letters was very emphatic, & stated that he (Seward) would not remain in the cabinet if he thought anything but peace contemplated."[39] With a solution at avoiding war believed to be genuine, the general also tried to appeal to Lee's ambitions; he told Lee that he would soon be promoted to colonel and that he wanted Lee to help others revise the army regulations. Furthermore, in an attempt to alleviate any angst, Scott informed Lee that he would not, for the time being, be placed under war orders. Scott also went on to hint that he was too feeble to take the field and would recommend Lee as his second in command.[40]

Following the meeting, Lee returned to Arlington to await developments. In both houses of Congress in Washington City, as well as in Richmond, Virginia, cooler heads seemed to be making progress toward averting war. In Congress, an amendment attempting to soothe Southern fire-eaters by preserving slavery in the states that had it (which would have included Delaware and the border states) had already passed the House on February 28th and subsequently received a two-thirds vote approval in the Senate the day after Lee had returned home from Texas. Meanwhile, the Virginia secession convention rejected the motion to leave the Union. While the delegates disagreed at that time on secession, they were in agreement that Virginia would not be party to any "coercion" on the part of the Federal government to bring any Southern state that had seceded back under Federal control. The vote was a reflection that many Virginians still held dear the

Courtesy Library of Congress

Winfield Scott

"I am impelled to make special mention of the services of Captain R. E. Lee, engineers. This officer, greatly distinguished at the siege of Vera Cruz, was again indefatigable during the operations, in reconnaissances as daring as laborious, and of the greatest value. Nor was he less conspicuous in planting batteries, and in conducting columns to their stations under the heavy fire of the enemy."

Winfield Scott, in a report on the Mexican War

York, 1947), p. 8; Simpson, "Lee West of the River," *Simpson Speaks on History*, p. 98.

[37] The exact date of the meeting is not known, but it was clearly long before the due date of April 1st. See William Allan, "Memoranda of Conventions with General Robert E. Lee," in Gary W. Gallagher, ed., *Lee the Soldier* (Lincoln, 1996), pp. 9-10, and 12.

[38] Keyes, *Fifty Years' Observations of Men and Events Civil and Military*, p. 206.

[39] William Allan, "Memoranda of Conversations with General Robert E. Lee," in Gary W. Gallagher, editor, *Lee the Soldier*, p. 9.

[40] Allan, "Memoranda of Conversations with General Robert E. Lee," *Lee the Soldier*, p. 10.

ideals of anti-Federalist Jeffersonian democracy. Then, Lincoln's March 4th inaugural address made it clear that he was going to do whatever necessary in order to, in his view, uphold the Constitution by invoking the protection clause. Lincoln intended to preserve the Union by holding all government property in the South, and by insisting on the executive power of collecting taxes even in states that had seceded. Clearly, Lincoln meant to employ all the powers of his office. This interpretation and clear denial of any right to secession indicated that, for the immediate moment, the choices would be either a war to preserve the Union or a political reconciliation with the Deep South.

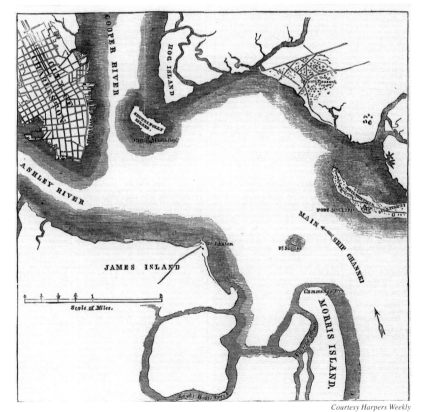

Courtesy Harpers Weekly

City of Charleston, South Carolina

Shortly after Lincoln's inaugural address, Lee received—and ignored—an offer from Confederate Secretary of War Leroy Pope Walker naming him as a brigadier general (the highest rank then being offered by the Confederate Congress). Lee still considered himself as an officer of the United States and the offer from Walker was not something a citizen of a state still in the Union could consider. About two weeks later, on March 28th, Lee received and accepted his new commission to the rank of colonel, signed by Abraham Lincoln. With his promotion, Lee became commanding officer of the 1st Cavalry. Even though the newly-minted colonel understood the purpose for the timing of his promotion, Lee repeated what he had said before: he hoped the Union would be preserved, but would adhere to the course decided upon by Virginia. Revealing his innermost convictions to Mary's cousin, Lee declared: "There is no sacrifice I am not ready to make for the preservation of the Union save that of honour."[41] For Lee, it would soon come to just such a dilemma.

Courtesy Harpers Weekly

Map of Charleston Harbor

While Lee awaited events in Washington and in his state capital, President Lincoln, the day after his inauguration, received a report from Major Robert Anderson, commanding the 80-odd Federal soldiers and four-to-five dozen laborers who were now closed up inside Fort Sumter located in Charleston Harbor, South Carolina. The pentagon-shaped brick fort had been under construction when South Carolina declared itself an independent republic on December 20th, 1860; six days later, for the sake of protecting his men, Anderson moved his command—then stationed at Fort Moultrie on Sullivan's Island—to Sumter. The unfinished fort occupied an artificial island inside the entrance to Charleston Harbor, and Anderson knew that if his tiny command were to stay, he needed help, and fast. He warned the President that unless massive amounts of reinforcements and supplies embarked soon, the fort would have to be surrendered. Lincoln had

---

[41] Avery Craven, ed., *"To Markie": The Letters of Robert E. Lee to Martha Custis Williams from the Originals in the Huntington Library* (Cambridge, 1933), p. 59.

come to a critical crossroads. If he did not send help, Sumter would fall without a shot being fired, and the blow to the authority of the Federal government, while embarrassing, would lack passion-raising drama. On the other hand, Lincoln could try and force the issue by creating the conditions by which the secessionists would, in essence, convince themselves that they had to fire on the garrison, thus initiating a war. For weeks, Lincoln and his cabinet debated the issue until the President, over the objections of General Scott and many advisers, determined to "maintain the authority of the Government." Lincoln decided to let it be known to the Confederate authorities in Montgomery that an expedition was to be ready to leave New York by April 8th, not with arms and men, but only with "provisions [that] would be sent to Sumter peaceably, otherwise by force."[42]

With this communiqué, Lincoln had, at least for the moment, shifted the onus of starting a war onto Jefferson Davis and the secessionists, and Lincoln had a pretty good idea how those firebrand Southerners, filled with bravado, might respond. Only two months earlier, the secessionists fired on a single relief ship sent by President Buchanan as it approached Fort Sumter. Therefore, by letting the Confederates know ahead of time that a full-scale expedition would be steaming out of New York and bound for Charleston, Lincoln was calculating that the secessionists would fire on Major Anderson's garrison before the relief ships arrived. Lincoln's instincts were excellent.

Those at the forefront of The Cause had very little patience. Rather than applying cool reason to the full scope of the diplomatic problem confronting the objective of Southern independence—a goal that might still be achieved without starting the shooting—Jefferson Davis and the firebrands did the opposite. Rather than ignore the presence of the Sumter garrison, thereby turning back onto Lincoln the damaging and damning onus of igniting the war, Davis pressed ahead as if he were fearful his chance for war might slip away. Anxious to demonstrate that the seceded states were independent and sovereign republics, Davis believed that the situation demanded a military solution: the diminutive Federal garrison would have to be removed from Southern soil, regardless of its questionable military value. In doing so, the minor irritant of a handful of Federal gunners in Charleston Harbor became the catalyst for a foolish self-inflicted wound, akin to firing a pistol at a fly on a wall and hitting yourself with the ricochet in the foot. To Davis and those puffed-up Southern firebrands, the Stars and Stripes flying above Fort Sumter represented something far more than a militarily insignificant command in the South Carolina harbor—it flouted the symbolism of Confederate sovereignty. Pride demanded that something be done. After 30 years in the long concatenation of events, war's powder keg was about to be lit by a cavalier match.

One member of Jefferson Davis' cabinet, Robert Toombs of Georgia, strongly disagreed with Davis and many others who were in favor of firing on Fort Sumter. According to one eye-witness, Toombs told Davis that opening fire on the Federal garrison would be "suicide...[as] it is unnecessary, it puts us in the wrong, it is fatal."[43]

Courtesy Harpers Weekly

Francis W. Pickens, Governor of South Carolina

Courtesy Library of Congress

Robert Toombs

"Wars begin when you will, but they do not end when you please."

—Niccolo Machiavelli

---

[42] *Charleston Mercury*, Thursday, December 13, 1860, "Our Harbor 'Defenses;'" *Charleston Mercury*, Friday, December 21, 1860, "Our Harbor Defenses—Fort Sumter." The numbers in Anderson's command vary, but appear to have been 10 officers and 74 to 76 enlisted. The number of laborers shrank during the ordeal. Ernest B. Furguson, *Freedom Rising: Washington in the Civil War* (New York, 2004), p. 73; Freeman, *R. E. Lee*, vol. 1, p. 435; Dowdey, *The Land They Fought For*, p. 89; William C. Davis, *Jefferson Davis*, p. 322; Pollard, *The Lost Cause*, pp. 108-109.

[43] See this account in William C. Davis, *Jefferson Davis: The Man and His Hour* (Baton Rouge,

Bombardment of Sumter

Courtesy Harpers Weekly

Courtesy Harpers Weekly

Charleston Rooftop Image

Horace Greeley

Courtesy Library of Congress

Davis ignored the objections of his cooler-thinking cabinet member, instead sending orders through Secretary of War Walker for General Pierre Gustave Toutant Beauregard to demand the immediate evacuation of the fort. Anderson told Beauregard's emissaries that surrender at this time was out of the question, but that he would soon be starved out and promised to evacuate Fort Sumter by noon on April 15th if he had not received other orders from Washington. Rather than wait the three days, Beauregard ordered the immediate removal of the Federal garrison in accordance with Davis' orders. On April 12th, Confederate batteries opened fire on Fort Sumter's garrison; on the 14th, Major Anderson surrendered the tiny command without the loss of life on either side.[44]

Receiving news of Sumter's fall, Lincoln issued a proclamation calling for 75,000 volunteers "to suppress said combinations," meaning the secession, and "to cause the laws to be duly executed," meaning to collect the taxes due the Federal government from the seceding states.[45] In plain language, Lincoln was calling for an army to invade the "Cotton States" and bring them back into the Union (whereby they would resume paying their taxes). Had Lincoln issued such a call without the Southerners firing on Fort Sumter, Northern passion for coercion and tax collection would have been tepid at best. Lincoln wisely kept his hounds of war close at hand; it was Davis and the firebrands who unleashed them, and that latter fact meant everything.

Lincoln's call-to-arms appealed to Northerners to save the Union, and they did not disappoint him. Volunteers flooded Northern recruiting offices as war fever engulfed the 16 Union states. For example, Ohio was supposed to furnish a contingent of 13 regiments. The turnout in that Midwest state was so great that the Ohio governor wrote: "Without repressing the ardor of the people, I can hardly stop short of twenty regiments." In New York City, newspaper mogul Horace Greeley claimed that the entirety of the President's 75,000-man quota could be raised in that city alone.[46]

As the tidal wave of men rushed forward, Lincoln recognized that his call for armed invasion might quickly force the hand of the so-called border states of the Upper South that, up until that point, had remained in the Union. Lincoln's announced plans for invasion and his summons for each state, including those of the upper South to furnish its quota for the confrontation (Virginia, for example, was to furnish 2,340 of the 75,000 volunteers) confirmed the policy of coercion. Naturally, the upper South neither wanted to be part of an invading force, nor wished to acquiesce to allowing Federal troops to utilize their territories, taxes and other resources to invade sister states. The very nature of the fiercely independent

1991), p. 323; Dowdey, *The Land They Fought For*, pp. 89-90.

[44] Furgurson, *Freedom Rising: Washington in the Civil War*, p. 73; Eisenhower, *Agent of Destiny*, p. 367. Two men of the Federal garrison were killed after the surrender when the gun with which they were firing a ceremonial salute exploded.

[45] *The War of the Rebellion: A Compilation of the Official Records of the Union and Confederate Armies*, 130 volumes (Washington, D. C., 1880-1901), Series III, vol. 1, pp. 67-68. Hereafter cited as *Official Records*.

[46] Eisenhower, *Agent of Destiny*, p. 369.

Southerner would not allow such a thing. With neutrality impossible, and in accordance with their sympathies, Arkansas, North Carolina, Tennessee and Virginia declared for the Confederacy; it would be not only disgraceful, but dishonorable to step aside and let Lincoln's legions pass southward.[47]

The Unionist majorities in those states "suddenly dissolved once the choice shifted from supporting the Union or the Confederacy to fighting for or against fellow Southerners." The theme emanating from these states was consistent. "I can be no party to this wicked violation of the laws of this country," penned Governor John W. Ellis of North Carolina. "Kentucky will furnish no troops for the wicked purpose of subduing her sister Southern States," wrote Kentucky Governor Beriah Magoffin. "In such an unholy crusade no gallant son of Tennessee will ever draw a sword," declared Governor Isham Green Harris. From Atlanta, Confederate Vice President Alexander H. Stephens boastfully predicted that it would "require seventy-five times the 75,000 volunteers to intimidate the South." To these Southerners, it was now revolution in the face of tyranny. Davis and Lincoln got a war that each had a significant hand in creating, and Robert E. Lee knew what that meant for him.[48]

Responding to Lincoln's threatening measures, the Virginia Convention went into secret session on April 16th. Two days later, with still no word from Richmond on whether or not the convention had reached a decision to lead Old Dominion out of the Union, Lee had come to his own crossroads. The colonel had received on the 17th two pieces of correspondence, one from General Scott ordering him to his office the next day, and the other from a Washington cousin, John Lee. The relative communicated that the famous publicist, political power broker and distant relative, Francis Preston Blair, Sr., desired to meet with Lee the next morning at the Washington home of Blair's son.[49] Lee decided to see Blair before reporting to Scott.

Leaving the majestic views of the front porch of Arlington that cool Thursday morning, Lee traveled down the hill and over Long Bridge that spanned the Potomac into Washington. As he made his way into the capital city with the cherry trees in full bloom, Lee knew the manner of the man he was about to meet. For the past 35 years, the elder Blair had proved to be one of the most powerful behind-the-scenes figures in American politics. By the time Andrew Jackson won the Presidential election of 1828, Blair had emerged as one of the most influential men of the newly-founded Democratic party. Named as political editor of The Congressional Globe, the recognized organ of the Democrats, Blair wielded considerable power in that party for almost two decades. By the late 1840s, Blair had become disappointed with the direction of the Democrats and subsequently helped found the Republican party; he was instrumental in securing the nomination of Abraham Lincoln for the 1860 election. Therefore, when he accepted Blair's invitation, Lee surmised that Blair had the sanction to speak for the new President of the United States.[50]

Courtesy Library of Congress

Blair House

Courtesy Library of Congress

Francis Preston Blair, Sr.

---

[47] Please consult the *Official Records*, Series III, volume 1, p. 69 for details concerning the quotas each state was to furnish towards the goal of 75,000. North Carolina and Tennessee were to furnish 1,560 each, whereas Arkansas was to contribute another 780.

[48] *Encyclopedia of the Confederacy*, William L. Barney, "Secession," vol. 3, p. 1383; Eisenhower, *Agent of Destiny*, p. 370.

[49] Freeman, *R. E. Lee*, vol. 1, pp. 435-436; Dowdey, *Lee*, p. 133. Francis Preston Blair, Sr., was Lee's third cousin-in-law, once removed. See: Eicher, *Robert E. Lee*, p. 212.

[50] Robert K. Krick, *Civil War Weather in Virginia* (Tuscaloosa, 2007), p. 23. Shortly after the war, Blair repudiated the cruelty of Reconstruction politics as implemented by the radicalized

Lee arrived at the younger Blair's house on Pennsylvania Avenue, diagonally across from the White House.[51] The elder Blair was waiting, and as soon as they sat down behind closed doors, came right to the point. War was coming—fast. Volunteers were swamping recruiting offices throughout the North and soon a large army would be fielded around Washington City, its purpose to carry out the President's directives to enforce Federal law, which could only be done by marching the army south. Blair had been authorized by President Lincoln to sound out Lee, and empowered by Secretary of War Simon Cameron to ask Lee if he would accept its command, and with it, another promotion.[52]

Had Lee been a man driven primarily by ambition, he might have accepted the offer. However, such characteristics had long been subordinated by Lee's disciplined mind—duty and honor always came first. After Mr. Blair outlined the President's proposal, Lee gave him his answer. In writing about the events of that day, Lee offered these succinct thoughts on the interview with Blair: "After listening to his remarks, I declined the offer he made to me to take command of the army that was to be brought into the field, stating candidly and as courteously as I could, that though opposed to secession, and deprecating war, I could take no part in an invasion of the Southern States."[53] Blair's account of the meeting was consistent on the main points, with some additional details: "I told [Lee] what President Lincoln wanted him to do. He wanted him to take command of the army. Lee said he was devoted to the Union. He said, among other things, that he would do everything in his power to save it, and that if he owned all the negroes in the South, he would be willing to give them up and make the sacrifice of the value of every one of them to save the Union . . . but he did not know how he could draw his sword upon his native state."[54] For Lee, the crux of the issue came down to the dictates of honor, and his words define that understanding: "As an American citizen, I prize the Union very highly & know of no personal sacrifice that I would not make to preserve it, save that of honour."[55]

Leaving the Blair home, Lee "went directly" to General Scott's office in the War Department across the street. As soon as Lee saw the 75-year old

Courtesy Library of Congress

**War Department Building,
Washington City**

Republican party, and eventually rejoined the Democrats before he passed away in 1876.

[51] Blair's house was No. 1651 Pennsylvania Avenue, which was across from the War Department; Furgurson, *Freedom Rising*, p. 75; Freeman, *R. E. Lee*, vol. 1, p. 436.

[52] *Southern Historical Society Papers*, Rev. J. William Jones, "The Friendship Between Lee and Scott," vol. 11, p. 420; Elbert B. *Smith, Francis Preston Blair* (New York, 1980), p. 283.

[53] *Southern Historical Society Papers*, Jones, "The Friendship Between Lee and Scott," letter dated February 25, 1868, from Lee to the Hon. Reverdy Johnson, United States Senate, vol. 11, p. 421.

[54] Freeman, *R. E. Lee*, vol. 1, Appendix 1-1, p. 634. Another version of Blair's story as relayed by his son is given in Freeman's *R. E. Lee*, vol. 1, Appendix 1-1, p. 635. Also see: Doris Kearns Goodwin, *Team of Rivals: The Political Genius of Abraham Lincoln* (New York, 2005), pp. 349-350 and footnotes on p. 813.

[55] Robert E. Lee to his son, Rooney Lee, written from San Antonio, Texas, December 3, 1860, George Bolling Lee Papers, Virginia Historical Society.

general, he sensed Scott's interest in what had already happened that morning. Lee "told him of the proposition that had been made" and his response to Mr. Blair. Lee and Scott discussed the matter, during which time Scott indicated that he could still plan a campaign, but he knew that his age and physical condition would prevent him from taking the field. Scott therefore believed that Lee was the best man to lead the new Federal army: victory, greatness and glory would follow. Despite the truth of Scott's words, Lee's view of honor would not allow him to lead an invading army that would make war on his family, relatives, friends and fellow Southerners. For Scott, who had greatly admired Lee's qualities as a soldier and with Lee "had developed something close to a father-son relationship," the meeting ended on a very sad note. Scott no doubt understood Lee's feelings, but disagreed. As his long-time mentor and friend, Scott strongly suggested to Lee that if was going to resign, he should do so "at once."[56]

Virginia State Flag

Winfield Scott's advice regarding the resignation was sound, and Lee knew it. The 75,000 volunteers would soon to be brought into the field and would be officered by those in uniform, with Colonel Lee being called on for such duty. Since he had already expressed his feelings on this matter, if he remained in uniform and was ordered to duty that he could not conscientiously perform, Lee would face the disgraceful choice of resigning under orders. These thoughts, and many others, were undoubtedly racing through Lee's mind as he said goodbye to General Scott, "rode out of Washington, across the bridge and up the quiet hills to the home whose white columns he could see for most of the way."[57] That night must have been a restless one for Robert E. Lee.

The following day, April 19th, Lee traveled to Alexandria on business. That afternoon, Lee learned that the Virginia delegates had voted to secede by a margin of two-to-one. Although a majority vote by the citizens of the state was needed to officially ratify the ordinance of secession, Lee knew that "once the dam of conservatism was broken, the referendum was moot." Virginia's break from the Union meant Lee had to act at once. Returning to Arlington, Lee demonstrated that his mind was preoccupied with his impending decision. When guests came over to the Lee home later that evening, Lee slipped away to walk by himself outside. Later, alone in his upstairs room, Lee paced the floor for hours, weighing in his mind the consequences

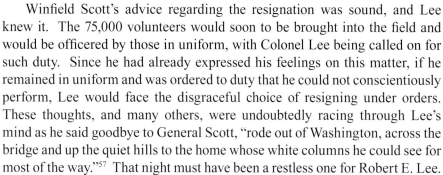

Courtesy Library of Congress

Wartime Alexandria

of a divided nation gone mad and his place in it. During this time, from her chair downstairs, the invalid Mrs. Lee could hear her husband pacing back and forth; another heard him fall on his knees in prayer, then get back on his feet and repeat the process. Mrs. Lee remembered that, for her husband, the night was "the severest struggle of his life."[58] Sometime after midnight

[56] Furgurson, *Freedom Rising*, p. 75; Freeman, *R. E. Lee*, vol. 1, p 437.
[57] Freeman, R. E. Lee, vol. 1, p. 438.
[58] Mary Custis Lee, "Mary Custis Lee's 'Reminiscences of the War.'" Edited by Robert E. L.

"I told McPherson we were going to fight for our 'liberty.' That was the view the whole South took of it. It was not for slavery but the sovereignty of the states, which is practically the right to resume self government or to secede.

"I think it is even now admitted by all candid & unprejudiced Northern writers that when the states formed the Union by the adoption of the Constitution they reserved their sovereignty in that instrument itself. And it is beyond dispute that some of the states in their acts adopting the Constitution even more expressly stated that they reserved sovereignty—Massachusetts I think is one of these. But in such a partnership any right expressly reserved by one is equally the right of all...

"We had the right therefore to secede whenever we saw fit, & it was truly for our liberty that we fought. Slavery brought up the discussion of the right in Congress & in the press, but the South would never have united as it did in secession & in war had it not been generally denied at the North & particularly by the Republican party."

Edward Porter Alexander

on April 20th, 1861, less than 15 hours after receiving positive information that the delegates had voted for Virginia to leave the Union, Lee resigned his commission. He then penned an explanatory note to his loyal friend and superior officer, General Scott.

> Arlington, Virginia
> 20 April 1861
>
> Hon. Simon Cameron
> Secretary of War
>
> Sir:
>
> I have the honour to tender the resignation of my commission as Colonel of the 1st Regt. Of Cavalry.
>
> Very respectfully, Your Obedient Servant,
> R. E. Lee
> Col. 1st Cavalry

> Arlington, Virginia
> 20 April 1861
>
> General:
>   Since my interview with you on the 18th instant, I have felt that I ought no longer to retain my commission in the Army. I therefore tender my resignation, which I request you will recommend for acceptance. I would have presented it at once, but for the struggle it has cost me to separate myself from a service to which I have devoted all the best years of my life and all the ability I possessed.
>   During the whole of that time—more than a quarter of a century—I have experienced nothing but kindness from my superiors and a most cordial friendship from my comrades. To no one, General, have I been as much indebted as to yourself for uniform kindness and consideration, and it has always been my ardent desire to meet your approbation. I shall carry to the grave the most grateful recollections of your kind consideration, and your name and fame will always be dear to me.
>   Save in defense of my native State, I never desire again to draw my sword.
>   Be pleased to accept my most earnest wishes for the continuance of your happiness and prosperity, and believe me, most truly yours,
>
> R. E. Lee

Lee later recalled that as he wrote his explanatory note, he still held out hope "that peace [would be] preserved; that some way would [be] found

deButts, Jr. *Virginia Magazine of History and Biography* 109, No. 3 Spring, 2001; Furgurson, *Freedom Rising*, p. 75.

to save the country from the calamities of war," and wished "to pass the remainder of [his] days as a private citizen."[59] In another letter written later that day, Lee summed up his decision to his sister, Mrs. Anne Marshall of Baltimore. "The whole south is in a state of revolution, into which Virginia, after a long struggle, has been drawn . . . in my own person I had to meet the question whether I should take part against my native state . . . [and] I have not been able to make up my mind to raise my hand against my relatives, my children, my home . . . and believe that I have endeavored to do what I thought right." Lee's words expressed what many other Southerners, in and out of uniform, felt as they wrestled with the issue of secession and their place with regards to allegiances that pulled at them from opposite directions. For Lee and countless other Southerners, it was a decision made not of hot defiance, but of duty and honor.[60]

THE REBEL GENERAL LEE.—[PHOTOGRAPHED BY BRADY.]

Courtesy Harpers Weekly

Lee in the Alexandria Gazette

Anticipating that the secession of Virginia would "cause an immediate resignation" of the many officers from Old Dominion, the editors of The Alexandria Gazette wasted no time in letting their readers know what they thought of Robert E. Lee: "We do not know, and have no right to speak for or anticipate the course of Colonel Robert E. Lee," the April 20th edition stated. "Whatever he may do, will be conscientious and honorable . . . no man [is] his superior . . . no man more worthy to head our forces and lead our army. There is no man who would command more of the confidence of the people; [his] is a name surrounded by revolutionary and patriotic associations and reminiscences."[61] In the eye of many Virginians, the mantle of George Washington had been passed.

Revolutionary fervor hung in the air on April 21st as Lee made his way to Sunday morning service in Alexandria, his first day as a civilian after more than 35 years in uniform (which included his West Point years). A large Bonnie Blue Flag flew high above the Marshal House Hotel, under which the townspeople celebrated. They rejoiced "at the secession of Virginia as if it meant deliverance from bondage. In their enthusiasm they fancied they were repeating the drama of 1776 and that the spirit of a Washington gave its benediction to a new revolution."[62]

Courtesy Library of Congress

Marshall House Hotel in Alexandria

Lee took no part in any of the unseemly and naïve celebrations. Although hoping that war could somehow still be averted, Lee realized that his decision to follow Virginia would almost certainly cost him and his family dearly, including the abandonment of their estate at Arlington. Furthermore, Lee long believed that if war did come, the struggle would be protracted, and its price in blood and treasure incalculable. So while most Virginians in this part of the state shared with their Southern brethren the indulgence in an unfettered emotionalism, Lee kept

[59] *Southern Historical Society Papers*, Jones, "The Friendship Between Lee and Scott," letter dated February 25, 1868, from Lee to the Hon. Reverdy Johnson, United States Senate, vol. 11, p. 421. Also see Lee's 20 April 1861 letter to his brother, Captain Sydney Smith Lee, of the United States Navy, in Robert E. Lee, Jr., *Recollections and Letters* (New York, 1904, reprinted 2004), p. 21.

[60] Robert E. Lee, Jr., *Recollections and Letters*, Robert E. Lee to *"My Dear Sister,"* April 20, 1861, pp. 20-21.

[61] *The Alexandria Gazette*, April 20, 1861.

[62] Freeman, *R. E. Lee*, vol. 1, p. 446; Furgurson, *Freedom Rising*, p. 91.

his head. Arriving at Christ Church, Lee briefly paused outside the historic brick walls that had served as George Washington's place of worship before going inside for the morning service.

The scripture for Episcopal churches in Virginia that Sunday morning was from the second chapter of Joel, verses 18 through 20: "Then will the Lord be jealous for his land, and pity his people. Yea, the Lord will answer and say unto his people, Behold, I will send you corn, and wine, and oil, and ye shall be satisfied there within; and I will no more make you a reproach among the heathen. But I will remove far off from you the northern army, and will drive him into a land barren and desolate, with his face toward the east sea, and his hinder part toward the utmost sea, and his stink shall come up . . . ." To many in the congregations across Virginia, this was taken as a prophecy.[63]

Courtesy Library of Congress

Christ Church in Alexandria

Later that evening at Arlington, a messenger arrived. Governor John Letcher wanted to see Lee in Richmond the next day. Lee must have known what this meant: he was going to be offered command of Virginia's revolutionary forces. Without hesitation, he agreed to go. On the morning of April 22nd, Lee left Arlington, where he and Mary Custis had been married 30 years earlier and their seven children had been born. He would never return. In looking back on this decision following the war, Lee never wavered from his conviction that he had acted the only way he could. "Every brave people who considered their rights attacked and their constitutional liberties invaded would have done as we did... And if it all were to be done over again, I should act in precisely the same manner."[64]

Lee's decision was central to his concept of honor. Despite the uncomfortable rapidity in which events were unfolding in the spring of 1861, Lee repeatedly stated that he "could have taken no other course without dishonour" in resigning his commission with the United States Army. Lee's decision had far-reaching ramifications. Rather than choose the course of remaining in the uniform that would have assured him of position, fame and fortune, Lee now risked all; honor would never allow him to make war on his kin. Mrs. Lee knew what her husband had been through making his decision when shortly afterwards she wrote a friend: "My husband has wept tears of blood over this terrible war, but as a man of honor and a Virginian, he must follow the destiny of his state." Two of Robert E. Lee's most renowned 20th century biographers conclude that Lee had no choice but to act as he did. In his epic, four-volume biography of Lee, the Pulitzer prize-winning Douglas Southall Freeman stated that Lee's decision was "the answer he was born to make." Clifford Dowdey described Lee's siding with his native state thusly: "It was not that the anguished man had any choice. The decision was made with his birth."[65]

Courtesy Library of Congress

Virginia Governor John Letcher

---

[63] Sallie B. Putnam, *Richmond During the War: Four Years of Observation by a Richmond Lady* (New York, 1867), pp. 20-22; *Holy Bible*, Book of Joel, 2: 18-20.

[64] Freeman, *R. E. Lee*, vol. 1, p. 442; Furgurson, *Freedom Rising*, p. 83; Robert E. Lee to Wade Hampton, June 1868; Dowdey, *Experiment in Rebellion*, p. xx.

[65] Rister, *Robert E. Lee in Texas*, p. 166; Freeman, *R. E. Lee*, vol. 1, p. 431; Dowdey, *Lee*, p. 134; Robert E. Lee to Wade Hampton, June 1868.

Understandably, it is difficult for some Americans generations removed from these events, to empathize with Lee's decision, or to context how the moral weight of the phrase "save that of honour" dictated Lee's course. In 19th century society, honor for many—in the South as well as in the North—was inextricably linked with family connections, public reputation and a keen desire to avoid shame. As mentioned, Lee believed his honor meant never raising his sword against his family and the kinsmen of his state, even if his decision risked his and his family's personal welfare. To Lee, family represented his primary allegiance, and the place his family called their "native country" was Virginia. Engaging in a war against one's own family was a violation of a fundamental law as old as recorded history. Indeed, from before the time that Tacitus wrote *Germania*, the commandment that family defense was inextricably linked to one's honor provided underpinning to the cardinal principle that helped drive the states of the Upper South out of the Union.

Courtesy Library of Congress

The Capitol at Richmond

After all, most Southerners had more kinsmen in the so-called "Cotton States" than in the North. Furthermore, Lee's view was rooted in the American ideals of Jeffersonian democracy and the interpretation of the vital importance of personal liberties, tied to the sovereignty of the states that had brought the Federal government into existence. For Lee, honor would not allow him to coerce other Southerners, even though he disagreed with them on their decision to secede. Therefore, when it comes to the final analysis on the issue of how Lee viewed honor, readers should well consider taking him at his word.

Lee's decisions to first resign his commission and then, once Virginia seceded, to fight for the Confederacy, have become targets of revisionist historians seeking to attack Lee's moral compass. These critics see Lee's sense of honor and duty as flawed, and feel that he owed a higher allegiance to the cause of the Federal government. Self-righteously, these detractors do not grant the right that, when confronted with a difficult moral decision and facing controversial constitutional issues, reasonable men may disagree. Hence, the complaint itself is parochial as it is absent the context of the historical time. Also, in a selective reading backwards designed to be prejudicial, the revisionists see Lee's decisions as encompassing a deliberate choice to fight for the preservation of slavery. Yet contingency tells us that many, many decisions had to be made before the abolitionist agenda became Federal policy: certainly Northern Democrats did not sign on initially to support a war to end slavery, but rather to preserve the Union. Well over 100,000 men had yet to die before the Emancipation Proclamation would be issued. Any number of alternatives and possibilities existed for this war that had hardly begun to unfold, including, to name just two, a spirited defense of the South followed by a negotiated settlement, or, as Lincoln argued, a purchase of the slaves by the Federal government; talk of gradual emancipation had been long

"We have never seen so much excitement and so general an exhibition or joy as there was yesterday, after the reception of the news that Virginia had joined our Confederate States. Houses were illuminated, bells were rung in all directions, and especially on our steamboats. Crowds were gathered together, and speeches were made. Guns and pistols were shot off in all directions, and there was a general disposition to make a noise. The Cadets and the Rifles turned out and fired volleys. In the evening, the excitement increased, and a meeting was held at the corner of St. Francis and Royal Streets, where the enthusiasm seemed to culminate."

The Mobile Tribune, **April 19, 1861,** describing the scene upon receiving the news of Virginia's secession

Thus when secessionists protested that they were acting to preserve traditional rights and values, they were correct. They fought to protect their constitutional liberties against the perceived northern threat to overthrow them. The South's concept of republicanism had not changed in three-quarters of a century; the North's had. With complete sincerity the South fought to preserve its version of the republic of the founding fathers—a government of limited powers that protected the rights of property, and whose constituency comprised an independent gentry and yeomanry of the white race undisturbed by large cities, heartless factories, restless free workers, and class conflict. The accession to power of the Republican party, with its ideology of competitive, egalitarian, free labor capitalism, was a signal to the South the northern majority had turned irrevocably toward this frightening, revolutionary future.

James McPherson, from his Pulitzer Prize-winning *Battle Cry of Freedom*

gaining momentum, particularly in the Upper South. Interestingly, in order to tether slavery to a critique of Lee's character, one must deliberately disavow Lincoln's paramount aim to preserve the Union with or without slavery. Thus, in the detractors' interpretation, both Lee and Lincoln must be seen as hypocrites—a remarkable presumption—rather than men forced to make decisions in a national tragedy.

Others suggest that Lee had another viable alternative to preserve his honor, namely, to have exiled himself from the conflict, essentially watching the invasion of Virginia from the porch of his Arlington home. Such a course represented a coward's way out—something that Lee never seriously entertained, having interpreted his allegiance as belonging to his home state. Or, in another critique, Lee should have acted differently—just as some other fellow officers hailing from Virginia did when they decided to stay in Federal uniform. The fellow-officer examples mentioned always include Lee's mentor, the elderly Winfield Scott, as well as George Thomas, with whom Lee had ridden the Texas plains with the 2nd Cavalry. Naturally, both Scott and Thomas suffered social ostracism as a result of their decision, suggesting that Lee may have lacked something when he did not turn his back on his family and home in favor of the Union. What is utterly missed in such a comparison is that significant differences existed between men and the choice each confronted. For instance, Scott's rejection of the Confederacy came as no surprise. The fact that Scott utterly despised Jefferson Davis, owing to a series of events that culminated in a very public and ugly feud while Davis was Secretary of War, was perhaps best summed up in his comments about the Confederate President. "There is contamination in his touch," Scott said of Davis. "If secession was 'the holiest cause that tongue or sword of mortal ever lost or gained,' he would ruin it!" Considering the nastiness with which Scott and Davis went at each other in their mutual hatred, General Scott would have jumped into Perdition's flames before siding with Jeff Davis. Interestingly, Scott's family seemingly did not take that episode into consideration when they all but disowned the distinguished general. Thomas' family did disown him, and in so doing, asked George to change his last name. Neither man, however, had the extraordinary and extensive family connections to Virginia and her rich history as did Robert E. Lee.[66]

But these examples aside, passing negative judgment upon Lee's agonizing decision, as affected by secession, requires the critic or moralist to be completely unsympathetic to the context of the moment, how things were in the mid-19th century South. Even though Lee disagreed with the course of the "Cotton States," he was always consistent in his view of standing by Old Dominion, and Virginia's secession from the Union had the effect of withdrawing the allegiance and loyalty of Virginia's sons. Hence, a sovereign state's perceived right and decision to secede released, *ipso facto*, her citizens from the Federal government, as the relation of the citizen to the Federal government was believed at that time by most Southerners to be through the State. In most cases, these critics are interested in undermining Lee's reputation and clouding a rational evaluation of his generalship.

---

[66] William C. Davis, *Jefferson Davis*, pp. 228-230; Freeman Cleaves, *Rock of Chickamauga: The Life of George H. Thomas* (Westport, 1974 reprint), pp. 5, 67-69; John S. D. Eisenhower, *Agent of Destiny: The Life and Times of General Winfield Scott* (New York, 1997), pp. 332-333; Allan Peskin, *Winfield Scott and the Profession of Arms* (Kent, 2003), p. 243.

The New Washington

Lee understood full well that he was about to become a revolutionary, and there is no doubt that he drew on the experiences of George Washington as his guide. He viewed his decision to follow Virginia as that of honor and patriotism. "I need not tell you," Lee wrote to Pierre G. T. Beauregard, "that true patriotism requires of men sometimes, to act exactly contrary at one period, to that which if does at another; & that the motive which impels them, viz, the desire to do right, is precisely the same." George Washington "at one time...fought against the French, under Braddock, in the service of the King of Great Britain; at another he fought with the French at Yorktown . . . against [the British]."[67]

Courtesy Library of Congress

Washington Crossing the Delaware

The reality of the situation facing Virginia must have weighed heavily on Lee as he rode the train into Richmond on Monday, April 22nd. At stops along the way, Lee saw that euphoria was still intoxicating most of the citizens of Old Dominion. Vocal crowds of Virginians jammed the rail platforms, calling for a glimpse of the famous soldier who they now looked upon as the heir to George Washington's revolutionary mantle. At other times during the journey, Lee sat quietly, looking out the window at the passing countryside. Just how many times he must have wondered how the sectional differences had led to the current crisis and how events had unfolded to place him in the position that he now found himself, we will never know. However, for a man as deeply religious as Lee, he no doubt trusted his fate to a God into whose hands he did not understand what role he would play.[68]

Arriving in Richmond on the unusually warm afternoon of April 22nd, Robert E. Lee easily stood out in the crowded city. Wearing a crisp civilian suit topped by a high silk hat, Lee did not look like a typical 19th century 54 year-old man. Contemporaries wrote before and during the war that Lee was either the handsomest or "the noblest-looking man" they had ever seen. "General Lee was an unusually handsome man," recalled James Longstreet, "even in his advanced life. He seemed fresh from West Point, so trim was his figure and so elastic his step." Henry J. Hunt, who would rise to command of the army artillery reserve in the Federal Army of the Potomac, served with Lee prior to the Mexican War. In Hunt's eyes, Lee was "as fine-looking a man as one would wish to see, of perfect figure and strikingly handsome." Lieutenant Colonel Arthur Fremantle of the Coldstream Guards, who traveled to North America and caught up with the Army of Northern Virginia as it was moving northward into Pennsylvania the latter part of June, 1863, thought that Lee was: "The handsomest man of his years I ever saw." One of Fremantle's fellow countrymen had held a similar view. Colonel Garnet Wolseley, later

Courtesy Library of Congress

Colonel Garnet Wolseley

---

[67] Robert E. Lee to Pierre G. T. Beauregard, as quoted in McCaslin, *Lee in the Shadow of Washington*, p. 77.

[68] While there were Virginians in the uniform of the United States who did not resign their commissions, it is interesting to note that none called Lee's honor into question. This was a decision that might not have been agreed on by all his contemporaries, but they all respected Lee's view of what honor meant to him. Interestingly, in their blind hatred to label Lee as dishonorable, not one Lee detractor cites a contemporary army officer of Lee who does the same.

Field Marshal Viscount Wolseley, visited Lee during the October, 1862, and noted that the Confederate was blessed with "one of the most rarely handsome faces I ever saw." Cadmus Wilcox, the officer Lee would personally instruct regarding his brigade's attack on a hot July afternoon during the second day's battle at Gettysburg, said that Lee was "known as the handsomest man in the army," while others claimed Lee possessed "strikingly handsome features, bright and penetrating eyes" with "the highest type of manly beauty" that made him "handsome beyond all men."[69]

Courtesy Library of Congress

George Washington Statue in Richmond

Lee stood five feet eleven inches in height, with his dark hair beginning to gray, beardless with a full mustache that was still nearly black, and sporting an athletic body weighing about 170 pounds. Lee's physique was exceptional, and his appearance was complimented by a voice that richly resonated with a lower middle register indicative of a man in superb health. To augment these faculties, Lee possessed impeccable social graces. With a similar echo made by Erasmus Keyes, long-time aide Walter Herron Taylor summed up Robert E. Lee thusly: "He appeared every inch a soldier and a man born to command."[70]

While Lee's aura exuded confidence, authority and fair-mindedness, he also projected a deep humility and self-assured calm. Never pretentious, Lee's behavior was absent patrician hauteur. He seldom lost control of his temper unless greatly provoked, and when it did erupt, it would be preceded by blood vessels protruding from his temples. Free of all forms of self-aggrandizement, Lee was courteous, honest, realistic, considerate, fiercely loyal to his friends and remarkably consistent in treating with respect all people from every level of society. Perhaps this is why he seldom incited envy in those who knew him.[71]

Courtesy Harpers Weekly

View of Richmond

Stepping down at the Virginia Central depot at 17th and Broad Street, Lee took a carriage to the new and elegant Spotswood Hotel. After taking a room and eating an early supper, he hurriedly left the hotel. Walking through the noisy streets, past the equestrian statue of George Washington in Capitol Square on his way to see Governor Letcher, Lee heard in the distance the catchy air of a minstrel song named "Dixie" as well as the French Revolutionary "La Marseillaise." The lively music was carried by a breeze that stirred countless new flags, many of them the single-starred "Bonnie Blue

---

[69] Krick, *Civil War Weather in Virginia*, pp. 21 and 23. The weather that day in Richmond was in the mid-80s; Thomas, *Robert E. Lee: An Album*, p. 19; Freeman, *R. E. Lee*, vol. 1, p. 450; James Longstreet, "'The Seven Days,' including Frayser's Farm," *Battles and Leaders of the Civil War*, 4 volumes (New York, 1889), vol. 2, p. 405; Arthur Lyon Fremantle, *Three Months in the Southern States April—June, 1863* (New York, 1864), p. 248; Cadmus Wilcox, as quoted in Thomas, *Robert E. Lee: A Biography*, p. 145; Walter Taylor, *General Lee: His Campaigns in Virginia, 1861-1865* (Lincoln, 1994 reprint of the 1906 original), p. 25; *Southern Historical Society Papers*, "Robert E. Lee," by Jefferson Davis, vol. 17, p. 362; Armistead Lindsay Long, *Memoirs of Robert E. Lee: His Military and Personal History, Embracing a Large Amount of Information Hitherto Unpublished* (New York, 1886), pp. 66-67. For one of the best collections of images of Robert E. Lee, please consult: Roy Meredith, *The Face of Robert E. Lee in Life and in Legend* (New York, 1947), as well as the portrait of General Lee by Benjamin F. Reinhardt in the R. W. Norton Gallery in Shreveport, Louisiana.

[70] Taylor, *General Lee*, pp. 21-22.

[71] Freeman, *R. E. Lee*, vol. 4, "Appendix IV-7," pp. 521-522; *Southern Historical Society Papers*, "Robert E. Lee," by Jefferson Davis, vol. 17, p. 362.

	The Secession of the Southern States		
State	Secession Ordinance	Popular Ratification	Joined the Confederacy*
South Carolina	December 20, 1860	None	April 3, 1861
Mississippi	January 9, 1861	None	March 29, 1861
Florida	January 10, 1861	None	February 26, 1861
Alabama	January 11, 1861	None	March 13, 1861
Georgia	January 19, 1861	None	March 16, 1861
Louisiana	January 26, 1861	None	March 21, 1861
Texas	February 1, 1861	February 23, 1861	March 23, 1861
Virginia	April 17, 1861	May 23, 1861	April 27, 1861
Arkansas	May 6, 1861	None	May 10, 1861
Tennessee	May 6, 1861	June 8, 1861	May 7, 1861
North Carolina	May 20, 1861	None	May 20, 1861

* With the exception of Virginia and Tennessee, these are the dates that the secession conventions ratified the Confederate Constitution. Ten days after the Virginia convention passed its Ordinance of Secession, it invited the Confederate government to shift its capital from Montgomery, Alabama, to Richmond. On May 7, 1861, Tennessee Governor Isham Harris committed his state to a military alliance with the Confederacy.

Flag" that flew from windows and porches of almost every house and building. Without calling attention to himself, Lee did not go in the front entrance, but instead entered a side door into the Capitol and climbed the stairs to the office once occupied by his father. Entering the governor's office and after exchanging greetings, Lee took a seat near Letcher's desk. The governor was known to many as a level-headed, conservative Democrat who had resisted the rhetoric of the firebrands who had called for Virginia to secede when the "Cotton States" went out. Letcher recounted to Lee how his considerable efforts to avert secession had ultimately gone for naught once Lincoln called for armed invasion. When that happened, Letcher wired Lincoln of his disapproval and the majority of Virginia convention delegates then voted the only way they believed they could—secession. The governor went on to tell Lee that immediately after the state's delegates voted to secede, an ordinance was passed calling for a commander of Virginia's military forces, with the rank of major general, to serve under the authority of the governor. Letcher wanted Lee for the job. Lee immediately "accepted" the leading role in what he described as "the dire calamity of this fratricidal war."[72] The governor hurriedly sent a message to the convention before it adjourned for the night: Robert E. Lee had resigned from the United States Army and was hereby nominated by Letcher for the post of commander of Virginia's army and navy. The convention responded at once and Lee was unanimously approved.[73]

The next day, April 23rd, the celebrated son of Virginia was officially installed as its military commander. In an acceptance speech that editor Edward A. Pollard described as being "Washington-like in its modesty," Lee took up "Washington's mantle" as the role of revolutionary general. For Lee, it was the beginning of a bizarre series of relationships heavily influenced by the strange bedfellows driving Southern politics, many of whom lacked any appreciation for the gravity of what they had gotten into, nor how to correctly and fully utilize the man who was Abraham Lincoln's first choice to command a major army.

"The Virginia Convention, to its honor be it said, did not hesitate an instant in tendering the supreme command of their land and naval forces to this eminent Virginian. Conscientious and honorable as he is brave and experienced, he did not hesitate to accept the post of honor and of danger. If our military, when brought into the field under his guidance, do not win the victory, then we shall conclude that right and justice is thenceforth powerless against the oppressor. Of him it was said before his appointment, and of him it may well be said, no man is his superior in all that constitutes the soldier and the gentleman — no man more worthy to head our forces and lead our army. There is no one who would command more of the confidence of the people of Virginia than this distinguished officer, and no one under whom the volunteers and militia would more gladly rally."

The Richmond Daily Dispatch, May 1, 1861

[72] *Southern Historical Society Papers*, Jones, "The Friendship Between Lee and Scott," letter dated February 25, 1868, from Lee to the Hon. Reverdy Johnson, United States Senate, vol. 11, p. 421; Furgurson, *Freedom Rising*, p. 83.
[73] *Journal of the Virginia Convention of 1861*, pp. 184-185; *Ordinances Adopted by the Convention of Virginia in Secret Session in April and May, 1861*, p. 9.

Politicians, Fantasies and Lee

Despite Robert E. Lee's initial opposition to secession, the abstract right of secession was held as a constitutional maxim in the South.[74] This widely-held belief had been conveyed through the experiences of early Americans who had forged the new nation, most notably Thomas Jefferson and other founding fathers known as the Anti-Federalists whose criticism of the proposed, new Constitution influenced the formation of the Bill of Rights. Long before Jefferson served as the country's third President, the belief that the states had the freedom to withdraw from the Federal compact was evidenced in the legacies of multiple state Constitutional conventions, especially New York and Virginia.[75]

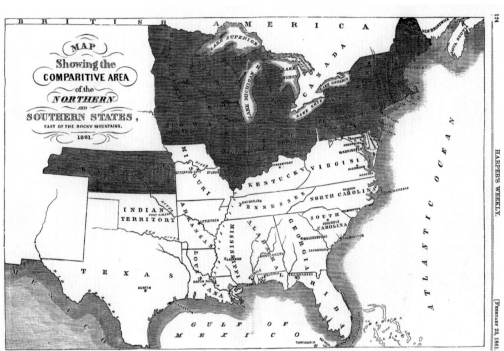

Courtesy Harpers Weekly

Map of the Southern States

Despite his opposition to this widely-held understanding, Lee was fair-minded enough to respect the views of those who advocated secession, even when he believed the exercise of such rights was neither necessary nor wise. The salient issue for Lee, as with most Southerners in the upper South, was coercion, or the attempt to hold together the Union at the point of the bayonet. Thus, few Southerners viewed Lincoln's announced plans to invade the "Cotton States" as legal. Indeed,

[74] One of many examples on this point is hereby illustrated. In November, 1865, Lee had an interview with a British visitor, Herbert C. Saunders. In July of the following year, Saunders sent Lee a manuscript of an article he proposed to publish. Lee refused to be quoted in the article, but he did revise Saunders' manuscript. Whereas Saunders had written: "This right [of secession] he [Lee] told me always he always held as a constitutional maxim. . . . As to the policy of secession on the part of the South he was at first opposed to it, and it was only until Lincoln issued a proclamation for 75,000 men to invade the South which he deemed clearly unconstitutional that he had then no longer any doubt what course his loyalty to the Constitution, and to his State required him to take." Lee made various changes, including striking totally from the statement the reference to "doubt" in his mind. The last sentence, as finally revised by Lee, read: "As to its exercise [the right of secession] at the time of the part of the South, he was distinctly opposed, and it was not until Lincoln issued a proclamation for 75,000 men to invade the South which was deemed clearly unconstitutional that Virginia withdrew from the U. States." See citation and story in Freeman, *R. E. Lee*, vol. 1, p. 423, fn 54.

[75] The Form of Ratification, which was read and agreed to by the Convention of Virginia, stated, in part: "that the powers granted under the Constitution, being derived from the people of the United States may be resumed by them whensoever the same shall be perverted to their injury or oppression." The Ratification of the Constitution by the Convention of the State of New York expressly stated, in part: "That the powers of government may be reassumed by the people, whensoever it shall become necessary to their happiness." In the Convention of the Delegates of the People of the State of Maryland, one of the proposed amendments also addressed secession. See: *The Debate on the Constitution: Federalist and Antifederist Speeches, Articles, and Letters During the Struggle over Ratification*, contents, headings and notes selected by Bernard Bailyn, 2 parts (New York, 1993), part 2, pp. 536, 553-554 and 557.

Lincoln's call in April for 75,000 volunteers to enforce Federal law, followed on May 3rd by a second call for another 42,000 men, had the effect of forcing the hand of the states of the upper South to rally behind "The Cause" for Southern independence. The impact of Lincoln's calls to arms cannot be minimized because the states of the upper South had previously either rejected calling for conventions of secession, or had voted against holding a convention. Beginning in April, 1861, all of that changed. Within weeks of Lincoln's first announcement for volunteers and the stories of war fever sweeping the North, the wildfires of secession rekindled across the South. Virginia, Arkansas, Tennessee and North Carolina cast their lot with the Confederacy: the nation was now truly a house divided.[76]

Courtesy Library of Congress

Manassas Junction

A considerable number of politicians of the South who led their region to secession and war, followed by destruction and occupation, had been influenced to initiate the secession movement under the expectation that their states could withdraw from the Federal compact legally and without the North going to war over the issue. Separation from the old (what was to them) compact was preferable to continuation as a subservient minority. After all, these Southern aristocrats believed in the superiority of their ruling class over the North's. In addition, these firebrands convinced themselves that if somehow there was a war, one or more foreign nations would not long hesitate in intervening on the South's behalf in order to insure the uninterrupted supply of cotton: salvation would soon follow—an attitude diametrically opposite to the view held by Robert E. Lee. This fatal combination of ideas comprised a large part of the foundation on which many Southern politicians advocated their new republic. So strong was the implicit belief of this combination of ideas and expected results that its effect on most Southern politicians resulted in them neglecting to take stronger measures to properly defend the Confederacy that—if they had been taken during the first year of the war—might well have proven the steps necessary to successfully establish the new nation.

Courtesy Library of Congress

Manassas Henry House Hill

Therefore, while Lee extolled that the power of the United States was so daunting that every Southerner would have to do his full part to achieve

---

[76] The Virginia convention passed the ordinance of secession on April 17, which was ratified by popular vote on May 23. Arkansas went out of the Union when its state convention passed the secession ordinance on May 6. Tennessee's convention passed its secession ordinance the same day as Arkansas. However, the citizens of Tennessee had to vote on the measure, and secession ratification was passed on June 8. North Carolina's secession convention was the last to pass its secession ordinance, which was done on May 20, 1861. Please note that these dates vary somewhat from those often listed as to when states "joined the Confederacy," which were the dates when the state secession conventions ratified the Confederate Constitution.

the political imperative, the majority of Southern politicians saw things very differently. Secessionists failed to recognize that the adamant beliefs among Northern abolitionists—financed largely by powerful interests—ran as deep as the bellicose beliefs of the powerful planter-élite minority in the South. And while Lee understood the depth of Northern resolve, most secessionists tended to believe that the Yankees lacked the courage or conviction to sustain much bloodletting. As a result, most influential politicians in the South deliberately staked the issue of creating their sovereignty on the wishful combination of a lack of resolve by the North, as well as the intervention of foreign governments knuckled under by King Cotton. Unrealistic political expectations along with a failure to review and reconsider their assumptions blinded Southern leaders and their constituents as to the likelihood of a long

Courtesy Harpers Weekly

Confederate troops leaving for Manassas

and difficult path before them; this continued to be the hallmark of a doggedly inflexible stance taken by many planter-*élite* Southern firebrands. Indeed, the primary cause for the defeat of the Southern Confederacy stemmed from these unrealistic expectations and corresponding poor decisions made by Southern political leaders during the first year of the war. Napoleon once said that, "I may lose a battle, but I shall never lose a minute." The Confederacy wasted the better part of a year, and the largest of those failings— incomprehensible in hindsight—was leaving their most outstanding soldier, Robert E. Lee, in a nearly useless bureaucratic role.[77]

Secession leaders convinced their region that the European powers of Britain and France would somehow save the South over the want of cotton. Therefore, while Lee espoused that Southerners alone would have to secure their independence, firebrands argued that if the North were foolish enough to actually go to war, it could not possibly exist for a long time because of the enormous efforts needed to invade and subjugate the expansive geographical region of the South. This latter point, in turn, fed their previous argument, because they believed that the quantity of cotton then in Europe would become exhausted by the beginning of February, 1862. Once that date came, intervention on the part of Britain or France would be inevitable, or so reasoned many Southern politicians. Since intervention was, in their minds, certain, extensive measures for defense were unnecessary beyond the initial preparations: anything more would only inconvenience and unduly alarm the good citizens of their region.[78]

---

[77]One of many Civil War history books that discuss tax and money issues as central to the causes of the conflict is: Kenneth Stampp, *And the War Came: The North and the Secession Crisis, 1860-1861* (Baton Rouge, 1950).

[78] More than three-fourths of the cotton used in the textile industries of England and France came from the states comprising the Southern Confederacy. One-tenth of England's wealth was invested in the cotton textile industry, and between one-fifth to one-quarter of the English population depended in some way on the textile industry, and at least half of the export trade of England consisted of cotton textiles. Southern politicians calculated that the European dependence on cotton along with their estimates of the supply of cotton running out in Europe by early 1862 would force England's and France's hand; they were wrong. At the outbreak of the war, there was an overabundance of cotton in Europe. But even if the Southern politicians were right about the supply of cotton, they totally miscalculated Europe's stance towards a new republic that had the institution of slavery. This can be seen in how the South failed to appreciate

This short-sighted, optimistic attitude resulted in extraordinarily limited preparations for war made by the Confederate Congress that first assembled at Montgomery, Alabama in early 1861; the pattern continued once the seat of government was shifted to Richmond in June of that year. This complacency among politicians continued well into the autumn of 1862—a fact that in and of itself is hard to comprehend in the wake of the massive Federal build up prior to, followed by the blood-shed of the 1862 summer campaigns, both of which clearly demonstrated that Abraham Lincoln was fully committed to prosecuting the war.[79]

Courtesy Library of Congress

Battle of Manassas

In fairness to those involved with these decisions, up until the Battle of Manassas on July 21st, 1861, very few people North or South (Robert E. Lee being one of the few exceptions), believed that once war did come, the fighting would not be "either of great extent or long duration."[80] This grievous error, first evidenced by the politicians of the deep South believing that they could leave the Union without consequences, then seconded by Lincoln's and Davis' confrontational handling of the Fort Sumter crisis, followed immediately thereafter by Lincoln's call for volunteers to invade the "Cotton States" and collect the taxes due the Federal government, was indicative of each side believing that the other would blink first.

Advocates for Southern independence reasoned that the righteousness of their constitutional views would eventually have to be accepted as the truth by their foes and the world. After all, how could the Federal government legally send an army of invasion into the South with the purpose of forcing one or more sovereign state republics back into the Union? Wasn't it understood, argued politicians who believed in Jeffersonian-style democracy, that the Constitution had been ratified by the state conventions—especially those in Virginia and New York—with the express understanding and explicit verbiage written into their states' Constitutional conventions that the union of the states was an experiment and that any state could withdraw at any time? Wasn't the Doctrine of Nullification, which came out of the Tenth Amendment and combined with the Ninth Amendment, valid? These beliefs combined to seduce many Southern politicians into the critical oversight of refusing to accept the stated views of their political opponent. Southern politicians, therefore, did not acknowledge the effect Lincoln's oath of office had on Lincoln's reaction

---

the May, 1862, communiqué sent through Count Mercier, a minister of Emperor Napoleon III, and French Consul Paul, that France would declare in support the Confederate war effort *only if* a bill was passed in Richmond outlining *when* emancipation would be granted, even if it "was a gradual abolition of slavery in 50 or 60 years." If that were done, whereby the French people would be satisfied that abolition of slavery was in the future, Napoleon III would immediately acknowledge the Confederate States of America. See the *Southern Historical Society Papers,* "Foreign Recognition of the Confederacy," by James Lyons, vol. 7, pp. 353-359; *Encyclopedia of the Confederacy,* vol. 1, pp. 415-420.

[79] Charles Marshall, *Lee's Aide-de-Camp* (Lincoln, 2000 reprint of the 1927 original), p. 11.

[80] Marshall, *Lee's Aide-de-Camp* p. 11.

to secession. That oath called for the President to preserve and protect the Constitution, and with it, maintain the "sacred Union" that in Lincoln's view legally bound all states to the Federal compact.[81]

The result of the prevailing Southern political winds greatly impacted Robert E. Lee once he took the field, for it played an important part in the decision by the Confederate Congress to undertake only the most limited measures to organize an army and prepare its nation for war. Short-sighted politicians thought that the enthusiasm of the Southern people would be enough to resist the initial onslaught made by the Federal government. After all, it was reasoned that adequate numbers of eager Southern soldiers could be concentrated at any place as rapidly as Lincoln's new army. Further, with communications comparatively open between North and South during this time, no secrets could be sustained long enough to exploit the element of surprise. So when Federal authorities sent their newly-formed army southward to brush aside Confederate forces on their way to capture the Confederate capital city, the opposing sides collided only a few miles from Washington City along Bull Run Creek near Manassas, Virginia, on July 21st, 1861; the battle resulted with the rout of the Federal army, with no pursuit by the victors. In a bizarre explanation, seemingly too paradoxical to make real sense, Confederate co-commander Joseph E. Johnston thought that the victorious Southern troops were "more disorganized by victory than that of the United States by defeat." The claim was echoed by a Federal observer who claimed that the Confederates were too demoralized by the victory to make the pursuit. "To that disorganization, and that demoralization the safety of Washington was due," a Federal officer later wrote.[82] In part, this shock came from the deflation of ludicrous Confederate expectations prior to the fighting about cowardly Yankees and easy victories. It turned out that the Federals not only could fight, but damned near won the day. Battle itself held horrors that Walter Scott seemed to have largely omitted from his glorious novels. While Southern

Courtesy Library of Congress

Infantry Charge at Manassas

---

[81] *The Debate on the Constitution: Federalist and Antifederist Speeches, Articles, and Letters During the Struggle over Ratification,* part 2, pp. 536, 553-554 and 557. Under its terms of the 1845 annexation, Texas was the only state ever admitted to the Union with the explicit condition that it could subdivide into five states anytime in the future by virtue of a popular vote of its citizens.

[82] Joseph E. Johnston, "Responsibilities of the First Bull Run," *Battles and Leaders of the Civil War,* vol. 1, p. 252; Benjamin Franklin Cooling, *Symbol, Sword and Shield* (Shippensburg, 1991), pp. 52-53; Nicolay, *The Outbreak of Rebellion,* p. 198-205. The Confederates had four brigades (Ewell, Early, Holmes and Jones) undamaged from the fighting, yet were not used for any sort of pursuit. The term "Yankee" was in use in the South and by Southerners decades before the outbreak of the War. One of many examples is a letter from Dick Ewell (West Point Class of 1840) to his brother, Benjamin, upon the former's arrival at the academy. Ewell mentions that the "Yankees" were over all better prepared academically for the challenges of West Point, especially in mathematics, and consequently attained relatively higher rankings as cadets than those from Southern states.

soldiers had at last gotten a dose of reality, the victory at Manassas could not have had a worse effect on Confederate politicians. Clearly, more bombast would be needed to quell any sinking fears.

Thus, in the wake of the rout of the Federal army, a residue of false security was layered on top of false hopes that only fed further delusions. Already believing that the existing, limited measures implemented by the Confederate government were all the action needed to raise an effective army, the victory at Manassas reinforced the notion that soon-to-be-expected diplomatic actions across the Atlantic would insure Southern independence. "President Davis, after the battle, assured his intimate friends that the recognition of the Confederate States by European powers was now certain," wrote newspaper editor and historian Edward A. Pollard. "The newspapers declared that the question of manhood between North and South was settled forever; and the phrase of 'one Southerner equal to five Yankees' was adopted in all speeches about the war—although the origin or rule of the precise proportion was never clearly stated."[83] The half-measures already taken were soon relaxed, and an air of overconfidence spread like a putrid fever with its deleterious effect: a fall off in enlistments immediately followed because it was believed that peace was at hand.

Nothing could have been further from the truth. While Lee was in Richmond, thankful for the victory at Manassas, and while Southern politicians made claims based on bravado rather than on fact, "on the very day that Washington was crowded with fugitives from the routed army . . . the [U.S.] House of Representatives [Congress being in special session] passed unanimously the following resolution:

> 'Resolved, That the maintenance of the Constitution, the preservation of the Union, and the enforcement of the laws, are sacred trusts which must be executed; that no disaster shall discourage us from the most ample performance of this high duty: and that we pledge to the country and the world the employment of every resource, national and individual, for the suppression, overthrow, and punishment of rebels in arms.'"[84]

Abraham Lincoln supported this resolution with his pledge to prosecute the war to its fullest. Calling for 500,000 men to serve for three years, Lincoln's announcement sent shock waves through the South and around the world: the mobilization represented the largest to date in modern history.[85] Thus, by the summer of 1861, the intent of the government of the United States could not be misunderstood. The invasion of the Southern states would soon be undertaken on many fronts in order to subjugate what was viewed in the

---

[83] Pollard, *The Lost Cause*, p. 153.

[84] Pollard, *The Lost Cause*, pp. 153-154.

[85] Lincoln's appeal for a half million men eclipsed any call—volunteer or conscription—previously known. Lincoln's goal far exceeded the mass conscription of the Jacobins and the *sans-culottes* of the French Revolution 1793 *levee en masse* that brought an additional 300,000 men into the French army. See *Official Records*, Series III, vol. 1, "General Orders, No. 49," August 3, 1861, pp. 380-383.

North as "The Rebellion," and was going to restore the Union by force. Yet, persistent denial of this unpleasant reality continued throughout the South.

An inveterate reader of Northern newspapers, Lee grasped Republican resolve. His perception differed dramatically from most Southern politicians; most strangely failed to comprehend the consequences of failing to initially match numbers with the Unionists for their fledgling country's defense, which remains one of the most stupefying contrasts of the war. Rather than taking the bold, necessary, and corresponding steps to respond to Lincoln's unprecedented call to arms, most Southern politicians did the unthinkable—nothing beyond calling for "any number of volunteers, not exceeding 400,000." Instead of action that at least matched Federal numbers, they called for fewer men than their adversary, all the while ridiculing Lincoln and trying to convince themselves and their constituents that everything would somehow turn out happily. To foster this latest fantasy, most Southern politicians spread the tales of how the people of the North would not come forth in such numbers, or if they did it would be impossible to either assemble, arm or organize such a force, or that the finances of the United States would be unable to meet to such demands. All of these assumptions proved to be wishful thinking.[86]

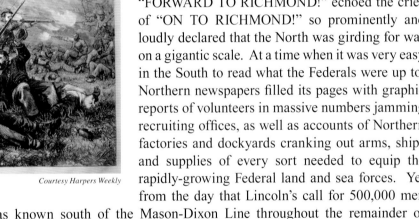

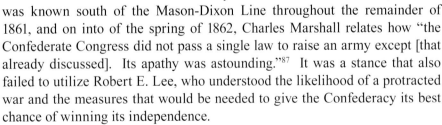

Courtesy Harpers Weekly

"On To Richmond!"

While Confederate politicians dreamed, massive preparations in the United States proceeded. The repeated newspaper headlines of "FORWARD TO RICHMOND!" echoed the cries of "ON TO RICHMOND!" so prominently and loudly declared that the North was girding for war on a gigantic scale. At a time when it was very easy in the South to read what the Federals were up to, Northern newspapers filled its pages with graphic reports of volunteers in massive numbers jamming recruiting offices, as well as accounts of Northern factories and dockyards cranking out arms, ships and supplies of every sort needed to equip the rapidly-growing Federal land and sea forces. Yet from the day that Lincoln's call for 500,000 men was known south of the Mason-Dixon Line throughout the remainder of 1861, and on into of the spring of 1862, Charles Marshall relates how "the Confederate Congress did not pass a single law to raise an army except [that already discussed]. Its apathy was astounding."[87] It was a stance that also failed to utilize Robert E. Lee, who understood the likelihood of a protracted war and the measures that would be needed to give the Confederacy its best chance of winning its independence.

---

[86] *Official Records*, Series IV, vol. 1, "An Act further to provide for the public defense," August 8, 1861, p. 537.

[87] *New York Tribune*, 25 June 1861; the demand by Horace Greeley was echoes in other papers across the North; Marshall, *Lee's Aide-de-Camp*, p. 13.

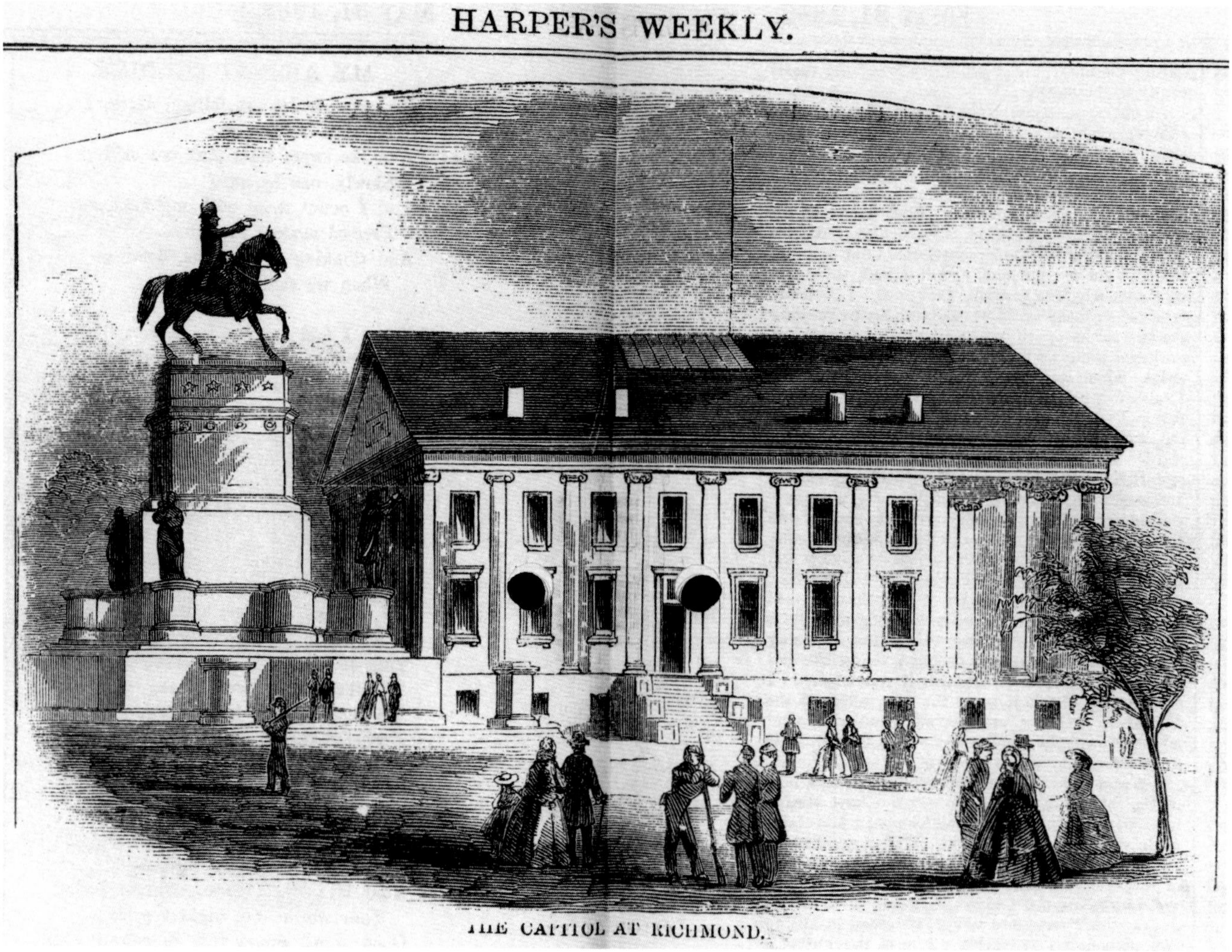

HARPER'S WEEKLY.

THE CAPITOL AT RICHMOND.

Courtesy Harpers Weekly

Capitol Square, Richmond

Rank Without Command

Robert E. Lee toiled throughout the first year of the war underutilized and underappreciated. Why Lee's talents went mostly untapped for so long by the Confederate President when his counterpart across the Potomac had already proved that he was very anxious to make full use of them remains one of the most curious decisions in American history.

At first, Lee's talents seemed appreciated both by Lincoln and Virginia Governor Letcher. After all, once Lincoln did not get his man, Governor Letcher and the Virginia representatives were both grateful and anxious to name Lee to head its military forces. However, Lee's inauspicious start could be traced to the time during which he held the anomalous title as "commander," acting under the authority of the governor and convention. While this position was a logical one for Lee immediately following Virginia's secession, Jefferson Davis' withholding Lee from field command once the state troops came under the authority of the central government seems inexplicable. So singular was this mistake by Davis that it can be argued that the Confederacy paid the ultimate price with its failed bid for independence. We know this in hindsight. In fairness, however, a detailed examination and analysis of how this came to be is required in order to see if Davis' decision can be explained or justified by the exigencies of the moment.

Lee's early-war roles are perhaps the least discussed of his war-time career, eclipsed, no doubt, by his accomplishments as an army commander beginning in June, 1862. When Lee was suddenly thrust into the role as "commander" of the Virginia forces, he took on a formidable task. Responsible for the safety of almost 1.6 million citizens spread over an area of 67,230 square miles, or roughly the size of all the states comprising New England, Lee was charged with organizing Virginia's state troops and protecting her expansive territory. In 1861, the borders of the state that had served, according to one prominent historian, as "the cradle that had rocked Washington, Jefferson, Madison, Monroe and a galaxy of other leaders," stretched from the Atlantic Ocean in the east to the Big Sandy River in the west, a distance of 425 miles, and from the "Panhandle counties" in the north near Pittsburg to North Carolina on its southern border, or a distance of 300 miles. Old Dominion was the most populous state in the South (prior to secession, the fifth largest in the Union) and its manufacturing capacity was almost as great as that of the original seven "Cotton States" states of the Confederacy combined. Raising and organizing Virginia's mostly untrained citizens into military units, protecting her borders and assets when no adequate defensive preparations existed were enormous undertakings, and Lee immediately set about to bring order to the state. He did not have a lot of time to get things done, given Lincoln's timetable.[88]

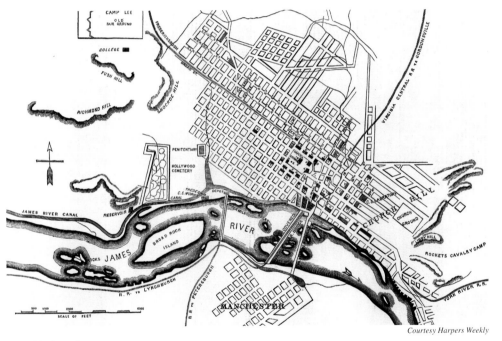

Courtesy Harpers Weekly

Map of Richmond

In Lincoln's proclamation of April 15th that called for 75,000 volunteers, he demanded that the secessionists "retire peaceable to their respective abodes within twenty days."[89] This gave rise to the wide-spread belief that Lincoln would wait until May 5th before invading the South. If true, that meant Lee had only 12 days—from April 23rd to May 5th—in which to ready Old Dominion before the inevitable invasion. Outside of enthusiasm exhibited by his fellow Virginians, Lee had precious little resources readily at hand. There was almost no Virginia navy, and the numerous volunteer infantry companies had to be quickly armed by emptying the arsenals across the state, as well as making other accommodations to speed along the mustering process. In addition, Lee tackled the issues of how to properly effect training, organize the companies into larger units, and recommend high ranking officers for their assignments of duty. The troops needed to be logically disposed to effectively meet an initial Federal thrust. In addition, Lee considered a wide variety of naval-related issues that ranged from what to do with the very vulnerable shipyards and valuable machinery at Norfolk (a most difficult task, considering that the Federals held Hampton Roads), as well as to how to defend Virginia's vulnerable tidewater region from water-born invasion. All this and much more Lee addressed in only a matter of days.

---

[88] Ernest B. Furgurson, *Ashes of Glory: Richmond at War* (New York, 1996), p. 39.
[89] *Official Records*, Series III, volume 1, "By the President of the United States: A Proclamation," p. 68.

By the end of May, 1861—only eight days after the voters of Virginia ratified the ordinance of secession and about six weeks after assuming his new role—Lee had put 30,000 Virginians into the field; two weeks later, the number increased to 40,000.[90] In early June, the Confederate Congress conferred the rank of general on Lee, and he and his Virginia troops passed to the authority of the central government. However, once that occurred, Lee did not readily receive any notice from Jefferson Davis about his future, and thought that his career as an officer might possibly be at an end.[91] Then came surprising news: instead of receiving a field command, Lee was to be an advisor to Davis—a position that carried no corresponding authority. It was a most curious assignment. In his self-professed confusion, Lee told his wife: "I do not know what my position will be . . . My movements are very uncertain, and I wish to take the field as soon as certain arrangements can be made."[92]

* * *

Most Southerners of this period would never be so direct as to put on paper why Jefferson Davis failed to promptly and properly employ Robert E. Lee (thus providing a first-hand explanation for historians). Davis and Lee maintained silence on this point. Circumstantial analysis strongly suggests that Davis delayed in utilizing Lee, naming him instead to a nebulous post when his record and history demanded otherwise, for a mix of political and personal reasons. Neither of these motives sheds much credit on Davis' leadership.

The political factors certainly appear to have been numerous. One prominent factor seemed to surface almost immediately after Virginia's secession convention voted to leave the Union. From many of the more vocal advocates of separation there arose a clamor for an armed invasion of Maryland in order to secure "Virginia's sister" for the Confederacy. The political reasoning behind this desire was rooted in the long-standing bond that had always been shared between Maryland and Virginia. In the presidential election of 1860, Maryland had voted for John C. Breckinridge, a Southern Democrat. Furthermore, the state legislature in Maryland was controlled by Democrats sympathetic to the South, and the legislative body was slated to meet in Frederick on April 26th (only three days after Lee assumed his role as "commander" of Virginia's military forces) for the purpose of voting on secession. Additionally, Lincoln had already made it known that if Maryland's politicians voted to secede, he would react swiftly and decisively. President Lincoln's stated that he would suspend the ancient writ of *habeas corpus*, imprison all those suspected of aiding, as he termed it, "The Rebellion," and would order "the bombardment of their cities."[93]

Courtesy Harpers Weekly

Chief Justice Roger B. Taney

---

[90] Long, *Memoirs of Robert E. Lee*, p. 103; Robert E. Lee, *The Wartime Papers of R. E. Lee*, edited by Clifford Dowdey and Louis H. Manarin (Boston, 1961), number 59, "To John Letcher," June 15, 1861, p. 51.

[91] Robert E. Lee to Mary Custis Lee, June 9, 1861, as quoted in Richard B. McCaslin, *Lee in the Shadow of Washington*, p. 87.

[92] Robert E. Lee, Jr., *Recollections and Letters*, Robert E. Lee To His Wife, June 9, 1861; Robert E. Lee To His Wife, June 24, 1861, pp. 29-30.

[93] Abraham Lincoln to General Winfield Scott, April 25, 1861, *The Collected Works of Abraham Lincoln*, edited by Roy P. Basler, et al., 8 volumes (Rutgers, 1953), volume 4, p. 344. The clause in the Constitution providing for the suspension of the writ of *habeas corpus* appears in Article I, Section 9, and states that "The privilege of the writ of *habeas corpus* shall not be suspended, unless when in cases of rebellion or invasion the public safety may require it." While it was purposeful why Lincoln carefully chose to use the term "The Rebellion" in connection with the secession crisis, the issue of suspending *habeas corpus* is in the article that deals with the authority of Congress, not the President. This was a fact that President Thomas

"Northern politicians do not appreciate the determination and pluck of the South, and Southern politicians do not appreciate the numbers, resources and patient perseverance of the North."

—**Robert E. Lee, in a May, 1861 interview**

The Federal executive's threats had their desired effect: the Maryland legislature avoided the secession vote. Lincoln, however, soon decided to proceed with suspending *habeas corpus* and allowed his military commanders the freedom to arrest and imprison indefinitely without indictment, judicial hearing, or trial any and all suspected secessionists in Maryland, confiscating their property in the process.[94] Lincoln's interpretation of the use of executive powers, based on his responsibilities to the protection clause of the Constitution, drew the ire of Chief Justice Roger B. Taney and further embittered many in the South who viewed this and other prior acts by Lincoln as coercive and outside his constitutional authority.[95]

Lincoln's actions provided the catalyst for increasing popular opinion in Virginia for an immediate invasion to succor Maryland. An in electrified Richmond, a grand celebration parade, replete with speech makers calling for Maryland to join the Confederacy, had whipped the crowds into a frenzy. "In less than sixty days," proclaimed one speaker, "the flag of the Confederacy will be waving over the White House." From the frenzied crowd, one shouted: "Yes—in less than thirty days!" Sallie Ann Brock Putnam, a young lady of Richmond society, wrote of the moment: "A stranger suddenly transported to the city, without knowledge of preceding facts, would have imagined the people in a state of intoxication or insanity."[96]

The firebrands looked to Lee, as "commander" of Virginia's forces, to help facilitate an invasion. In the minds of these Southerners, such an aggressive act would, in Clifford Dowdey's characterization of rampant expectations, "send the Yankees hurrying back to their money counters."[97] Lee would have none of it. His outright rejection of such a hare-brained scheme, choosing instead

Author's Collection

1855 Harpers Ferry Rifled Musket

to focus on legitimate defensive concerns confronting Virginia, prompted an unfair reaction from the less militarily inclined. While these critics failed to grasp Lee's prudent course to prepare Virginia's defenses and properly train "the poorly armed, undisciplined and unbrigaded uniformed civilians," they used the incident to circulate totally unfounded rumors that the "commander"

Jefferson acknowledged in 1806 when he sought to bring Aaron Burr to justice in the wake of Jefferson's accusation that the former Vice President had headed a conspiracy against the United States. Interestingly, Jefferson's view of the Constitution—in this respect that Congress alone possessed the power to suspend the writ—was reiterated by none other than Chief Justice John Marshall, who confirmed this interpretation in an 1807 opinion, *Ex parte Bollman*, dealing with the legal claims of two other citizens accused of participating in the Burr conspiracy.

[94] Abraham Lincoln to General Winfield Scott, April 27, 1861, *The Collected Works of Abraham Lincoln*, edited by Roy P. Basler, et al., volume 4, p. 347. One of the Maryland men incarcerated by Federal soldiers was John Merryman, a wealthy landlord and state legislator, who became the subject of the famous 1861 *Merryman* opinion written by Chief Justice Taney.

[95] In his *Merryman* opinion, Chief Justice Taney maintained with certitude that every source, including Constitutional text, Court precedent, treatise, history, common law roots and more, conclusively supported his position that Lincoln had acted illegally by suspending the writ of *habeas corpus*. There was only one problem—no wartime president has ever, nor would ever, accept an impotent Constitutional role; Lincoln was no exception, *and* he commanded the armed forces. In summarizing this unique event, historian Ernest B. Furgurson wrote: "Constitutionally, Taney may have been right, and Lincoln wrong. But Lincoln had the army, and Taney did not. The president simply defied Taney's ruling, and nothing displayed the temper of the times more clearly than the vociferous support that came from the Republican press, lashing the chief justice as if he were Jefferson Davis in person." See Furgurson, *Freedom Rising*, p. 97.

[96] Putnam, *Richmond During the War*, pp. 20-22.

[97] Dowdey, *Lee*, p. 148.

of Virginia's forces was not properly committed to The Cause. President Davis could not have taken this news well, because in addition to what he heard from the stump, Davis himself indulged in some of "the wildest, most belligerent prophecies . . . as he predicted the destruction [of] Northern cities and even Washington."

Southern newspapers egged on the President. One Richmond paper predicted that Davis would lead the invading Southern legions to victory. "President Davis will soon march an army through North Carolina and Virginia to Washington," declared its editors. The Richmond Examiner cried in excited italics: "There is one wild shout of fierce resolve to capture Washington."[98]

While politicians and newspaper editors were engaging in flights of fantasy and exciting the Southern populace to believe that the war—if there was indeed any fighting—would be short and/or that European powers would come to their aid,

Courtesy Harpers Weekly

Confederate Forces Swearing In

Lee remained of a different mind. To go with his initial focus on Virginia's defensive measures, Lee insisted that Southerners alone would have to bear the responsibility for winning their independence, and as such the struggle against the powerful United States would be very costly and long—much longer and more costly than what their forefathers endured during the American Revolution. Only eight days after arriving in Richmond, Lee wrote his wife that: "The war may last ten years." Lee indeed understood what was at stake for assuming the role of a revolutionary. He knew that he and his fellow Southerners were risking all, "save honour." Paradoxically, nothing could be spared in terms of effort if they did not want to lose everything in the attempt to secure independence. Incredible as it may seem in retrospect, Robert E. Lee singularly voiced the most accurate assessment of the military situation confronting the South. According to Walter Taylor, who served with the general longer than any other aide, Lee was "alone, of all the men known to me" to have "expressed his most serious apprehensions of a prolonged and bloody war." Taylor also remembered that Lee foresaw "a determined and bitter conflict" owing to "those traits of the Anglo-Saxon race . . . when liberty and honor are involved."[99]

Lee spoke openly and honestly about this issue to many with whom he came in contact, and during the time in which he was organizing Virginia's defenses, he gave further warnings in letters to family and friends. When

---

[98] Dowdey, *Lee*, p. 148; William C. Davis, *Jefferson Davis*, p. 328.

[99] Walter Taylor, *Four Years With General Lee* (New York, 1878, Indiana University Press reprint 1996), pp. 11-12; Lee to Mrs. Lee, April 30, 1861, as quote in Freeman, *R. E. Lee*, vol. 1, p. 475.

firebrand Edmund Ruffin—the man who claimed the credit for firing the opening shot of the war upon Fort Sumter—showed up in Richmond on May 14th, he got a dose of reality when Lee tried to explain to him what hardships the South could expect from the coming conflict. Ruffin was insulted by such talk, and two days later displayed his utter lack of understanding of what war meant when he wired Jefferson Davis (who was then in Montgomery, Alabama) to come to Richmond at once and take over Lee's job.[100]

At least three other reports emanating from Richmond had few, if any, encouraging words to say about Lee. One such report came from D. G. Duncan of Montgomery, Alabama, who was sent to Richmond in late April to act as a spy for Davis and Secretary of War Leroy Pope Walker. Duncan spoke to Lee shortly after the latter's appointment. Reporting back to his superiors then in Montgomery, Duncan claimed that Lee "wishes to repress enthusiasm of our people." Others who knew of Lee's appraisal heard instead the voice of Cassandra. Albert Taylor Bledsoe, an old friend of Davis from West Point days and a bombastic faculty member of the University of Virginia, wrote to the President that Lee was "too despondent" and that his remarks "dispirit our people . . . [for] he does not know how good and how righteous our cause is, and consequently lacks one quality which the times demand."[101] That reputed quality, of course, was conviction, and Davis later heard another complaint about Lee, this time offered up from rabid secessionist and Governor Francis Pickens of South Carolina. "Lee is not with us at heart," Pickens wrote Davis, "or he is a common man, with good looks, and too cautious for practical Revolution."[102]

Courtesy Harpers Weekly

Volunteers for The Cause

Many of these observations about Lee, however unfair, came about the same time as Lee's turning down Davis' untimely summons in early May for the general to drop what he was doing and come to Montgomery to discuss the defense of Virginia and define Lee's role in the new nation's military. Lee's wire back to Davis answering that he "cannot be spared" from the pressing issues at hand, deliberately risked upsetting the vainglorious and stiff-necked President who was being told by his sycophants in Richmond that he—Davis—was the one great man that the South could turn to "in this great crisis" and only he "can save her." Therefore,

[100] *Official Records*, Series I, vol. 51, part 2, Supplement, Edmund Ruffin to Jefferson Davis, telegram, Richmond, May 16, 1861, p. 92.

[101] *Official Records*, Series I, vol. 51, part 2, Supplement, D. G. Duncan to Leroy Pope Walker, Richmond, April 26, 1861, p. 39. Also, see: Albert Taylor Bledsoe to Jefferson Davis, University of Virginia, May 10, 1861, in Lynda Lasswell Crist and Mary Seaton Dix, editors, *The Papers of Jefferson Davis*, volume 7 (Baton Rouge, 1992), pp. 160-162.

[102] Pickens, as quoted in William C. Davis, *Jefferson Davis*, p. 337.

instead of Lee going to Montgomery, it was Davis who did the traveling. In a move that many believed was to demonstrate the value of Old Dominion, the Confederate Congress voted on May 20th to move the seat of government to the storied city of Richmond, where "the lordly planters of Tidewater built their winter houses" and "the tobacco men their mansions." Nine days later, Davis led the vanguard of his administration into the new capital.[103]

When Davis reached Richmond that Wednesday, he was met with resounding greetings from the curious and the enthusiastic. Lee was not among them, and Davis could not have been pleased. In every town along the tracks from Montgomery to Richmond, crowds cheered Jefferson Davis northward with an enthusiasm that one historian described "as if he were going to drive away the Yankees with his own sword." All along the way, Davis kept looking for Lee. At Atlanta and Augusta in Georgia, and at Wilmington and Goldsboro in North Carolina, the presidential train stopped for Davis to address the crowds, and all along the way Davis was expecting Lee to have taken a train southward to meet the President in route. When Davis' train pulled into the Richmond & Petersburg station shortly after dawn on May 29th, Lee was not there to greet him. Davis wasn't going to forget it.[104]

Lee's whereabouts do leave room for some interpretation of his motives, although no hearsay or letters suggest he was doing anything other than his duty. It is easy to see how Lee's actions could have led to a serious and fateful misunderstanding. Having little use for the festivities surrounding his own arrival in Richmond, Lee had no desire to stand among the sycophants awaiting Davis. Thus, the general had departed Richmond the day before to inspect troops at Manassas Junction; he also spent part of the 29th at Fairfax Courthouse. Lee's absence either from meeting Davis in route, or at the time that Davis was scheduled to arrive in Richmond, reflected Lee's deep concerns concerning the challenges of meeting the needs to properly defend his home state. In all likelihood, Lee had embarked on a fact-finding mission in order to brief Davis fully. Time pressures meant that Lee could not be chained to his desk in Richmond. When he arrived at Manassas Junction, Lee saw troops in every possible state of efficiency. Although there was encouraging news about the increasing numbers, the overall situation could not have improved Lee's existing assessment of the formidable task facing the military. He went to Fairfax Courthouse, made some disposition adjustments, then returned to Manassas Junction to do the same. The new dispositions were designed to more effectively observe the nearby enemy while giving the Federals reason to be cautious about any advance towards Harpers Ferry—where important work was going on with the disassembling and transporting of the machinery of the former national armory—or towards Manassas where the principal Virginia army was gathering.[105]

His brief inspection tour over, Lee boarded a train for the trip back to Richmond. When the train reached Orange Court House, it stopped briefly and in the tradition of the day, a crowd gathered and called for Virginia's favorite son to emerge from the car to say a few words. Lee demurred. When the locals persisted, Lee emerged to issue a few sober words that reflected the concerns of a preoccupied mind burdened by a massive workload brought on

---

[103] William C. Davis, *Jefferson Davis*, p. 337; *Official Records*, Series I, vol. 51, part 2, Supplement, D. G. Duncan to L. P. Walker, May 7, 1861; Dowdey, *Experiment in Rebellion*, p. 9.

[104] Furgurson, *Ashes of Glory*, p. 49; William C. Davis, *Jefferson Davis*, pp. 337-338.

[105] *Official Records*, Series I, volume 2, M. L. Bonham to General Lee, May 25, 1861, p 43; R. S. Garnett to Jefferson Davis, May 28, 1861, pp. 890-891; Lee to Joseph E. Johnston, May 30, 1861, p. 894 and June 1, 1861, p. 897.

Courtesy Library of Congress

Joseph E. Johnston

"If Joe Johnston is not a general, I don't know where to find one."

Jefferson Davis

by a race against time. Lee commented on how every Southerner had to be earnest and spend every moment preparing for war and the protection of themselves and their families. Lee's reality-based comments did little to inspire the citizens, let alone the reporter from The Richmond Whig.[106] As the Richmond-bound train pulled out of Orange Court House, Lee must have felt the added weight of public expectations to his already heavy responsibilities.

In addition to the press of time, Lee faced other challenges. He was concerned with the proper positioning of troops to protect the frontier while at the same time appear poised in such a manner as to induce caution amongst the Federals so as to buy more time to further prepare for the coming conflict. The difficulty in effectively stationing the units was compounded by the growing conflict of authority between Virginia and the Confederate Government. These friction-filled circumstances were brought about by the rise in authority of Joseph E. Johnston, and the growing military role assumed by President Davis.

Despite his position as "commander" of Virginia military forces, Lee's authority began to undergo serious erosion as early as the middle of May when the Confederate War Department began to assert its power over troops that Lee was supposed to be directing. To effect this override, Joe Johnston was ordered by the Montgomery authorities on May 15th to take command of the assembling troops at Harpers Ferry as well as other formations that Lee had previously earmarked for deployment elsewhere. In addition, other Southern forces moving into Virginia were not to report to Lee, according to directives from the central authorities, a situation in which Lee had no authority to alter the dispositions, or countermand movements authored by the central government's newest rising star, Joe Johnston.[107]

Standing at five-foot, seven-inches "and rail thin," his face and body not having "a distinguishing characteristic,"[108] Joe Johnston tried to compensate for his lack of striking physical features by way of his actions. He carried himself with a self-assured, exaggerated swagger, complete with puffed-up chest and stiff back to give the appearance of someone stouter. Either while walking or standing, Johnston often rose up on the balls of his feet to provide the illusion of someone taller. The unmistakable side effect of these demonstrative actions was that Johnston often exuded a stuffy, haughty air. While many of his peers considered him intelligent and a good conversationalist who was mindful of the welfare of his men, his serious nature seemed to be the reason that a permanent scowl crossed his face.[109]

When Virginia's convention voted for secession, Johnston, a career army man who had graduated from West Point in the Class of 1829, resigned his commission and repaired to Richmond. Upon arrival he found Robert E. Lee already a major general and in command of the state's military forces. Realizing that Johnston was one of the senior officers in the old army, Governor Letcher decided to also name Johnston as a major general. The Virginia Convention, however, thought that one was enough and he was reduced to brigadier general.

[106] Virginia Historical Society, *Richmond Whig*, June 7, 1861, p. 2, columns 3-4.
[107] *Official Records*, Series I, volume 51, part 2, D. G. Duncan to L. P. Walker, May 24, 1861, pp. 103-104; John W. Ellis to Robert E. Lee, May 24, 1861, pp. 106-107; and F. W. Pickens to Jefferson Davis, May 29, 1861, pp. 119-120.
[108] Craig L. Symonds, *Joseph E. Johnston: A Civil War Biography* (New York, 1992), p. 10. To give the reader a sense of historical comparison, Johnston was only one inch taller than Napoleon, who stood five-foot, six-inches.
[109] Symonds, *Joseph E. Johnston*, p. 10.

The demotion in the state army, and being a rank lower than Lee, did not sit well with Johnston. He therefore left Richmond and traveled to Montgomery for the express purpose of seeking a separate appointment with the central government. In this, he met success. Johnston attained his commission as a brigadier general in the Confederate States army, and then received orders to return to Virginia and take command of the Southern forces assembling around Harpers Ferry. Johnston wanted the more prestigious command of the forces gathering around Manassas Junction, but that command had been earmarked for the hero of Fort Sumter, General Beauregard. However, once he and his staff arrived at the Ferry, Johnston decided that he wanted to retreat.[110] Of course, Johnston's idea for speedy abandonment of Harpers Ferry without pressure from the enemy ran counter to that of General Lee, Thomas Jonathan Jackson, and Confederate President Davis.[111]

Thomas Jefferson vividly described the natural setting of Harpers Ferry. After visiting the place in 1783, the prominent Virginian wrote: "The passage of the Patowmac [Potomac] through the Blue Ridge is perhaps one of the most stupendous scenes in Nature."[112] In 1861, that vista still retained all its majesty, but had attained increasing strategic importance. As the northernmost point of the Confederacy, Harpers Ferry was the gateway to northwestern Virginia, which Old Dominion was desperately trying to retain, and provided an important political bolster to Maryland, which the Confederacy hoped to add to its list of states. Also, Harpers Ferry was the opening towards the Shenandoah

Author's Collection

Confluence of the Potomac and Shenandoah rivers

Valley. Although the Ferry was not the geographical key to the Shenandoah Valley (that distinction belonged to Winchester), within its invaluable fields of grains and corn was a network of hardened roads that made for a natural invasion route for both sides. Moreover, the valley was far more useful for the Confederacy in that respect, for its geographical layout served as a sharp knife pointed directly at Washington and Southern forces in the valley would threaten the right flank of any Federal force moving on Manassas.

Harpers Ferry rests at the confluence of the northward-flowing Shenandoah River and the southward-flowing Potomac River. These rivers cut their way through the Blue Ridge Mountains (the view of which Jefferson wrote) to form a natural pass for the Chesapeake & Ohio Canal along the northern bank of the Potomac, and for the Baltimore & Ohio Railroad that joins the Winchester and Potomac Railroad. Confederate possession of these rail lines significantly impaired Federal communications with the Midwest. This ease of access provided by water, along with the locale far removed from the threat of foreign invasion, were the primary reasons that President George Washington located

---

[110] *Official Records*, vol. 2, p. 471 and pp. 880-881.

[111] Before his departure from Montgomery, President Davis attempted to impress upon Johnston the importance that Harpers Ferry had to the Confederate cause at this point in the war.

[112] Thomas Jefferson, *Notes on the State of Virginia*, Query IV "A Notice of Its Mountains," as reproduced in *Thomas Jefferson: Writings, Autobiography, A Summary View of the Rights of British America, Notes on the States of Virginia, Public Papers, Addresses, Messages, and Replies. Miscellany, Letters* (New York, 1984), pp. 141-142; Dave Gilbert, *A Walker's Guide to Harpers Ferry, West Virginia* (Harpers Ferry, third edition, 1991), pp. 8 and 42.

this national armory in Harpers Ferry before the turn of the 19th century. More than 60 years later, few munitions factories then existed within the borders of the Southern states, making the Harpers Ferry armory's warehouses and factory for small arms a priceless possession for the Confederacy. Thus, the fortuitous seizure of the United States Armory and Arsenal at Harpers Ferry by Virginia state troops on April 18, 1861, provided much of the tools, machinery and stock for two future arsenals—the Virginia Armory, later known as the Richmond Armory, and the Fayetteville Armory in North Carolina. Finally, the seizure of the Ferry had netted valuable rolling stock belonging to the B&O Railroad.[113]

Courtesy Harpers Weekly

Harpers Ferry Vista

Soon after the capture of Harpers Ferry, Lee ordered Thomas Jackson, then a colonel of Virginia state troops and a former professor at Virginia Military Institute, to proceed to Harpers Ferry and take command of that post. In addition to organizing and training the volunteers sent to that place, Lee instructed Jackson to "expedite the transfer of the machinery to this place, ordered to the Richmond Armory." Lee also told Jackson that any partially constructed rifles be assembled "as fast as possible," and then "such arms, machinery, parts of arms, raw material, etc., that may be useful" be removed without delay whereby they "must be sent into the interior." Jackson wasted no time implementing Lee's orders with regards to organizing and instructing the troops. Moving the machinery, however, proved to be a more difficult matter. Jackson initially had trouble procuring transport, but by early May, he had started moving the armory's assets to Richmond—a process that would take "probably six-weeks to remove." The transfer was still ongoing when Joe Johnston arrived with the authority from the central government to assume command.[114]

Courtesy Harpers Weekly

US Armory, Harpers Ferry

Despite the obvious importance of Harpers Ferry to the Confederates at the time, Johnston didn't seem to appreciate it. On May 26th, within three days of his arrival at the Ferry, Johnston wrote that the position was "untenable."[115] That indeed might well have been the case if the numerically

---

[113] The 44-man Federal garrison that was in Harpers Ferry on April 18, 1861, set fire to some of the buildings and munitions as the Virginia state troops arrived. Although some of the buildings and 10,000 weapons were destroyed or heavily damaged by the blaze, the Virginians did manage to save most of the structures along with the vitally important machinery; the Virginians also spared 5,000 weapons from the fire. James I. Robertson, Jr., *Stonewall Jackson: The Man, The Soldier, The* Legend (New York, 1997), p. 221.

[114] *Official Records*, Series I, vol. 2, Robert E. Lee to Thomas J Jackson, April 27, 1861, pp. 784-785; C. Dimmock to Robert E. Lee, April 27, 1861, pp. 785-786; Frank E. Vandiver, *Mighty Stonewall* (New York, 1957), p. 136; Frank E. Vandiver, *Ploughshares into Swords: Josiah Gorgas and Confederate Ordnance* (Austin, 1952), p. 62.

[115] *Official Records*, Series I, vol. 2, J. E. Johnston to R. S. Garnett [Lee's adjutant-general],May 26, 1861, pp. 880-881; Joseph E. Johnston, *Narrative of Military Operations* (Bloomington, 1959 reprint of the 1874 original), p. 16. In a report dated May 28th, engineer officer W. H. C. Whiting gave his opinion that the defense of the Ferry and its surrounding area would "require a force of from twelve to fifteen thousand men." See *Official Records*, Series I, vol. 2, W. H. C. Whiting [to Lee in Richmond], "Consultation on the condition of Harpers Ferry and its defenses reduced to writing," May 28, 1861, p. 890.

superior Federals in the region were threatening the Ferry or maneuvering against its sensitive flanks. Although that was not yet the case, Johnston still wanted to abandon this place post haste. In Johnston's mind, Harpers Ferry was only a point on a map—a town wedged between two rivers and dominated by a trio of surrounding heights that seemed to make the place serve only as a trap—as if the Ferry could only be defended by stationing troops in the shadows of those hills, and as if the Confederacy could afford to prematurely abandon the machinery still being removed from the grounds of the former national armory. The situation was made

Courtesy Harpers Weekly

Confederate recruits

worse by Johnston's impolitic handling of the men under his command. He held in low esteem the enthusiastic but unproven volunteers assembled there, and he let them know it. Only days after Johnston assumed command at the Ferry, he thoughtlessly remarked as the 2nd Virginia marched by: "I wouldn't give a company of regulars for the whole regiment!" With that utterance, many officers of the future "Stonewall Brigade," including Jackson, were understandably concerned about the measure of the man who future historians would dub as "Retreatin' Joe."[116]

Joe Johnston's view of Harpers Ferry contrasted sharply with that of Robert E. Lee. While the process of removing the vital machinery from the former national armory was ongoing, Johnston received two telegrams from Lee in Richmond dated June 1st, 1861. These advised Johnston that "a large force" of Confederates then gathering "in front of Alexandria" would serve as a deterrent to the Federals in moving against Johnston's right flank. Furthermore, Lee related to Johnston that additional troops had "been directed to report to you as soon as practicable," and that others "from the valley" would follow. With these added reinforcements, Lee hoped that Johnston could maintain his front for as long as it was feasible because "the abandonment of Harpers Ferry" before all the war-making machinery had been removed and developments in northwestern Virginia could be better determined "would be depressing to the cause." Lee further emphasized to Johnston the need to improve his defensive method through the use of maneuver by making his "column moveable." In realizing that conditions may change at any time, Lee advised in his communiqués for Johnston to use his "good judgment" that should he "be attacked by a force which you may be unable to resist at all points," Johnston was to "destroy everything that cannot be removed… deprived them the use of the railroad, take the field, and endeavor to arrest their advance up the valley…" by contesting the enemy's "approach step by step into the interior."[117]

---

[116] *Southern Historical Society Papers*, Hunter McGuire, "General T. J. ("Stonewall") Jackson, vol. 25, p. 103. The term, "Retreatin' Joe," was coined by Clifford Dowdey.
[117] *Official Records*, Series I, vol. 2, Robert E. Lee to Joseph E. Johnston, June 1, 1861, pp.

These telegrams provide a window to Lee's nuanced thinking. Pragmatically, Lee saw it as imperative that Harpers Ferry be stripped of every bit of war-making industrial equipment, and that this factor alone necessitated that Johnston be strongly encouraged to maintain a bold front for as long as possible. The Confederacy could ill-afford for its field commander to be spooked out of the position, leaving valuable assets behind to the enemy and potentially harming the new nation's morale and ability to make implements of war. Thus, given the limitations of his authority, Lee tried to reason with Johnston that, given present circumstances, his position was relatively secure; he also tried to ameliorate Johnston's fears about being outnumbered by advising that reinforcements were on the way. Furthermore, Lee recognized the nature of command, control, and operational friction by using terms of contingency, stating that help would arrive as soon "as practicable," rather than stating a completely impossible-to-predict arrival timetable. Both men knew that these reinforcements, having received their orders, would be expected to make haste to the Ferry as soon as they could.[118]

Strategically, Lee also explained that Harpers Ferry and its thinly-guarded flanks could be defended by other means than simply positioning troops in static positions. Although Lee did not underestimate the vulnerability of the Harpers Ferry position—indeed it has the feel of a box canyon where a force could easily be trapped—his telegrams clearly pointed out to Johnston that the Ferry and the troops defending it were part of a broader picture. While Johnston fretted about his flanks and the sense of being easily trapped, Lee understood that the Southern force being assembled in front of Alexandria indirectly protected Johnston's right, and he took the pains to explain this. Johnston did not understand the reverse—that abandoning his position would expose the left flank and rear of the Manassas front. To better protect both flanks of Harpers Ferry, and to have the effect of augmenting his smaller numbers, Lee emphasized to Johnston the need to make his forces maneuverable. This principle of war—whereby audacious maneuver is utilized to confuse the enemy and create opportunity—remains important for a numerically smaller side. In these communications Lee revealed his core philosophy and, in the insightful words of biographer Clifford Dowdey, "the aggressive military cast of his mind. His first thought on a threatening enemy was not how to avoid but how to get at him."[119]

MAJOR-GENERAL PATTERSON.—FROM A PHOTOGRAPH.

MAJOR-GENERAL PATTERSON.

Courtesy Harpers Weekly

Major-General Robert Patterson

Johnston's defensive-minded military philosophy could not have been more opposite in spirit to Lee's aggressive cast of mind. In his replies to Richmond, Johnston revealed his desire to leave Harpers Ferry rather than trying to implement any ideas communicated by Lee. Accordingly, Johnston sought to justify a withdrawal, even though he was not being pressured by the enemy. Aside from his protestations typical of almost every commander at this point in the war concerning a lack of supplies of all sorts—complaints that were often valid—Johnston carped that the "general plan of campaign" had not been spelled out to him. He was fearful that separate Federal forces under Brigadier General Robert Patterson and Major General George B. McClellan would "very soon" swoop down upon him whereby his command "must be captured or destroyed." This fear fed off rumors that McClellan would soon bring reinforcements to join Patterson. Accordingly, Johnston

---

897-898.
[118] *Official Records*, Series I, vol. 2, R. S. Garnett to J. E. Johnston, May 30, 1861, and Robert E. Lee to J. E. Johnston, June 3, 1861, p. 894.
[119] Dowdey, *Lee*, p. 153.

asked if he and his troops could be ordered away "to some point" where they could "still be useful." Johnston revealed a rigid mind tethered with a fearful imagination. Despite Lee's urging for him to make the effort to make his command maneuverable, Johnston struggled with military semantics; he could not figure out if his "troops constitute a garrison or a corps of observation." Johnston also complained that he did not have enough reinforcements, and the ones that did arrive were like the troops already at the Ferry—lacking "instruction or subordination."[120]

Harpers Ferry Arsenal

Despite his wish to do otherwise, Johnston felt the distant pressure from Lee and others in Richmond to remain for the time being around Harpers Ferry. However, by June 10th, Johnston could no longer resist the compulsion to retreat. A newspaper from Hagerstown, Maryland, heralded the advance of a sizable Federal force under the command of 69 year-old Robert Patterson. The War of 1812 veteran had moved his forces from Chambersburg, Pennsylvania, to Hagerstown, only six miles from the Potomac at Williamsport. If Patterson crossed the river at that point, he would be as close to Winchester as Johnston. Also, the Hagerstown paper published the complete list of the 24 regiments comprising Patterson's command, making it possible for Johnston to immediately calculate that Patterson's force numbered about 18,000—almost three times as many as his own. Three days later, a Federal force comprising a portion of the command under McClellan raided Romney, Virginia, some 43 miles west of Harpers Ferry. Although Johnston did not learn of the Romney raid until the 16th, Patterson's advance from Chambersburg convinced Johnston that Harpers Ferry should be abandoned. The labor-intensive job of removing the machinery from the former national armory had not yet been completed, and no plans were in place to save the rolling stock of the B&O Railroad when Johnston—who had been in command at Harpers Ferry for three weeks and had been itching to leave since the second day after he had arrived—gave the orders to retreat. On June 14th, Confederate troops wrecked the remaining machinery, started blowing up the railroad bridges, and destroyed some of the valuable railroad engines of the

Destroying the Bridge at Harpers Ferry

B&O Railroad that Jackson had not already commandeered. The following day, the buildings of the old armory were set a fire: Johnston quickly pulled back, giving the excuse that "the want of ammunition has rendered me very timid."[121]

---

[120] *Official Records*, Series I, vol. 2, J. E. Johnston to Robert E. Lee, June 6, 1861, pp. 907-908; J. E. Johnston to Robert E. Lee, June 12, 1861, p. 922; John G. Nicolay, *The Outbreak of Rebellion*, "Campaigns of the Civil War," (New York, 1882), p. 160.

[121] *Official Records*, Series I., vol. 2, J. E. Johnston to Samuel Cooper, June17, 1861, p. 934.

On the 16th, anticipating a swift advance by Patterson's Federals once they seized Harpers Ferry, Johnston deployed his command now numbering about 7,000 just north of Bunker Hill, Virginia, about 15 miles west of Harpers Ferry, halfway between Martinsburg and Winchester. Around noon, Confederate scouts brought word to Johnston that Patterson's men had indeed crossed the Potomac only to suddenly and inexplicably re-cross the river. The bizarre retrograde movement of Patterson's command, combined with the news that a portion of McClellan's command was now 43 miles to the west, spurred Johnston to continue his retreat. He fell back to Winchester, where, according to one biographer, "Johnston felt that he could congratulate himself on a timely escape and on foiling the enemy offensive."[122]

* * *

Even though the authority given to Robert E. Lee by Virginia Governor Letcher and the state's convention was destined to be of only a limited time, the actions by Jefferson Davis and the central government accelerated the process. Johnston's assignment to Harpers Ferry and other correspondence emanating from the War Department had the effect of either ignoring or bypassing

Courtesy Harpers Weekly

Richmond, Virginia

Lee's state authority. Starting with the end of May, after he returned to Richmond from his inspection tour around Manassas, Lee saw his influence continually shrink each day until it vanished once Jefferson Davis and his various central government departments took over the responsibilities for the new nation. By June 9th, the day after Virginia forces were officially transferred to the Confederate States, Lee was a brigadier general in the Confederate army. President Davis made no mention to Lee of any future assignment, even though he had had more than 10 days to do so. Lee, in the meanwhile, thought that inquiring about his status and future would be tantamount to immodest place-hunting. However, silence did not relieve the angst about his uncertain future. "I do not know what my position will be," Lee confessed to his wife, "but if I can be of service to the state or her cause, I must continue."[123]

With no formal announcements forthcoming from Davis, and no one from the War Department stepping into all the responsibilities involving Old Dominion, affairs along coastal Virginia and in northwestern Virginia had no official guidance. Lee took it upon himself to continue to provide direction for those seeking help along the coast. Davis, meanwhile, initially fixated his attention on the Manassas front, then expanded it to Harpers Ferry, and lastly to northwestern Virginia, where Lee was still involved by attempting to give advice regarding the organization of the forces in that area. This unofficial and awkward situation continued for a few days until Davis grew comfortable working with Lee. The President had every reason to be pleased with what he saw from Lee, for the general proved an ideal subordinate—professional, extremely hard-working, modest, efficient, knowledgeable, courteous and respectful. After a few days, Davis seemed to overcome his initial hesitancy regarding Lee, but still refrained from awarding him a field command. Davis instead had other ideas. By June 12th, word was circulating around the War Department that the President had decided that all the brigadier generals holding a regular Confederate army commission would be elevated to full general, and that Lee would be third in seniority among these officers (the Adjutant and Inspector General, Samuel Cooper, and the President's hero,

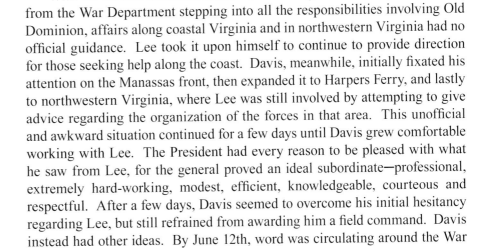

---

122 Symonds, *Joseph E. Johnston*, p. 109; Nicolay, *The Outbreak of Rebellion*, pp. 155-168.
123 Robert E. Lee, Jr., *Recollections and Letters*, Robert E. Lee to His Wife, June 9, 1861, p. 29.

Sidney Johnston, ranked ahead of Lee). Furthermore, rumor had it that Lee would remain in Richmond to aid the direction of the central government's war effort.[124]

Thus began for the Southern Confederacy what can be arguably called "The Lost Year of Opportunity," as Robert E. Lee remained in various advisory or administrative roles, often without authority, instead of employed with an active army command. The man Abraham Lincoln and Winfield Scott had handpicked to lead the Federal government's new army found himself seemingly abandoned by destiny.

No Authority—No Results

The same day that the War Department rumor about Lee was making its rounds, (Provisional) Brigadier General Beauregard, the commander of the Confederate forces assembling around Manassas, wrote a letter to Davis, giving it to Lieutenant Colonel (later, Major General) Samuel Jones of his staff for delivery to the President with more extensive oral explanations. The letter outlined two variants, the first involving a grandiose Confederate offensive into Maryland that had no basis in reality of logistics or the capabilities of his forces. Further, Beauregard's offensive vision made wild assumptions regarding cooperative Federal action. Then, to cover himself if the offensive did not work to his expectations, the general assumed the Federals would themselves immediately advance on the Confederate capital. Beauregard went on to state that "with 35,000 men, properly handled" he would "crush in rapid succession and in detail" some "50,000 of the enemy." In either scenario, Beauregard called for Johnston's forces from the Valley to join his (the only aspect of his scheme that made any sense) and presumed once Johnston's forces arrived that Johnston, who held a regular commission, would be subordinated to him.[125]

Beauregard, generally not regarded as the delusional sort, came away from the Mexican War deeply embittered against Winfield Scott for not giving him more commendations than Robert E. Lee. Nevertheless, Beauregard had considerable experience as an army engineer, and with powerful politicians advocating for him, secured an appointment from Jefferson Davis in February, 1861, as a provisional brigadier general in the Confederate army. Subsequently sent to Charleston Harbor, Beauregard accomplished, according to historian Clifford Dowdey, what "any militia artillery captain could have [with] the futile bombardment on Fort Sumter." Forever associated with the dramatic declaration of independence, the "small thin man" was hailed as the "Hero of the South," and cut a public image of greatness complete with olive skin and a smart mustache.[126] However, beneath the veneer, the 1838 graduate of West Point was, according to Dowdey "actually a specious hero"—an extremely

Courtesy Library of Congress

Perhaps the most recognizable photo of Beauregard

---

[124] John Beauchamp Jones, *A Rebel War Clerk's Diary,* edited by Earl Schenk Miers (New York, 1958 reprint of the 1866 original: *A Rebel War Clerk's Diary at the Confederate States Capital*), p. 27. The newly authorized rank of full general was a Confederate States rank, as opposed to a state commissioned rank.

[125] Crist and Dix, *The Papers of Jefferson Davis*, vol. 7, Beauregard to Davis, June 12, 1861, pp. 197-198. *Official Records*, Series I, vol. 2, Jefferson Davis to Beauregard, June 13, 1861, pp. 922-923. Since Beauregard held a provisional commission as brigadier general, he was outranked by Johnston, who held a regular commission as brigadier general.

[126] *Southern Historical Society Papers*, Thomas R. R. Cobb, "Extracts From Letters to His Wife, February 3, 1861–December 10, 1862," vol. 28, p. 287; Dowdey, *Lee*, p. 155.

conceited man who, as an officer and according to biographer Craig Symonds, had "an abiding tendency to accept conventional abstract theory rather than imaginative pragmatic execution as the measure of military performance."[127]

The next day, the President carried "on extensive conversations with Jones" before answering Beauregard.[128] Crafting a response in a tone as polite and non-confrontational as was possible from him, Davis never called into question the weaknesses of the proposal, focusing instead on other matters that included the need to "have many alternatives." In the end, Davis expressed his faith in Beauregard and in "the expectation that you will know how to use" his men to maintain his front at Manassas, while Johnston remained for the time being in the Valley.[129]

Courtesy R. W. Norton Gallery

Jefferson Davis

Despite the gentle handling by the President, Beauregard stung from the rejection. Convinced of his genius and in the brilliance of his plan, Beauregard regarded Davis' dismissal as an act of a "stupid fool."[130] There is little doubt that the slight got back to Davis and the relationship between Beauregard and the President soured from there. Over the next few weeks, Davis began poking fun at Beauregard's schemes as well as members of his staff; meanwhile, Beauregard became more convinced of his genius and the need to pursue even more grandiose plans than what he previously proposed.[131]

On July 14th, Beauregard dispatched Colonel John S. Preston of his staff to take a new plan to Davis and to "urge [the President of] the absolute and immediate necessity of adopting the plan of operations." Within a few hours, Beauregard thought of yet a better plan and sent another member of his staff, James Chesnut, Jr. an old Senate colleague of the President, and a South Carolina member of the Confederate Congress, to urge Davis to approve its adoption. Chesnut found the President in his sick bed, racked with trigeminal neuralgia "that almost blinded and paralyzed him." Not having yet received Preston and not knowing of the proposal carried by him, Davis mustered up enough energy to receive "with great kindness and cordiality" his old friend. Listening to the latest fantastical proposition must have sent Davis' already-hurting head into a spin, for he asked Chesnut to return that evening so that he could explain the proposal to two senior officers—Samuel Cooper and his brother-in-law Robert E. Lee.[132]

---

[127] Dowdey, *Lee*, p. 155; *Encyclopedia of the Confederacy*, vol. 1, p. 146.

[128] Steven E. Woodworth, *Davis & Lee at War* (Lawrence, 1995), p. 32.

[129] Davis to Beauregard, June 13, 1861, *The Papers of Jefferson Davis*, vol. 7, pp. 199-200.

[130] William C. Davis, *Jefferson Davis: The Man and His Hour* (New York, 1991), p. 345.

[131] Mary Boykin Chesnut, *Mary Chesnut's Civil War*, edited by C. Vann Woodward (New Haven, 1981), pp. 62 and 80.

[132] Alfred Roman, *The Military Operations of General Beauregard in the War Between the States, 1861-1865*, 2 volumes (New York, 1884), pp.- 84-87; Douglas Southall Freeman, *Lee's Lieutenants: A Study in Command*, 3 volumes (New York, 1944), vol. 1, p. 42; Freeman, *R. E. Lee*, vol. 1, p. 536; Chesnut, *Mary Chesnut's Civil War*, p. 100.

The two generals and the President met Chesnut in the parlor of the Spotswood Hotel at the agreed hour. Chesnut detailed the utterly fantastical scheme. As envisioned by Beauregard, Confederate forces in northwestern Virginia and in the Shenandoah Valley would combine forces, cross into Maryland and strike from the rear the Federal army covering Washington City, while Beauregard with his army assailed the Federals from the Virginia side. After defeating the Federals in front of Washington, Confederate forces would return to the Valley and destroy Patterson's Federals. All this Beauregard predicted "could be completed brilliantly in from fifteen to twenty-five days." Independence would certainly follow.[133] Lee, Cooper and Davis listened with "respectful and earnest consideration" before "two leading objections" were pointed out "by the President and by General Lee." Aside from the fact that Beauregard believed the Confederate forces in the Valley to be far stronger than they were, the fantasy called for the Federals to cooperate by giving battle at a disadvantage, rather than falling back on their reserves, or to within the fortifications already under construction around Washington.[134]

Robert S. Garnett

Beauregard's scheme must have been quickly dismissed from Lee's disciplined mind, but he used tact in disagreeing. When Lee said the plan "might be brilliant in its results, if we should meet with no disaster in details," it was his patrician way of saying that it was not based in reality. Insofar as the portion of the plan that concentrated the commands of Beauregard and Johnston, Lee observed "that the time for its execution had not yet arrived."[135]

Besides, news of far greater importance arrived that same day from northwestern Virginia. Brigadier General Robert S. Garnett was dead and his crudely-equipped and poorly-organized "army" routed at Rich Mountain. It was bad news for the Confederacy, but it could not have come as a total a surprise to Lee. Garnett had been Lee's adjutant at West Point and had served as his adjutant general following Virginia's secession. The situation in northwestern Virginia had grown ominous by early June when the scant, ill-equipped and poorly-officered Confederate forces were driven out of that far corner of the Commonwealth. Lee sent Garnett to try and get control of the situation. Within a month of his arrival, and after attempting to organize the troops that Garnett had found "in a miserable condition as to arms, clothing, equipment, instruction and discipline," the new commander also discovered that his forces were amidst a population largely "opposed to the South" and through which it was "almost impossible to get accurate information concerning the position of the enemy." Certainly, the deep-seated political disaffection in the region caused considerable

Courtesy Harpers Weekly

Battle of Rich Mountain

difficulties, but Garnett somehow believed that the Federals would not try and press their advantage. This curious misperception overlooked northwestern Virginia's vital importance to the United States; Union control of this part of the country was paramount to the security of the Baltimore and Ohio Railroad that connected the eastern theater of war to the Midwest states. Writing to

---

[133] *Official Records*, Series I, vol. 2, James Chesnut, Jr. to Beauregard, July 16, 1861, pp. 506-507; Roman, *The Military Operations of General Beauregard*, p. 87.

[134] *Official Records*, Series I, vol. 2, James Chesnut, Jr. to Beauregard, July 16, 1861, pp. 506-507; Beauregard's plan called for Johnston to "loan" him 20,000 men when the latter had only 11,000 under arms.

[135] Crist and Dix, *The Papers of Jefferson Davis*, vol. 7, Lee to Davis, November 24, 1861, pp. 425-427.

MAJOR-GENERAL McCLELLAN, U.S.A.—FROM A PHOTOGRAPH.—[SEE PAGE 487.]

Courtesy Harpers Weekly

George B. McClellan

Lee's assistant adjutant general on July 6th, Garnett did not believe that the Federals would "attempt to attack" his forces that numbered between 4,500 and 5,300 effectives, as he supposed that the enemy had occupied "as much of northwestern country as he probably wants."[136]   Lee saw things much differently.   "I do not think it probable," he responded to Garnett on July 11th after communicating that commander's thoughts to the President, "that the enemy will confine himself to that portion of the northwest country which he now holds, but, if he can drive you back, will endeavor to penetrate as far as Staunton.   Your object will be to prevent him, if possible, and to restrict his limits within the narrowest range, which, although outnumbered, it is hoped by skill and boldness you will accomplish."[137]

Lee's appraisal again reflected the cast of his military mind, or philosophy, as well as his use of the English language.   Lee knew Garnett had inferior numbers and that in order to contain the enemy, Garnett would have to employ the well-known military maxim to maneuver his smaller force by using "skill and boldness."   Lee also correctly foresaw the potential goal of the Federal advance being Staunton, an objective George McClellan already had in mind.[138]   Therefore, in order for Garnett to have the best chance possible to deny the enemy its goals of defeating the Confederate forces and capturing more territory, Lee's used the phrase "if possible," that was typical of the manner of communications among educated men of this time as well as that between superior and subordinate officers, and clearly indicated that Garnett was to try to prevent the Federal advance.   Military language of the day, given the absence of modern reconnaissance tools and lack of instant communications, out of necessity, had to recognize that unforeseen contingencies could arise during the message's transit time.   In this instance, just such a dramatic situation occurred.

Thus, Lee's advice never reached Garnett.   Before the latter's July 6th message got to Richmond, General McClellan was comfortable enough with his dispositions and superior numbers to do what Lee predicted.[139] Ironically, McClellan planned his attack by employing the same operational execution developed by Robert E. Lee at Cerro Gordo during the Mexican War.   "If possible," McClellan wrote prior to his offensive, "I will repeat the maneuver of Cerro Gordo."[140] McClellan's attempt was successful.   The Federals advanced unnoticed and surprised part of Garnett's forces at Rich Mountain on July 11th, then pushed on towards Beverly.   With his flank now turned, Garnett attempted to withdraw to a suitable position with the rest of his command.   Pursued by the blue coated troops, the Confederate rearguard was cut off two days later at Carrick's Ford on the Shivers fork of the Cheat River, where Garnett was killed and his force utterly defeated.   Although the Confederates

Courtesy Harpers Weekly

Death of General Robert S. Garnett

[136] *Official Records*, Series I, vol. 2, R. S. Garnett to George Deas, July 6, 1861, p. 241; Freeman, *R. E. Lee*, vol. 1, p. 533.   Deas was at the time Lee's assistant adjutant general.

[137] *Official Records*, Series I, vol. 2, Robert E. Lee to R. S. Garnett, p. 242.   Please also consult the *Southern Historical Society Papers*, vol. 16, "Narrative of the Service of Colonel George A. Porterfield," May 17, 1888, pp. 82-91.

[138] *Official Records*, Series I, vol. 2, McClellan to E. D. Townsend, p. 201.

[139] McClellan had about 11,000 combatants under his command.   Please see: Stephen W. Sears, *George B. McClellan: The Young Napoleon* (New York, 1988), p. 88 and footnote 27 on p. 421; Frank J. Welcher, *The Union Army, 1861-1865: Organization and Operations*, 2 volumes (Bloomington, 1989), vol. I, The Eastern Theater, pp.1058-1061.

[140] *Official Records*, Series I, vol. 2, McClellan to E. D. Townsend, July 5, 1861, p. 198.   Note McClellan's use of the phrase "if possible," indicating that McClellan was going *to try* to accomplish what he stated.

lost less than 1,000 men, discipline seemed to unravel completely. Most of the survivors of Garnett's tiny army were, according to Douglas Southall Freeman, "demoralized and scattered" while those who remained with the colors "precipitately withdrew over successive strong positions to Monterey, thirty-five miles southeast of Beverly." These few were all that stood between McClellan's command and Staunton, Virginia, in the heart of the Shenandoah Valley. Whether or not three days of hard marching would have put McClellan in position to do what he described as "break the backbone of secession," such an advance would have undoubtedly spelled serious consequences for the Confederacy. However, prior to his attack, McClellan asked General Scott for advice on how far he should advance; the far-removed Scott admonished McClellan against outrunning his communications, but left the decision up to McClellan on how far and fast to go once the action had begun. The cautionary note had its effect on McClellan: no further advance occurred once Garnett's force was scattered.[141]

Courtesy Library of Congress

General Pierre G.T. Beauregard

Lee received news of the Rich Mountain defeat on the 14th and acted promptly by advising the local acting commander "to oppose the advance of the enemy" in order to deny the Federals the capture of Staunton and the terminus of the Virginia Central Railroad. On the 17th Lee learned fully the extent of the "disastrous retreat of Garnett's command," and sent notes to the separate columns under Generals John B. Floyd and Henry A. Wise to support what remained of Garnett's force.[142] The situation indeed called for a strong, guiding hand of a superior grade officer to take control, and there is no doubt that Lee "would have gone at once in person to attempt to redeem the evil." Writing to his wife on July 12th, Lee vented his frustrations on being held in Richmond: "I am very anxious to get into the field," he told his wife, "but am detained by matters beyond my control." President Davis was in control of such matters and in response to the latest crisis, he considered, as one historian described it, his own "military experience and instincts the most important contributions he could offer his new nation." Thus, Davis decided to detain Lee in Richmond for what can only be described as suspicious reasons.[143]

Between the times that he made his various proposals to Richmond advocating fantastical offensives, Beauregard had organized his growing number of regiments into brigades and had placed them in advance of the

[141]Freeman, *Lee's Lieutenants*, vol. 1, pp. 35-37; Freeman, *R. E. Lee*, vol. 1, pp. 534-535; *Official Records*, Series I, vol. 2, McClellan to E. D. Townsend, July 7, 1861, p. 201; E. D. Townsend to McClellan, July 9, 1861, pp. 201-202; McClellan to E. D. Townsend, July 10, 1861; 9 a.m., July 12, 1861, p. 202; 8 p.m., July 12, 1861, p. 203; and July 13, 1861, pp. 203-204. The total Federal forces in the immediate area numbered more than 12,000, although those readily at hand under McClellan numbered more than 8,000. For a narrative of McClellan in western Virginia campaign, please consult: "McClellan in West Virginia," *Battles and Leaders of the Civil War*, vol. 1, pp. 126-139.
[142] *Official Records*, Series I, vol. 2, M. G. Harman to Robert E. Lee, July 14, 1861, with enclosure of Colonel Scott's note of the 12th, p. 244; Robert E. Lee to M. G. Harman, July 14, 1861, p. 245; Robert E. Lee to H. R. Jackson, July 16, 1861, p. 254; Samuel Cooper to John B. Floyd, July 17, 1861, p. 981; Samuel Cooper to Henry A. Wise, July 17, 1861, p. 981.
[143] Freeman, *R. E. Lee*, vol. 1, p. 535; Robert E. Lee, Jr., *Recollections and Letters*, Robert E. Lee to His Wife, July 12, 1861, p. 30; Thomas, *Robert E. Lee*, p. 198.

defensive line selected by Lee. The forward positioning—occupying an indefensible line held by immobile regiments—only invited trouble. On the 17th Beauregard reported to President Davis that his outposts had been assailed "in heavy force" and that he had fallen back to the defensive positions devised by Lee "on the line of Bull Run." Beauregard, who had only a few days before fancied his army crossing the Potomac and attacking Washington, then advised the chief executive that he planned to "make a stand at Mitchell's Ford" and asked for reinforcements from Joe Johnston in the Valley and Theophilus H. Holmes at Fredericksburg.[144]

The Creole did not have to urgently call for reinforcements; both Lee and Davis knew he was outnumbered. Beauregard's Army of the Potomac (not to be confused with the later Federal army by the same name) in front of Manassas numbered over 21,000 present and under arms, while General Irvin McDowell's Federal army was known to be substantially larger. Even allowing for McDowell leaving some troops in the Washington defenses as a reserve, Lee and Davis had every reason to estimate that McDowell was moving with at least 30,000 men. Beauregard needed help, and fast. The President wasted no time in summoning reinforcements. A hurried telegraph to Joe Johnston, commander of what was now called the Army of the Shenandoah, advised: "General Beauregard is attacked. To strike the enemy a decisive blow a junction of all your effective force will be needed. If practicable, make the movement..." Johnston remembered the "telegraphic dispatch informing me that the [Federal] Northern Army was advancing upon Manassas, then held by General Beauregard, and directing me, if practicable, to go to that officer's assistance...I at once determined to march to join General Beauregard."[145] After arranging for his sick, Johnston set out on the 18th by transporting his infantry by rail while his cavalry and artillery marched. At noon on the 20th Johnston arrived at Manassas with the van of his 11,000-man army. Meanwhile, every other available regiment that could be transported by rail rushed forwarded to Beauregard in anticipation of a great battle.[146]

As expectations over the impending clash of armies grew, Lee wanted to get to the front, "but the President thought it more important that" he remain in Richmond. On Sunday morning, July 21st, while Lee was forced to endure inaction, Davis overcame the effects of his illness and took a special train to Manassas Junction, where he arrived in the afternoon with the battle raging in the distance. By the time the President reached the vicinity of the front sometime after 4:00 P.M., the Johnston-Beauregard combination of sending troops to the right points and inspiring their efforts, along with the exhaustion of the Federals and the good fortunes of battle, had already turned the tide in the Confederates' favor. Seeing the panicked Federals in full flight, Davis had enough battle sense to seek a crushing pursuit. In his black suit, the adrenaline-charged President apparently crossed Bull Run to push the troops forward, only to find that many of the Confederates were pitifully ill-equipped

---

[144] *Official Records*, Series I, vol. 2, G. T. Beauregard to Jefferson Davis, July 17, 1861, pp. 439-440.

[145] *Official Records*, Series I, vol. 2, Samuel Cooper to J. E. Johnston, July 17, 1861, p. 478; "Reports of J. E. Johnston . . .", October 14, 1861, p. 473; "Abstract from field return, First Corps of [the Confederate] Army of the Potomac, July 21, 1861 [Dated September 25, 1861], p. 568; Robert Matteson Johnston, *Bull Run: Its Strategy & Tactics* (Boston, 1913, reprinted 1996), pp. 97-98 and 110. Note the use of the phrase, "if practicable," by both Jefferson Davis and Joe Johnston. As used, the phrase clearly indicated that both men understood that Johnston was *to try* and effect a junction of his command with that of Beauregard.

[146] Johnston, *Bull Run: Its Strategy & Tactics*, p. 110; *Official Records*, Series I, vol. 2, Jefferson Davis to G. T. Beauregard, July 18, 1861, p. 981.

and had not eaten all day. They were in no condition to go any further. Fresh formations that had fought little or not at all could have pursued if valuable time had not been wasted by some officers. As a result, virtually no pursuit ensued. Congratulating the troops and consoling the casualties, Davis eventually re-crossed the stream and rode to Johnston's headquarters. Well after nightfall, the President wrote a brief, though partly exaggerated, dispatch to Richmond: "We have won a glorious though dear-bought victory. Night closed on the enemy in full flight and closely pursued."[147]

Lee admitted that he "almost wept for joy" about the news of "the glorious victory," but could not suppress his warrior spirit in a letter to his wife. "I wished to partake in the former struggle," he wrote on July 27th, "and am mortified at my absence [from the fighting], but the President thought it more important I should be here…I could have helped, and taken part in the struggle for my home and neighborhood."[148] Despite not being on the field of battle, Lee did have a significant role in the victory. More than one quarter of the troops present at Manassas were Virginian, and as such, had been raised and brought into the field under Lee's direction. Without detracting "from the merits of others," Jubal Early accurately captured the essence of one part of Lee's war contribution when he stated, "but for the capacity and energy displayed by General Lee in organizing and equipping troops to be sent to the front, our army would not have been in a condition to gain the first victory at Manassas." Lee selected the defensive line along Bull Run, but more importantly deserves a large part of the credit in fashioning the idea of mutual support and the operational junction of Beauregard's and Johnston's armies. As historian Douglas Southall Freeman insightfully pointed out: "[It] was not whether the one force should join the other, but when." Insofar as when that happened, it was President Davis "who made the decision and consequently deserves the credit."[149]

An euphoric Davis, though weakened by his exertions over the past days, returned to Richmond on Tuesday, July 23rd, to proclaim the greatness of the Confederate victory. Davis not only took credit for fashioning the strategy that won Manassas, he also fed the delusion that the victory had won the war and secured Southern independence by assuring "his intimate friends that the recognition of the Confederate States by the European Powers was now certain." To the cheering throngs at the Richmond train shed at Broad Street and 16th, as well as in front of the Spotswood Hotel at the southeast corner of Main Street and 8th, the President proclaimed: "We have taught them a lesson in their invasion of the sacred soil of Virginia." Diarist Mary Chesnut (whose husband, recall, served on Beauregard's staff) wrote that: "The President took all the credit to himself for the victory," while at the same time paid tribute to the heroism of the Confederate soldiers and their officers. For the latter, the President also approved a resolution from Congress more than a week later honoring Beauregard and Johnston for their role in the victory.[150]

"President Davis returned to Richmond last evening. An immense concourse of people assembled in front of the Spotswood House, and vociferously called for his appearance. He finally presented himself, and addressed the multitude in glowing and eloquent allusions to the brilliant occurrences of Sunday.

He described the brilliant movement of Gen. Johnston from Winchester to Manassas, and with fervid feeling drew a graphic picture of the struggle of the wearied soldiers of that gallant command for seven hours with the heavy columns of the enemy. --After paying a most honorable tribute to Gen. Johnston, who seized the colors of a regiment and rallied them to the flag of the Confederacy, he alluded to the glorious manner in which Gen. Beauregard came to the support of his comrade in arms, and at a late hour relieved him of the odds against which he was contending. Each of these two able and consummate commanders, though not imprudently or idly exposing their persons where it was unnecessary, yet, when their presence was demanded, gallantly dashed before the lines, and by their personal courage and example reanimated the ranks whenever they were shaken.

"The President, in a delicate manner, alluded to his own appearance upon the field, in order to pay a tribute to the devotion of the soldiers to the Confederacy. Men, he said, who lay upon their backs, wounded, bleeding and exhausted, when they saw him pass, though they could do

---

[147] Reverend J. William Jones, D. D., *Personal Reminiscences of General Robert E.* Lee (New York, 1875, reprinted 1994), p. 384; William C. Davis, *Jefferson Davis*, p. 351; Freeman, *Lee's Lieutenants*, vol. 1, pp. 71-75; *Official Records*, Series I, vol. 2, Dispatch from Jefferson Davis to George Washington Custis Lee, July 21, 1861, p. 986. G. W. C. Lee was Robert E. Lee's oldest son and the aide that Davis left in charge of his office in Richmond. The aide that accompanied the President to the battle was his nephew, Joseph.
[148] Freeman, *R. E. Lee*, vol. 1, p. 538; Robert E. Lee, Jr., *Recollections and Letters*, Robert E. Lee to His Wife, July 27, 1861, p. 31.
[149] Jones, *Personal Reminiscences of General Robert E. Lee*, p. 2; Freeman, *R. E. Lee*, vol. 1, p. 540.
[150] Pollard, *The Lost Cause*, p. 153; *Richmond Enquirer*, July 24, 1861; Chesnut, *Mary Chesnut's Civil War*, p. 105; "Resolution" of Confederate Congress, August 6, 1861. When

nothing else, waved their hats as they lay, and cheered for Jeff. Davis and the South. Where the ranks had been broken and the men were somewhat scattered, when they saw the President of the South in their midst, shouted that they would follow him to the death, and rallied once more for the last and the successful onslaught.

"The President alluded also to the immensity and extravagance of the outfit which the enemy had provided for their invasion. Provisions for many days; knapsacks provided with every comfort; arms the most perfect; trains of wagons in numbers which the mind could scarcely comprehend, and ambulances for the officers stored with luxuries that would astonish our frugal people whom these minions of the North had taxed for seventy years, attended their marching columns. But the columns themselves were scattered and chased, like hares, from the battle ground, throwing away and leaving behind everything they could get rid of, and leaving us all the equipments we have described as the trophies of victory.

"The President concluded with a glowing tribute to the gallantry of the soldiers of our army, invoking the praise and blessing of the country upon them. He reminded the people, however, that the enemy was still in strong force, and that much hard fighting was yet before us, urging the country to unremitted diligence in pushing on the war."

The Richmond Daily Dispatch,
July 24, 1861

Davis relished in his role in the battle. Enthusiastic journalists "compared Manassas with the decisive battles of the world" thus further raising the Southern populace's expectations that independence was at hand. The Confederate Congress likewise got swept up in the high-tide of elation further raising unrealistic hopes. Passing a resolution the day after the battle, the politicians proclaimed: "We recognize the hand of the most High God, the King of Kings and Lord of Lords, in the glorious victory with which he has crowned our armies at Manassas, and that these people of the Confederate States are invited by appropriate services on the ensuing Sabbath to offer up their united thanksgiving and prayer for this mighty deliverance." Amidst this tidal wave of euphoria, Lee again seemed to be the lone voice of realism. In his July 27th letter to Mary Lee, the general believed that "the battle will be repeated [at Manassas] in greater force." What Robert E. Lee could not predict was the strange path his career would take before ascending to army command and leading his men onto the plains of Manassas where his prophecy would indeed be fulfilled.[151]

Lee In Northwestern Virginia— The Cheat and Sewell Mountains Campaign

"After the first battle of Manassas," wrote Charles Marshall, "the aspect of affairs was completely changed."[152] Exhilaration in the South had been stoked and overheated with foolish rhetoric. The bombast of politicians and journalists magnified a single battlefield victory—one absent the destruction of the opposing army—into one of the decisive victories in world history. Ordinarily reasonable men now mistook Davis, Johnston and Beauregard as the worthies of Hannibal, Caesar and Napoleon. The impact of this widespread delusional euphoria would be catastrophic to The Cause; for the South, the first victory was nearly fatal.

With their deliverance believed to be at hand and with, as Southern historian Edward A. Pollard noted, "politicians actually commenced plotting for the Presidential succession, more than six years distant," exertions to insure the security of their new republic declined. In that ill-advised relaxation of resolve, volunteer enlistments slackened. In short, the Confederacy dropped its guard. Meanwhile, one Southerner did not slacken in his efforts. Robert E. Lee spent his "whole time" occupied with the matters of war. "All my thoughts and strength," he wrote his wife less than a week after Manassas, "are given to the cause to which my life, be it long or short, will be devoted." Lee's temperament was indeed similar to the one driven "with infuriate energy" emerging from across the Potomac.[153]

The outcome of the Battle of Manassas galvanized the North to the

Mrs. Davis came into Mary Chesnut's room to announce the victory, she said: "A great battle has been fought—Jeff Davis led the center, Joe Johnston the right wing, Beauregard the left...." One story in *The Richmond Whig* stated that Davis had directed the battle itself. Five days later, the same paper corrected the error, stating that Davis had not commanded in person, but had arrived in time to witness the Federal flight. Davis evidently did not comment when the corrected story was published.
[151] Pollard, *The Lost Cause*, p. 153; Luther W. Hopkins, *From Bull Run to Appomattox: A Boy's View* (Baltimore, 1908), p. 36; Robert E. Lee, Jr., *Recollections and Letters*, Robert E. Lee to His Wife, July 27, 1861, p. 31.
[152] Marshall, *Lee's Aide de Camp*, p. 12.
[153] Pollard, *The Lost Cause*, p. 154; Robert E. Lee, Jr., *Recollections and Letters*, Robert E. Lee to His Wife, July 27, 1861, p. 31.

same degree that it opiated the South. From the President, to the Congress, to the officers and men in uniform, the unexpected rout of the Federal army on July 21st served to further the awareness for needed sacrifice and raised determination to preserve the Union. Needing some immediate success, northwestern Virginia became one of the geographic areas the Federals looked to for a victory, especially as it had been infused with troops and capable commanders.

The rugged and remote Allegheny region protected vital Federal communications between east and midwest. By late July, when word of the defeat along Bull Run was received in the wild, George McClellan was still trying to put together a plan for an advance out of the mountains and descending on Staunton (he could have easily accomplished that with a prompt pursuit following his victory at Rich Mountain). Informed by General Winfield Scott that the "finely-appointed and admirably-led army" of Irvin McDowell had been defeated and "transformed into a mob," McClellan was ordered to "come hither without delay" to Washington as the city had been thrown into a near panic. The "Young Napoleon" was to leave "Rosecrans or some other general" with the job of further solidifying the [northwestern Virginia] region.[154]

The Federals had a tight hold on the portion of northwestern Virginia already in their possession. Far better supplied and organized than the Confederate forces in the area, the more numerous Federals enjoyed the benefits of more qualified senior officers, unity of command, and a better intelligence network, thanks to the support of the region's sturdy mountaineers. With these advantages, the Federal's lack of pursuit following Rich Mountain had prevented the rag-tag and separated Confederate forces from total defeat and had spared the fall of Staunton. Even with the gift of this respite, Confederate fortunes were not improving, and soon after Manassas, President Davis thought he knew best how to remedy the situation.

The Mississippian was well aware that Old Dominion's population and politicians hailing from east of these mountains wanted the northwestern counties expunged of Yankees. Davis agreed—especially since any Federal advance towards Staunton and the Shenandoah Valley had to be strongly resisted. Further, recovery of the northwestern counties would significantly turn the tables on the Federals and put them on the defensive to protect their vital rail communications. In the wake of the Confederate triumph at Manassas, President Davis thought the time was right to try and seek a remedy for the troubling northwestern Virginia situation. Apparently, he first asked Joe Johnston to try his hand at turning things around, but the co-victor of Manassas declined the offer, citing that he was needed on his existing front since he predicted that an even larger army of Federals would advance again "before the end of fall." Johnston could well have believed what he said. More likely, his candid reason for turning down the assignment was that he saw the northwestern Virginia job as "much less important" service and a potential career-damaging pitfall. Davis then turned to Robert E. Lee, and the duty-conscious general, of course, accepted. Importantly, however, rather than sending off Lee with command authority over the three so-called "armies" in the region—authority that would give Lee a more realistic chance to successfully rid northwestern Virginia of the current occupying Federal forces—President Davis violated one of the key tenets of the principals of war by completely undermining any unity of command. As Napoleon famously put it during

"If any one had told me that the next time I traveled that road would have been on my present errand, I should have supposed him insane."

Robert E. Lee, on his mission to western Virginia

Courtesy Library of Congress

William Wing Loring

---

[154] *Official Records*, Series I, vol. 2, Winfield Scott to George McClellan, July 22, 1861 at 1 A.M., L. Thomas to George McClellan, July 22, 1861, and Thomas A. Scott to Joseph K.F. Mansfield, July 22, 1861, at 2:30 A.M.

his early career, "an army is better commanded by one bad general than two good ones." Thus, Davis dispatched Lee, without any formal authority, on a nebulously-defined mission of "coordinating" the three commanders in the region. Lee's position seemed further ludicrous in that he held the titular command of all the military forces of Virginia, but no longer had any forces to command (since they had already passed into Confederate service). As his aide Walter Taylor described it: "It was hoped [by Davis] that the presence of General Lee would tend to harmonize" the three commands. If Davis thought that Lee's prestige alone would be enough for other general officers to listen to him, he miscalculated. The absurdity hit home with Lee before "he rode into Loring's camp at the advance base in the dirty mountain village of Huntersville," where he "received a very cool welcome."[155]

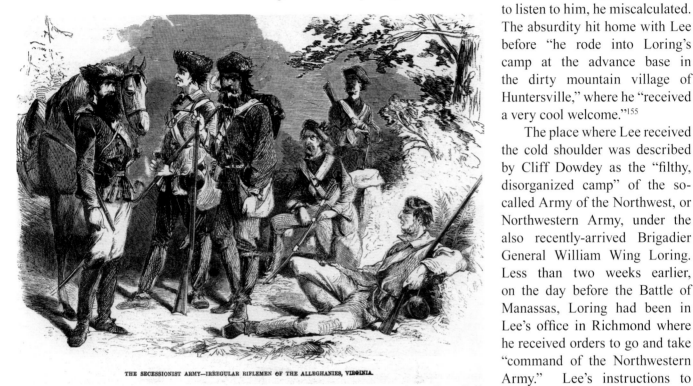

THE SECESSIONIST ARMY—IRREGULAR RIFLEMEN OF THE ALLEGHANIES, VIRGINIA.

Courtesy Harpers Weekly

Western Virginia Infantry

The place where Lee received the cold shoulder was described by Cliff Dowdey as the "filthy, disorganized camp" of the so-called Army of the Northwest, or Northwestern Army, under the also recently-arrived Brigadier General William Wing Loring. Less than two weeks earlier, on the day before the Battle of Manassas, Loring had been in Lee's office in Richmond where he received orders to go and take "command of the Northwestern Army." Lee's instructions to Loring were specific with regards to "preventing the advance of the enemy," emphasizing the importance of "restraining [the Federals to] the other side of the Alleghany Ridge." Lee informed Loring that the other forces in the area had been "directed to move" as to effect "a union of all forces" in order to strike "a decisive blow, and, when in your judgment proper, it will be made."

Loring, along with his staff, left Richmond on Saturday, July 22nd, the day after the Battle of Manassas, and arrived in the small village of Monterey about 60 miles west of Staunton on July 24th. He was in the process of organizing and provisioning his command when Lee suddenly appeared, and "took Loring by surprise."[156]

Despite his many years in the army, Loring could not bring himself to understand why Lee was suddenly standing before him, although he certainly should have known. Loring was a life-long soldier whose service record extended back to the days in which he had enlisted in the Florida militia at age 14 and fought in the Second Seminole War during the 1830s. He had

---

[155] *Official Records*, Series I, vol. 5, Jefferson Davis to Joe Johnston, August 1, 1861, p. 767; Special Orders, No. 239, issued by R. E. Lee, August 5, 1861, p. 770; Johnston, *Narrative of Military Operations*, p. 59; Dowdey, *Lee*, pp. 166-167; Taylor, *General Lee*, p. 27. Lee's first inspection of Loring's camp was on August 3rd.

[156] Dowdey, *Lee*, p. 167; *Official Records*, Series I, vol. 2, Robert E. Lee to W. W. Loring, July 20, 1861, p. 986; Long, *Memoirs of Robert E. Lee*, pp. 117 and 120. Lee used the English spelling "Alleghany" in his letter, whereas the French spelling "Alleghany" is also correct.

received his first commission as a second lieutenant when he was 18 years-old, and when the war with the Seminoles was winding down, Loring was sent to school, passed the bar exam to become an attorney, and then failed in a bid for a seat in the Florida legislature. When the war with Mexico broke out, Loring was commissioned a captain in the new regiment of Mounted Rifles. Brevetted for gallantry at Cerro Gordo—a battle fought and won accordance with Lee's daring plan—Loring later lost his left arm storming Chapultepec. Continuing his service after the war, Loring had marched a column across the continent, commanded the 11th Military District that covered a large portion of the Pacific Northwest, became the youngest line colonel in the army in 1856 at age 38 (while Lee was still a lieutenant colonel with the 2nd Cavalry) and defeated the Gila Apaches in New Mexico. Five years later in answering the call of his native Florida during the secession crisis, Loring was, by far, the youngest of the line colonels to resign his commission. After a brief stint as a Confederate colonel, Loring received his brigadier general's star in May. His position and rank in the Old Army suggested that he would be a valuable Confederate officer, but his roughhewn personality often counteracted his experience. Tan with black hair, Loring was fractious, conceited and ambitious to a fault. His pre-war seniority convinced him of his importance, and he openly displayed his resentment that Robert E. Lee now outranked him.[157]

The petulance displayed by Loring, unbecoming from an officer of his experience but not an uncommon petty reaction among officers, took no account of the fact that Lee had been ordered to the scene by Lee's superior. More importantly, Loring had no reason to feel threatened by Lee on any level, for Lee certainly understood that when he left Richmond he had no command authority to direct operations once he arrived in northwestern Virginia. This singular fact was no secret at the time (but somehow was lost on the public as well as on many historians), and was printed in at least one newspaper. Three days after Lee departed Richmond, the July 31st, 1861, edition of The Richmond Examiner, correctly reported that General Lee was on "an inspector-general's job" to "tour to the West, looking after the commands of Generals Loring and Wise…His visit is understood to be one of inspection, and consultation on the plan of campaign."[158]

When Lee first arrived, he was told by Loring that an advance by Colonel William Gilham with the 21st Virginia Infantry had discovered an open road at Valley Mountain into Tygart's River Valley that lead to the west and in the rear

Courtesy Library of Congress

Henry A. Wise

Courtesy Harpers Weekly

Arkansas Emblem

---

[157] *Official Records*, Series I, vol. 2, W. W. Loring to George Deas, July 30, 1861, p. 1009; *Encyclopedia of the Confederacy*, vol. 3, p. 947; Dowdey, *Lee*, p. 166-167; Ezra J. Warner, *Generals in Gray: Lives of the Confederate Commanders* (Baton Rouge, 1959), pp. 193-194. Lee wasn't the only Confederate superior with whom Loring did not get along. In early 1862, Loring got into a violent disagreement with Thomas J. "Stonewall" Jackson over the location of winter quarters in the Romney Expedition. That disagreement was essentially his ticket out of the eastern theater and he eventually found himself in the west in John C. Pemberton's Army of Vicksburg, where as a major general in command of a division, he soon became at odds with his superior. Shortly following the vitally important battle of Champion Hill that all but sealed the fate of the Vicksburg army—a battle where Loring acted with seemingly suspicious motives— Lieutenant William Drennan, a staff officer in Brigadier General Winfield S. Featherstone's Brigade of Loring's Division, wrote his wife: "There is quite a feud existing between Loring and Pemberton—so far as Loring is concerned. . .in fact it amounted to that degree of hatred on the part of Loring that Captain [William] Barksdale and myself agreed that Loring would be willing for Pemberton to lose a battle provided he would be displaced." See: Letter, William A. Drennan to wife, May 30, 1863, Mississippi Department of Archives and History, Jackson, Mississippi.

[158] *The Richmond Examiner*, July 31, 1861, p. 3, columns 3 and 4. At the forefront of the legion of historians that miss the mark with regards to Lee's command authority in the western Virginia campaign is none other than the legendary Lee biographer, Douglas Southall Freeman. For details, please see: Freeman, *R. E. Lee*, vol. 1, pp. 552-553.

of the Federal position on Cheat Mountain. Why the Federals had left the vital road unguarded seemed inexplicable, and Loring told Lee that he intended to take advantage of this opportunity, but only after he had established a sufficient supply base that, in his opinion, would properly support the 18-mile movement. This meant rather than immediately seize the fleeting opportunity that would have required the men carrying their own rations, Loring decided to wait at Huntersville for more supplies that could have been brought up after the move was underway. Here, President Davis' limitations on Lee proved fatal. Absent command authority, Lee knew that the mission on which he had been sent was a fool's errand—something Lee realized before he ever arrived at Loring's camp. Writing his wife on August 4th, Lee remarked:

> I reached here yesterday, dearest Mary, to visit this portion of the army. . . It is difficult to get our people, unaccustomed to the necessities of war, to comprehend and promptly execute the measures required for the occasion. . . A part of the road, as far as Buffalo Gap, I passed over in the summer of 1840, on my return from Saint Louis, after bringing you home. If any one had told me that the next time I traveled that road would have been on my present errand, I should have supposed him insane.[159]

Unable to override Loring, Lee had no choice but to act within his orders, and this meant that he could only counsel Loring to act more swiftly, while time and opportunity slipped away. Four days later, Lee was still waiting. Finally, when on August 12th Loring stood ready to move, the Federals had discovered their omission and had taken possession of the pass that controlled the Valley Mountain Road into Tygart's River Valley. With the opening now shut, Lee advised against a frontal attack: Loring agreed.[160]

Jefferson Davis had placed Robert E. Lee in a straitjacket. With his capacity limited to that of only an advisor, Lee intended to use every diplomatic and social skill he possessed to encourage and to advise. Furthermore, beyond Loring resenting his presence and advice, Lee also discovered that the other two commanders in the area, political appointees Henry A. Wise and John B. Floyd, wanted nothing to do with Loring—or each other!

In addition to this intolerable mess of a command arrangement, the Confederate situation also eroded due to conditions in the camps. "The soldiers everywhere are sick," Lee wrote in his August 4th letter to his wife. "The measles are prevalent throughout the whole army, and you know that disease leaves unpleasant results, attacks on the lungs, typhoid, etc., especially in camp, where accommodations for the sick are poor." Also, those in the ranks under Wise and Floyd carried arms, equipment and transportation in a poor state of readiness, which almost all of the men, including those of Loring's command, were "without tents or camp equipage, and with but the clothing upon their backs." Brigadier General Henry R. Jackson, a senior commander under Loring, also observed that "the horses of the artillery and cavalry are jaded and galled." The lack of equipment, feebleness of the men and horses, combined with the feuding commanders and a mostly inhospitable citizenry all contributed to the bleak environment in which the Confederates expected to wage war in northwestern Virginia. Writing to his brother-in-law,

Courtesy Library of Congress

John B. Floyd

---

[159] Robert E. Lee, Jr., *Recollections and Letters*, Robert E. Lee to His Wife, August 4, 1861, pp. 32-33.
[160] Freeman, *R. E. Lee*, vol. 1, pp. 552-554; Long, *Memoirs of Robert E. Lee*, pp. 119-121.

Adjutant General Samuel Cooper, about the unenviable situation into which he had been sent to "coordinate," Lee confided that "their command [Loring, Wise, Floyd] will not prove very effective."[161]

Lee, however, felt duty-bound to try something. In order for the Confederates to have a chance to recover the portion of northwestern Virginia previously lost to McClellan in July, and with an easily-traversed route no longer open to flanking the enemy, Lee knew that he would have to find a less obvious way to envelop the Federal position. Lee wanted a way to achieve close coordination between the area's three commanders as a substitute for unity of command. Finding a way to flank an enemy position was one challenge; realizing the latter would be another. While Loring ostensibly was a professional soldier, the other two senior officers owed their rank and position solely to the whim of a politician. If Jefferson Davis' appointment of Wise and Floyd—each a former Virginia governor and fierce political rivals—as general officers wasn't strange enough, then the President's assigning them to serve in the same vicinity remains puzzling. These decisions by the chief executive not only negated Governor Letcher's efforts to keep unqualified, prominent citizens out of command authority in Virginia, but the presidential assignments violated common sense as well. Even though Wise had been governor during the John Brown raid, the closest contact he had to anything military was "his relationship as brother-in-law to the Federal general, George Gordon Meade." Floyd's credentials were only slightly better. Like President Davis, he was a former Secretary of War, and this perhaps played a part in Davis commissioning Floyd to raise a brigade of infantry in direct competition with the regular recruiters of the state. Floyd's political need to impress others led him to style his diminutive command as the 'highfalutin' Army of the Kanawha.[162]

Following a series of exchanges with the commanders, Lee surmised that the existing northwestern Virginia command team was already fractured. Lee therefore set about to figure out the best way to overcome this and the other significant difficulties facing him. To formulate a plan of action, Lee needed information. With but a handful of cavalry and an unsympathetic local population, Lee decided to become his own intelligence officer to formulate a concerted plan of action. The first order of importance in this regard was to ascertain if somehow the opportunity discovered by Colonel Gilham days ago still existed by way of some other avenue in Tygart's River Valley. Lee soon discovered that the opportunity that supposedly existed four days earlier had indeed passed; therefore, a new plan of campaign would have to be concocted. Lee required an alternative route to get at the enemy, and that "the only way of finding such a route, if one existed, was to reconnoiter with the greatest care." As in Mexico, Lee would have to do a lot of riding through inhospitable country to examine the ground. Though older, Lee remained a truly superb horseman: it had always been his favorite form of exercise. As he adroitly rode through the difficult and wet northwestern Virginia countryside, Lee thoughtfully eyed the ground in order to exert every "means to prevent unnecessary loss of life." Through the near-pathless mountains, along the bog-like roads and across the rain-soaked valleys, Robert E. Lee searched the countryside, sometimes with Walter Taylor of his staff "to find a practicable route leading to the rear

Courtesy Library of Congress
Armistead Lindsay Long

---

[161] Robert E. Lee, Jr., *Recollections and Letters*, Robert E. Lee to His Wife, August 4, 1861, p. 32; *Official Records*, Series I, vol. 2, Henry R. Jackson to George Deas, July 24, 1861, pp. 997-998; Dowdey, *Lee*, pp. 166-167. Please note Lee's use the term "*their* command [not *my* command] will not prove very effective."

[162] Dowdey, *Lee*, pp. 166-167; *Official Records*, Series I, vol. 5, John B. Floyd to Henry A. Wise, September 1, 1861, p. 826.

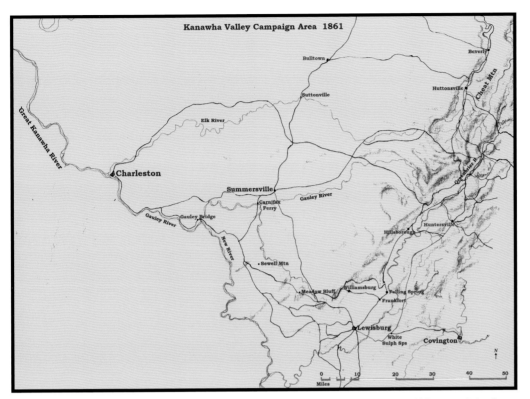

Kanawah Valley Campaign of 1861

of the Cheat Mountain" position.   Miserable weather hindered the search. On August 29th, Lee described the weather in a letter to his daughter: "It rains here all the time, literally...But the worst of the rain is that the ground has become so saturated with water that the constant travel on the roads has made them almost impassible, so that I cannot get up sufficient supplies for the troops to move. It is raining now. Has been all day, last night, day before, and day before that, etc., etc."[163]

In addition to personal reconnaissance, Lee also used every opportunity possible to visit the troops in order to learn their condition and evaluate the competency of their officers. Lee also ascertained the pitiful state of his intelligence network and evaluated potential Federal offensive action. He had to thwart the designs of the enemy while procuring time to come up with a plan to recover the previously lost territory. According to Douglas Southall Freeman, early every "morning Lee went out; often wet and weary, it was late when he returned." In performing this rigorous work, and the general learned more with each day; the daunting challenges facing the Confederates in northwestern Virginia equaled what he had anticipated while on the road to Buffalo Gap. Fortunately, Lee found that he could count on the spirit of the men—despite their hunger, fatigue and deprivations—who consistently voiced their eagerness for action. Major Armistead Lindsay Long, the talented chief of artillery and inspector-general for Loring, agreed. "The troops were in fine spirits, and desired nothing more than to be led against the enemy," Long wrote, to which he added his opinion: "The troops were well armed and equipped, all of them were accustomed to the use of arms, and many were expert marksmen." To lead the men, a few noteworthy officers emerged such as Lindsay Long, Edward Johnson and Lee's second son, William Henry Fitzhugh ("Rooney") Lee. Overall, the officer quality, troop conditions, discipline and training in Loring's command largely exceeded that of Floyd and Wise.[164]

Even with his detailed scouting missions, and even with the enemy's tents on the mountainous elevations "in full view" of the Confederates, Lee recognized that "reliable information of the strength of the enemy in our

---

[163] Robert E. Lee, Jr., *Recollections and Letters*, Robert E. Lee to His Daughters, August 29, 1861, p. 35.

[164] Freeman, *R. E. Lee*, vol. 1, p. 555; Johnson was colonel of the 12th Georgia Infantry, while "Rooney" Lee was a major in the 9th Virginia Cavalry, and he, along with one squadron (one source says that it was a battalion of the 9th Virginia Cavalry) were detached for service under the command of Loring. See Long, *Memoirs of Robert E. Lee*, pp. 118 and 121-122; *Official Records*, Series I, vol. 51, part 2 Supplement, Alfred Beckley to Robert E. Lee, August 21, 1861, pp. 244-245.

front or that may be in reserve to his rear within supporting distance" was "impossible" due to the combination of the difficult terrain, small numbers of mounted troops that could also scout, and the loyalties of most citizens. Despite these difficulties, Lee kept searching for an opportunity in order to have a chance to get at and defeat the enemy.[165]

Lee certainly understood that any attack against the Federals would have to overcome the most evident terrain advantage—the area's key geographical position, Cheat Mountain. The blue coated troops occupying the heights after their victory at Rich Mountain had settled into their camps since the Confederates had not attempted to dislodge them. The summit of Cheat Mountain, 15 miles west from the crest of the Alleghenies, controlled, according to Freeman, "one of the historic highways of Virginia, the Staunton-Parkersburg turnpike, which joined the two towns its name hyphenated." By holding Cheat, the Federals occupied the central position in the area. Possession of Cheat Mountain also could serve as a springboard to first seize and block all important passes, thereby making any obvious Confederate offensive movements virtually impossible. Once that was accomplished, the Federals would have the freedom to advance on Staunton by one of three routes: the first due east along the Staunton-Parkersburg turnpike; the second, by a slightly indirect route that called for masking the Confederates opposite Cheat and moving southeast to Huntersville and then to Millboro; and, the third, by a more indirect route that required marching south up the Kanawha Valley (moving south was called "moving up" this valley as well as the Shenandoah) before turning east towards the Shenandoah. Regardless of the route by which the Federals advanced, if Staunton fell, it would be "a major Confederate disaster," because the Federals would, at a minimum, cut the Virginia Central Railroad that connected eastern Virginia with the grain-rich Shenandoah Valley.[166]

CAMP ON CHEAT MOUNTAIN SUMMIT.

Courtesy Library of Congress

Federal Camp on Cheat Mountain

On the other hand, an opportunity existed if the Confederates did not wait for the numerically superior Federals to attack, but instead seized the initiative by discovering a route to take the offensive. By defeating the Federal forces defending Cheat Mountain, no major obstacle would exist between the Ohio River and the important Baltimore and Ohio Railroad. In this respect, the editors of The Richmond Daily Dispatch grasped the importance of what Lee wished to accomplish. In the August 30th edition of the paper, the editors wrote: "The importance of the movements of General Lee consists, besides driving the enemy out of our State, in getting possession of the Baltimore and Ohio Railroad and thus cutting off the most direct communications between Cincinnati and St. Louis with Washington City." Alternatively, they could block the Kanawha Valley with Floyd and Wise; meanwhile, Loring's command would mask Cheat Mountain and advance along one of two avenues north or south of Cheat if such an advance was done prior to the Federals seizing and fortifying the critical passes. Logistics for those moves would have to be worked out, but the benefit of either option was tempting, as either could present the Confederates with the opportunity to be in a position to defeat the Federals on ground more favorable to the Southerners. If the Confederates

---

[165] *Official Records*, Series I, vol. 51, part 2 Supplement, Robert E. Lee to John B. Floyd, September 4, 1861, p. 271; Freeman, *R. E. Lee*, vol. 1, p. 555; excerpt from *The Savannah Republican*, "From the Georgia Twelfth Regiment," Camp Alleghany, Pocahontas County, Va., 28 July 1861, as published in the *Southern Historical Society Papers*, vol. 17, pp. 161-165; Long, *Memoirs of Robert E. Lee*, p. 122. Rosecrans' knowledge of Confederate dispositions and strengths can be found in *Official Records*, Series I, vol. 5, "Reports of Brig. General Williams S. Rosecrans," August 28, 1861, pp. 118-119.

[166] Freeman, *R. E. Lee*, vol. 1, pp. 545-547.

managed to pull this off, they "would effectively free the greater part of western Virginia from the grip of the enemy." Aware of these options, Lee escalated his efforts to gain more information. Individual scouts and some trustworthy inhabitants of the area augmented Lee's extraordinary and risky labors. Finally, Lee's "endless reconnaissance trips paid off," wrote Freeman. "In early September, the general found a narrow stock trail path that led to a point known as West Crest on the Staunton-Parkersburg Turnpike about two miles west, or behind, the Federal position on Cheat Mountain."[167]

Courtesy Library of Congress

3rd Arkansas Volunteer Infantry

Lee's reconnaissance gem—the exact piece of information he needed in order to turn the enemy flank by an advance from Valley Mountain—echoed his discovery across the Pedregal in Mexico. As Lee was ascertaining exactly how the attack could be executed in conjunction with troops from the camp at Monterey (Virginia), General Loring forwarded a local surveyor's report of another route leading west from Monterey that wound through the mountains "to a point that overlooked the Federal defenses" immediately in "the rear of the Cheat Mountain Pass." According to the surveyor, he had made the trip undetected. Lee wanted to be sure that troops could make the move over the ground, so on a follow-up trip, the surveyor was accompanied by Colonel Albert Rust of the 3rd Arkansas Volunteer Infantry. When these men returned, they expressed the utmost enthusiasm about Confederate prospects. They insisted that an attacking force "could move along the route and open a surprise attack…that would turn the Federal position." Lee had the confirmation he sought. All he had to do now was formulate a plan that would take into consideration all the known factors, including overcoming the already obvious and existing difficulties, as well as other daunting obstacles.[168]

The northwestern Virginia skies had turned dark in the latter part of July and from the clouds there poured forth daily a steady amount of rain. The precipitation was not a warm, summer rain, but rather a cold, piercing wet that chilled men to their bones. It had turned the scenic mountainous terrain gloomy, the roads into mud-laden quagmires, and had made Lee's scouting missions all the more difficult. As early as August 10th, after 20 successive days of rain, the roads had become virtually impassable. "Time and again," wrote Walter Taylor, "could be seen double teams of horses struggling with six or eight barrels of flour" due to the wagon being sunk in mud up to the axles. By the middle of the month, the rainy weather turned colder and ice formed during the night. These miserable conditions continued as the end of August approached. "It rains here all the time, literally," Lee wrote in an August 29th letter to his two daughters. "It is raining now…But we must be

Courtesy Library of Congress

Albert Rust

---

[167] *Richmond Daily Dispatch*, August 30, 1861; Freeman, *R. E. Lee*, vol. 1, p. 548.

[168] *Richmond Daily Dispatch*, August 30, 1861; Freeman, *R. E. Lee*, vol. 1, p. 548. The Federals, meanwhile, were having their own challenges in gathering accurate intelligence, and were misinformed about the numbers of Confederate troops they were facing. "The *Cincinnati Commercial* credited Lee with 40,000 to 50,000 men," as cited in Freeman, *R. E. Lee*, vol. 1, p. 557, fn 8. Also, General McClellan, former commander of the Federal forces in this area and writing from Washington on August 16th, urged his successor, General Rosecrans, to attack the Confederates before they could concentrate and "attack your main column." See *Official Records*, Series I, vol. 5, George McClellan to W. S. Rosecrans, August 16, 1861, pp. 563-564; Long, *Memoirs of Robert E. Lee*, p. 122; Clayton R. Newell, *Lee vs. McClellan: The First Campaign* (Washington, D.C., 1996), p. 222.

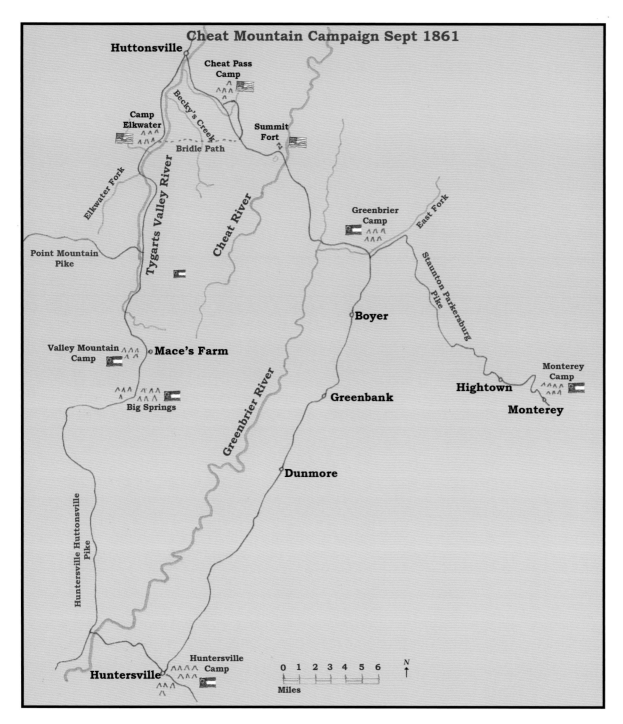

Cheat Mountain Campaign Sept 1861

Position of opposing forces prior to Confederate offensive

patient." His patience must have been tried, because the bad weather brought all meaningful operations to a virtual standstill, merely one of several issues Lee could not alter. Sickness ravaged the ranks. The "troops, being new and unaccustomed to camp-life, began to suffer from all the camp-diseases. Typhoid fever, measles, and home-sickness [spread rapidly] so that in the course of a few weeks nearly one-third of the army was rendered *hors de combat* by sickness." With so many already dead, and with the other men wet, shivering and always hungry, the number of those present and under arms with Loring at Valley Mountain numbered only about 6,000, while those in General Henry R. Jackson's Division near Monterey stood at about 5,000. Lindsay Long noticed that in the midst of all the challenges, Lee managed to keep "his equanimity and cheerfulness" in an effort "to ameliorate as much as possible the sufferings of the men." The men weren't the only ones suffering. The rain and cold severely impacted the health of the horses, and they "grew thin and pitiful."[169]

In addition to the weather and sickness, Lee confronted the ominous terrain of the Alleghenies and the constant supply shortages. The steep ground along the proposed attack routes was treacherously difficult for a large body of troops trying to move across. Lacking accurate maps, Lee had done as much as possible to discover the position and numbers of the enemy. The Federals under Brigadier General Joseph J. Reynolds occupied two positions about eight miles apart from each other—at Elkwater and Cheat Mountain—and Lee saw that the nature of the difficult terrain rendered the Federal positions isolated from each other, and as such, they were not mutually supporting. The prospective attacking Confederates under Loring waited in two camps about 10 miles apart, likewise separated by terrain. Effective close coordination between attacking columns would require clear-thinking commanders possessing initiative. Finally, supply difficulties only seemed to be increasing with the worsening weather, which meant that further delays only lengthened Confederate odds. In the face of all these challenges, Lee realized that if the Confederacy had any chance at recovering the northwestern counties, they had no realistic alternative but to attack—now. President Davis had only days before communicated to Lee "of the importance of your presence in Western Virginia so long as might be necessary to carry out the ends [of recapturing the northwestern counties.]" No longer could the offensive be delayed. If the Confederates did not attack, they would have to withdraw. Favoring audacity and risk over caution and certain defeat, Lee wanted a bold attack.[170]

Of course, Lee's desire to impose his will on the enemy and assume the offensive had to overcome the biggest obstacle of the campaign—his lack of command authority. Despite the fact that Lee was confirmed as a full general in the regular army of the Confederate States on August 31st, no amount of prestige could fully neutralize General Loring's massive ego, testing Lee in ways most officers of his rank would have been incapable of handling. However, instead of complaining to Richmond or usurping Loring's command authority, Lee concentrated on what he could accomplish within his constitutional authority. He visited with the troops often, during which time his modesty and sincerity won the confidence and hearts of the men. His refined, gentlemanly manners and obvious commitment to duty went a long way in smoothing over Loring's needlessly jealous and easily-bruised feelings. Walter Taylor was of the opinion that "no trait of his appears to greater advantage or impresses one more profoundly than his utter self-abnegation." Accordingly, the detailed attack orders dated September 8, 1861, diligently crafted by Lee, tactfully bore the name of General Loring.[171]

---

[169] Taylor, *Four Years With General Lee*, p. 17; Robert E. Lee, Jr., *Recollections and Letters*, Robert E. Lee to *"My Precious Daughters,"* August 29, 1861, p. 35; Long, *Memoirs of Robert E. Lee*, p. 122-123; Freeman, *R. E. Lee*, vol. 1, p. 557.

[170] Freeman, *R. E. Lee*, vol. 1, pp. 561-562; Long, *Memoirs of Robert E. Lee*, pp. 122-123; Taylor, *Four Years With General Lee*, pp. 22-23. *Official Records*, Series I, vol. 5, S. Cooper to Robert E. Lee, September 4, 1861, pp. 828-829.

[171] *Southern Historical Society Papers*, vol. 20, "Davis and Johnston...How Lee Came to be Put over Johnston," p. 98; Taylor, *General Lee*, p. 32; *Official Records*, Series I, vol. 51, part 2 Supplement, "Confidential" Orders, September 8, 1861, pp. 282-283. According to Douglas Southall Freeman, the wording of General Lee's orders were "detailed, well-drafted, and very simple in form," as cited in *R. E. Lee*, vol. 1, p. 562. These orders are presented here in their entirety.

CONFIDENTIAL

Headquarters,
Valley Mountain,
September 8, 1861

First. General H. R. Jackson, commanding Monterey Division, will detail a column of not more than 2,000 men, under Colonel Rust, to turn the enemy's position at Cheat Mountain Pass at daylight on the 12th instant, Thursday. During the night preceding the morning of the 12th instant, General Jackson having left a suitable guard for his own position, with the rest of his available force will take post on the eastern ridge of Cheat Mountain, occupy the enemy in front and co-operate in the assault of his attacking column should circumstances favor. The march of Colonel Rust will be so regulated as to obtain his position during the same night, and at dawn of the appointed day (Thursday, 12th) he will, if possible, surprise the enemy in his trenches and carry them.

Second. The pass having been carried, General Jackson, with his whole force, will immediately move forward toward Huttonsville, prepared against an attack from the enemy, taking every precaution against firing upon the portion of the army operating west of Cheat Mountain, and ready to cooperate with it against the enemy in Tygart's Valley. The supply wagons of the advancing column will follow, and the reserve will occupy Cheat Mountain.

Third. General Anderson's brigade will move down Tygart's Valley, following the west slope of Cheat Mountain range, concealing his movement from the enemy. On reaching Wyman's or the vicinity he will report his force unobserved, send forward intelligence officers to make sure of his further course, and during the night of the 11th (Wednesday) proceed to Staunton turnpike where it intersects the west top of Cheat Mountain, so as to arrive there as soon after daylight on the 12th (Thursday) as possible. He will make dispositions to hold the turnpike, prevent re-enforcements reaching Cheat Mountain Pass, cut the telegraph wire, and be prepared if necessary to aid in the assault of the enemy's position on the middle top of Cheat Mountain by General Jackson's division, the result of which he must await. He must particularly keep in mind that the movement of General Jackson is to surprise the enemy in their defenses. He must, therefore, not discover his movement nor advance beyond a point before Wednesday night, when he can conceal his force. Cheat Mountain Pass being carried, he will turn down the mountain and press upon the left and rear of the enemy in Tygart's Valley, either by the old or new turnpike or the Beckytown road, according to circumstances.

A Tennessee Flag

Fourth. General Donelson's brigade will advance on the right of Tygart's Valley River, seizing paths and avenues leading from that side to the river and driving back the enemy that might endeavor to retard the advance of the center along the turnpike or turn his right.

Fifth. Such of the artillery as may not be used on the flanks will proceed along the Huttonsville turnpike, supported by Major Munford's battalion, followed by the ——, of Colonel Gilham's brigade in reserve.

Sixth. Colonel Burks' brigade will advance on the left of Tygart's Valley River in supporting distance to the center, and clear that side of the valley of the forces of the enemy that might [be] obstructing the advance of the artillery.

Seventh. The cavalry under Major Lee will follow, according to the nature of the ground, in rear of the left of Colonel Burks' brigade. He will watch the movements of the enemy in that quarter, give notice, and prevent if possible, any attempt to turn the left of the river, and be prepared to strike when opportunity offers.

Eighth. The wagons of each brigade, properly packed and guarded, under the charge of their respective quartermasters, who will personally superintend their movements, will pursue the main turnpike under the general direction of the acting quartermaster, in rear of the army and out of cannon range of the enemy.

Ninth. Commanders on both lines of operations will particularly see that their escorts wear the distinguishing badge; that both officers and men take every precaution not to fire on our own troops. This is essentially necessary, as the forces on both sides of Cheat Mountain may unite. They will also use every exertion to prevent noise and straggling
from the ranks, correct quickly any confusion that may occur, and cause their commands to rapidly execute their movements when in the presence of the enemy.

By command of
Brigadier-General Loring:
C. L. Stevenson,
Adjutant General

The plan called for the six Confederate brigades of Loring's Army of the Northwest to emerge from their two widely separated bases and move undetected in five separate columns over difficult terrain against two different objectives, then simultaneously initiate a surprise attack on September 12th against an undetermined number of Federals, some of whom were probably entrenched. Success depended on timing and determination. One of the columns issuing from Valley Mountain would follow the stock trail discovered by Lee, while another column emerging from the Monterey camp and approaching Cheat Mountain from the east would take the path confirmed by Colonel Rusk. Lee's verbiage clearly explained to all commanders their expected role, and "each of the brigade commanders was determined to carry out his portion of the plan." Both Lee and Loring would accompany different columns advancing from Valley Mountain. Finally, Lee issued his "Special Orders," exhorting "the troops to keep steadily in view the great principles for which they contend."[172]

---

[172] *Official Records*, Series I, vol. 51, part 2 Supplement, "Confidential" Orders, September 8, 1861, pp. 282-283; Clayton R. Newell, *Lee vs. McClellan: The First Campaign* (Washington,

GENERAL ORDERS, No. 10

Headquarters, Army of the Northwest
Valley Mountain, September 8, 1861

The following organization of the Army of the Northwest is published for the information of all concerned:

First Brigade, Brig. Gen. H. R. Jackson—12th Georgia, 3rd Arkansas, 31st Virginia and 52nd Virginia Regiments, Hansbrough's battalion, Danville Virginia Artillery, and Jackson's Cavalry.

Second Brigade, Brig. Gen. S. R. Anderson—1st Tennessee, 7th Tennessee, and 14th Tennessee Regiments, Hampden Virginia Artillery, and Alexander's company of cavalry.

Third Brigade, Brig. Gen. Donelson—8th Tennessee, 16th Tennessee, 1st Georgia and 14th Georgia Regiments, Greenbrier Cavalry.

Fourth Brigade, Col. William Gilham—21st Virginia, 6th North Carolina, 1st Battalion of Confederate States Provisional Army, Georgia Troup Artillery.

Fifth Brigade, Col. William B. Taliaferro—23rd Virginia, 25th Virginia, 37th Virginia and 44th Virginia Regiments, Rice's Virginia Artillery and the Lee Virginia Artillery.

Sixth Brigade, Col. J. S. Burks—42nd Virginia and 48th Virginia Regiments and Lee's cavalry.

For field service, a section of the Hampden Artillery will be assigned to the Third Brigade, and one from the Troup Artillery with the Sixth Brigade. Commanders will send to the headquarters as soon as practicable a return of their respective brigades.

By order of General Loring:

C. L. Stevenson,
Adjutant General[173]

SPECIAL ORDERS, No. ——

Headquarters of the Forces
Valley Mountain, Western Virginia
September 9, 1861

The forward movement announced to the Army of the Northwest in Special Orders, No. 28, from its headquarters, of this date, gives the general commanding the opportunity of exhorting the troops to keep steadily in view the great principles for which they contend and to manifest to the world their determination to maintain them. The eyes of the country are upon you. The safety of your homes and the lives of all you hold dear depend upon your courage and exertions. Let each man resolve to be victorious, and that the rights of self-government, liberty, and peace shall in him find a defender. The progress of this army must be forward.

R. E. Lee,
General, Commanding

D.C., 1996), p. 226; *Official Records*, Series I, vol. 5, "Special Orders" September 9, 1861.

[173] *Official Records*, Series I, vol. 51, part 2 Supplement, "General Orders, No. 10," September 8, 1861, pp. 283-284.

Glad that all the deprivations might at last lead to real action, the Confederates began their widespread approach movements on September 10th. By the night of the 11th, despite marching for two days on short rations, the brigade commanders had succeeded in getting all five of the Confederate columns to their assigned positions. Green troops and untested officers had indeed overcome forbidding terrain and wet, bone-chilling weather that taxed the endurance of the men to the limit. Despite orders, rations did not reach all the men: One Tennessean remembered the plight of Donelson's brigade, entrusted with the eventual envelopment of the Federal rear via Huttonsville:

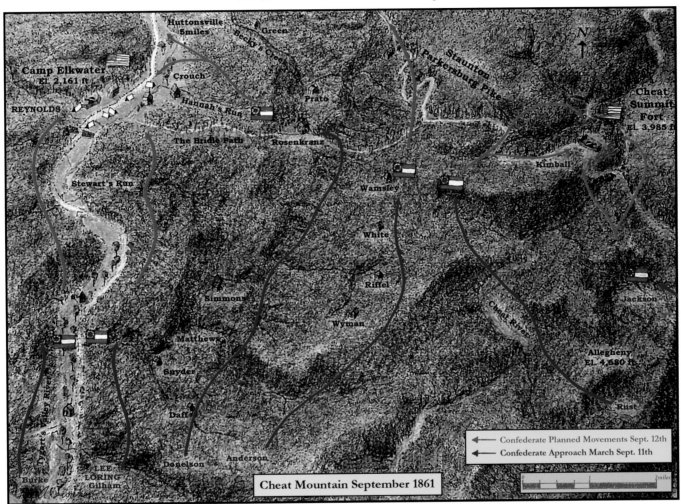

Lee's Plan of Operations for Cheat Mountain

Next morning, the 11th of September, by daylight, the two regiments were quietly aroused, and without a single thing to eat, we were soon into line and began to move out again, with orders to maintain the strictest silence, and to keep 'closed up ranks.' The fates were against us again, as usual. Promises were made that at some designated point our cooking men would meet us with our two days' ration, and then we would get something to eat. To add to our discomfort, it soon began to rain. We marched out in a northwestern direction, and down hills and up hills, across branches and small creeks, still avoiding all roads or anything like a road. Wet, hungry, muddy, on we marched without a murmur, expecting every few minutes to be halted to receive our rations; but still they came not.[174]

174 Joseph G. Carrigan, Cheat Mountain: Or, Unwritten Chapter of the Late War (Nashville,

As the soaked, exhausted Confederates fell on their arms on the night of September 11th, the officers and men were anxious to attack in what Walter Taylor promised to be "certain victory." With every one of the columns in their assigned place, a foggy and rainy night concealed the Confederates' close proximity to the Federals. The first phase of Lee's attack plan had gone as well as possible. The only thing for the officers and men to do now was to try and get some rest before forming up in the morning and wait for the signal from Colonel Rust's 3rd Arkansas that would open the attack.[175]

As the cold morning of September 12th dawned on Cheat Mountain, the 3rd Arkansas moved towards the unsuspecting enemy. The regiment advanced at the head of Rust's column of "1,500-1,600 men" when it came upon a few surprised Federal pickets. Several shots rang out and a few Federal pickets and teamsters were taken prisoner. Upon interrogation, the captives claimed

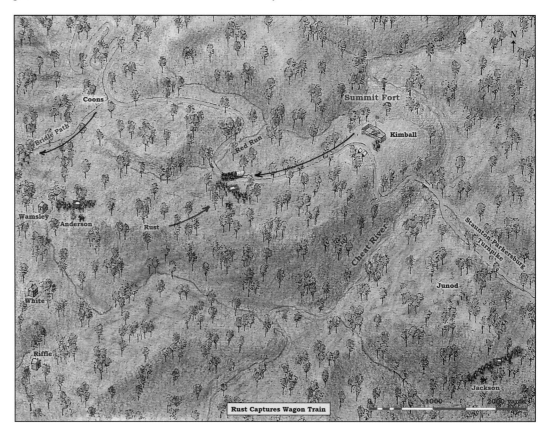

Rust Advances

that the size of their command lurking beyond the mountain pass "was between 4,000 to 5,000 men," a remarkably heady claim to make under the circumstances, considering that only 300 men in blue were nearby. Indeed, the exchange of fire had alerted the Federals to the presence of Confederate forces, and distant drums could be heard in the Federal camp. But how many bluecoats were really there? Colonel Rust, who had been given the honor to lead the all-important column designated to trigger the Confederate attack lacked military experience, and the prisoners' claims immediately went to work on his imagination. Believing surprise was lost and that a large number of the Federals awaited, and hearing what he presumed were enemy artillery pieces moving into action, Rust lost his resolve. According to the colonel's official report, he hurriedly called together "all the field officers" of his command who "declared it would be madness to make an attack." So rather than push forward as ordered, the numerically superior Arkansans lost the opportunity to defeat 300 Federals. Rust timidly withdrew his command without attempting to confirm the prisoners' claim. In this manner, the Confederacy had lost the best opportunity of the campaign, and Rust's refusal to risk his command

1885), p. 74.
[175] Newell, *Lee vs. McClellan*, pp. 227-229; Freeman, *R. E. Lee*, vol. 1, pp. 564-565; Taylor, *Four Years With General Lee*, pp. 27-28; and Long, *Memoirs of Robert E. Lee*, p. 123; Dowdey and Manarin, *The Wartime Papers of R. E. Lee*, number 77, "To His Wife," September 17, 1861, p. 73.

despite clear orders compromised the entire Confederate operation. While Rust's career would essentially be ruined, a stain of dishonor attached to him, the 3rd Arkansas, led by a more able Colonel Vannoy ("Van") Hartrog Manning, would later win laurels on many battlefields from Pennsylvania to Georgia as part of the famed "Texas Brigade."

The decision negated the efforts of the army that had undergone so much in order to get into a position to have a chance to succeed. By 10:00 A.M., the long-awaited fusillade to signal the assault by Rust failed to materialize. Trying to salvage something out of the situation, Lee decided to interject himself into the action by riding toward Donelson's Brigade. Descending from the heights with his aide Lieutenant Walter Taylor and a few cavalry escorts, where Lee had just observed "the enemy's tents on [Tygart's] Valley River at the point on the Huttonsville road just below," a scouting party of Federal cavalry came upon Lee and his group. The Federal cavalry bore down on them, only to suddenly turn away when the horsemen saw the head of Donelson's Brigade nearby. Spurring his mount up to the brigade, Lee cut an image that one company commander remembered as that of a "gallant officer and most exemplary man." Lee ordered the brigade to attack immediately to try and take advantage of whatever surprise still remained. The officers and men responded, but just barely. By then, everyone knew the intended attack by Rust had not happened. With a listless, half-hearted effort, the Confederate attack achieved a short-lived, limited success only because the Federals had indeed been surprised. However, the Confederates, sapped of aggressive leadership, were quickly thrown back when the Federals gathered themselves and counterattacked. Riding close to the front, Lee encouraged the officers to get their men in hand, but to no avail. Confederate morale had already plummeted and the attack completely unraveled from the point of first failure.[176]

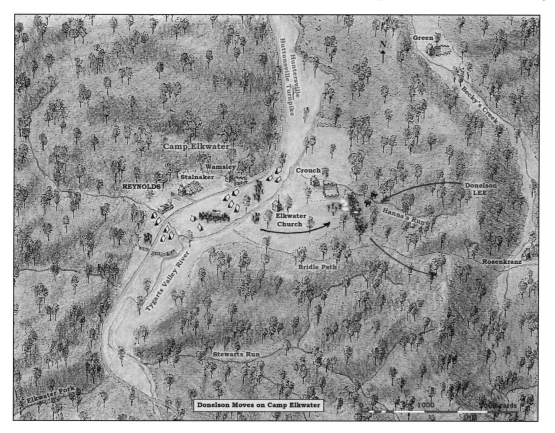

Donelson Moves on Elkwater

---

[176] *Official Records*, Series I, vol. 5, Albert Rust to W. W. Loring, September 13, 1861, pp. 191-192; in the *Official Records*, Series I, vol. 5, Joseph J. Reynolds to L. Thomas, September 17, 1861, p. 185, Reynolds states that had only three Federal regiments were in the vicinity, and from those only four companies numbering 300 serving as detachments were opposite Rust's column; Taylor, *Four Years With General Lee*, pp. 28-29; Freeman, *R. E. Lee*, vol. 1, pp. 567-568; Long, *Memoirs of Robert E. Lee*, pp. 123-124; and Robert E. Lee, Jr., *Recollections and Letters*, Robert E. Lee to Governor Letcher, September 17, 1861, p. 39. The Federal prisoners had done their duty well, as they exaggerated the strength of their command. See: Newell, *Lee*

In Donelson's column advancing from Elkwater some seven miles distant, the lack of firing from Rust's column indeed had caused command hesitation. Brigadier General Daniel Smith Donelson, who graduated 5th in the West Point Class of 1825, had quit the service after only five months to focus on a career as a planter, and had risen to become Speaker of the Tennessee House of Representatives. As a brigadier in the state militia, Donelson had the dubious distinction of being asked to approve the two sites, Fort Donelson and Fort Henry, which, despite his own misgivings, he did. At Cheat Mountain, Donelson now found himself involved in yet another mess. Private Garrigan of the 8th Tennessee gives his after-war recollection of that day (the night of the 11th):

> General Donelson, Cols. Fulton and Savage and our guide had by this time passed to the front, and were with the advance as we descended this mountain. A brief consultation was here held, the guide insisting, as we understand, that we must push on and into the camps of the enemy that night.
> Cols. Savage and Fulton, with a cool, deliberate judgment, protested and urged that something had gone wrong; that a mistake had occurred somewhere, and that such an attack, with men in the condition we were in, was folly and nonsense.
> In a short time the word was quietly passed along the line to 'about face' and move out.[177]

Although his planned efforts for the attack on the 12th had gone unrealized, Lee knew that the men, although demoralized and exhausted, were not actually defeated and casualties had been minimal. In Lee's mind, all was not lost. Even with the Federals now fully alerted to the Confederate activity, Lee still hoped to find a way to salvage the campaign, and the only way that was possible was to flank the enemy positions in the Tygart's Valley River. If this could be done, Federal lines of communication with Cheat Mountain would be seriously threatened and the campaign would continue. Needing information about the feasibility of turning the still vulnerable Federal right that rested at Elkwater, Lee sent out reconnaissance parties on September 13th. One party consisted of Lee's 24 year-old son, Major William Henry Fitzhugh ("Rooney") Lee, along with some members of the 9th Virginia cavalry and Lieutenant Colonel John Augustine Washington, the senior aide de camp of General Lee and great-nephew of George Washington. The colonel had often wanted to go on reconnaissance missions, and this was the first time Lee assented. When the group unexpectedly came upon a concealed Federal picket line within 20 yards of them, a volley rang out. Many bullets found their mark at such a short range. Three musket balls hit Washington, killing him, along with one of the troopers. Bullets whizzed by "Rooney" without hitting the general's son. His horse wasn't as lucky, as three bullets struck the animal. The major was able to escape by adroitly leaping on Washington's horse and galloping away.[178]

The news of Washington's death, coming on the heels of the failed attack against Cheat Mountain, hit Robert E. Lee hard. Not only had six weeks of tireless effort within the nonsensical confines of Jeff Davis' command restraints

Col. John A. Washington

"News from General Lee's camp confirm the Federal report of the death of this officer, who was an aid to Gen. L. He was shot near the Fort of Cheat Mountain. Col. W. was the owner of Mount Vernon prior to the sale to the M V. Association."

The Richmond Daily Dispatch, September 18, 1861

---

vs. McClellan, pp. 229-231.
[177] Carrigan, Cheat Mountain, pp. 75-76.
[178] Jack Zinn, *R. E. Lee's Cheat Mountain Campaign* (Parsons, 1974), pp. 186-192; Newell, *Lee vs. McClellan*, p. 231; Dowdey and Manarin, *Wartime Papers of R. E. Lee*, number 77, "To His Wife," September 17, 1861, p. 74; Robert E. Lee, Jr., *Recollections and Letters*, Lee to Governor Letcher, September 17, 1861, p. 40.

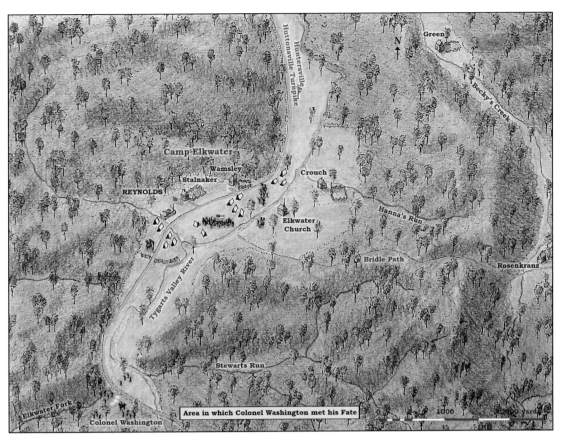

Area in which Colonel Washington met his fate

severely crippled Confederate designs at recovering the region, Lee now had to come to terms with the death of a dear family friend. In writing to Washington's daughter a few days later, a grieving Lee told Miss Louisa Washington that her father "fell in the Cause to which he had devoted all his energies, and in which his noble heart was warmly enlisted." Lee decided to call off any further attempts to force the Federal positions, and the following day, September 17th, he reported the news of the failed attack on Cheat Mountain to his wife and to Governor Letcher. Lee wrote that he could not begin to express his "regret and mortification at the untoward events that caused the failure of the plan," especially after he "had taken every precaution to ensure success" and that he "was very sanguine of taking the enemy's works" as he "had considered the subject well."[179]

Given the brevity and nature of the action, the casualties from the Cheat Mountain affair were light. Federal losses amounted to nine killed, about 25 wounded, along with 70 taken as prisoners and two missing. The Confederate losses are more difficult to pinpoint, but seem to be less than 100 wounded and killed, including Colonel Washington, along with about 20 taken prisoner.[180]

* * *

Lee wasn't the only general officer in western Virginia who knew that he had traveled from Richmond with no command authority in hand. Following an initial disapproval in having Lee on scene with the Army of the Northwest, General Loring had become more receptive to Lee's suggestions, but that was only after Lee's confirmation as a full general, along with Lee's extraordinary efforts to assure Loring of his position and importance. However difficult the situation with Loring was for Lee, the relationship involving generals Floyd and Wise proved more so, largely because of Davis.

[179] Robert E. Lee, Jr., *Recollections and Letters*, Robert E. Lee to His Wife, September 17, 1861, p. 38, and Lee to Governor Letcher, September 17, 1861, p. 39.

[180] These numbers are a compilation of the available sources. *Official Records*, Series I, vol. 5, Joseph J. Reynolds to L. Thomas, September 17, 1861, pp. 184-186; Robert E. Lee, Jr., *Recollections and Letters*, Robert E. Lee to His Wife, September 17, 1861, and Lee to Governor Letcher, September 17, 1861, pp. 38-40; *Southern Historical Society Papers*, vol. 17, "Robert E. Lee" by Jefferson Davis, p. 367.

From the time that Lee arrived in the theater of operations in early August, he had urged simplicity and unity when it came to Floyd and Wise working together in the Kanawha Valley: Unfortunately for Lee, something more was required in order to control two cantankerous, feuding ex-politicians. John Floyd, as senior commander to Henry Wise, was to "advance west of Lewisburg to Meadow Bluff," continuing to move "to the Gauley, if desirable," and was supposed to unite with Wise "for the protection of the Virginia Central Railroad" as well as "the Virginia and Tennessee Railroad." However, Floyd and Wise became more interested in seeing "the other annihilated" rather than the enemy. So while Lee was giving the bulk of his attention and efforts before Cheat Mountain, the Federals expanded their stronghold on the Gauley Bridge in the Kanawha Valley, about 70 miles to

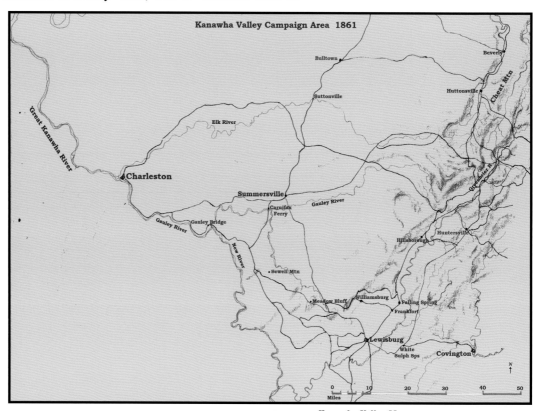

Kanawha Valley Map

the southwest, against two commanders who refused to be good comrades. The two former governors had continued their mindless feuding, and that uncooperative air was all too evident when, two days before the aborted action at Cheat Mountain, the Federals attacked Floyd's brigade at Carnifax Ferry. Floyd was slightly wounded in the arm during the action, but his brigade "held firm." Believing he was significantly outnumbered, Floyd repeatedly called for Wise, some 12 miles away, to come to his support. Wise refused or ignored each request. Floyd meanwhile retreated to the southern bank of the Gauley while Wise claimed in a letter to General Lee that his "force was not safe under his [Floyd's] command." When Lee read this nonsense, he decided to go see what insolence was afoot. Advising Loring to "leave a sufficient force to watch the enemy at Cheat Mountain, and move the rest of his army to the Kanawha Valley," Lee, accompanied by Walter Taylor and some cavalry acting as an escort, rode for several days through the cold mountains before reaching Floyd's headquarters at Meadow Bluff on September 21st. Upon arrival, Lee learned from Floyd that Wise was still refusing to cooperate and that the juncture of Confederate forces had not happened.[181]

---

[181] Tim McKinney, *Robert E. Lee at Sewell Mountain: The West Virginia Campaign* (Charleston, 1990), pp. 37-40; *Official Records*, Series I, vol. 5, Robert E. Lee to Henry A. Wise, August 3, 1861, p. 768 and Robert E. Lee to Henry A. Wise, August 5, 1861, pp. 771-772, and Henry A. Wise to Robert E. Lee, September 11, 1861, p. 149; *Official Records*, Series I, vol. 51, part 2, Robert E. Lee to John B. Floyd, August 3, 1861, p. 211; *Official Records*, Series I, vol. 5, Mason Mathews to Jefferson Davis, September 19, 1861, p. 864, and W. H. Syme to Jefferson Davis, September 19, 1861, p. 865; Freeman, *R. E. Lee*, vol. 1, pp. 581-587; Taylor, *Four Years With General Lee*, pp. 32-33; Zinn, *Cheat Mountain*, pp. 201-202; Newell, *Lee vs. McClellan*,

When Lee arrived in the Kanawha Valley area, he possessed more than just the prestige with which he had arrived at Loring's camp some seven weeks earlier. Partially in response to Lee's, and other, reports to Richmond about the sorry state of command affairs in western Virginia, on the day that the abortive Confederate attack against Cheat Mountain took place, the President had finally consented to empower Lee with some limited authority; namely, being able to transfer Wise and his command anywhere Lee wanted. Additionally, General Cooper had sent word to Lee about what troops had been designated to replace Wise's men. Thus, when Lee rode up to Floyd's headquarters on the 21st he had the authority to resolve the command impasse.[182]

However, despite the previous friction Lee had encountered with the political generals soon after his arrival in the theater of operations in August, and despite the news coming out of the Kanawha Valley, Lee remained fair-minded. Rather than assuming anything before giving any orders to Wise, Lee once again recognized that he had to quickly learn the strengths and intention of the enemy. Faced with an active foe, both Floyd and Wise disagreed about who occupied the better position. Lee urged Wise "if not too late, that the troops be united, and that we conquer or die together," and that his feuding with Floyd be dropped in "the interest of our Cause."[183]

Outside of writing this communiqué from Floyd's camp at Meadow Bluff, the situation demanded action. Without hesitation, Lee once again assumed the role of his own intelligence officer. Leaving Floyd's headquarters and scouting the forward area of Sewell Mountain the next day, September 22nd, Lee readily ascertained that the enemy's cavalry was active, and that the Sewell Mountain position occupied by Wise was indeed stronger than was Floyd's at Meadow Bluff. Lee also detected that the "few inferior roads" that ran north and south of Wise's position offered an aggressive enemy commander the opportunity to flank this position. Confederate cavalry outposts, or vedettes, added nothing to Lee's observations and could not provide intelligence as to whether or not the Federals were moving directly against Sewell, or intending to conduct a flank march and attack Floyd at Meadow Bluff. All this gave cause for Lee to seek more information before deciding where the best position would be to unite the commands.[184]

Returning to Meadow Bluff on the 23rd, and after spending part of the day listening to Floyd expound on his theory that the enemy were flanking Wise and heading for him, coupled with the absence of reliable information from the cavalry vedettes, Lee decided to head back to Sewell Mountain. When Lee arrived at Wise's camp at Sewell on September 24th, he "found the enemy in sight," only a mile and a half away. Incredibly, no one in the disorganized and demoralized command seemed to know anything about the nearby Federal forces. The chaotic situation infuriated Lee, as evidenced when one of the green lieutenants of Wise's command approached him to ask an inane question. T. C. Morton of the 26th Virginia Battalion was nearby and later recalled the scene. Lee was "standing in the rain by a log fire," his image that of a "martial figure . . . with his breeches tucked in his high cavalry boots,

---

pp. 235-236; Taylor, *Four Years With General Lee*, p. 32; Thomas, *Robert E. Lee*, p. 207. In Walter Taylor's *General Lee*, he states that it was only General Lee was only accompanied by himself during this journey on horseback to the Kanawha Valley.

[182] Thomas, *Robert E. Lee*, pp. 207 and 432, footnote 22; *Official Records*, Series I, vol. 5, Mason Mathews to Jefferson Davis, September 19, 1861, p. 864, and W. H. Syme to Jefferson Davis, September 19, 1861, p. 865.

[183] *Official Records*, Series I, vol. 5, Robert E. Lee to Henry A. Wise, September 21, 1861, p. 868.

[184] *Official Records*, Series I, vol. 5, Henry A. Wise to J. P. Benjamin, October 26, 1861, p. 162.

his hands behind his back, a high, broad-brimmed black hat, with a gilt cord around it, on his head, which was bowed as if in deep thought. " Suddenly, a young lieutenant came up to him, saluted, and asked: "who was the ordnance officer and where was the [ordnance] train?" Morton could "never forget" the look in Lee's eyes as the general first "quietly eyed his intruder a moment," then proceeded to reprimand the questioning officer. "I think it very strange, Lieutenant, that an officer of this command, which has been here a week, should come to me, who am just arrived, to ask who his ordnance officer is, and where to find his ammunition. This is in keeping with everything else I find here—no order, no organization; nobody knows where anything is, no one understands his duty; officers and men are equally ignorant. This will not do." Then pointing to a tent and some wagons on a knoll a few hundred yards off, "There you will find what you are looking for, sir, and I hope you will not have to come to me again on such an errand."[185]

Lee knew firsthand of his men's trials and deprivations; according to Walter Taylor, "he preferred to share discomfort with his men." Like many other nights, he slept covered by only his overcoat before resuming his reconnaissance duties the next dawn. His morning ride confirmed again in his mind that Wise, either out of luck or by instinct, had indeed selected a better position on Sewell Mountain than had Floyd at Meadow Bluff. Lee faced an obvious dilemma. How would Floyd react if Lee told him that the uncooperative Wise was correct in holding onto Sewell, especially since Floyd expected Lee to make Wise obey Floyd's previous request? Even absent the authority to send Wise where he saw fit, how could Lee, after conducting his reconnaissance missions, order Wise to quit Sewell Mountain when he was correct in not giving up the position?[186]

Lee handled the matter as tactfully as possible. In a written letter to Floyd dated September 25th, Lee advised Floyd that his morning reconnaissance had counted "five or six regiments" to Wise's front, but that he could not "see the ground in their rear where others may be." Lee noted "a large wagon train of supplies, independent of the regular supply train" supplemented "by rows of barrels piled outside" that gave him cause to believe that a "large number of troops [stood] before" the Confederate position on Sewell. Lee saw no indications of the Federals being "on the roads to our right or left" that would have tipped their hand at an attempt to flank Sewell Mountain. Therefore, Lee felt that the enemy's main force "was before" Wise. "An enterprising enemy," reasoned Lee, could still flank Sewell Mountain, and Floyd was cautioned to "better have [those roads] well guarded." Lee explained to Floyd that the strength of the Sewell position was compelling because the Federals "can get no position for their artillery, and their men I think will not advance without it." Finally, in order to strengthen the Confederate hold on Sewell Mountain, Lee pointed out that food and forage were required as men were in need and "the horses are suffering." Then, in a postscript, Walter Taylor, acting as Lee's Assistant Adjutant-General, instructed Floyd that he was to forward "three days' rations."[187]

The response to Lee's message came back in an unexpected form. Floyd forwarded a brief but tersely-worded dispatch by the War Department that had been issued five days earlier. President Davis ordered General Wise "to turn

"I begin to fear that the enemy will not attack us. We shall therefore have to attack him."

—Robert E. Lee to John B. Floyd, September 30, 1861

---

[185] Freeman, *R. E. Lee*, vol. 1, p. 590; *Southern Historical Society Papers*, vol. 11, "Anecdotes of General R. E. Lee," by Captain T. C. Morton, pp. 518-519.
[186] Taylor, *General Lee*, p. 32.
[187] *Official Records*, Series I, vol. 51, part 2, Supplement, Robert E. Lee to John B. Floyd, p. 312.

"I am sorry, as you say, that the movements of the armies cannot keep pace with the expectations of the editors of papers. I know they can regulate matters satisfactorily to themselves on paper. I wish they could do so in the field. No one wishes them more success than I do & would be happy to see them have full swing. Genl Floyd has the benefit of three editors on his staff. I hope something will be done to please them."

—Robert E. Lee in a letter to his wife, October 7, 1861

over all troops heretofore immediately under your command to General Floyd, and report yourself in person to the Adjutant-General in this city [Richmond] with the least delay." Lee forwarded the dispatch to Wise without comment. The former governor was embarrassed to be relieved of command, and thinking about defying Davis' recall, Wise asked Lee "for counsel." Lee, of course, advised Wise "to obey the President's order." A few hours later, Wise left for Richmond, but not before he drafted a farewell notice that entrusted "the safety and honor of my legion" with General Lee. Lee would see Wise in the field again, as they would "share the ordeal of Appomattox."[188]

Fully realizing the numerical inferiority of the Confederate forces in the area, Lee expected a Federal attack momentarily. In the days following Wise's departure, Lee employed his skill as an engineer to direct operations in strengthening the Sewell Mountain position. The constant cold rains hampered progress on the Confederate works on Sewell Mountain. Meanwhile, Floyd strengthened the possible approaches on the roads that skirted by Sewell, but he could do little about the inadequate number of wagons and teams available to move even the minuscule amount of supplies available the 16 miles from Meadow Bluff to Sewell Mountain. Indeed, Lee's constant pleas for food and fodder reflected an already failed Confederate supply system more than it revealed General Floyd's inability to do his duty. The men and the animals lived from day to day on what they could find and what arrived from Floyd, which meant that no reserve supplies could be gathered for an offensive. The malnourished animals survived on the verge of breaking down when word arrived on September 29th that Loring's advance guard had finally reached the vicinity.[189]

With the arrival of additional troops, Confederate numbers on Sewell increased to about 8,000 to 9,000. General Lee gained renewed hope for assuming an offensive that could lead to the recovery of western Virginia. The following day, Lee once again resumed his reconnaissance. Moving along steep slopes and negotiating large crags while perilously exposing himself to the enemy, Lee inspired many who saw the general in this role. Taylor recalled that Confederate troops "marveled at the sight" of Lee, who was spoiling for a fight and intently seeking a way to get at the enemy.[190]

Despite Lee's anxiety to rid the northwestern counties of "those people," he recognized that the formidable barriers of terrain in front of Sewell Mountain, combined with the horrible conditions of the roads, posed obstacles of the most serious sort. Little hope existed if supplies were not forthcoming in sufficient quantities to support a flanking movement that would negate the strength of the Federal position. With each passing day, scrawny teams pulling meager numbers of supply trains labored up the muddy road to Sewell Mountain. The wagons bore just enough food to keep the men from serious hunger and barely enough forage to keep the horses from starvation. With this routine, no chance existed of creating a reserve of supplies needed to sustain an offensive in the wet, miserable, fall weather. Lee reluctantly had no choice but to wait for the Federals to attack him.[191]

The Federals took no such action, denying Lee a battle. Sometime during

188 *Official Records*, Series I, vol. 5, Henry A. Wise to Robert E. Lee, September 25, 1861, and answer from R. E. Lee, September 25, 1861, p. 879; *Official Records*, vol. 51, part 2, Supplement, General Orders No. 106, September 25, 1861, p. 313; Freeman, *R. E. Lee*, vol. 1, p. 593.
189 *Official Records*, Series I, vol. 5, John B. Floyd to the Secretary of War, October 16, 1861, p. 900; McKinney, *Robert E. Lee at Sewell Mountain*, p. 77.
190 McKinney, *Robert E. Lee at Sewell Mountain*, p. 78; Taylor, *Four Years With General Lee*, p. 33.
191 Freeman, *R. E. Lee*, vol. 1, p. 596; Taylor, *Four Years With General Lee*, pp. 34-35.

the night of October 5th-6th, the cautious General Rosecrans had come to the conclusion that it would be unwise for his 5,200-man Federal force to assail the strong Confederate positions on Sewell, and therefore decided to shorten his line of communications for the upcoming winter. Marching away from the Confederates under the cover of darkness, the Federals slipped far away before the Southerners realized what had happened. Lee immediately ordered his cavalry to pursue in order "to ascertain their movements and position." However, the animals were too feeble for the job. The Confederate infantry followed up as well, but their movement, initiated without provisions, was slow and labored. Later that day, Lee ascertained that it would be impossible to overtake Rosecrans and called off the pursuit. The weakened condition of the men and animals, as well as the difficulty of the ground and the lack of supplies had forced his hand. Dejected, hungry, and shivering, the Confederates tramped back to the desolate, wind-swept slopes of Sewell Mountain. With this, Walter Taylor observed, "the campaign in western Virginia was virtually concluded."[192]

* * *

William Rosecrans

Once Rosecrans retreated and with the prospects for future operations during the current season nil, Lee contemplated a return to Richmond. Before departing, Lee reviewed the best way to defend the approaches to Staunton. He subsequently wrote Floyd of the necessity to return Loring's troops "to the Huntersville line" and reposition other troops from Sewell Mountain back to Meadow Bluff. Lee also thought it necessary to visit the wounded in the hospitals at Blue Sulphur, where he found it "badly managed" and gave "all necessary instructions" to put things right. Lee then advised that he would stop at the hospitals at Lewisburg and White Sulphur and then "proceed thence to Richmond."[193]

Accompanied by Taylor, Lee reached the Confederate capital on the afternoon of Thursday, October 31st. He still looked like a tower of strength, and he let grow a beard "which added to the solemn dignity of his appearance." Lee's return was not heralded, especially by the fire-eaters who had previously voiced their suspicions that Lee was not fanatically enough committed to The Cause. Regardless of how others viewed him, Lee's comments made in letters to his wife at the beginning of the campaign as well as to his daughter afterward, reveal that he considered the expedition, given the constraints placed on him by Jefferson Davis, to be a forlorn hope. Certainly, the President had the right to know and wanted details, and when Lee went to report to Davis, he pressed Lee for an explanation about what had gone wrong. This afforded Lee the first opportunity during the war to reveal his strong belief that fellow officers, regardless of their shortcomings, were never to be officially criticized so that such statements could be used either in the press or by members of the government. Consequently,

Richmond, Virginia

---

[192] *Official Records*, Series I, vol. 5, W. S. Rosecrans to E. D. Townsend, October 8, 1861, p. 615; *Official Records,* Series I, vol. 51, part 2, Supplement, Robert E. Lee to Officer Commanding Cavalry, October 6, 1861, p. 335; Taylor, *Four Years With General Lee*, p. 35. Lee tried yet again to organize another offensive, but the lack of transport, fodder and food, combined with the bitter cold weather and all-but impassable roads, prevented the plan from being executed. By October 20th, Lee gave up the idea of taking the offensive. See *Official Records*, Series I, vol. 5, Robert E. Lee to John B. Floyd, October 20, 1861, pp. 908-909.
[193] *Official Records*, Series I, vol. 51, part 2, Supplement, Robert E. Lee to John B. Floyd, October 29, 1861, pp. 361-362.

Lee "exacted a promise" from Davis "not to repeat his statement, as he would rather rest under censure himself than injure in the public esteem any who were bravely striking for the common cause." Once the President "pledged this, Lee reviewed the campaign verbally." Therefore, with Davis' promise of silence, Lee told the President how and why things had gone awry. Lee's willingness to publicly take the blame for what had happened in western Virginia over the past three months, even though the President had never entrusted him with the authority he required in order to have a reasonable chance at success, is noteworthy. Lee shouldered all the recriminations, and much more, in silence. This episode clearly illustrates that Lee was truly a man of unique qualities— qualities to which the prideful Jeff Davis ever so slowly and reluctantly began to appreciate, a season too late.[194]

"Another forlorn expedition"— Lee is sent to South Carolina

It was not until August 31st that Davis finally decided how the originally appointed five brigadier generals in Confederate service would be promoted, and in what order would be their seniority: first, the man who would served as Adjutant General in Richmond, Samuel Cooper; second, the man most idolized by Jefferson Davis and who was just returning from his antebellum army post in the far west, Albert Sidney Johnston; third, Robert E. Lee, at that time temporarily on duty in western Virginia; fourth and fifth, the co-victors of Manassas, Johnston and Beauregard, respectively. Therefore, when Lee reported back to Richmond, he was conspicuous for being the only full general without important duty or command.[195]

On November 4th, Lee had a long conference "till after 11 P.M." with the "new Secretary of War, the brilliant Judah P. Benjamin, who had succeeded the overworked and disillusioned" Leroy Pope Walker. The main topic focused on the already toppling South Atlantic coastal defenses. Federal ships roamed off the Southern coastline, her officers picking and choosing where to send ashore landing parties that committed "depredations along the rivers, showing the vulnerability of the region." Furthermore, Benjamin informed Lee that a large Federal fleet previously gathered around Hampton Roads (the mouths of the James, Nansemond and Elizabeth rivers) that had been feared to be an indication of an enemy offensive on Norfolk, or up the Virginia Peninsula, had instead sailed into the Atlantic. Benjamin was convinced that the enemy's destination was Port Royal Sound and the barrier island of Hilton Head, South Carolina. Southern land forces in and around that superb anchorage and rich area of the country were spread thin and the naval forces were virtually non-existent. With Federal amphibious expeditions already enjoying limited successes, this news aroused fear from every quarter. A sufficient Federal force landing would be able to wreck the important Charleston and Savannah Railroad, and Benjamin wanted Lee to ascertain as to the seriousness of the trouble he believed was afoot.[196]

"We learn that General Robert E. Lee left this city yesterday morning for Beaufort, South Carolina. He was accompanied by several naval officers, and is charged with the command of the coast defences south of Virginia."

The Richmond Daily Dispatch, November 7, 1861

Courtesy Library of Congress

Judah P. Benjamin

194 McCaslin, *Lee in the Shadow of Washington*, p. 91; Freeman, *R. E. Lee*, vol. 1, p. 603; Jones, *Personal Reminiscences of General Robert E. Lee*, p. 168.
195 *Official Records*, Series I, vol. 1, "An Act to Provide for the Establishment and Organization of the Army of the C. S. A.," 6 March 1861; *Southern Historical Society Papers*, vol. 20, "Davis and Johnston:…How Lee Came to be Put over [Joseph E.] Johnston," p. 95-108.
196 Robert E. Lee, Jr., *Recollections and Letters*, Robert E. Lee to His Wife, November 5, 1861,

President Davis recognized the vulnerability of the Southern coast. He knew that Federal possession of Port Royal Sound offered the enemy a superb refueling and refitting station for blockading squadrons, as well as a base that posed a dagger aimed at Charleston, Savannah and the heart of one of the richest cotton districts in the South. Realizing that he had to do something, and fast, to demonstrate that the central government would try and protect all potentially threatened parts of the new republic, Davis thought the best way to counter the news of the Federal move on Port Royal Sound was to order Lee to South Carolina with the mission to improve coastal defenses. Furthermore, Davis decided to organize the area as a single administrative department.[197]

The morning after Lee met with Benjamin, the general went to have another conference with the President. News had arrived confirming what Benjamin had feared. A Federal quartermaster's steamer named Union, "one of the fleet," had run aground about 16 miles from Fort Macon on the night of the 2nd after a heavy gale had scattered the Federal ships. From its wreckage, the Confederates had rounded up 73 prisoners, and they admitted that the Federal expeditionary force of 75 warships and transports under Admiral Samuel F. DuPont carrying more than 12,000 infantry and artillerists under Brigadier General Thomas W. Sherman were "destined for Port Royal." Davis believed that such news demanded presidential action, and before the conference ended, he had decided what to do: Lee would immediately depart for South Carolina "for the purpose of directing and supervising the construction of a line of defense along the southern coast" of the newly-created Department of South Carolina, Georgia and East Florida. Fully aware of the intensely independent and provincial nature of the Southern governors, Lee suspected that Francis Pickens of South Carolina and Joseph E. Brown of Georgia would bristle at the idea of having their state troops ordered about by a general outside their respective state control. Further, Lee had no desire to repeat the command fiasco he had been forced to endure in western Virginia. Lee, therefore, modestly and tactfully insisted that Davis define what position he would hold, and with what authority he was entrusted. Davis instantly responded, telling Lee that he would go as a full general of the regular army of the Confederate States, the senior officer of the new department, with complete authority to command, and do so with the support of the central government.[198]

Courtesy Harpers Weekly

Charleston, South Carolina

p. 46; Freeman, *R. E. Lee*, vol. 1, p. 606; *Official Records*, Series I, vol. 51, part 2, Supplement, J. P. Benjamin to R. C. Gatlin, October 28, 1861, p. 360; the Federal fleet arrived on November 3rd, see *Official Records*, Series I, vol. 6, "Circular" dated November 4, 1861, and report of R. Saxton to Brigadier General Thomas W. Sherman, November 9, 1861, pp. 185-187; and J. P. Benjamin to Governor Pickens, November 9, 1861, p. 313.

[197] *Official Records*, Series I, vol. 5, Jefferson Davis to Joseph E. Johnston, September 8, 1861, pp. 833-834, and *Official Records*, Series I, vol. 6, "Special Orders, No. 206," XII, p. 309.

[198] Freeman, *R. E. Lee*, vol. 1, p. 607; *Official Records*, Series I, vol. 51, vol. 2, Supplement, R. C. Gatlin to S. Cooper, November 4, 1861, p. 369; Robert E. Lee, Jr., *Recollections and Letters*, p. 46; *Official Records*, Series I, vol. 6, "Special Orders, No. 206," XII, p. 309.

Lee possessed familiarity with the southern coast, especially Savannah. His first assignment as a young Brevet Lieutenant in the antebellum army had been to assist in preparing the foundation for a "third system fort" of what became Fort Pulaski on Cockspur Island, at the mouth of the Savannah River. Lee departed Richmond on a rainy Wednesday, November 6th. Leaving on such short notice cancelled any hope he had in seeing his wife who was then visiting "Shirley" on the James River. He considered it "a grievous disappointment" to have missed Mary, but duty demanded otherwise.[199]

As General Lee arrived in Charleston on the morning of November 7th, it might have seemed strange to an observer that one of the Confederacy's five full generals and new department commander got off the train accompanied by only a single officer: Lieutenant Walter Taylor, the remaining member of his military household from the prior campaign. Operating a military department demanded a larger staff, and upon his arrival, Lee initially named four other men, all members of the noblesse: Captain Thornton A. Washington became departmental assistant adjutant-general, having served General Twiggs in similar duties that Lee observed from his days with the 2nd Cavalry. Well educated, Washington had attended Princeton before graduating from West Point in 1849. Lee appointed Captain Joseph Christmas Ives as his chief engineer, another West Pointer of the Class of 1852, already famous as a topographical engineer and renowned explorer of the Colorado River. Lieutenant Colonel William G. Gill became Lee's ordnance officer, and civilian volunteer aide-de-camp, Joseph Manigault, would further assist the general.[200]

Courtesy Harpers Weekly

Charleston and Savannah Railroad through the Swamps

The following day, the small entourage took a special train to Coosawhatchie, the station on the Charleston and Savannah Railroad nearest to

---

[199] Krick, *Civil War Weather in Virginia*, p. 40; Robert E. Lee, Jr., *Recollections and Letters*, Robert E. Lee to His Wife, November 18, 1861, pp. 46-47; *The Richmond Examiner*, November 7, 1861, p. 3, col. 1. For details on Lee's duty on Cockspur Island, and his role in the construction of what became Fort Pulaski, please see: Thomas, *Robert E. Lee*, pp. 57-59. At the time of its construction, "third system forts" were masonry in construction and widely considered as invincible. The advent of rifled artillery would drastically alter that perspective.

[200] *Official Records*, Series I, vol. 6, "General Orders, No. 1," November 8, 1861; *Official Records*, Series II, vol. 1, Earl Van Dorn to L. P. Walker, March 26, 1861, p. 38; Freeman, *R. E. Lee*, vol. 1, Appendix I-4, "The Staff of General Lee, Third Period—The South Carolina Operations," pp. 640-641; *Richmond Daily Dispatch*, November 8, 1861, p. 3, col. 6, from Charleston, Nov. 7, "Gen. Lee arrived this morning;" *Southern Historical Society Papers*, vol. 30, "Graduates of the United States Military Academy at West Point, N. Y., Who Served in the Confederate States Army....", pp. 34-76; *Southern Historical Society Papers*, vol. 35, "Officers of Gen. R. E. Lee's Staff," pp. 25-28; *Southern Historical Society Papers*, vol. 38, "List of General Officers and Their Staffs in the Confederate Army....", pp. 156-183; Robert E. L. Krick, *Staff Officers in Gray: A Biographical Register of the Staff Officers in the Army of Northern Virginia* (Chapel Hill, 2003), pp. 297, 329, 335 and 342; Walter Taylor, *Lee's Adjutant: The Wartime Letters of Colonel Walter Herron Taylor, 1862-1865*, edited by R. Lockwood Tower (Columbia, 1995), p. 9. General Lee had the habit of calling Taylor "Captain," referring to Taylor's rank in the Provisional Army, although he was only a first lieutenant of infantry in the Regular Army of the Confederate States. Taylor was officially promoted to the rank of captain on December 10, 1861.

Port Royal Sound. After finding the officer commanding the few Confederate troops in the vicinity, Lee learned that the Federals already occupied Port Royal and had overwhelmed two nearby forts with firepower. (That brief contest graphically illustrated how the war pitted brother against brother. The Confederate land forces defending forts Walker and Beauregard were commanded by Brigadier General Thomas F. Drayton; his brother, Commander Percival Drayton, held command of the Federal steamer Pocohontas that took part in the attack on these forts.) Once Lee arrived, he issued orders to area troops before returning to the "decrepit and deserted village" of Coosawhatchie, where he established his headquarters in an abandoned house. With time short for preparing the defense of the area, Lee immediately went to work on analyzing his scant resources and how best to utilize them.[201]

One of the more famous Florida flags

Lee's mission meant cobbling together a defense plan for a department with a coastline over 360 miles long from South Carolina southward to the mouth of the Saint Johns River in northeastern Florida. Georgetown, South Carolina, represented the most important spot in this stretch. The historic seaport on Winyah Bay at the confluence of the Pee Dee River, Waccamaw River, and Sampit River ranked as one of the largest rice exporting ports in the world; its protection added another 60 miles of coastline that ran from the North Carolina border to below Georgetown. Further southward, a series of sounds and bays included a multitude of islands that, in 1861, represented the home to some of the most wealthy and powerful rice planters and "sea-island" cotton growers in the South. In addition to these plantations, Lee's responsibilities included the city of Charleston with all its symbolic importance, as well as the rich seaport of Savannah, Georgia, from which the Confederacy shipped thousands of bales of cotton to world markets. The critically important 100 mile-long Charleston and Savannah Railroad connected these two cities. This stretch of track ran across dozens of bridges and "a number of rivers that could be ascended by light vessels to within a few miles of the railroad bridges." With the Federals in complete control of the waterways, Lee knew that their naval task forces combining heavy ships and gunboats could control deeper channels as well as probe the upper stretches of the rivers. Whenever the numerous and unwelcome Federal ships chose to appear, Confederate naval vessels in the area numbered a paltry "four converted steamers, armed with two guns each."[202]

Lee also found out that about 12,000 Southern land forces within his new department had been spread thin to mollify the planter-*élite* who insisted on their property being protected. Adhering to the assumption that the military cost of a pragmatically useless defensive presence still had redeeming political value, South Carolina Governor Francis Pickens and Georgia Governor Joseph E. Brown parceled out their state-controlled troops in answer to the call from every quarter for protection. In truth, the mostly ill-equipped and often marginally-trained regiments scattered here and there all along the coast and supported by "scarcely any efficient field artillery," were incapable of stopping even a modest Federal raiding force. Furthermore, the Confederates in the department lacked cavalry and transport. Those wants—coupled with the

---

[201] *Official Records*, Series I, vol. 6, Report of Brigadier-General Thomas F. Drayton, November 24, 1861, pp. 6-13; By December, Commander Drayton commanded the gunboat *Pawnee*. See: *Official Records*, Series I, vol. 6, T. W. Sherman to Lorenzo Thomas, December 22, 1861, p. 210; Taylor, *General Lee*, pp. 39-40; Freeman, *R. E. Lee*, vol. 1, pp. 608-609; Dowdey, *Lee*, p. 175.

[202] Freeman, *R. E. Lee*, vol. 1, p. 609.

news of the small and ineffective sea island forts Walker and Beauregard being silenced the day before his arrival—did not bode well for attempts to challenge landings within gun range of Federal ships, or for that matter, the fate of other permanent fortifications and static garrisons that the Federal fleet wished to bring within gun range. With the Federals possessing the means and the initiative to move unchecked by water and bring the firepower necessary to secure their landing, Lee recognized that the enemy could strike quickly up river and, under the cover of gunboats, wreck havoc almost at will. A strike at the Charleston and Savannah Railroad loomed inevitable.[203]

Top: South Carolina Bank Note
Bottom: South Carolina $2 Rail Ticket

The alarming state of affairs required a new system of defense, clearly delineated and decisively executed. Lee would have to personally inspect the coastal defenses to come up with specifics, but before he could do that, he instinctively sketched out what he knew had to be done. First, intelligence gathering had to start, and fast. Lee instructed one of the local general officers "to push the cavalry as close to the enemy as may be prudent, to watch his movements and circumscribe his operations." Second, the inland passes to Charleston had to be closed and the other waterways leading inland that the Federals were likely to send their forces on raids had to be obstructed. Third, the batteries and forts protecting Charleston, Savannah and other places along the waterways needed to be strengthened. However, the multitude of approaches from the sea meant there were not "enough guns with enough range to cover every channel, sound, and creek." Fourth, rather than present the Federals with an easily pierced defensive shell, Lee called for a mobile defense. This last concept required the previously scattered Confederate formations not manning forts or field works to be withdrawn from the barrier islands and concentrated further inland and thus out of range of Federal gunboats, but close to the points most likely for the Federals to strike at the Charleston and Savannah Railroad. Ordering these measures, Lee called for activity on every level. He admonished his subordinates that "the enemy's fleet. . . may visit your coast at any time" and that "every measure must be taken to prevent the enemy using the inland navigation … and all the armed troops" in South Carolina and Georgia must be "brought into the field."[204]

---

[203] *Official Records*, Series I, vol. 6, Robert E. Lee to J. P. Benjamin, November 9, 1861, pp. 312-313; Freeman, *R. E. Lee*, vol. 1, pp. 609-610. Also see in *Official Records*, Series I, vol. 6, "Abstract from monthly returns of the Department of Georgia…for October, 1861," on pages 304-305; Governor Pickens exaggerated returns of South Carolina troops in the department in his November 19, 1861, letter to Robert E. Lee on p. 326 of the same volume, and Thos. F. Drayton's "indorsement" (sic) on page 331.

[204] *Official Records*, Series I, vol. 53, Supplement, Robert E. Lee to Secretary of War [J. P. Benjamin], November 11, 1816, p. 186; Robert E. Lee to Thomas F. Drayton, November 11, 1861, p. 186, Robert E. Lee to A. R. Lawton, November 11, 18161, pp. 186-187, and Robert E.

While Lee's plan of defense provided for the greater good of the department's defense, the most powerful members of the noblesse reacted angrily when they heard the news that their tidal plantations would now be at the mercy of the enemy. The Federals did not waste much time in taking advantage of the situation. "The vicissitudes of war" fell upon countless islands and plantations as Federal raiding parties conducted predatory excursions against civilian property. Lee suffered to hear of these deprivations, but his concern rested in defending the vital points in his department. To many influential persons in South Carolina and Georgia, the man labeled as "Granny" Lee, a failure in western Virginia, the man who would withdraw troops from posts guarding rich plantations, was not the man to conduct a vigorous defense of the Southern Atlantic coast. Their complaints to Richmond— some registered before Lee ever stepped off the train in Charleston—prompted Davis to defend his decision in sending Lee and advised governors Pickens and Brown of his confidence in the new department commander.   Surprisingly, the usually cantankerous Brown supported Lee (probably out of relief that he did not have to answer for those difficult choices), and he told Davis that he held Lee in "highest confidence." Two weeks after Lee's arrival, and following his tour of the meandering tidal streams, wide channels and numerous sounds bounded by salt marshes, Lee had determined where best to set up his coastal defenses. He reported his findings—all of which validated his plan on how to best defend the department—during a three-day meeting with Governor Pickens. From those meetings held November 13th-15th, Pickens criticized Lee's plan of defense as "over caution."[205]

Courtesy Harpers Weekly

Top: Fort Pulaski
Bottom: Fort Pulaski

Lee recognized how his talents were being utilized. Writing on November 15th to his youngest daughter, Mildred, who was then at school in Winchester, Virginia, Lee thought that the mission Davis had assigned him was: "another forlorn hope expedition. Worse than West Virginia." A week later in another letter written to two other daughters, Agnes and Ann ("Annie"), Lee lamented that: "It is difficult to get our people to realize their [desperate] position." Nevertheless, Lee pushed forward with his mission and the implementation of his plan. Making haste, Lee constantly rode in the field supervising the work and inspecting the troops. Often traveling on horseback as much as 35 miles

---

Lee to Colonel Dilworth, November 12, 1861, p. 187; Thomas, *Robert E. Lee*, p. 212.
[205] Jefferson Davis, *Rise and Fall of the Confederate Government*, 2 volumes (New York, 1881), vol. 1, p. 437; Robert E. Lee, Jr., *Recollections and Letters*, To Annie, December 8, 1861, p. 49; William C. Davis, *Jefferson Davis*, p. 382. South Carolina Governor Pickens was critical of the central government and the army leadership In Virginia for the lack of activity by principal army following the victory at Manassas. Pickens argued that it was the lack of activity by Joe Johnston as the reason why the Federals believed it possible they could send expeditionary forces to South Carolina, rather than using them to defend Washington. Pickens certainly had a valid point.

a day, Lee's grueling work schedule stretched from early morning "till eleven or twelve o'clock at night."[206]

One of the horses that carried Lee on his duties was a handsome colt that had first caught the general's eye only weeks earlier in western Virginia during the Sewell Mountain campaign. The horse had won two first prizes at the Lewisburg (Greenbrier County) fairs in 1859 and 1860. A powerfully-sized animal, standing 16-hands high, with a muscular figure that complimented his beautiful iron-gray coat with black points, mane, and long tail, caused Lee to say of him: "Such a picture would inspire a poet." Lee thought he had seen the last of the horse when he departed western Virginia, but when the owner of the colt was transferred with his unit, the 60th Virginia, from western Virginia to South Carolina in the late fall of 1861, he took the horse with him and their paths again crossed with General Lee. When the general saw the horse near Pocotaligo, South Carolina, he had reacted the same as he had whenever he saw the horse in western Virginia: Lee playfully referred to the horse as "my colt." The owner knew the general really liked the animal, and offered him as a gift. Lee could not accept a gift as valuable as a horse; he instead bought him for $200, and shortly thereafter renamed him Traveller.[207]

In the course of commanding his department, Lee needed more qualified officers for his staff. The most notable of the additions was Major Armistead Lindsay Long, formerly of General Loring's staff, who impressed Lee during

Lee on Traveller   *Courtesy Library of Congress*

the Cheat Mountain campaign. Lee took a liking to Long: a fellow Virginian and West Pointer, Class of 1850, Lee appreciated his elegant manners, articulate speech and intelligence. Long had dark hair and his finely-trimmed moustache exuded a somewhat dandified aura. Like Lee, his family was torn by the war, as his father-in-law was Federal Brigadier General Edwin V. Sumner. Prior to resigning his commission on June 10th, 1861, Long had spent his army career as an artillerist and trained under the gifted Henry Hunt, his life-long friend and the future artillery commander

---

206 Robert E. Lee, Jr., *Recollections and Letters,* Robert E. Lee To Mildred, November 15, 1861, p. 47; Robert E. Lee To Agnes and Annie, November 22, 1861, p. 48; Robert E. Lee To His Wife, December 25, 1861, p. 51; *Official Records,* Series I, vol. 6, Robert E. Lee to S. Cooper, November 21, 1861, p. 327; Freeman, *R. E. Lee,* vol. 1, p. 615.

207 *Southern Historical Society Papers,* vol. 19, "General Lee's War Horses," pp. 333-335; vol. 35, "General Lee's War Horse: A Sketch of Traveller by the Man who Formerly Owned Him," by Thomas L. Broun, pp. 99-101; *Richmond Daily Dispatch,* Aug. 10, 1886, "General Lee's War-Horse," by Thomas L. Broun, as published in McKinney, *Robert E. Lee at Sewell Mountain,* Appendix "A," pp. 117-119; Blake A. Magner, *Traveller & Company: The Horses of Gettysburg* (Gettysburg, 1995), pp. 4-5. Before Lee obtained the animal, it was named "Jeff Davis." The horse was turned into a gelding.

of the Federal Army of the Potomac. In addition to all these attributes, Long's astute eye for terrain in the placement of artillery, as well as his overall professionalism during the western Virginia expedition, earned Lee's confidence.[208]

While Lee was on the southeastern Atlantic coast, on November 8th, 1861, the Federal navy fired on and intercepted the British steamer *Trent* out of Havana, Cuba, that was carrying Confederate commissioners John Slidell and James M. Mason. An armed crew of Federals went aboard and forcibly removed Slidell and Mason from the ship. The commissioners were bound for Britain and France to press for diplomatic recognition from those European powers. Many in the South received the news with indignation and satisfaction, believing that Britain would certainly do more than file a protest. The press inflamed the incident, with the Northern papers flaunting its perceived rights and the Southern papers doing the same and stirring emotions as far away as Europe. With the time approaching that cotton supplies were projected to be exhausted (February, 1862), the Trent Affair was seen by many in the South as the catalyst for Britain's intervention—and the Confederacy's salvation.[209]

Robert E. Lee held out no general expectations for foreign salvation, and placed no faith that the conflated *Trent* incident would change things. Although the incident became a difficult one for the Lincoln administration to handle, Lee held to his previously-stated beliefs. "You must not build your hopes on peace on account of the United States going to war with England," Lee wrote his wife on Christmas day, 1861. "She will be very loath to do that, notwithstanding the bluster of the Northern papers. Her rulers are not entirely mad, and if they find England is in earnest, and that war or a restitution of their captives must be the consequence, they will adopt the latter. We must make up our minds to fight our battles and win our independence alone. *No one will help us* [emphasis added]. We require no extraneous aid, if true to ourselves …"[210]

Lee continued to persevere with the implementation of his defense plans, but foresaw what would happen when the Federals struck. Despite an increase in the number of troops in the department, too many "deep estuaries, all accessible to their ships" provided avenues along the coast. "The strength of the enemy, as far as I am able to judge," Lee told Governor Pickens on December 27th, "exceeds the whole force that we have in the State. It can be thrown with great celerity against any point, and far outnumbers any force we can bring against it in the field." Pickens eventually seemed to appreciate Lee's efforts, but, in the midst of hot-blooded times, Pickens and others thought Lee's *sangfroid* ill-suited for a revolutionary. When Brigadier General Roswell S. Ripley made public, derogatory remarks about Lee, Pickens incredulously told President Davis that Lee was culpable for Ripley's disrespect. Lee is "all that a gentleman should be," Pickens wrote Davis, but because he was "quiet and retiring," and this "reserve" was interpreted by some "disadvantageously."[211]

---

[208] Long, *Memoirs of Robert E. Lee*, p. 134; Freeman, *R. E. Lee*, vol. 1, Appendix I-4, "The Staff of General Lee, Third Period—The South Carolina Operations," p. 640; Chesnut, *Mary Chesnut's Civil War*, p. 101; *Official Records*, Series I, vol. 6, Robert E. Lee to J. C. Pemberton, March 14, 1862, pp. 406-407. Long arrived in Charleston on December 11, 1861, and reported to General Lee just as the great fire of that date was spreading.

[209] *Encyclopedia of the Confederacy*, vol. 4, "*Trent* Affair," pp. 1619-1621.

[210] Robert E. Lee, Jr., *Recollections and Letters*, To His Wife, December 25, 1861, pp. 51-52.

[211] Lee penned many letters about the situation facing him in defending the Southeastern coast. For a few examples, please consult: Dowdey and Manarin, *The Wartime Papers of Robert E. Lee*, To Judah P. Benjamin, February 10, 1862, No. 110, p. 112, To Joseph E. Brown, February 10, 1862, No. 111, p. 113, To General Nathan G. Evans, February 15, 1862, No. 112, p. 114, and To General Henry C. Wayne, February 15, 1862, No. 113, p. 114; Robert E. Lee, Jr., *Recollections and Letters*, To Annie, December 8, 1861, p. 49; *Official Records*, Series I, vol.

In the course of the four frustrating months he spent on the Southeastern coast, Lee repeatedly demonstrated the value of his cool level-headedness. He realistically assessed subjects ranging from the capability of staff officers to that of troop formations, and from scouting terrain to dictating engineering tasks. Lee also disclosed his talents for diplomacy as well as exercising authority, whether it was dealing with, as described by Dowdey, "the outrage of citizen-soldiers whose ideals of chivalric war he offended, [or] the plantation princelings and the city dandies [who] found digging with picks and shovels alien to the pageantries of war," or the Ohioan-turned-South Carolinian, Roswell Ripley, the South Carolina district commander, who was "as contumacious as Loring had been." However, whereas Lee in western Virginia had to use courteous suggestions and amiable exchanges in absence of authority, here he commanded, and Ripley consequently "received the same treatment as any soldier."[212]

When it came to the execution of his duties, Lee went about his business with an innate authority inherent in his presence that gave reassurance to men who had been uprooted from their previous lives to serve The Cause. Nevertheless, as the weeks passed, Lee remained anxious about the progress of the defenses lest the Federals attack. Writing from Savannah to Mary on February 8th, the general privately admitted: "I have more here than I can do…It is so very hard to get anything done, and while all wish well and mean well, it is so different to get them to act energetically and promptly…The news from Kentucky and Tennessee is not favorable, but we must make up our minds to meet with reverses and overcome them. I hope God will at last crown our efforts with success. But the contest must be long and severe, and the whole country has to go through much suffering. It is necessary we should be humbled."[213]

Real War Begins

"While Lee was struggling with inertia, incompetence, and a multitude of troublesome duties," wrote Douglas Southall Freeman, "the Confederate cause elsewhere had suffered two disasters." On February 6th, 1862, while Lee was in Savannah attending to matters of his department, almost 600 miles to the west the Federals captured Fort Henry, a poorly-designed, earthen structure on the lower Tennessee River, which sliced into western Tennessee. Partially-flooded and mounting outdated guns, the undermanned fort was doomed. Ten days later, nearby Fort Donelson fell. That fort, located at Dover, Tennessee, sat on the Cumberland River 10 miles from Henry along the stretch where the Cumberland paralleled the Tennessee River as the rivers enter the state. Donelson had been invested by Federal land and flotilla forces a week following the capture of Fort Henry. After two days of fighting, most of the 15,000-man Confederate garrison surrendered on February 16th to a

---

6, Robert E. Lee to Francis W. Pickens, December 27, 1861, pp. 356-357. Lee specifically told Pickens that garrisons for the forts and static field works that were not mobile formations were "not therefore included in the force for operations in the field." Lee told Samuel Cooper of the impracticality of defending Brunswick, Georgia, in Dowdey and Manarin, *The Wartime Papers of Robert E. Lee*, Robert E. Lee To General Samuel Cooper, February 18, 1862, No. 114, p. 115; *Official Records*, Series I, vol. 6, F. W. Pickens to President Davis, January 7, 1862, p. 366.

[212] Dowdey, *Lee*, pp. 178-179.

[213] Robert E. Lee, Jr., *Recollections and Letters*, Robert E. Lee To His Wife, February 8, 1862, pp. 55-56.

no-nonsense Federal general named Ulysses Simpson Grant. With the fall of these forts, two major water transportation routes—the Cumberland River and the Tennessee River—bounded in the east by the Appalachian Mountains and in the west by the Mississippi River, were opened into the heartland of Tennessee and the Confederate west. These became principal water highways for the movement of Federal troops and materiel. Furthermore, the fall of the river forts severed Kentucky from potentially joining the Confederacy as well as exposed much

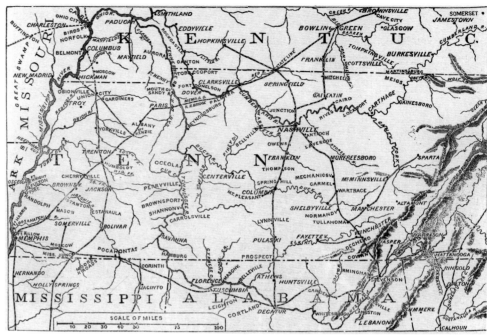

Courtesy Harpers Weekly

The Confederate Heartland

of Tennessee to Federal occupation. Nashville became uncovered, and on February 25th, 1862, the first state capital of the Confederacy fell. Aside from the loss of morale and having the state government flee to Memphis, the tangible loss of Nashville's railroad hub, 73 factories and major supply depots marked a notable blow to the Confederate western war effort.[214]

As the Federal offensive opened in the west, another overpowering Federal combined operation launched in the east. Naval and land forces descended on strategically located Roanoke Island, the key to the inland waters of North Carolina. On February 8th, Federal forces overwhelmed Henry Wise's 3,000 men, killing the son of the ex-governor while also rendering *hors de combat* two-thirds of the Confederate command. The victory gave the Federals control of the mouth of Albemarle Sound, at the confluence of the

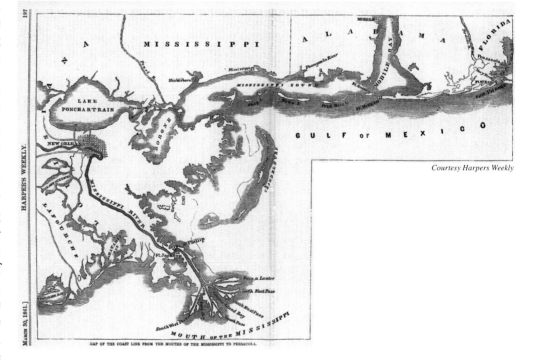

Courtesy Harpers Weekly

New Orleans Gulf Coast

Chowan and Roanoke rivers. Lee recognized that the effect of the Henry and Donelson defeats, combined with what the Federals had already accomplished along the coast, meant, according to one historian, that "most of Virginia east of the Chesapeake and west of the Shenandoah was in Yankee hands," and that the Federal navy was tightening its blockade grip on the South.[215]

---

214 Freeman, *R. E. Lee*, vol. 1, p. 625; *Encyclopedia of the Confederacy*, vol. 3, p. 1107.
215 Furgurson, *Ashes of Glory*, p. 111.

News of these reverses reverberated throughout the South, and morale plunged. The early-war Confederate victories at Big Bethel, Ball's Bluff, and, especially Manassas, had lifted morale so unrealistically high, that when substantial reverses followed, morale dropped precipitously. "Disasters seem to be thickening around us," Lee wrote to his wife on February 23rd. "It calls for renewed energies and redoubled strength on our part." Indeed, the losses of Henry, Donelson and Roanoke publicly exposed Confederate inability to counter Federal combined operations. In response to these reverses, the Confederate War Department redeployed troop formations to replace those lost in Tennessee. Lee's department soon sent 4,000 men traveling west for duty with Albert Sidney Johnston's army. As these troops were being reassigned, Lee called upon those who remained to step up their efforts. However, he was not satisfied with those he described to his daughter Annie as "slow workmen," or with those who thought that manual labor was beneath them and "endeavored to prove that they ought to do nothing." Lee was especially anxious about the Savannah sector, where the Federals were slowly girding up for their long-expected offensive. The general went about his business evaluating new defensive measures, monitoring existing projects such as the obstruction of waterways, while ordering a further pull back of troops for better concentration (while exposing more private property in the process), all of which was for a better defense of the department.[216]

One evening after finishing letters to Mary and his daughter Annie about the critical state of affairs facing the Confederacy, Lee received the following telegram:

Richmond, Virginia, March 2, 1862.

General R. E. Lee,
Savannah:

If circumstances will, in your judgment, warrant your leaving, I wish to see you here with the least delay.

....

Jefferson Davis.[217]

Davis' succinct telegram contained obvious urgency. After making arrangements for most of his staff to continue the work not yet completed, Lee wrote detailed instructions on March 3rd, urging the department commander in Georgia "that the work at every point should be pushed forward with the utmost vigor and the closest attention given to the whole subject of the defense of [Savannah]." Then, taking along Walter Taylor as the sole member of his

---

[216] Furgurson, *Ashes of Glory*, p. 111; Robert E. Lee, Jr., *Recollections and Letters*, Robert E. Lee To Annie, March 2, 1862, p. 57; *Official Records*, Series I, vol. 6, J. P. Benjamin to Robert E. Lee, February 18, 1862, p. 390; Robert E. Lee to S. Cooper, February 18, 1862, p. 390; Robert E. Lee to Joseph E. Brown, February 18, 1862, p. 391; Robert E. Lee to J. H. Trapier, February 19, 1862, pp. 393-394; Robert E. Lee to R. S. Ripley, February 19, 1862, p. 394; Robert E. Lee to N. G. Evans, February 20, 1862, pp. 394-395; Robert E. Lee to John C. Pemberton, February 20, 1862, p. 395; J. P. Benjamin to Robert E. Lee, February 24, 1862, p. 398; Robert E. Lee to J. H. Trapier, February 24, 1862, pp. 398-399. For the Federal preparations to attack Savannah, please see: *Official Records*, Series I, vol. 6, T. W. Sherman to the Adjutant-General, February 15, 1862, p. 226; T. W. Sherman to George B. McClellan, February 23, 1862, p. 235; W. T. Sherman to the Adjutant-General, February 27, 1862, pp. 235-236.

[217] *Official Records*, Series I, vol. 6, Jefferson Davis to Robert E. Lee, March 2, 1862, p. 400..

military household, Robert E. Lee boarded the train on the evening of the 3rd, reached Charleston the next day, then departed for Richmond on Wednesday, March 5th. On the train ride to his home state, Robert E. Lee must have wondered if President Davis had in mind for him some sort of duty more meaningful than his last two assignments.[218]

Courtesy Old State House Museum

"Dallas Artillery" Flag

Confederate Envelope

218 *Official Records*, Series I, vol. 6, Robert E. Lee to A. R. Lawton, March 3, 1862, pp. 401-402; *Charleston Mercury*, March 5, 1862.

Lee's Wasted Year—
Summary and Analysis of His Use and Performance, April 1861 to April 1862

Based on Lee's writings and communiqués to family members, Lee, a realist to the core, even in his self-assessment, believed that Jefferson Davis had dramatically curtailed his ability to contribute to the conduct of the war. After all, Lee had rejected command of the new Federal army being formed around Washington City, which amounted to the highest field command of the most important army in Federal Service. Contrasting that offer to Lee's employment status south of the Potomac is shocking. Instead of Virginia's heralded favorite son being placed in a position of command, whereby he could begin molding an army and its staff to meet the Federal onslaught, the best President Davis could do was to send Lee to western Virginia in a role analogous to a modern-day consultant. Subsequent to Lee's not being able to achieve the near impossible absent authority, Davis then entrusted Lee to oversee the southeastern coast. Lee essentially had to administer the bad news of the Confederacy's military reality to a deluded planter-aristocracy who were bringing pressure on both state and central government politicians to protect their property. In assigning these tasks, Davis found in Lee the one man who could perform thankless tasks without letting his ego and exaggerated sense of honor get in the way. With failure all but ensured in western Virginia, Lee and his military reputation would surely suffer, ironically relieving Davis of any pressure to otherwise utilize Lee's skills. Not until the Confederacy had suffered irremediable triple disasters did Davis yield to the outcry of the Confederate Congress and recall Lee—who, had proven he could suffer failure silently in order to start earning Davis' trust—and even then Davis failed to place Lee in a fitting command. Only a Federal bullet along with a fragment from an artillery shell would eventually turn Lee's career around from Davis' incompetent squandering of Lee's leadership.

Courtesy RW Norton Gallery

**Portrait of Jefferson Davis
by Benjamin Franklin Reinhardt**

Historians have long dodged this one question that begs to be answered fully: why did Jefferson Davis employ Robert E. Lee in the manner that he did for almost one full year when the man Winfield Scott declared as the antebellum army's "finest soldier" had been offered command of the principal Federal army? The answer must lie in four areas: the intense, personal animosity that existed for more than the previous dozen years between Jefferson Davis and Winfield Scott; Jefferson Davis' personal history with Robert E. Lee; Jefferson Davis' awareness of his military record when compared to Robert E. Lee from the time both attended West Point; and the deep recesses of Jefferson Davis' tortured ego.

The slightly built President hailing from Mississippi with prominent cheek bones, thin lips and deep-set eyes, who carried himself with an unnatural—yet somehow dignified—stiffness and had a personality described by one biographer as "priggish," exuded a haughty air and severe manner of mind that could be both indecisive and stubbornly inflexible at the same time. Davis considered his achievements as the stuff of legend. After all, he was a graduate of West Point, a Mexican War hero, a former United States Senator and Secretary of War. While in Montgomery after the formation of the Confederacy, and following Virginia's secession, his sycophants had wired and written him more than a few times that he was the only man that could save the Confederacy by coming and taking over preparations for war in Richmond because Robert E. Lee wasn't doing things to their satisfaction. And he believed it. Certainly, those who were not as impressed with Davis walked a fine line at offending the new President. Once he was offended, he harbored that offense for a long time. This meant that in almost any circumstance whereby someone might possibly say or do something that Davis might construe as an act less than that of total fealty, he took it personally.[219]

Despite his flaws, Davis became the region's leading advocate after the passing of John C. Calhoun. Whereas Calhoun evolved his aggressive states' rights stand by perceiving state independence as the only way to insure the South with protection against growing Northern financial domination, Davis generally glossed over the broader economic reasons for his position. As the spokesman for the cotton princes, Davis advocated aristocratic guidance within the Democratic system of government, for he believed in the superiority of the planter-*élite* class adamantly, but in a different way than Royalists believed in the divine right of kings. Clifford Dowdey described the difference: "the Stuarts were born to their belief; Davis learned his," and this impacted his later interaction with Lee. Davis hardened his attitude while in grief and seclusion following the death of his first wife, the daughter of Zachary Taylor. According to Dowdey, Jefferson Davis "was as touchy about his opinions as a reformed madam about her respectability, and to attack his opinion was to attack him." Davis "knew nothing of the necessity of compromise, he did not admit its possibility." However, Davis was totally devoted and hard-working, and his tireless advocacy for states rights translated to most Southerners as honestly believing they had selected the right path in choosing secession. No one appeared more devoted to The Cause than Davis. Most Southerners initially believed Davis to be the perfect man to lead them. Confederate Vice President Alexander Stephens, on the other hand, never shared the common enthusiasm, and saw from the outset a man "weak and vacillating, timid, petulant, peevish [and] obstinate." Davis' public image proved deceptive. He frequently took bitter exception when he believed someone might be questioning him. In these occasions—and there were many—

Courtesy White House Historical Association, White House Collection: 64

**Portrait of Zachary Taylor
by Joseph Henry Bush**

Davis' true character flaws revealed, according to biographer William C. Davis, "the turmoil seething inside this terribly contained man." These deep-seated flaws included what the same biographer described as "vanity, obstinacy, imperiousness, pettiness, petulance, and more [that] all revealed their substantial presence in his makeup."[220]

* * *

Life has always had a way of opening or closing doors of opportunity based on a myriad of factors. Sometimes, these factors are a direct result of a person's actions or inactions. Sometimes, these factors are not a direct result of anything the person most affected does or has not done, but are simply due to circumstance, luck, or a combination thereof—that something referred to by William Shakespeare as "the slings and arrows of outrageous fortune." Usually, the doors of opportunity are intertwined with intricate, almost innumerable details involving careers and often wrapped around politics between individuals that developed as a result of alliances or clashes with others. It is necessary to recall some of these details in order to understand how all of it affected Robert E. Lee and his first year in Confederate uniform.[221]

---

[219] William C. Davis, *Jefferson Davis*, p. 38.
[220] Dowdey, *Experiment in Rebellion*, pp. 4, 6-7; William C. Davis, *Jefferson Davis*, pp. 172 and 230. For one example of Davis' emotions in this regard, please see the controversy between Davis and Mississippi's other senator, Henry S. Foote, beginning in 1847, in William C. Davis, *Jefferson Davis*, pp. 170-172.
[221] William Shakespeare, *Hamlet*, Act III, Scene 1.

Jefferson Davis served in the Mexican War under his former father-in-law, "Old Rough and Ready" Zachary Taylor (Davis had married Taylor's daughter a decade before, only for her to tragically die three months after the wedding). Up until early 1847, General Taylor and been friends with General Winfield Scott, but that friendship was torn asunder prior to Taylor's victory at Buena Vista. Davis, of course, closely identified with Taylor and so Davis believed as Taylor believed—that Scott was to blame for the breakup of the friendship when Scott assumed command of troops previously earmarked for Taylor's army (Scott claimed Taylor had moved his army too far away from him, and so it only made sense that he incorporate the troops into his command). With this incident, Davis' resentment of Winfield Scott seemed to grow in proportion equal to his loyalty to his former father-in-law. Thanks to Taylor, Davis returned from the war a hero of Buena Vista, and Davis intended to combine that status with his new political power to damage General Scott.

Courtesy United States Army Art Collection

Winfield Scott

The Mississippi legislature presented Davis with a sword of honor, and appointed him to fill an unexpired United Stated Senate seat. Davis went to Washington, where he soon became one of two Democratic senators loudly condemning Scott's conduct in a war in which the general had displayed nothing less than superb leadership in conducting one of the most remarkable campaigns in American military history, that being from Vera Cruz to Mexico City. President James K. Polk, also a Democrat, was persuaded by the condemnations and recalled General Scott, who, not coincidentally, had presidential aspirations as a member of the rival Whig political party. The purpose behind the recall of General Scott was transparent to many members of the army in Mexico. Colonel Ethan Allen Hitchcock wrote: "We all see the enormity of the conduct of the President—deplore and abhor it." Scott was forced to deal with a court of inquiry involving charges he had brought against subordinate officers when they broke army regulations by writing for civilian publications, among other specifications. Scott, however, had powerful political enemies, and through them the proceedings dragged on into the summer. Eventually, the verdict came down acquitting the subordinate officers that was described by historian John S. D. Eisenhower as "through the sheer manipulation of governmental power." While Scott was busy with these proceedings that included defending his honor and war record, the Whig presidential convention met, and Zachary Taylor was nominated as its candidate for the upcoming 1848 election. When Taylor won the presidency, Jefferson Davis escorted him to the inaugural ceremonies the following March 5th—a symbolic moment. Meanwhile, Scott believed that he had been done a gross injustice, and knew that Davis had played a major part in those events.[222]

Jeff Davis' roles in forcing Scott's recall from Mexico resulted in Scott ultimately being denied the Whig presidential bid in 1848. This proved to be but the opening of one of the most bitter personal feuds in American political history. In 1849, a Congressional bill called, in part, for Scott to be promoted to the rank of lieutenant general. No officer since George Washington had held that lofty rank and Davis fought the bill, making his personal vindictiveness a public spectacle. Then, in early 1851, with the aforementioned bill not yet passed, Congress introduced a resolution to confer upon General Scott the honorary title

---

[222] Eisenhower, *Agent of Destiny*, pp. 307-320. To read Davis' ungracious remarks about Scott's performance during the Mexican War, and why Davis did not believe Scott to be worthy of the honorary title, please see: William C. Davis, *Jefferson Davis*, p. 210. Also see Eisenhower, *Agent of Destiny*, p. 333.

of lieutenant general. Davis came out in opposition, making the invidious claim that Zachary Taylor's Mexican War achievements outweighed Scott's and that Scott had not earned such an honor. One wonders if Davis had read the Duke of Wellington's assessment of General Scott's campaign from Vera Cruz to Mexico City, claiming that Scott was "the greatest living general." In the petty opposition, Davis made a complete fool of himself. A year later, having learned nothing, Davis took on Scott again. The Whig party had Winfield Scott as its candidate for president (Taylor had died in office, and the Vice President, Millard Fillmore, who then became President, was cast aside in favor of Scott), and Davis was campaigning for one of his Democratic friends, Franklin Pierce. While on the stump, Davis made numerous uncomplimentary remarks about Scott. When Pierce won the election, Davis was rewarded for his role in the victory by being named as Secretary of War. On paper, Davis indeed had the credentials for the lofty office. However, rather than rise to the level of this assignment, and put the country above all, Davis used the new office as another platform for bedeviling Winfield Scott, and he wasted little time in manufacturing a controversy. "Old Fuss and Feathers" took the bait. Thus beginning in 1853, within months of taking the job, Davis initiated what became an unnecessary, long and nasty public feud with Scott over whether or not the general was due reimbursement for specific travel expenses in connection with the infamous Mexican War recall, as well as back pay for his rank as brevet lieutenant general, and more. For the next two years, the caustic fighting continued. Tempers boiled—in which Davis stooped to imply the ridiculous—that Scott was a thief and a coward. Finally, in 1855, Congress stepped up and sided with Scott, first granting him the rank of brevet lieutenant general from the bill that had been submitted in 1849, then passed a joint resolution appointing Scott with the permanent rank of lieutenant general, with full pay and allowance retroactive to March 29, 1847, the day Scott received the surrender at Vera Cruz. Scott won a signal victory in his war with Davis. Devastated and dejected, the Secretary of War acted so petulantly over the lost political battle that he refused to sign President Pierce's order.[223]

There had then been so much emotional blood spilled between these adversaries that there was no stopping it. Over the next six years, Scott and Davis continued to take swipes at each other in the press, some of it related to their old feud, and some of it over the growing sectional crisis. Not coincidentally, Scott held a diametrically opposite view of slavery and its expansion to new territories than Davis. Therefore, when Davis took the oath of office in Montgomery, Alabama, as President of the Confederate States of America on February 18, 1861, General Scott did not shy away from offering up his opinion. Scott called Davis "a Judas, who would betray Christ, the Apostles, and the whole Christian church" for political gain. None of what passed between Scott and himself ever escaped Jefferson Davis' memory.[224]

Unfortunately, the animus between Davis and Scott served to cloud Davis' personal relationship with Lee from the outset. Scott's lofty praise for Lee antagonized the sensitive ego of Davis. Objectively, Lee's war record exceeded that of Davis' record; Scott's comments, along with the praise in the Richmond papers and other places, stoked the Confederate President's insecurity and jealousy. Southern cultural factors, involving the two-fold nature of Southern aristocracy and the new President's social anxieties, further prejudiced Davis, who believed himself to be self-made, while Lee seemed to be the embodiment of the patrician. Up until the spring of 1861, Robert E. Lee's life had intersected with a great many other Americans who were part of forging the young nation. His extensive family ties, and his service in the army that included his close association with Winfield Scott had resulted in Lee being among the better known personalities of the antebellum army. If Dowdey saw Davis as having acquired his radical aristocratic beliefs rather than having been born to them, Lee inherited a sense of noblesse oblige, and did not share Davis' arrogance. The associations Lee formed with family, friends and army compatriots, beginning prior to his attendance at West Point and continuing in the army up to the time of Virginia's secession, all played a part in shaping Lee's life and his career opportunities. Thousands of Americans with whom General Winfield Scott had come in contact from the time the Mexican War concluded, through his presidential bid in 1852, and continuing with the army up and including the outbreak of hostilities with the Civil War, knew that he considered Robert E. Lee the soldier's soldier. Scott repeated his claims to everyone that Lee was largely responsible for the Mexican War's victorious outcome, and Lee foremost should be entrusted with the safety of the country should a foreign invader came to America's shores. Furthermore, Scott believed

---

[223] William C. Davis, *Jefferson Davis*, pp. 210, 229-231; Eisenhower, *Agent of Destiny*, pp. 332-333.
[224] Timothy E. Johnson, *Winfield Scott: Quest for Military Glory* (Lawrence, 1998), p. 224; Charles Winslow Elliott, *Winfield Scott: The Soldier and The Man* (New York, 1937), pp. 690-691.

Battle of Buena Vista by Carl Nebel

Lee would "prove himself the greatest captain in history" if ever given the opportunity, and he left no doubt as to Lee's deserving reputation among those in the social, military and political circles in which the influential Scott circulated. Given these facts, it is no exaggeration to assert that Scott considered Lee his protégé. Lincoln, who lacked military qualifications or expertise, eagerly listened to Scott and authorized the offer issued through Francis Preston Blair, Sr. for Lee to command the main Federal army. However, Lee's association with Scott did not have a positive effect on everyone, particularly the man so many would later claim was Lee's friend.[225]

In order to be a great leader, Davis should have been expected to set aside his personal prejudices. Indeed, it is difficult to determine what, if any, acts of friendship were made by Jefferson Davis to Robert E. Lee prior to Lee achieving fame as the commander of the Army of Northern Virginia. Davis' life and actions intersected with Lee's career on several distinct occasions up to the time of the Civil War. The first was when they attended West Point (Davis graduated in 1828; Lee graduated the following year). The second was in 1850 when Lee was working on Fort Carroll in Baltimore following the Mexican War when he found it necessary to travel to Washington to consult with Jefferson Davis, then a senator and chairman of the committee on military affairs. The third was when he was commandant of West Point and Davis was Secretary of War as the two worked on matters related to the academy between March, 1853, and March, 1855. The fourth time was during the Civil War.

During the first of these occasions, there does not seem to be any surviving letters from either Lee or Davis written while they were both at West Point that contained revealing references about the other. As cadets, however, they could not have contrasted more sharply. Lee's conduct and academic record at the academy were, and still are, legendary and exemplary; Davis' were not. The Mississippian's final standing

---

[225] *Southern Historical Society Papers*, Jones, "The Friendship Between Lee and Scott," vol. 11, p. 424; Scott Bowden and Bill Ward, *Last Chance for Victory*, pp. 67-70.

in his class was 23rd out of 33, and his conduct in the corps as a whole was 163rd out of 208. Davis never really wanted to attend West Point and only did so chiefly to appease and silence his brother Joseph; therefore, he lacked Lee's determination to excel. Davis' ego did not take well to discipline, and he resented authority to the point that his record of offenses repeatedly showed difficulty in taking orders. Perhaps it was his preference to exercise his spirit of independence that he did not suffer criticism well. Perhaps it was his obsession never to be in error that he denied wrongdoing, even when he was caught in the act, preferring instead to resort to bizarre technicalities to exonerate himself. Regardless, Davis came out of West Point an infantryman, as those who finished in the lower ranks of their classes at the academy always did during that era.[226]

The second time Lee and Davis' paths crossed was in February, 1850—almost 22 years after Davis graduated from West Point. Much had transpired in that intervening time. Lee was still a soldier, of course. He had married into one of the most influential families in Virginia, and had saved the city of Saint Louis by an impressive reengineering of a course change for the Mississippi River, along with emerging as a three-brevet hero of the Mexican War. Davis, in the meanwhile, had served on the frontier as a young officer before resigning his commission, marrying and losing Zachary Taylor's daughter. He then moved to Mississippi where his brother propped him up as a planter like himself, became involved in politics during which time he revealed a talent for oratory, remarried, returned to military service for the Mexican War by raising a volunteer regiment from Mississippi and was wounded at Buena Vista. His former father-in-law made sure that the after-action reports gave deserved praise to Davis, and he returned to the United States a war "hero."[227]

Turning again to politics, Davis was appointed to an unexpired United States Senate seat. Serving as chairman of the Committee on Military Affairs, Davis became interested in Cuban affairs when an exiled Cuban revolutionary junta led by General Narciso Lopez arrived in Washington in early 1850. The Cubans had fled to the United States two years earlier, and were seeking help in overthrowing what they considered to be Spanish misrule. Many Southern politicians were sympathetic to the plight of the revolutionaries, most probably because these lawmakers coveted the annexation of Cuba to the United States as an additional slave state. As a leading advocate for expansion into Cuba, Davis was repeatedly on the floor of the United States Senate, filibustering against the Spanish. News of Senator Davis' position, combined with his war record, encouraged the Cubans to look for help from the Mississippian. However, Lopez' junta wanted more than Davis' words: they wanted him to command an expedition aimed at overthrowing their Spanish masters. Davis might have talked a good game on the Senate floor, but he had no interest in becoming a mercenary general. Informing Lopez that: "I deem it inconsistent with my duty" to leave Washington, Davis then did a curious thing: he urged the junta to go see Robert E. Lee and ask him about leading an invasion of Cuba. The revolutionaries accordingly went to Baltimore to seek an audience with Major Lee who was working on the construction of Fort Carroll (Sollers' Point). Knowing who it was that had suggested that the Cubans see him, Lee listened only to the broad outline of their proposal before stopping the interview "on a consideration of personal honor." Frostily, Lee informed the Lopez-led junta that as a commissioned officer of the United States, he had a problem entertaining a proposal from another government, and before any details of the proposal were opened up, he wanted to visit with the man who had suggested the meeting. Accordingly, on a mid-February day in 1850 (there does not seem to be a recording of the exact date) Lee traveled into Washington City where he and Davis "confidentially discussed the matter." Unfortunately, the particulars of the conversation and Davis' explanation are not recorded. However, what is known is that Lee held "the strictest view of his duty" and declined to further consider the Cuban's proposal.[228]

While no written explanation why Davis suggested that the junta ask Lee to do something that the senator felt was "inconsistent with my duty," it presages an alarming pattern in their relationship. Davis seemed to relish the tactic of sending Lee on a fool's errand that Davis himself recognized as too dangerous for his own position. Indeed, Davis' actions seem exploitative and disingenuous in nature, even arrogant. Alternatively, perhaps Davis was infatuated with the idea of adding Cuba as a slave state and wished for

[226] William C. Davis, *Jefferson Davis*, pp. 37-38.

[227] William C. Davis, *Jefferson Davis*, pp. 158-160 and 163.

[228] William C. Davis, *Jefferson Davis*, p. 197; Freeman, *R. E. Lee*, vol. 1, pp. 306-307; Long, *Memoirs of Robert E. Lee*, pp. 72-73; Thomas, *Robert E. Lee: A Biography*, p. 148; McPherson, *Battle Cry of Freedom*, p. 105. Some sources mistakenly list this activity in late 1849. The center of the Cuban junta activity was in New York.

one of America's leading soldiers to risk everything for the expansion of plantocracy. But, based on his past behavior, it is unlikely that Davis actually admitted Lee's superior military merits. The far more likely explanation for why Davis suggested that Lopez ask Lee to lead the rebels back to Cuba was that Davis knew full well the political attachment Lee had to General Scott—a political affiliation for which Davis cared not a lick. At that precise moment, Davis was embroiled in his bitter fight to deny Scott his promotion to lieutenant general. Consequently, Jefferson Davis was not about to do Winfield Scott's favorite officer any favor by sending the Cubans to see Lee. Therefore, in either explanatory case, for Davis to suggest that Scott's *protégé* be the hireling for the Cuban junta indicates a crass indifference to Lee's sense of duty as an officer and to his status as one of the most decorated soldiers to emerge from the Mexican War, as well reflective of Lee's connection with General Scott—a person totally at odds with Davis' former father-in-law and himself.[229]

The third time that these men's careers crossed came during Lee's stint as superintendent at West Point. Lee began his duty at the academy on September 1st, 1852, and just a little more than six months later, Jefferson Davis became Secretary of War for the new President Franklin Pierce. The respective positions held by each mandated their cooperation. For the next two years, the men worked together on matters West Point related, and the relationship seemed to work well. Lee certainly understood Davis' constitutional authority, and he always treated Davis with the utmost deference and courtesy. The working relationship ended with the 1855 formation of the new regiments for frontier service. General Scott told Davis that Lee was the best qualified officer to command the 2nd Cavalry. The recommendation made no impression on Davis, as he was embroiled in an ugly feud with the general. Davis instead appointed Albert Sidney Johnston, his old friend and Lee's senior, as colonel; Lee was assigned as the regiment's lieutenant colonel.[230]

By the time the Civil War began, all the factors involving Davis' feud with Scott, his dealings with Lee, and Davis' own sense of self, had created the conditions for all these variables to manifest a toxic effect. Soon after Virginia's secession, while Lee was working furiously as commander of Old Dominion's forces to prepare for war, Davis called for Lee to drop what he was doing and travel to Montgomery, Alabama, to discuss Virginia's defense, the importance of the state in the new nation, and Lee's role once Virginia's troops were transferred to the central government. Lee's sense of duty dictated his reply: Virginia could ill afford to have its ranking officer away from his duties. Several weeks later, once it was determined that the capital of the Confederacy was to be moved to Richmond, Davis again expected Lee to suspend his duties to travel and meet him while the President was in transit to Richmond. When that did not happen, Davis must have been mortified that Lee was not waiting at the platform in Richmond when the presidential train pulled into the shed. Instead of traveling to Montgomery, instead of taking a southbound train and meeting Davis somewhere—anywhere—either in Atlanta, or Augusta, or Wilmington, or Goldsboro, instead of being at the train shed in Richmond when Davis arrived, Lee did not spare one second of his time or spend an ounce of energy to go out of his way to see the chief executive before the situation warranted. Only after Davis arrived in Richmond (Lee was at that time on an inspection tour of the Manassas front) did Lee, upon his return to the new capital city, visit Davis as part of his duties.

Lee understood, perhaps more than anyone, the gravity of the situation facing Virginia and the Confederacy. Furthermore, he possessed as high a sense of duty as anyone in uniform, North or South. In considering both these factors, and from what Walter Taylor tells us, Lee stood as one of the very few men south of the Potomac preparing for a long and bloody war. With many people on both sides indulging in an almost a carnival atmosphere, Robert E. Lee, the supreme realist, believed every Southerner needed to get ready for war. As a result, one can understand how the conscientious Lee resisted any other activity that might take him away from his duties.

In addition to this point, however, there existed the unspoken cut—the silent, yet loudly-speaking actions by which aristocratic Southerners spoke (and continue to do so today). Certainly, it would have been inefficient for Lee to have left Virginia to travel to Montgomery on Davis' whim, or for Lee to have boarded a train and met Davis while in route to Richmond. Each of those acts would have needlessly taken Lee away from vital duties for days, and Davis, in expecting such a meeting, had perhaps exaggerated his

---

[229] William C. Davis, *Jefferson Davis*, p. 153; also consult page 165.

[230] Ellsworth Eliot, Jr., *West Point in the Confederacy* (New York, 1941), pp. 364 and 377.

own self-importance over the crisis in readying for Virginia's defense. Davis had already been inundated with the kind of supplications that Joe Johnston undertook to gain his position, and Davis took offense when Lee refused to be obsequious. When the President's train pulled into the Richmond & Petersburg Railroad shed shortly after dawn on May 29th, Lee was not in the city to meet him. That singular act spoke volumes. Lee, who had no use for political toadying, believed he needed to fully and properly apply himself to his duties.

Courtesy Harpers Weekly

Inauguration of Jefferson Davis in Montgomery, Alabama

Slighting Jefferson Davis casts some interesting questions onto the widely observed trait of humility that so many saw in Robert E. Lee. He was a supremely confident officer, and his impressive martial abilities, displayed over the course of a three decade-long career, were never lost on his mind. Furthermore, Lee knew of Davis' deep attachment to Zachary Taylor and the shameful political machinations Davis had pulled in his long and tortured feud with Winfield Scott. Lee knew that Davis' sending the Lopez junta to see him in Baltimore in early 1850 about leading a mercenary force to Cuba only served the interests of Jeff Davis and other politicians. Lee knew that Davis had chosen a close friend of his holding the position of a paymaster to command the 2nd Cavalry when a very strong case existed for him to command. Lee knew Joe Johnston had left Richmond in a huff shortly after Old Dominion's secession and that Davis awarded his lobbying in Montgomery with a commission from the central government. Lee knew that this appointment resulted in Johnston's command at Harpers Ferry and how troubling signals already indicated that Johnston's actions were at odds with Lee's direction of Virginia's forces prior to their transfer to Confederate service. Lee knew that Davis' speeches about Confederate troops marching into Maryland to succor Virginia's sister state were not grounded in reality, and Lee knew that Davis' amateurish sycophants were running around Richmond, taking exception to anyone not as enthusiastic as were they about invading Maryland. Lee knew that Davis' repeated summons to drop his duties and travel to consult with the new chief executive was the stuff of false pride. Lee also knew his duty and how to voice his displeasure in his tidewater, aristocratic way. As a result, when the President stepped off the train in Richmond that Wednesday morning, Lee's snub spoke so loudly that Jeff Davis, replete with his entourage and his conquering hero entrance into Richmond, could not have failed to grasp the meaning of Lee's actions.

Davis did not have to say a thing to repay Lee for the perceived slight. By June 9th, the day after Virginia's forces were officially transferred to the Confederate States, with Lee a brigadier general in the Confederate army without authority or command, the President had remained mum regarding any future assignment for Lee. This mind boggling silence by Davis, even though he had plenty of time and opportunity to advise Lee how he intended to employ him, reveals much about Davis' character and leadership. Instead of utilizing Lee in a useful command capacity, Davis kept the general in Richmond doing next to nothing for another two months. Lee did keep busy, performing work and giving advice without having been instructed. The admirable work ethic had the effect of letting Davis know of Lee's in-depth knowledge of Virginia and the forces thus far organized for war. However, what was being accomplished by Lee during that time was a job that other officers could have performed while Lee did more important duty. Jeff Davis, however, did not allow that, and following Manassas, the President decided to send Lee on what amounted to a fool's errand.[231]

* * *

Western Virginia was a mess and everyone in Richmond knew it. Even Jeff Davis, the man responsible for appointing two incompetent former governors as general officers and sending them into this region to command "armies" in close proximity to each other, understood not only the importance of this territory with regards to threatening Federal communications, but also grasped the growing threat that could come from the enemy using this area as a staging ground for a thrust towards the vital Shenandoah Valley. Therefore, it would have only made sense to have ordered Lee to western Virginia with the authority he would need to positively effect cooperation between the three commands in the region (those belonging to generals Loring, Floyd and Wise). Certainly, Davis would not have dispatched Joe Johnston, the co-victor of Manassas, to western Virginia without command authority. Such an obvious situation makes it all the more strange that when Johnston turned down the assignment, Davis sent Lee to the Allegheny Mountains with nothing but his reputation. "In his underestimation of Lee, Davis not only wasted the Virginian's great gifts for the new nation," wrote Clifford Dowdey, "but sent him on an assignment . . . dealing with those vainglorious clowns bickering away the Confederacy's chances in western Virginia." It is difficult to conceive of a more revealing example of how badly Davis could have violated Napoleon's well-known Maxim: "Nothing is so important in war as an undivided command." Three months later, when Lee returned to Richmond without having accomplished the success Davis had wished for, the President wasted little time sending Lee off again. He was ordered to the southeastern Atlantic coast to command a newly-created department, but Lee knew it was "another forlorn hope expedition ... worse than West Virginia."[232]

It has, for a very long time, been fashionable in the historical community to refer to Robert E. Lee and Jeff Davis as friends, and that the relationship between the President and the general was one of confidence and trust between two respecting and friendly comrades. The number of authors referring to these men as friends before the war is lengthy indeed, and to include samples from all would be outside the purview of this study. Curiously, none examine Davis' feud with Scott, or any of the other factors impacting Davis' underutilization of Lee. Instead, the writers who describe Lee and Davis as friends prior to the war reads like a who's who of American history. For example, in the early 1850 episode when the Cuban junta sought out Jeff Davis for him to lead their army back and overthrow their Spanish masters, Davis declined on the basis that such a job was outside his duties. Davis then recommended Lee, who James McPherson describes as "his friend," to do the dirty work of a mercenary; no friend of Lee's would have done something so insulting or foolish. Three years later, Lee had been the commandant at West Point for a few months and was having trouble with the War Department with regards to the method of disciplining of cadets. Once Davis became Secretary of War in March, 1853, Douglas Southall Freeman believed: "Lee's troubles were accordingly reduced. On the foundation of old friendship [emphasis added], new confidence and respect between himself and Davis were built so stoutly in two years that all the strains of the War Between the States could not overthrow them." Another of the myriad of examples is seen with the coming of the war, and despite Davis refusing to employ Lee in any meaningful way, Davis biographer William J. Cooper paints a picture Davis' valuing Lee so much as to why: "Davis kept Robert E. Lee by his side."[233]

In examining Davis' actions with regards to Lee up until the time of his recall from the Atlantic coast, there is absolutely no evidence that would in any way either suggest or support the notion that Davis considered Lee a friend. If Lee was his friend, on what is that assertion based? Certainly none of their meetings up to March, 1862, suggest anything resembling friendship, and Lee's assignments and treatment

---

[231] Lee considered it a fool's errand because Davis sent him to western Virginia *without* command authority.

[232] Dowdey, *The Land They Fought For*, p. 127; Napoleon I, *The Military Maxims of Napoleon* (London, 1901), Maxim LXIV; Robert E. Lee, Jr., *Recollections and Letters*, Robert E. Lee To Mildred, November 15, 1861, p. 47.

[233] McPherson, *Battle Cry of Freedom*, p. 105; Freeman, *R. E. Lee*, vol. 1, p. 327; William J. Cooper, Jr., *Jefferson Davis, American* (New York, 2000), pp. 354-355; Dowdey, *Lee*, p. 180, misjudges Davis' view of Lee in March, 1862, by saying that the President "greatly admired [Lee]."

by Davis up to that point in the war certainly are not reflective of how one treats a friend. The only example prior to the war in which one can begin to attempt to make an argument for Davis having a high opinion of Lee is when Davis named Lee as second in command of the new 2nd Cavalry in 1855. However, that appointment offered no endorsement by Davis considering Lee as a friend. General Scott openly told everyone, and specifically Davis, that Lee was the best man to command the regiment—not be second in command. Yet, Jeff Davis was not about to listen to Winfield Scott. The Secretary of War instead kept is own counsel by naming his old friend, Sidney Johnston, who was at that time a major holding the job of paymaster to frontier posts, as commanding officer. Davis could not have taken the heat of public opinion that would have been turned up by Winfield Scott had he failed to appoint the Old Army's finest officer as second in command of the 2nd Cavalry, and Lee was so named.

From the moment of Virginia's secession in April, 1861, to the recall of Lee to Richmond in March, 1862, and extending through the end of May, Davis' use of Lee defies conventional documentary analysis, and has escaped a plausible motive by historians. Despite ample opportunity to appreciate Lee's qualities related through his performance in the Mexican War and while working with Lee as Secretary of War, Davis' refusal to put Lee in command of troops cannot be defended as a viable decision. Worse still, whether deliberate or not, Davis' assignments could not have been better calculated to ensure that Lee faced nothing but frustration and "forlorn" missions. Can a case be made that Davis took military advice from Lee, since this ostensibly was Lee's job once he was recalled to Richmond? If the answer is "not really," or "not much," the next question becomes: why have a military advisor if he was not going to be fully utilized? While the circumstances involving Lee's recall to Richmond and Davis' outmaneuvering the Confederate Congress with regards to Lee's official position has already been covered in detail, clearly, Davis' adhering to his "strategy of defense by dispersal" bears no marks of Lee's methods; only Lee's interactions with Jackson give a glimpse of Lee as an advisor. However, on the most important decisions facing the Confederacy, Lee's advice was unsought or mostly ignored. Perhaps only a man convinced of his own genius, stoked by circumstances toward a near messianic view of himself as savior of The Cause, could habitually ignore a military advisor of Lee's capacity. Davis, unfortunately, seemed remarkably susceptible to the puffery of sycophants extolling his military genius, and his behavior after First Manassas seems to be a convincing example of this dangerous vanity.

The summary of facts regarding Lee's assignments reaffirms a disturbing portrait of Davis as a leader. First, Lee had been offered command of the principal Federal army at the war's outbreak—an offer that should have alerted Davis and his inner circle as to Lee's qualities and reputation, but which instead, to the firebrands, cast doubt as to his loyalties. Second, upon Old Dominion's secession from the Union (and Lee resigning his command), Virginia lawmakers placed Lee in command of all Virginia forces, which, instead of reaffirming Lee's wide regard, prompted Davis to appoint a lesser light from Virginia, Joe Johnston, to one of the field commands Lee should have received. Third, during the war with Mexico, Lee had performed brilliantly in the field, overshadowing Davis' own commendable record and likely inciting his envy. Fourth, negative feelings about the secession of the Cotton States, and continuing sobering assessments of the Confederate early war effort, enabled ardent secessionists, who confused bombast with competence, to portray the audacious Lee as timid and defeatist. Fifth, Winfield Scott considered Lee the best soldier on the North American continent; Davis could not separate Scott's professional endorsement from his own personal animosity for Scott—another example of Davis' pettiness in the face of a task requiring greatness. As a result of these factors, President Davis chose to employ Robert E. Lee as a glorified errand boy during the first year of the war.

The unanswered question of "why" has been so disturbing to historians that it has been virtually ignored; yet it is one of the most critical questions of the war. Again, what caused Jefferson Davis to neglect the talents of Robert E. Lee from June, 1861, until the following June? Absent a simple unifying theory of the Mississippian's motivations, Davis' misuse of Lee—arguably the single biggest mistake made by the Confederacy during the war—leaves two disturbing scenarios (not necessarily mutually exclusive). One, Jefferson Davis was completely blind in failing to see what most everyone, including Lincoln, clearly recognized; or, two, Davis was so riven with vanity, and poisoned by his blind hatred of Winfield Scott and Lee's connection to Scott as the great general's protégé, that he could not set aside his emotions for the benefit of a higher cause. Worse, for all the deserved Lost Cause praise that Davis garnered for his devotion, sacrifice and hard work, Davis never possessed the wisdom to subordinate his massive ego to his daunting mission. Ultimately, the evidence is overwhelming that Davis' dealings with Lee from the moment the war began until he was forced to elevate Lee to army command were the lingering result of a debilitating malaise deep within Jefferson Davis' inflexible mind and self-centered reasoning.

* * *

During the first year of the war, Lee's role changed several times, and each time that his role changed, his authority within his assigned duty changed. Once Virginia seceded, Lee was named "commander" of her armed forces, and command them he did. As the Virginia troops passed from the authority of the state to the central government (June 8, 1861), Lee became a general with no command. Because President Davis refused to assign him to duty, Lee remained in Richmond in limbo, doing what he could to help the war effort and Jeff Davis. Later, when Davis sent Lee to western Virginia to try and coordinate the commanders in that region, Lee did what he could, absent the authority he needed from the President in order to have a realistic chance at success. Following that hopeless assignment, Davis sent Lee on another "forlorn hope" errand as the newly-designated department commander along the southeastern Atlantic coast until his recall to Richmond in March, 1862. Lee therefore held four duty posts during this time, each with different responsibilities and each with different authority. However, his combination of duties during the early war period does provide a view into a variety of his strengths and soldierly qualities, as well as foreshadows his operational plans when defending Virginia as commander of the Confederacy's principal army.

Lee demonstrated deep respect for constitutional authority. Despite enormous friction, Lee kept a cool head. With the exception of failing to meet Davis' train, Lee never did challenge, insult or in any way impugn the honor of his civilian superiors. Lee's discipline checked his emotions under trying circumstances as he worked tirelessly for the common goal—independence. And although there would be exceptions, Lee was usually able to keep his emotions under control. This coolness, or *sangfroid*, Napoleon deemed "the first qualification in a general-in-chief." During his limited time as "commander" of Virginia's military forces, to his hamstrug advisory role in western Virginia, to his near-meaningless departmental command role along the southeastern coast, Lee never allowed himself to be drawn into the highs and lows of good news or bad concerning the progress of the war. When the fire-eaters wanted to send Southern sons on an ill-conceived invasion of Maryland, Lee kept his focus on practical matters—arming, organizing and fielding Virginia's regiments. Several weeks later, prior to the battle at Manassas, Beauregard reiterated similarly grandiose and foolish designs to invade Maryland and capture Washington City. In making a pitch to President Davis, Beauregard's aide had the hare-brained scheme squashed by Lee. When Lee was sent to western Virginia in the summer of 1861 to deal with the three headstrong personalities commanding their respective "armies," Lee carried out his advisory role as energetically and professionally as possible. When Lee was reassigned in November as the new commander of the Department of South Carolina, Georgia and East Florida, Lee demonstrated his skill in dealing with cantankerous independent governors and other individualistic officers in South Carolina and Georgia, while at the same time showing "a courteous imperviousness to the outrage of citizen-soldiers whose ideas of chivalric war he offended" by having them take up a pick or a shovel.[234]

During the first year of the war, Lee also displayed excellent organizational skills for a man who loathed bureaucratic paperwork—in this aspect, Lee cannot be compared to a prolific communicator like Napoleon, who, out of necessity, dictated voluminous correspondence as head of state and army commander, even while in the field. Certainly, Lee did not care for desk jobs or paperwork; he considered such work tedious, mundane and sedentary, a necessity of duty, and some of his personal communications show signs of being abbreviated and hastily dashed off. However, without authority, and nowhere near enough staff, Lee seems to have fulfilled his duties; excessive missives from Lee would have been inappropriate to his position. The paperwork so prevalent with the West Point superintendent job (no doubt, one of the reasons he fought hard the assignment to that post) held absolutely no attraction for him, and because of these and "the thanklessness of the duty" at the academy, he bolted from the banks of the Hudson as soon as he could following his new assignment with the 2nd Cavalry. Despite Lee not being the clerk-type, he could take pride knowing that he had played a significant and guiding hand in organizing and fielding 40,000 Virginians for

---

[234] Napoleon I, *The Military Maxims of Napoleon*, Maxim LXXIII; Dowdey, *Lee*, p. 178.

the Confederacy between the day he was named as "commander" of Virginia's troops to early June. It was no small feat, confirming what Napoleon believed: "when a nation is without establishments and a military system, it is very difficult to organize an army." Based on that accomplishment, and considering that a quarter of the troops at the Battle of Manassas were Virginians, Lee certainly played a contributing role to the war's first important victory.[235]

Another striking feature of Lee's military character comes into focus during this period—his constant quest for information about the enemy. Whether he was behind a desk in Richmond, or overseeing engineering projects along the Atlantic coast, or in the field in western Virginia, Lee essentially served as his own intelligence officer and proved to be tireless in his efforts to seek information regarding all things related to the Federals. The general was a vociferous reader of newspapers, a ready source of political and public sentiment, as well as military information. Through his network of surrogates, informants and others who dutifully forwarded daily papers from around the region for his consideration, Lee was able to gauge many aspects of what was developing on the "other side of the hill." The reason for gathering as much useful intelligence on the opposition is obvious, and Lee's correspondence is replete with examples of him instructing local commanders to do whatever they could in order to gather accurate details about the countryside as well as on the enemy.

When Lee had to gather information himself, he proved to be as remarkable a horseman as he had shown while on the plains of Texas, and possessed as keen an eye for terrain as he had demonstrated during the Mexican War. In his daily routine in western Virginia, he exerted Herculean efforts in scouting accurately every available defile and pass throughout the countryside in order to gather all possible information needed in preparation for a plan of operation on how to best "get at 'those people.'" In his western Virginia duty, the 54 year-old revealed the conditioning and energy of a younger man, and whose zeal for duty could not be deterred by the cold, cruel weather. Naturally, there was a driving force behind Lee's physical stamina and mental capacities: his understanding of what was at stake, and his sense of duty. The former was part of his relentless pursuit of realism, while the latter was the cornerstone of his military personae. It was this sense of duty, combined with his physical characteristics, alert mind and intense self-discipline, that made possible his focused efforts, regardless of duty assignment. Yet, if anything troubling revealed itself, Lee may have been pushing himself too hard, in part out of his controlled rage at the folly of his assignments. Many noted how his hair had grayed significantly while in western Virginia. His sense of duty drove him, but at a physical cost. The South's most accomplished soldier had begun trading on his astonishing vitality; his inner resources may have seemed to some superhuman, but they could not be inexhaustible. Thus, the further tragedy of the wasted year is that Lee began to burn up his inner reserves. He had not used them all up by any means, but what had been accomplished by his sacrifices in western Virginia? "One has but a short time for war," Napoleon once said. Regrettably, Davis had not only wasted Lee's talents, he had also prematurely started the clock.

Beyond his drive, discipline and physical attributes, Lee's understanding of military operations can be seen emerging in 1861—a glimpse that foreshadows his operational methods as an army commander. Certainly, Lee had acquired knowledge of the art of war starting with the Great Captains. From this study and from his experiences in Mexico and in Texas, Lee's actions in 1861 and early 1862 demonstrate his understanding that the art of war is adaptable by grasping three major points of influence. The first point consists of adjusting the principles of war to the weapons and capabilities of the time. The second point includes the spirit of the age, a combination of the nature of the war, the politics underlying the conflict, and the character of the belligerents, including a detailed knowledge of one's own army. The third point concerns the evolution and methods of logistics. Each of these points must be grasped or understood by the commander, who develops a discernible and often systematic interpretation of these principles and the exigencies of his time and place. A "genius of war" or "Great Captain" emerges when a leader merges the art and the conduct of war in such a way that he may seem to have almost redefined the current operational art.

During the time he was "commander" of Virginia's military, Lee advised Joe Johnston of the importance of retaining Harpers Ferry long enough to effect the removal of the invaluable machinery from the former

---

[235] Napoleon I, *The Military Maxims of Napoleon*, Maxim LVII. Elizabeth Brown Pryor, *Reading the Man: A Portrait of Robert E. Lee Through His Private Letters* (New York, 2007), p. 212. For extensive details concerning Lee organizational abilities accomplishments during this time, please see: Freeman, *R. E. Lee*, vol. 1, pp. 472-526.

National Armory, as well as provide political support for those in Maryland who were advocating secession. The latter point was more abstract than the former, and Lee knew it. Nevertheless, he had to use every reason possible in order to influence Joe Johnston—who wanted to retreat from Harpers Ferry almost as soon as he arrived—even though there was no pressure being applied from the enemy and even though the desperately-needed machinery from the former armory had yet to be transported into the interior. In the course of advising Johnston, Lee knew that the Confederate forces in the area were outnumbered, and in order to augment their fighting power, Lee wanted Johnston to make his command as mobile as possible; ultimately, this maneuverability would prove vital at First Manassas.

Lee also demonstrated his understanding of the importance of concentration; 19th century logistics did not allow for permanent concentration of forces absent a huge transportation delivery system. Therefore, troops had to be dispersed to sustain themselves through non-operational periods, while retaining the ability to concentrate more rapidly than the enemy at the point of battle. As the outnumbered side, this speed of concentration was essential. Good intelligence and cavalry screening allowed commanders to concentrate more rapidly than their opponents. Absent information, a commander had to rely only on instinct.

Lee's advice to Johnston at Harpers Ferry is illustrative of his desire to concentrate troops in order to retain freedom of maneuver and maximize fighting power. When Lee was in command of the coastal department, he implemented another version of concentration, suitable with the local situation. Rather than keeping the troops spread out along the coast in dispersed, static roles designed to protect every sea island and inlet—troops that would be overwhelmed and defeated whenever and wherever the Yankees launched an expedition—Lee pulled back the exposed regiments, concentrating his troop strength at strategic points so that these would be able to maneuver and respond to any enemy attack. While Lee was effecting this repositioning, he also constructed what Walter Taylor described as "a system of defensive works" to augment troop capabilities. Wisely erected beyond the range of the Federal navy's big guns in order to protect vital points, Taylor thought that these strong points "constituted a monument to his skill as an engineer." Lee was able to effect proper security of the vulnerable Charleston & Savannah Railroad as well as provide protection from gunboats that might attempt to ascend the inland waterways. A brilliantly-devised scheme, neither Charleston nor Savannah, though constantly and heavily bombarded, fell from the seaward side. Only very late in the war did these cities succumb, and only then to overwhelming numbers of Federal troops.[236]

More than any other soldier, Lee understood the importance of the initiative, especially for a numerically inferior force. He had studied it in the campaigns and battles of the Great Captains. He had lived it time and again during General Scott's remarkable campaign from Vera Cruz to Mexico City. True to his understanding, Lee resolved to create the conditions to seize the initiative in western Virginia in order to have the best chance for victory. Through a combination of intelligence gathering and careful planning that utilized maneuver and surprise, Lee planned the Cheat Mountain battle as if it was straight out of Napoleon's Maxims, Number XIV: "The character of this mode of warfare [attacking in the mountains] consists [of getting] on the flanks or in the rear of the enemy, leaving him only the alternative of abandoning his position without fighting." However, Lee's lack of command authority ultimately proved the Confederates' undoing, as it did again soon thereafter at Sewell Mountain. Aside from the general discovering the robust work ethic of Walter Taylor and meeting the remarkably capable Lindsay Long—Loring's chief of artillery and inspector-general—along with a few other officers such as Edward Johnson, Lee made the best of it. Nevertheless, Lee did not publicly blame the President for having expected him to attain significant results without command authority. Lee explained to his wife: "I can not tell you my regret and mortification at the untoward events that caused the failure of the plan" at Cheat Mountain. To Governor Letcher, Lee never pointed fingers for the failed attack, instead assuring him that: "I can answer for my sincerity in the earnest endeavour I make to advance the cause I have so much at heart." Taking severe criticism in the Richmond papers, Lee never uttered one syllable of criticism towards his chief executive, the difficult Loring, or the timid Rust. Lee had indeed performed his duty as best he could within his constitutional limits.[237]

---

[236] Taylor, *General Lee*, p. 35. Savannah was taken from the land side by General Sherman in December, 1864; Charleston had to be evacuated soon thereafter, and was occupied by Federal forces in February, 1865.

[237] Robert E. Lee, Jr, *Recollections and Letters*, Robert E. Lee To His Wife, September 17, 1861, and Robert E. Lee To Governor Letcher, September 17, 1861, pp. 38-39.

After the war, Jefferson Davis eventually revealed his direct role in the western Virginia fiasco, and the impossible position into which he had placed Lee. Davis conjured up a disingenuous explanation, admitting that he had hoped that Lee would have only needed "his military skill and deserved influence over men" to retrieve Confederate fortunes in the region, despite undercutting him such that neither talent nor personality could retrieve the mess. If Davis had truly believed in Lee's "Military skill and deserved influence," he would not have wasted him in western Virginia. Furthermore, in short, Davis hereby admitted that Lee had no authority, something that Lee and everyone else in uniform understood. Writing from Valley Mountain on August 26th, 1861, Lee told John B. Floyd, the commander of the Army of the Kanawha: "General Loring, commanding the whole force of the Northwest Army, has his headquarters at this camp." Davis would never admit that in the absence of the needed authority, he had asked Lee to perform a miracle.[238]

Davis' admission, however, coming as it did after the war, did nothing to help Lee at the time of the event. As a result, newspaper editors essayed a series of unfounded attacks that Lee's reputation was inflated and that he was to blame for what had happened in western Virginia. The Richmond Examiner, known as the harshest critic of the Davis administration, had accurately reported in its July 31st edition that Lee was being sent to western Virginia for the purpose of "inspection, and consultation." However, once bad news started arriving, its editorial staff, always quick to point out ill-advised government policies, thoughtlessly turned on Lee for the failed campaign. The reason was no doubt connected to John Moncure Daniel, a 36-year-old, 120-pound bundle of nerves who doubled as one of the paper's editors as well as served as an aide to General Floyd. The paper's September 24th edition said that Lee's plan for Cheat Mountain was "said by military men to have been one of the most perfect pieces of strategy," but because of its failure "it will be useless to canvass its merits." Another edition of The Richmond Examiner described Lee as a general whose "excess of caution…has wrought, by mere delay, much of the mischief that was dreaded from defeat." Editors James Cowardin and John Hammersley of The Richmond Daily Dispatch in August mischaracterized Lee as being "in command of our army operating in that part of the state," described Lee's plan of battle for Cheat Mountain as possessing "too great circumspection," because "in mountain warfare, the learning of the books and of the strategists is of little value." The Richmond Enquirer pitched in as well, no doubt because Henry A. Wise owned a large portion of the paper and his son, Obediah Jennings Wise, was an editor and steadfastly supported Jeff Davis. Lee's plan for the unfought battle at Cheat Mountain can be criticized for being too elaborate. Yet, after painstaking lengths to gather accurate intelligence on the enemy, Lee designed a plan that represented the best chance the Confederates had at retaking the key geographical position in the region, even if it represented a long shot. Given the rugged terrain and mountainous passes that the Confederates had to negotiate in getting at the Federal positions in and around Cheat Mountain, as well as the nature of the weather and all other factors, Lee's plan actually stood on the verge of success. Indeed, consolidating and having fewer columns move against the Federal position was not an option, as the terrain greatly limited movement and access, plus the fact that to achieve success, the multiple columns needed to threaten, cut off and surprise the Federals. Of course, Lee read these newspapers and the criticisms. He wrote his wife soon thereafter: "I am sorry, as you say, that the movements of the armies cannot keep pace with the expectations of the editors of papers … I hope something will be done to please them." In three months, Virginia's favorite son and warrior, after having been so savagely attacked in the press, became known to many as "Granny Lee," a man too timid for the hard hand of war. That image would have never manifested itself had Jefferson Davis protected Robert E. Lee the way Lee protected his lieutenants and his chief executive.[239]

---

[238] Jefferson Davis, *Rise and Fall of the Confederate Government*, vol. 1, p. 434; *Official Records*, Series I, vol. 51, part 2, Supplement, Robert E. Lee to John B. Floyd, August 26, 1861, pp. 253-254.

[239] *The Richmond Examiner*, September 24, 1861; *The Richmond Examiner*, October 11, 1861; *The Richmond Daily Dispatch*, August 10, 1861 and September 26, 1861; the later quote can be seen in Freeman, *R. E. Lee*, vol. 1, pp. 576-577; Robert E. Lee, Jr., *Recollections and Letters*, Robert E. Lee To His Wife, October 7, 1861, p. 44; Furgurson, *Ashes of Glory*, p. 164. Sometime prior to the Battle of Sharpsburg, Lee was discussing the Sewell Mountain campaign with Brigadier General William E. Starke who had also in western Virginia at that time. After Lee explained the utter impracticality of continuing the pursuit of Rosecrans once he slipped away, Starke countered: "But your reputation was suffering, the press was denouncing you, your own state was losing confidence in you, and the army needed a victory to add to its enthusiasm." The remark lit a smile on General Lee's face as he replied: "I could not afford to sacrifice the lives of five or six hundred of my people to silence public clamor." See: Long, *Memoirs of Robert E. Lee*, pp. 493-494. To a friend, Lee stated that a victory that could have been won would have been a completely barren one, and added: "I would rather sacrifice my military reputation and quietly rest under undue censure than to unnecessarily

Davis' refusal in 1861 to own up to his part in the western Virginia fiasco in no small way fueled the journalists' frenzied attack on Lee, helping to create a lasting legacy of historians stressing Lee's culpability in the failed Cheat-Sewell mountains campaign. This is especially curious since it was accurately reported in the Richmond press beforehand that Lee had no authority, and that Davis finally confessed that he had sent Lee with only "his military skill and deserved influence over men." Typical of the writers who level invalid criticism against Lee in western Virginia is that characterized by Virginia Brown Pryor. Without acknowledging that Davis had failed to extend to Lee command authority, Pryor not only maintains that, "Lee faltered in his campaign to dislodge Union troops under General William Rosecrans," she makes the error of confusing Lee's very limited jurisdiction with his actions, as well as totally misreads how he later commanded the Army of Northern Virginia. "There were many excuses [why Lee was defeated]," Pryor states, "… [and] two critical elements presaged flaws that would remain with him to the end [of the war]. The first was a failure to coordinate movements effectively among various components of his army. The second was an inability to either issue clear orders to subordinates or replace those who hesitated in carrying out instructions."[240]

The idea put forth by Pryor, among others, that Lee failed to effectively coordinate the movements in front of Cheat Mountain ignores three important facts. First, it was not his army—it was Loring's. Second, the converging columns had done extremely well following the plan in getting into position the night before the proposed attack on Cheat. Third, the attack did not materialize as envisioned because Colonel Rust lost his courage. Further, the charge that the plan of battle (Pryor misses the point that these were drafted by Lee and issued under Loring's name) contained unclear orders is unsubstantiated (particularly given that the orders were in fact executed without confusion), and is a gross generalization leveled against General Lee that has taken on a life of its own. The only accusation with any element of truth is that Lee did not replace Wise in front of Sewell Mountain the first instant he had a chance. Perhaps this was because Lee had just received the authority for such action and wanted to gather all the facts before making a fair and fully-informed decision, or because a replacement was not readily available, or because Lee sensed some action regarding Wise would soon be forthcoming out from Richmond. Regardless, linking Lee's treatment Wise, or Floyd, or Loring in 1861 to Lee's handling of unsatisfactory subordinates when he was an army commander seems tenuous. Lee would always have to deal with a few officers who owed their rank—and often their position—through their political connections, including those with President Davis. In each of those cases, Lee always figured out ways to minimize those officers' impact or have them reassigned. However, Pryor's sweeping characterization ignores the historical pattern that General Robert E. Lee did not suffer fools for long in his army.

For some apparently inexplicable reason, the overwhelming majority of writers of this phase of Robert E. Lee's career fail to emphasize that Lee lacked command authority. Two notable exceptions, however, are Ellsworth Eliot, Jr., and Steven E. Woodworth. In his *West Point in the Confederacy*, Eliot correctly comes to the point of the general's sojourn: "The object of Lee's campaign was to promote the co-operation of the several forces in Northwestern Virginia in its defense. The campaign ended in failure, for which Lee was in no way to blame although its significance could neither be measured nor appreciated by the general public." In his *Davis & Lee at War*, Woodworth goes part of the way in accurately recounting Lee's lack of command authority. "The directions given and the authority granted [to Lee] were not adequate to realize such hopes, and even with the best of command arrangements it might have been impossible to salvage a situation in which the enemy had so many advantages and the Confederates had Loring, Wise and Floyd." Where Woodworth falls short, Lee's surviving aide from the campaigning, Walter Taylor, clearly highlights. With the action in western Virginia drawn to a close, "a large portion of the state was in possession of the Federals, including the rich valleys of the Ohio and Kanawha Rivers, and so remained until the close of the war. For this, however, General Lee cannot be reasonably held accountable."[241]

---

sacrifice the life of a single one of my men." See Eliot, *West Point in the Confederacy*, p. 46.

[240] Pryor, *Reading the Man*, p. 320. Of the many who mischaracterize Lee's authority in the western Virginia campaign, and consequently fault him for what happened at Cheat Mountain, see Ganville Davisson Hall, *Lee's Invasion of Northwest Virginia in 1861* (Glencoe, 1911), pp. 10-12, as well as Clayton R. Newell, *Lee vs. McClellan*, pp. 232-233, and Freeman, *R. E. Lee*, vol. 1, pp. 550-551.

[241] Eliot, *West Point in the Confederacy*, pp. 45-46; Woodworth, *Davis & Lee at War*, pp. 59-60; Taylor, *Four Years With General Lee*, p. 35.

CHAPTER THREE

"The Enemy is Pushing Us Back in All Directions"
The Confederacy On the Cusp of Disaster

*"I do not see either advantage or pleasure in my duties. But I will not complain, but
do my best. The enemy is pushing us back in all directions, and how far he will be
successful depends much upon our efforts and the mercy of Providence."*
—Robert E. Lee to his wife, the day after he was named as Davis' advisor[1]

A brisk chill clung to the air that Friday, March 7th, 1862, when General Robert E. Lee returned to Richmond. On every front, Federal forces were advancing; before them, Southern arms were reeling. Instead of the usual optimism prevalent with the coming onset of spring, the Confederate capitol felt gripped by the dispiriting aura of disaster.[2]

In the West, where the central territory of defense was the state of Tennessee that protected the "Cotton States," Confederate fortunes were unraveling at an alarming rate. Coming on the heels of the defeats at Fort Henry and Fort Donelson, Nashville had fallen. This loss had ineluctably dire consequences. With the eastern flank of the much-heralded Confederate strongpoint at Columbus, Kentucky—known as the "Gibraltar of the West"—suddenly uncovered and outflanked, it had to be evacuated. As the upper Mississippi River Valley subsequently became a Federal conduit, the next strongpoint stood 60 river miles down stream at Island No. 10. Already under siege from Federal combined naval and army forces, Island No. 10—given the nature of Confederate strategy—would inevitably fall, a question of time. Then Fort Pillow and Memphis would succumb. Meanwhile, the Confederate army in the theater, under the command of General Sidney Johnston, had abandoned Tennessee, stopping near the border at the railhead of Corinth, Mississippi, to regroup.

In the East, the principal Federal army busily reorganized under the command of George B. McClellan—a man who excelled in administration—its strength and capabilities burgeoning following the disastrous July engagement along Bull Run Creek. After its long hibernation, McClellan's host began stirring. Federal probes initially suggested a southwestwardly trek overland towards the main Confederate army based at Centreville and still lingering in the vicinity of Manassas. However, information from north of the Potomac indicated that the rumblings were preparatory to a move to Richmond, not overland but by sea to the Virginia Peninsula. Meanwhile, in the principal Confederate army, there had been only minor attempts at organizing the major commands, with the most notable change being that the Southerners were

---

[1] Robert E. Lee, Jr., *Recollections and Letters*, Robert E. Lee To His Wife, March 14, 1862, p. 58.
[2] Krick, *Civil War Weather in Virginia*, p. 51; *Richmond Daily Dispatch*, March 8, 1862.

now led by General Joe Johnston. Beauregard, the co-hero of Manassas, had enjoyed *entente cordiale* with Davis until he wrecked the situation with his official report of the battle. As a result, Beauregard fell out of favor with the President and was assigned to duty in the West, where Davis once again confused the principle of unity of command by sending Beauregard to Sidney Johnston's side.

Courtesy Harpers Weekly

Attack on Fort Henry

Meanwhile, Joe Johnston, just as he had demonstrated while at Harpers Ferry the previous late spring and summer, felt extremely uneasy about his numbers and vulnerable right flank, and had made it known that he would abandon his forward position at the first signs of a serious Federal advance. Certainly, Johnston did not have at his disposal the requisite manpower to execute a static defense along the long line from the Blue Ridge to the Potomac against McClellan's vastly superior numbers. The Confederate positions were further hopelessly extended by the Virginia coastline, which provided numerous access points for Federal landings. Thus, the Confederates' position could be turned by Federal combined operations involving disembarking troops below Johnston's right flank on the Potomac, or by a bolder move of landing troops in the Confederate rear on the Rappahannock.

Yet, while proclaiming his intentions to Richmond that he would not remain in the advanced position, Johnston made no meaningful plans for his army to leave the exposed and doomed Centreville base. While historians of the war have often portrayed Johnston as some sort of Quintus Fabius Maximus in gray, a master of retreat and delay, in reality, Johnston exhibited little true ability even in this regard. While understanding the futility of staying put, and while recognizing that retreat from Centreville was inevitable, Johnston expended remarkably little energy in preparing to make this and other retreats. His inexplicably contradictory mindset represents Johnston's most serious weakness as a commander, and undercuts any claims to competence. Apparently, Johnston did not have the leadership skills to roll up his sleeves and manage the details of such an operation, and his military career prior to the war had not made him as intimate with the nuances and details of military operations such that he could effectively manage such a highly difficult operation. Whereas Wellington, and later Lee, would manage every detail connected to such a task, being actively visible in checking upon the particulars and leaving nothing behind to the enemy that could be removed, "Retreatin' Joe" Johnston seemed content to spend his time at headquarters. No master of delay would abandon invaluable material assets needlessly—a key component in retrograde movements—and Johnston, having learned nothing from Harpers Ferry, repeated his error on an even grander scale in the early spring of 1862.[3]

Courtesy Sons of Confederate Veterans

Great Seal of the Confederacy

---

[3] For a good summary of the Beauregard-Davis feud, please consult: Eliot, *West Point in the Confederacy*, pp. 151-155.

Meanwhile, Federal combined operations along the Atlantic coast proved to be as effective as they were along the rivers in the heartland. Choosing where and when they wished to move, the Federals swooped down on the Confederate coastline, picking off strategic islands and anchorages, along with any static defenders, in the execution of the planned naval blockade of the South. What at the time went as an unsung achievement, Robert E. Lee stabilized the southeastern coastal defenses of Charleston and Savannah proper before his recall to Richmond. Therefore, without pomp or ceremony, Lee, who Lincoln would have long before placed in command of the Federal government's principal army a year before, returned to the Confederacy's capital city still looking for gainful duty.

Formula for Disaster—
Jefferson Davis and the
"Strategy of Defense by Dispersal"

George Washington Statue at Richmond

Courtesy Library of Congress

Prior to Robert E. Lee's return, Southerners began looking beyond army commanders and local leaders for who was to blame for the current state of affairs. Once they started looking, they looked to the top. After all, President Davis and other leaders had *promised* the South its independence following the victory at Manassas. With that pledge now clearly broken by events, the hope of firmly establishing the new republic seemed more distant than ever in the early months of 1862. Against that backdrop, Jefferson Davis' permanent inauguration for a six-year term took place on February 22, 1862, the 130th anniversary of the birthday of the great Revolutionary figure, George Washington. Below Washington's magnificent, equestrian statue in Richmond's Capitol Square, the Confederate President addressed, in miserable 40-degree and drizzling weather, what historian Clifford Dowdey described as "a crowd of shivering men and women who the year before had happily been citizens of the United States."[4]

Although there was no repining over their decision to break from the Union, given the course of developments in April 1861, something was much different among the citizens in Richmond on that dreary day as opposed to the jubilant May morning the prior year when Davis had made his triumphal entry into the city. It was a difference for which the weather could not have been to blame. Faith—that intangible act of will whereby a person, or a people, believe without any evidence in the sincerity and promises of their leaders—had fallen with the misfortunes of The Cause. The developing circumstances over the past several months had had the effect of humbling almost all of the sunshine patriots. Those who had made sport of Lee, who had misrepresented him as not being devoted enough to the independence of the new republic, were no longer to be heard. Silent, too, were the arrogant platform-soldiers who only 10 months earlier had proclaimed that "one Southerner equal to five Yankees"

"Little minds try to defend everything at once...He who defends everything defends nothing."

—**Frederick the Great**

---

[4] Krick, *Civil War Weather in Virginia*, pp. 46 and 48; Marshall, Lee's Aide-de-Camp, pp. 18-27; William C. Davis, Jefferson Davis, pp. 352-353; Dowdey, *The Land They Fought For*, pp. 125 and 145.

would result in the complete defeat of the United States in a matter of weeks, if not a few months. The hotheads who once professed that "Southern valor" more than negated Northern factories, Northern ports, Northern shipyards and the Federal navy no longer scoffed at the vast differences between an industrialized nation of 23 million people against an agrarian society of only nine million. Although still committed to their course, and still believing that they had the ability to win, those in Richmond for the inauguration were similar to other like-minded Southerners—they were deeply concerned as to why they were not winning.

In the face of the mounting crisis and the string of military defeats, Jefferson Davis always remained sure of himself and his convictions. That self-assuredness, combined with his expansive view of his constitutional role as commander-in-chief, insured that *his* military policy would be the path which the South followed. Yet, for all his prerogatives in creating military policy, Davis seemed to be remarkably unable to connect his decisions to the unfolding series of debacles. He demonstrated a remarkable capability to detach himself from culpability to any setbacks, while attaching himself to the victory at Manassas. As criticism mounted in the papers, and as heated conversations increased in the halls and parlors of the Confederate capital, Davis' approach to running the war grew more imperious. Like many embattled leaders, Davis clung stubbornly to his superior *resumé* in order to turn a deaf ear to his less-qualified critics; the critics may be right in point of fact, but armchair strategists, outcome-based second-guessers, and politically motivated journalists still did not possess status in Davis' eyes of deserving critics. After all: *he* was the former West Point graduate who knew war, *he* was the former veteran who had emerged from the conflict with Mexico as a hero; *he* was the former senator and chairman of the Committee on Military Affairs; *he* was the former Secretary of War; *he* was the major general of Mississippi troops once his state seceded; *he* was the President and he knew best how to handle the very difficult job of defending the vast expanse of the new nation. All this self-awareness reinforced what can only be described as Davis' Messianic vision of himself as *the* man who could lead the South to victory. Outside his offices, however, much had changed around Davis. Long passed were the previous summer days of Southerners basking in the glory of a victory won at Manassas—a victory that now rang hollow as neither European recognition nor intervention had ensued as Davis had promised, and independence was still something of dreams. Instead, by March, 1862, public awareness of the fatal flaws of Davis' military policy grew with each setback.[5]

As the curtain was quickly falling on the first year of the war, the Yankees were coming, armies of them. After the series of Federal successes beginning the month before, the ever-present question on Southern lips in March, 1862, was: 'how do we stop 'em?' The strategy then in effect wasn't working.

Months earlier, Jefferson Davis had decided to translate the Confederacy's political purpose of defense of its borders into a military policy, essentially a "cordon system," long-outdated by Napoleonic advances in grand-strategy and operational art of war. In pointing out its weaknesses conceptually, it can be described simply as "the strategy of defense by dispersal," whereby in defending all points, nothing gets defended at all. Oddly bureaucratic and administrative, Davis seemed to be drawing upon his experiences as a Secretary of War protecting frontier settlements from American Indians when faced with the challenges of the Presidency. Indeed, correct military logic clashed

---

[5] Scott Bowden and Bill Ward, *Last Chance for Victory: Robert E. Lee and the Gettysburg Campaign* (Cambridge, 2001), p. 16.

The Spirit of the South

The natural depression which followed the recent reverses to our arms has passed away from the public mind, and the South is now looking full in the face all the trials and perils of its situation, and accepting with stern determination the alternative which is really and truly presented to it, of "Liberty or Death." It has always been evident and it is now more clearly seen than ever by the Southern people that we are dealing with a foe who does not even know the meaning of magnanimity, and that we have no hope on earth for anything which earth has dear, except in the most united, determined, and unending resistance. The triumph of the North means the ruin of the South, in property, life, liberty, and honor. It means the spoliation of all we own, the confiscation of every dollar's worth of property, the emancipation of the serf and the enslavement of the master. The enormous debt which the North has contracted to carry on this bloody war – a debt which cannot be less this moment than twelve hundred millions of dollars, will be saddled entirely upon the South, in the event of its subjugation. In will be wrung from Southern staples by heavy export duties, and from the Southern people by grinding taxes, which will condemn Southern industry in every shape and form to the most terrible burthens. It will take from us all that we have – not only liberty, and property, and personal security, but the respect of all the world, and even our own self-respect. We should not only be trempled down and beggared, but disgraced and degraded in the eyes of all mankind. If we achieve our independence, thought it cost us hundreds of millions, and though it leave us poor, we shall be able again to begin the world with a soil whose rich products are our own with the spirit and energies of freemen, and with the inspiring influence of hope to cheer our hearts and animate our exertions. But if we succumb to Northern domination, we are reduced to a lower depth of poverty than any successful sacrifice for independence can cost us and lose besides honor and hope. We shall be the Parialie of civilization, the scorn and contempt of all mankind, the loathing and self-reproach even of our own hearts. The Southern mind comprehends all this, and it has resolved to perish rather than submit to such a fate. There never has been an hour from the beginning of this contest when a determination as profound has animated the souls of the Southern people. They can die, and they can die with dignity and glory, but they will never live to be slaves. In this sublime resolution they have rendered their subjugation an impossibility. Such a people cannot be conquered. The Yankees shall not take our country from us, our homes, our liberty, our farms, our wives and children, our honor. They shall not make us slaves, and, above all, slaves to the meanest, the most rapacious, and most cruel of mankind.

The Richmond Daily Dispatch,
March 6, 1862

with the political expediency of providing a show of force wherever wealthy civilians felt most threatened. Lee encountered the implications of dispersal first hand in Charleston and Savannah. Thus, Davis' so-called strategy indeed spread military forces along all points of the expansive South, including its enormously long coastline. This idea sat well, if only initially, with those near the frontier or along the coast who expected the government to provide for their security. However, it was on this promise of protecting all Southern soil that Davis completely surrendered the initiative to the Federals. Southern forces literally sat around waiting for the numerically superior Federals to decide where to inflict the next defeat. By committing himself to this course, Davis negated the natural advantages of defense, passing it off instead to an adversary already possessing significant advantages of numbers, materiel and transport. In other words, military forces placed in fixed positions that could provide local security to the populace facing Indian raiding parties might have been a viable garrisoning option for a peacetime Secretary of War, but it was nothing less than a recipe for disaster when waging a revolutionary war for existence. The stultifying policy of defending everywhere directly caused the significant losses suffered in the West as well as along the Atlantic coastline in early 1862. True, little could have been done to prevent the capture of Roanoke Island and Port Royal Sound. Both were very exposed points. However, the loss of these did not also have to carry with them the loss of significant numbers of invaluable Confederate manpower and ordnance. Yet, this is exactly the result of Davis' "strategy of defense by dispersal"—a policy which, to cite one example, turned a marginally competent general like Ambrose Burnside into the hero of Roanoke Island and New Berne—and which made well-executed Federal combined operations irresistible.[6]

Richmond stood next in line whenever the Federals decided to move against Confederate vitals. Close to Washington City by an overland route, and accessible by water, Richmond represented the one objective most critical to the Confederacy. If in place, Davis' policy would hamstring the field commander charged with the capital's defense, and with Johnston in charge, the flaws of the two men would prove synergistic. With significant numbers of troops sitting in garrisons, fewer troops stood available for concentration with the mobile armies; therefore, Johnson's calculus would lead to retreat after retreat. The results of Davis' strategy had become manifest. He had largely created the conditions whereby less Southern manpower would be available to concentrate and maneuver with the intent of retaining the operational initiative against the larger Federal armies. At the same time, the policy guaranteed that when the Federal armies moved, the passive, dispersed and numerically fewer Southern troops in their paths would be gobbled up or forced to give way. When the inevitable result came to pass,

Courtesy Harpers Weekly

Federal troops storming Confederate defenses on Roanoke Island

---

[6] The term, "strategy of defense by dispersal," was coined by Clifford Dowdey in his, *Death of a Nation: The Story of Lee and His Men at Gettysburg* (New York, 1958), p. 16. The fatuity of this so-called strategy is so obvious that the author took Dowdey's phrase and used it in *Last Chance for Victory*, pp. 12-18.

Southern politicians, who "had grown up in the mold, not of policy makers, but of policy critics," reacted to the cries of their constituents and decided that President Davis needed some help in running a war. After all, its course needed to be turned around, and fast.[7]

* * *

To paraphrase aristocratic Southern language of the time, it had become clear by early 1862 that directing the military defenses of the Confederacy was too much for one man already burdened by the challenges of civil administration. In a more realistic tone, some Southern newspapers of the time dared to speculate on the state of public affairs. One Georgia weekly journal said, "President Davis does not enjoy the confidence of the Southern people." Directly referencing the President's "strategy of defense by dispersal," the Georgia publication described Davis, "with a cold, icy, iron grasp, has fettered our people, stilled their beating pulses of patriotism, cooled their fiery ardor, imprisoned them in camps and behind entrenchments." *The Richmond Examiner* was much bolder, and denounced the chief executive "as the ultimate enemy of the South." The war's direction as provided by Davis, who had surrounded himself with civilian sycophants, was seen as the most obvious cause for falling Southern fortunes. One Virginian wrote in his diary: "Nothing can exceed the imbecility of President Davis. His obstinacy and self will are dreadful. He will not have about him men of talent and force." Major General Daniel "Harvey" Hill, brother-in-law to Thomas J. Jackson and a division commander who served under Joe Johnston and later Robert E. Lee, understood, at least during this time in the war, the folly of Davis' defensive policy and the results that limited the manpower serving with the mobile army. After retreating with Johnston to the outskirts of Richmond in May, 1862, Hill wrote Secretary of War George Wythe Randolph to ask if he could do anything to change the President's way of conducting war. "Why permit ourselves to be beaten in detail," Hill queried, "when we might throw our heavy masses with resistless force upon the enemy? I do not think that I am an alarmist . . . but the scattering of our forces makes me fear the worst." Perhaps Charles Marshall summed up the situation best after the war when he recalled that in the Spring of 1862 it "had become very general among the people of the Confederate States, that Mr. Davis was not competent to direct operations of the Armies."[8]

The Confederate Congress, its members just months earlier engaging in mindless babble about the war being over by February, 1862, failed to appreciate the potential irony of their boasts. If the war were to end soon, it would be the Federal juggernaut that would do it. Rather than realize that many urgently-needed defense-related issues required immediate correction—such as further efforts at raising and supplying troops, along with increasing terms of enlistments in order to keep the men with the colors—Congress focused on Davis.

The President had been very busy—as might be expected of someone with

"One of the falsest notions in war is to remain on the defensive and let the enemy act offensively. In the long run it is inevitable that the party which stays on the defensive will lose."

—Frederick the Great

Courtesy Library of Congress

George Wythe Randolph

---

[7] *Journal of the Congress of the Confederate States of America, 1861-1865*, 6 volumes (Washington, 1904), vol. 2, p. 47. Senate Bill 4 was "a resolution pledging the Government to maintain the territorial integrity of the Confederacy," but Davis' imagination was so limited that he took the pledge literally; William C. Davis, *Jefferson Davis*, p. 436.

[8] Dowdey, *The Land They Fought For*, pp. 157-158; *Official Records*, Series I, vol. 11, part 3, Daniel Harvey Hill to George Wythe Randolph, May 25, 1862, p. 544; Marshall, *Lee's Aide de Camp*, pp. 3-4.

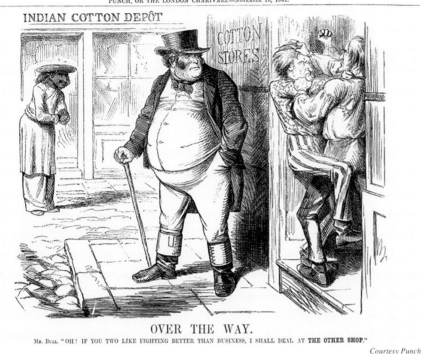

INDIAN COTTON DEPÔT

COTTON STORES

OVER THE WAY.

Mr. Bull. "OH! IF YOU TWO LIKE FIGHTING BETTER THAN BUSINESS, I SHALL DEAL AT **THE OTHER SHOP.**"

Courtesy Punch

Cartoon portraying England having to seek cotton elsewhere

a controlling personality—coupled with being plagued by trigeminal neuralgia. From this affliction, Davis suffered intermittent, severe pain that interfered with daily activities such as eating and sleeping. Tragically, it was the fear of suffering sudden, painful attacks that led to Davis' sleep deprivation and under-eating that must have contributed to his irritability and anxiety. Thus, to comfort himself, Davis spent virtually all of his time and energies in the field of his interest while relegating affairs of state to what amounted to second-tier considerations. Perhaps Davis felt that there was virtually nothing for the State Department to do. After all—and while Davis would not have described it this way—he had committed his government to the policy of bringing England to her knees and enticing her into the war on the side of the Confederacy by withholding cotton. However, by March, 1862, the fatuity of Davis' cotton policy became clearer to a growing number of folks inside and out of the halls of Confederate government. Foreign intervention was not imminent, especially if the Confederacy could not demonstrate the ability to defend itself.

Lee's return to the capital on Friday, March 7th had not been heralded by the chief executive who had suddenly summoned him. While Davis' March 2nd telegram clearly seemed to indicate the importance of Lee's return ("I wish to see you here with the least delay"), the President showed no particular excitement or concern about his arrival. For Lee, it felt as if the "wasted year" would soon stretch into a wasted war. Instead of immediately assigning Lee to duty, Davis did nothing. This did not sit well with many members of Congress who were of the opinion that Virginia's favorite son needed to be utilized in a meaningful way. A few days earlier, on Monday, March 3rd, as soon as word of Lee's recall reached lawmakers, the Confederate House of Representatives introduced "a bill to create the office of commanding general of the armies of the Confederate States." Passing quickly through the House that same day by a vote of 50 to 16, and subsequently the Senate a few days later, the bill had no intention, and no language, of altering the theoretical constitutional powers of the President as the commander-in-chief. Instead, Congress realized the impossibility of Jeff Davis and his staff continuing to exercise control of all movements of all armies in the field. The bill created a new grade in the service whereby a professional soldier holding the title of "Commanding General of the Armies" would have authority over all Confederate armies and their commanders, coordinating

Rolling Cotton on Board the "Tatum."

Courtesy Harpers Weekly

Images of the South's leading cash crop— cotton

their recruitments, training, movements and more. At the same time, the bill was *very clear* that the officer holding that position was subordinate to the President. Lawmakers created the position with the expectation that President Davis would name General Lee to the post as soon as the bill was signed. However, the legislators had misread the President.[9]

Jefferson Davis did not want Robert E. Lee—or any other general for that matter—in *his* war office. As discussed earlier in this work, the genesis of this attitude dated back to the Mexican War and continued through the secession crisis. During the late 1840s, and continuing in the 1850s when he was a Secretary of War, Davis spent inordinate energy in a vitriolic and absurd feud with Winfield Scott. Years later, the last thing Davis wanted was having Scott's *protégé* foisted upon him. Furthermore, the President considered this move by Congress a direct challenge to his constitutional authority. Indeed, the better-intentioned members of Congress merely wanted Robert E. Lee in a position whereby he could employ his talents. When word got back to Congress that Davis was cold towards the new bill, the behind-the-scenes political action heated up. Genuinely desirous of loosening Davis' iron grasp on the military and bringing in a real soldier to take charge of the country's failing defense, Congressional leaders let Davis know that they wanted Robert E. Lee in a position of authority. They also let the President know that if he returned the bill, they had enough votes to override his veto. Once the bill was overridden and became law, who else but Lee, reasoned the lawmakers, could fill the position as the new "Commanding General of the Armies?" With this applied pressure from lawmakers, Davis had no choice but to strike as much of a compromise as his personality dared.

Having taken Davis' communication as urgent, Lee left his departmental assignment and rushed to take the train back to Richmond, only to find himself languishing in the capital almost a week after his arrival, waiting for his new assignment. Davis' telegram of March 2nd that "I wish to see you here with the least delay" had been sent without any evident sincerity, if the President is to be judged by his actions. Instead, with the pressure from lawmakers firmly in place, Davis made a politically calculated move of astonishing disingenuousness. On Thursday, March 13th, the chief executive announced that General Lee was "assigned to duty at the seat of government; and, under

997

CONFEDERATE AUTHORITIES.

encampment for drill, &c. An assistant quartermaster-general will be in readiness at the place of general rendezvous to provide all the necessary outfit and subsistence. These regiments will elect their own officers. The staff of each regiment will recommend, which always amounts to an appointment, the regimental quartermaster, commissary, surgeon, &c. Any one wishing further information will receive it promptly by addressing me at Bonham, Fannin County, Tex. To give this a wider circulation in Texas I hope the patriotic editors of newspapers in the counties designated will insert it in their papers.

SAML. A. ROBERTS,
Assistant Adjutant-General, Provisional Army, C. S.

EXECUTIVE DEPARTMENT,
March 14, 1862.

To the SPEAKER OF THE HOUSE OF REPRESENTATIVES: .

Not being able to approve, I return with my objections, in accordance with the duty imposed by the Constitution, an act entitled "An act to create the office of commanding general of the armies of the Confederate States." The act creates an office which is to continue during the pleasure of the President, but the tenure of office of the general to be appointed is without any other limitation than that of the office itself. The purpose of the act, so far as it creates a military bureau the head of which, at the seat of government, under direction of the President, shall be charged with the movement of troops, the supply and discipline of the Army, I fully approve; but, by what I cannot regard otherwise than as an inadvertence on the part of Congress, the officer so appointed is authorized to take the field at his own discretion and command any army or armies he may choose, not only without the direction but even against the will of the President, who could not consistently with this act prevent such conduct of the general otherwise than by abolishing his office. To show that the effect of this act would be highly detrimental to the Army, it might be enough to say that no general would be content to prepare troops for battle, conduct their movements, and share their privations during a whole campaign if he expected to find himself superseded at the very moment of action. But there is another ground which to my mind is conclusive. The Constitution vests in the Executive the command in chief of the armies of the Confederacy; that command is totally inconsistent with the existence of an officer authorized, at his own discretion, to take command of armies assigned by the President to other generals. The Executive could in no just sense be said to be Commander-in-Chief, if without the power to control the discretion of the general created by this act. As it cannot have been the intention of Congress to create the office of a general not bound to obey the orders of the Chief Magistrate, and as this seems to be the effect of the act, I can but anticipate the concurrence of the Congress in my opinion that it should not become a law.

JEFFERSON DAVIS.

[Inclosure.]

AN ACT to create the office of commanding general of the armies of the Confederate States.

The Congress of the Confederate States do enact, That there shall be, and is hereby, created the office of commanding general of the

[9]*Journal of the Congress of the Confederate States of America, 1861-1865*, vol. 2, p. 47; *Official Records*, Series IV, vol. 1, "An Act to create the office of commanding general of the armies of the Confederate States," pp. 997-998; Marshall, *Lee's Aide de Camp*, pp. 3-5; Dowdey, *Lee*, pp. 180-181; Dowdey, *The Land They Fought For*, pp. 157-158.

the direction of the President, is charged with the conduct of military operations in the armies of the Confederacy." There were no details, no explanations. Lawmakers could only *assume* that Davis was voluntarily assigning Lee for meaningful duty along the lines and in the spirit of the bill just sent to the President. The following day, Davis returned the bill unsigned to the House of Representatives. With it, the President attached a letter to Speaker Thomas S. Bocock of Virginia, maintaining that the bill infringed on his legal rights. "The Constitution," Davis lectured those who already knew, "vests in the Executive the command in chief of the armies of the Confederacy." In Davis' mind, the bill reeked of intrusion and disrespect, as evidenced by his words "seems to be the effect of the act." Despite the fact that the bill contained no such infringement on Davis' constitutional powers, the President's assigning of Lee had the effect of defusing the situation.[10]

The completion of Davis' maneuver was revealed in the ending of his letter. "I can but anticipate the concurrence of the Congress in my opinion that it should not become a law," Davis entreated. House members by force of circumstance sustained the veto. They *believed* that President Davis had taken the steps that they were intending in the bill, and they *thought* the talents of Robert E. Lee were about to be employed in a meaningful way. At least one newspaper saw things clearly. Ten days after the House sustained the veto, the editors of *The Charleston Mercury* accurately described Lee as being reduced "from a commanding general to an orderly sergeant."[11]

In truth, President Davis out-foxed Congress to keep control of the war's defense policy. As a result, the implementation of his policy of defense would continue, and Jefferson Davis had reinforced to Congress "that he wanted to be Commander-in-Chief not only in law but in fact." For Davis, the only change, if you could call it that, was that Robert E. Lee was now officially in tow in an anomalous role with no authority unless specifically conveyed by the President. Lee had returned, like a repeating nightmare, to the same, senseless arrangement that had existed during the summer of 1861, except now it existed on a formal level.[12]

---

998   CORRESPONDENCE, ETC.

armies of the Confederate States, which office shall continue only during the pleasure of the President.

SEC. 2. *Be it further enacted,* That the said officer shall be appointed by the President by and with the advice and consent of the Senate. His usual headquarters shall be at the seat of government, and shall be charged, under the direction of the President, with the general control of military operations, the movement and discipline of the troops, and the distribution of the supplies among the armies of the Confederate States, and may, when he shall deem it advisable, take command in person of our army or armies in the field.

SEC. 3. *Be it further enacted,* That the pay of the commanding general aforesaid shall be $400 per month, without allowances; and if the officer appointed under the provisions of this act shall be an officer of the permanent Army the appointment shall not affect his rank as such, but he shall receive none of the pay and allowances of his grade as an officer of the permanent Army while holding the office created by this act.

SEC. 4. *Be it further enacted,* That the staff of the commanding general shall consist of a military secretary with the rank of colonel, four aides-de-camp with the rank of major, and such clerks, not to exceed four in number, as the President shall from time to time authorize. The pay and allowances of the military secretary and aides-de-camp shall be the same as those of officers of cavalry of the like grade, and the salaries of the clerks shall not exceed $1,200 per annum for each. Such offices, office furniture, fuel, and stationery shall be provided for the commanding general as the duties of his office may render necessary, to be paid for out of the appropriation for the contingent expenses of the War Department.

Passed House March 3, 1862. Vote, 50 to 16.
Passed Senate March 6, 1862. Vote not recorded.
[Veto sustained in the House by vote of 68 to 1.]

[MARCH 14, 1862.—For General Orders, No. 15, Adjutant and Inspector General's Office, publishing proclamation of Jefferson Davis, extending martial law over certain counties in Virginia, see Series I, Vol. LI, Part II, p. 502.]

Hon. W. M. BROOKS,   RICHMOND, VA., *March 15, 1862.*
        Marion Ala.:

MY DEAR SIR: If under other circumstances I might be willing to hear criticism of my acts, the condition of the country now too fully engrosses all my thoughts and feelings to permit such selfish impatience, and I have read yours of the 25th ultimo,* anxious to gather from it information, and thankful for your friendly remembrance and the confidence your frankness evinces. I acknowledge the error of my attempt to defend all of the frontier, sea-board and inland; but will say in justification that if we had received the arms and munitions which we had good reason to expect, the attempt would have been successful and the battle-fields would have been on the enemy's soil. You seem to have fallen into the most uncommon mistake of supposing that I have chosen to carry on the war upon a "purely defensive system." The advantage of selecting the time and place of attack was

Not found.

---

[10] *Official Records,* series I, vol. 5, "General Orders, No. 14," March 13, 1862, p. 1099; *Journal of the Congress of the Confederate States of America, 1861-1865,* 6 volumes, vol. 5, pp. 107-108.

[11] *Journal of the Congress of the Confederate States of America, 1861-1865,* 6 volumes, vol. 5, p. 108 *Official Records,* Series IV, vol. 1, "An Act to create the office of commanding general of the armies of the Confederate States," pp. 997-998; *The Charleston Mercury,* March 24, 1862. The House veto was sustained by a vote of 68 to 1.

[12] *Official Records,* Series IV, vol. 1, The Senate of the Confederate States, March 17, 1862; Marshall, *Lee's Aide-de-Camp,* p. 6; Dowdey, *The Land They Fought For,* p. 160. With the

Another New Position, But Still No Authority—
Lee's New Role

Robert E. Lee's realistic approach tolerated no illusions about the unrewarding position to which he had just been named, or the mounting difficulties facing the Confederacy. Lee knew that he worked for a President who operated his own staff and, in Davis' need of omnipotence, usurped many of the functions of the War Department. To be sure, Davis immediately gave Lee things to do, but they lacked defined purpose, were totally without authority, and, absent the sage advice offered up by Lee, could have been carried out by any competent junior officer. Lee's disappointment with his new position expressed itself poignantly; he offered his valued and trusted aide, Walter Taylor, "the choice between [serving elsewhere as part of] the adjutant-general's department of the service or an appointment as major and aide-de-camp" to a desk-bound general. The loyal Taylor "told him I would rather be an aide."[13]

Courtesy Harpers Weekly

The Confederate War Department

Lee's first day at his new position was a precursor of a typical one. Davis consulted at length with the general about defensive preparations that often had no basis in reality. With his charts and his maps that displayed the President's widely dispersed defensive garrisons, and in the face of an enemy who could operate against a static system without fear of counter-developments, Davis' strategy represented the virtual antithesis to Lee's understanding of war. Thus, Davis' long hours of work were bitterly ironic; the more he tried to control the war, the more he harmed The Cause, and Lee knew it. Writing to his wife from Richmond the day after receiving the new assignment, Lee confided his disappointment: "I have been placed on duty here to conduct operations under the direction of the President. It will give me great pleasure to do anything I can to relieve him and serve the country, but I do not see either advantage or pleasure in my duties. But I will not complain, but do my best...The enemy is pushing us back in all directions, and how far he will be successful depends much upon our efforts and the mercy of Providence...." Lee's self-control seems remarkable in that he penned those words at the moment when the chief executive was busily destroying the Confederacy through the folly of his arrogance.[14]

"It is always proper to assume that the enemy will do what he should do."

—Robert E. Lee to Jefferson Davis

Lee matter settled, Davis then hurriedly reorganized his Cabinet that had no Secretary of State and a War Secretary that was under fire for his role in the loss of Roanoke Island. Congress and many citizens were upset with how Judah Benjamin was handling his job as Secretary of War, as so Davis used this opportunity to shift Benjamin's vast talents out of the War Department and into the wasteland of the Confederate State Department, where, at least in theory, Benjamin carried the highest prestige. With Benjamin moved out of the War Department, Davis had to find a replacement. Two lawyers had already been Davis' Secretary of War, and neither had been able to suit Davis' or Congress' expectations. Consequently, on March 17, 1862, Davis named George Wythe Randolph, a grandson of Thomas Jefferson and popular Virginian as well as a relative of Robert E. Lee, as the new Secretary of War. Randolph would work with Lee over the course of the next eight months.

[13] Taylor, *General Lee*, p. 42.

[14] Robert E. Lee, Jr., *Recollections and Letters*, Robert E. Lee To His Wife, March 14, 1862, p. 58.

Among the challenges in Lee's professional life that tested his spirit, suffering as Davis' advisor ranks as paramount among them. Biographer Clifford Dowdey described "his heroic self-mastery of the less noble human traits which dog us all that gave to the total man a symmetry akin to the sublime in art." Lee exhibited incalculable discipline while pursuing his dedication to duty. Yet Davis triumphantly celebrated his political sleight of hand by reassigning the Old Army's "finest soldier" to an ignominious desk job that he *knew* Lee abhorred. The contrast in character between Lee and Davis seems stupefying. In Dowdey's words, "It must have required the patience of Job for Lee to endure this disrespect and waste of his talents, while seeing the Commander in Chief bring his native state to the brink of a disaster which had already befallen" so much of the country. While lesser men would have revolted at such treatment, Lee only deepened his humility and devoted himself as best he could to his new duties.[15]

Courtesy Museum of the Confederacy

Walter Taylor, General Lee's longest-serving aide-de-camp, shown in his Norfolk Militia uniform

---

[15] Dowdey, *The Land They Fought For*, pp. 160-161. Perhaps Lee's greatness of spirit that was used to deal with the circumstances of his newest and humiliatingly impossible job came from his devout religious faith. In the conclusion of his March 14th letter to Mary, Lee told of how in the early evening hours of the 13th, word came to him that Virginia's Episcopal Bishop, William Meade, wanted to see the general as soon as possible. Meade had been Rector of Christ Church in Alexandria during Lee's youth, and decades later from his death bed the bishop gave the Lee a blessing that moved the general greatly. See Robert E. Lee, Jr., *Recollections and Letters*, Robert E. Lee To His Wife, March 14, 1862, p. 59.

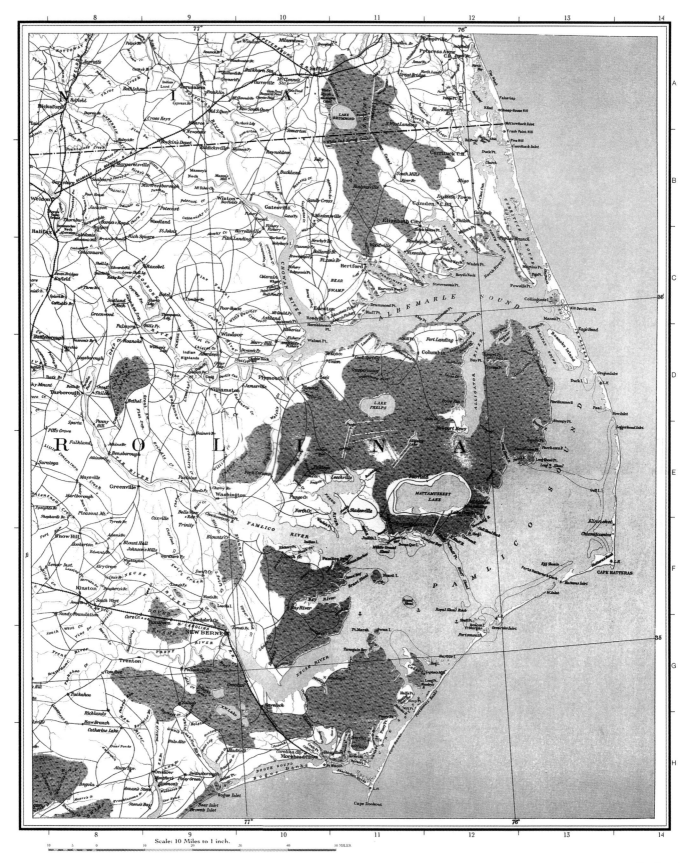

Map of Albemarle Sound and New Berne Area

Atlas, Official Records

* * *

On the day that Davis made the announcement of Lee becoming what amounted to an advisor, Confederate war fortunes in the East started to unravel. When the ever-so-slightest indication suggested that McClellan's army was beginning to move, General Johnston abandoned his position in far Northern Virginia. Johnston knew that McClellan could flank his Manassas defensive line on his way overland to Richmond, but thought a far more likely scenario involved McClellan transferring the Federal army to the Peninsula via water for combined operations against Richmond. Johnston therefore hastily departed his base at Centreville after making no serious advance plans for ensuring an orderly and efficient withdrawal. The hurried state of affairs conjured up memories of Johnston's harried departure from Harpers Ferry the previous June where he left invaluable rolling stock and other machinery behind. This time, incredibly, with his army in no discernible danger, Johnston put a torch to a million pounds of food and other supplies that his command desperately needed. The lowliest private could not have failed to notice the waste and incompetence. Compounding the wastage, Johnston thoughtlessly abandoned his heavy artillery that, despite the age of the ordnance and poor weather conditions, certainly could have been moved to Richmond for the city's defense. The loss of these guns, regardless of their age, was especially senseless at this point in the war, because it occurred at a time when Confederate government agents were scouring the countryside for metal so that the Tredegar Iron Works could deliver ordnance for The Cause.[16]

As meaningful as was the loss of supplies and guns along the Manassas line, other alarming news reached Lee's desk the first day of his new assignment. A Federal combined naval and army expedition commanded by Ambrose E. Burnside and carrying three brigades of infantry numbering 11,000 had descended from recently-captured Roanoke Island and landed near the North Carolina town of New Berne, an old community at the confluence of the Trent and Neuse rivers. The Confederate defense consisted of nine forts mounting 46 heavy guns, garrisoned by a 4,000-man brigade of Tarheels under Princeton graduate Brigadier General Lawrence O'Bryan Branch and supported by three batteries of field artillery. The Federals ran the river batteries and entered the Trent River, disembarking their troops behind the Confederate positions and on the opposite side of the river. Spending only a day to slog their way through the swamps and thickets to get guns and men into position, the Federals attacked on the morning of the 14th. After four hours of heavy fighting, the outnumbered Confederates were driven from the field, losing several hundred men in the process. The Burnside-led forces took possession of the nine forts, 46 heavy guns and 18 field artillery pieces. In securing New Berne, the Federals lost only about 550 killed and wounded. However, in their loss, the Federals gained another serviceable anchorage. New Berne also gave the blue clad forces a staging area for launching inland expeditions against the vital stretch of the Wilmington & Weldon Railroad— track that connected Richmond with the South Atlantic states—that ran through Goldsboro, less than 60 miles inland.[17]

BRIGADIER-GENERAL BURNSIDE.—[PHOTOGRAPHED BY BRADY.]

Courtesy Harpers Weekly

Ambrose E. Burnside

[16] *Official Records*, Series I, vol. 5, Johnston to Davis, February 22, 1862, p. 1079; Johnston to Whiting, February 27, 1862, pp. 1082-1083; Johnston to Davis, March 2, 1862, p. 1088; Marshall, *Lee's Aide de Camp*, p. 28; Dowdey, *The Land They Fought For*, pp. 164-165; Dowdey, *Lee*, p. 185.

[17] *Official Records*, Series I, vol. 9, "Reports of A. E. Burnside" dating March 16, 1862, March 21, 1862 and April 10, 1862; "General Orders, No. 17," March 15, 1862; R. C. Gatlin to J. P. Benjamin, March 14, 1862, p. 443; R. C. Gatlin to Samuel Cooper, March 14, 1862, pp. 443-

To this crisis, Davis overreacted.   Undeniably, some forces needed to be dispatched to the New Berne area as quickly as possible to prevent any significant Federal inland excursion and to protect the rail line. Davis therefore "authorized" Lee to redirect selected units and brigades from two commands in Virginia to the threatened area, as well as selected senior officers to accompany the units. The forces detached from the mobile Virginia commands were not immediately replaced, as Davis insisted on maintaining dispersed forces across the frontier as well as before the capital. Therefore, Davis' response to the Battle of New Berne was the first of many examples of his over-reaction to a given situation when more important objectives had to be kept in mind. When he was finished, Davis had detached more than 10 percent of the existing strength from the principal Confederate army. This shifting of troops to the threatened New Berne area would not have been needed had Branch's command been held slightly inland. In addition, Davis somehow believed that Lee would be a suitable commander for these detachments bound for the New Berne front (now to number approximately three brigades accompanied by two batteries) when several other lower-grade general officers were already present. However, the President soon changed his mind about sending a full general to command this small force and instead called upon an old West Point friend of his who he had already promoted to major general. Theophilus Hunter Holmes, a native North Carolinian, was sent to Goldsboro to organize that area's defenses. While this was being done, Confederate authorities in Richmond knew that the mammoth Federal army under George McClellan was poised to move.[18]

Lee was monitoring the latest enemy combined operations when he became involved with the organization and preservation of the Southern armies. He already recognized the dire situation facing the Confederacy, and knew that there was plenty of work to do keeping the armies intact in the face of expiring enlistments, along with the dangers which the existing laws presented to the army's efficiency. With things not going well across the South, combined with volunteers soon to decide on renewing their commitments, he feared the worst. Therefore, in order to correct some of the ills that already existed in order to avoid a collapse of the army which was the sole hope of the country, Lee unveiled some bold initiatives. Believing that the Confederacy had to look within for achieving its independence, Lee realized that the army *had* to be dramatically increased and its efficiency substantially improved.

On or about April 1st, in order to achieve both goals, General Lee directed the newest member of his staff, Lieutenant Charles Marshall, to prepare a

---

444; Henry T. Clark to J. P. Benjamin, March 15, 1862, pp. 444-445. While the town certainly may not have been defensible, what cannot be argued is that if Lee's strategy of concentration had been adopted around New Berne, and had Branch's command and fortifications been further inland, the town's loss would not have also meant the loss of 64 valuable guns and hundreds of men. See Harvey Hill's analysis of the New Berne defeat in: *Official Records*, Series I vol. 51, part 2, Supplement, D. H. Hill to G. W. Randolph, March 22, 1862, pp. 512-513. For details on the Confederate rail lines, see: Robert C. Black, *The Railroads of the Confederacy* (Chapel Hill, 1952), front maps and key legend on pp. xxii-xxix. For some details concerning the fighting, see: *Supplement to the Official Records of the Union and Confederate Armies*, Part I—Reports, Volume 1, Serial No. 1 (Wilmington, 1994), pp. 598-602.

[18] Robert E. Lee, Jr., *Recollections and Letters*, Robert E. Lee To His Wife, March 15, 1862, pp. 59-60; *Official Records*, Series I, vol. 9, Henry T. Clark to J. P. Benjamin, March 15, 1862, pp. 444-445, S. G. French to Robert E. Lee, March 18, 1862, pp. 448-449; Benjamin Huger to Robert E. Lee, March 20, 1862, p. 449; Robert E. Lee to B. Huger, March 21, 1862, pp. 449-450; *Official Records*, Series I, vol. 11, part 3, Robert E. Lee to J. B. Magruder, March 22, 1862, p. 391; *Official Records*, Series I, vol. 12, part 3, J. E. Johnston to Robert E. Lee, March 20, 1862, p. 832; *Official Records*, Series I, vol. 51, part 2, Supplement, Robert E. Lee to Jefferson Davis, March 21,1862, p. 512.

Charles Marshall

draft of a bill for the Confederacy to raise more men through conscription and to reorganize the armies by way of a number of improvements deemed best by the general. Marshall seemed to be the perfect man for the job, for he possessed a brilliant mind and a rare mastery of both the English language and mathematics. A native Virginian and kinsman of the former Chief Justice John Marshall, Charles earned a Masters Degree in English from the University of Virginia at the age of 18 where he achieved the institution's "highest honors." The bespectacled Marshall tackled the ambitious project, cleanly penning within just a few days all of Lee's objectives and goals. General Lee took Marshall's draft to the President, who gave it to Secretary of State Benjamin, who then recommended it to Congress for adoption. On April 16th, "An act to further provide for the public defense" was approved, but what Congress passed and the President signed into law was *not* the desperately needed reforms that Lee had submitted (see summary chart, next page).

Instead of the measures that Lee believed would dramatically improve the officers through a system of meritocracy, Congress opted to sustain the militia system of popular elections. Worse, instead of following Lee's advice about insuring the maintenance of the supply of officers and their execution of duties, and instead of passing a conscription law that was imminently fair to all able-bodied men between 18 and 45 years of age, Congress took the liberty of substantially reshaping the act, most egregiously allowing for substitutions, and later for allowing exceptions for members of the slave-holding class. President Davis signed on to what Charles Marshall described as "certain grave and most hurtful alterations, the effects of which" haunted the Confederacy "until the end of the war." So radically were General Lee's original ideas mutated that Marshall believed "that the provisions of the bill as it passed Congress did more to weaken the army, to impair its efficiency, and in fact to prepare the way for disaster, than any single cause." The irony of what Lee had initiated would, through the changes to his vision made by the Confederate Congress, become considerable obstacles for him as commanding general of the army.[19]

SOUTHERN "VOLUNTEERS".

Courtesy Harpers Weekly

---

[19] *Official Records*, Series I, vol. 6, Robert E. Lee letter of December 24, 1861, pp. 349-351; *Southern Historical Society Papers*, vol. 1, Letter of Robert E. Lee to Governor Letcher, December 26, 1861, p. 462. A detailed account of Lee's various initiatives that include his ideas of a conscription act as well as his attempted reorganization of the army, are detailed in Volume Four of this series.

To read the account by the man who wrote the original draft, please consult: Charles Marshal, *Lee's Aide-de-Camp*, Chapter II, "General Lee Attempts Reforms," pp. 28-43. Marshall's excellent job with this project earned him a rapid promotion to Major on April 21, 1862, as mentioned in Robert E. L. Krick, *Staff Officers in Gray*, p. 214. Another summary of Lee's ideas and how they were altered may be found in Freeman, *R. E. Lee*, vol. 2, Chapter III, "Lee and the Conscription Act," pp. 25-29. What the Confederate Congress passed was styled by Douglas Southall Freeman as "a worse law could hardly have been imposed on the South by the enemy." For some of the evils that Lee was trying to correct and overcome, see: *Official Records*, Series I, vol. 5, General Orders, No. 1, "An act providing for the granting of bounty

Confederate Conscription–Two Visions

Key Points of Conscription Bill	Lee's Proposals	Law as Enacted
Existing enlistment laws	Repealed & replaced	Repealed & replaced
Eligible men subject to draft	Ages 18 to 45	Ages 18 to 35
Term of service	Duration of the war	Three years from the date of original enlistment
Existing volunteers whose term of enlistment was soon to expire	Retained for duration of war	Retained for three years
Substitutions*	None	Allowed
Exemptions	Physically & mentally unfit	Many, including the slave-holder class**
Regimental/battalion/company officers	Appointments based on merit	Popular election
Maintaining supply of junior officers	Promote deserving NCOs	Popular election of NCOs
Promotions— All ranks below brigadier general	Through valor & skill	Stimulus for promotion through valor & skill rendered "almost useless;" as a result, promotions were based on seniority

* Specifically included in original bill as an accommodation for the slave-holding class.
** The Exemption Act became law five days after the enactment of the first conscription legislation. The specific exemption for the slave-holder class added by amendment in Fall, 1862.

"Strategy of Defense by Dispersal," Combined With Retreat, Brings a Nation to the Brink

While matters of administration and reforms attracted much of Lee's time following his appointment as Davis' advisor, the general's primary interest was with developments in the field. For sure, Lee recognized it could only be a matter of days before the Federal Army of the Potomac, estimated to number between 150,000 and 200,000 combatants, started its movements. To oppose Major General George McClellan's army stood Joe Johnston's principal Confederate army that on March 1st, 1862—prior to the detachment of Holmes to North Carolina, and including the forces under Major General Thomas J. "Stonewall" Jackson in the Shenandoah Valley—had only 47,617 effectives, and all of who were

and furloughs to privates and non-commissioned officers in the Provisional Army," pp. 1016-1017. Also, please see the extensive comments to this act in: Bvt. Maj. Gen. Emory Upton, *The Military Policy of the United States* (Washington, 1912) pp. 457-470. Upton was indeed correct when he stated that Lee was trying to remedy a bad situation and what Southern lawmakers had been previously passed should have been styled as "an act to disorganize and dissolve the provisional army." For more details, also consult: *Journal of the Congress of the Confederate States of America, 1861-1865*, vol. 1, House proceedings, pp. 690, 692, 695, 711, 847 and 848.

Fortress Monroe at Old Point Comfort

Courtesy Harpers Weekly

described by historian Bruce Catton as still in the throws of "trying to reorganize their troops all the way down to company and regimental levels." Given the disparity of the forces, combined with the nature of President Davis' strategy and General Joe Johnston's *modus operandi*, Lee recognized that George McClellan had the complete freedom of maneuver. On March 24th, Lee received a telegram from Major General Benjamin Huger (pronounced *you-jee*) in Norfolk, advising that a sizable number of steamers had come down the Chesapeake Bay and had begun disembarking Federal troops at the tip of the Peninsula at Old Point Comfort (Fortress Monroe). A little later that day, another telegram from Major General John Bankhead Magruder, the commander on the Peninsula, to Secretary of War Randolph, confirmed that he was confronted by a large Federal force of "not less, I think, than 35,000 men."[20]

Although the telegrams did not say that the troops were from the Army of the Potomac, Lee had to consider all possible Federal options and various Confederate responses. Lee therefore weighed these scenarios in a series of long and detailed discussions with President Davis and Secretary of War Randolph. Within two days of Lee receiving news of the landing at Old Point Comfort, he had used his powers of persuasion to get Davis' approval to concentrate as many troops as Davis would allow on the Peninsula, subject to proper caution before the enemy's plans were fully discovered. As it turned out, that was only half the battle. As Davis still would not give Lee any authority, the President instead told him to advise Johnston to get his army ready to respond to a "move at once" order. Lost days ensued in late March during which Lee and Johnston traded correspondence in which it became clear that Johnston would largely ignore the President's advisor.[21]

Evidence accumulated that a large portion of the Federal Army of the Potomac had indeed been transported by sea to the tip of the Virginia Peninsula,

[20] *Official Records*, Series I, vol. 6, Robert E. Lee letter of December 24, 1861, pp. 349-351; The Army of the Potomac actually had 185,420 present for duty; see *Official Records*, Series I, vol. 5, "Abstract from return of the Army of the Potomac, commanded by Maj. Gen. George B. McClellan, U. S. Army, for the month of February, 1862," p. 732; for the Confederate strength, please consult "Abstract from return of the Department of Northern Virginia, General Joseph E. Johnston, C. S. Army, commanding, for the month of February, 1862, " p. 1086; Bruce Catton, *Terrible Swift Sword* (New York, 1963), p. 264; *Official Records*, Series I, vol. 11, part 3, Benjamin Huger to Robert E. Lee, March 24, 1862, p. 394; *Official Records*, Series I, vol. 11, part 3, J. Bankhead Magruder to George W. Randolph, of March 24, 1862, pp. 392-393. Freeman, *R. E. Lee*, vol. 2, p. 13, states that the telegram from Huger arrived before the one sent by Magruder.

[21] *Official Records*, Series I, vol. 6, Robert E. Lee to Joseph E. Johnston, March 25, 1862, p. 397; *Official Records*, Series I, vol. 6, Joseph E. Johnston to Robert E. Lee, March 26, 1862, pp. 400-401; *Official Records*, Series I, vol. 6, Robert E. Lee to Joseph E. Johnston, 1 A.M. March 28, 1862, p. 408; *Official Records*, Series I, vol. 6, Robert E. Lee to Joseph E. Johnston, March 28, 1862, pp. 408-409.

and from there would soon march into action. The Herculean efforts of the men who built and sailed the ironclad *C.S.S. Virginia* bought time—only to be matched by the workers employed at the Delamater iron works in Brooklyn who had armored the *U.S.S. Monitor*. In early March, the *Virginia* steamed out of Norfolk, attacked, destroyed or ran aground several formidable, wooden-hulled Federal warships off Newport News. Fought to a standoff the next day by the *Monitor*, the *Virginia* remained afloat at the great naval base at Norfolk. As a consequence, the Federals dared not steam past her into the mouth of the James River. Thus the Federal fleet could not move up river to guard their army's left, or southern, flank. Meanwhile, the waterway on the north side of the Peninsula—the York River—was firmly closed by Confederate guns at Yorktown and Gloucester Point where the York was only 1,000 yards wide.[22]

Courtesy Harpers Weekly

C.S.S. Virginia

Lee was in favor of keeping the Federals in and around Old Point Comfort and therefore as far down on the Peninsula for as long as practicable. However, in order to realize that goal over a several-week period of time, Confederate forces already on the Peninsula had to be reinforced significantly and immediately. Even with the Federal commander acting systematically, Lee recognized that McClellan simply had too many soldiers, guns and ships to be bottled up forever by Magruder's diminutive command of 10,000 men. Failing reinforcements, the high-strung and imaginative Magruder would be forced to give way, and McClellan would then steamroll his way up the Peninsula to Richmond, eventually pulverizing any *static* Confederate army in range of his massive siege train. Meanwhile,

Courtesy Library of Congress

The Battle Between the *U.S.S. Monitor* and *C.S.S. Virginia*

another Federal force under the command of Irvin McDowell, consisting in part of the First Corps of McClellan's army that he did not take with him by sea to the Peninsula, remained around Washington and would be available to move overland towards Richmond if President Lincoln perceived that there was no threat to the Federal capital. With McClellan and the majority of the Army of the Potomac pressing up the Peninsula, and with McDowell and his augmented First Corps descending from the north to form a junction near Richmond, the Confederate capital and the rebellion's center of gravity would be taken in one blow, thereby giving a knockout to the hastily improvised compact

---

[22] The Confederates had lifted the sunken Federal steamer *Merrimack*, armored her with iron plates from the Tredegar works, increased her firepower and rechristened her the *C.S.S. Virginia*.

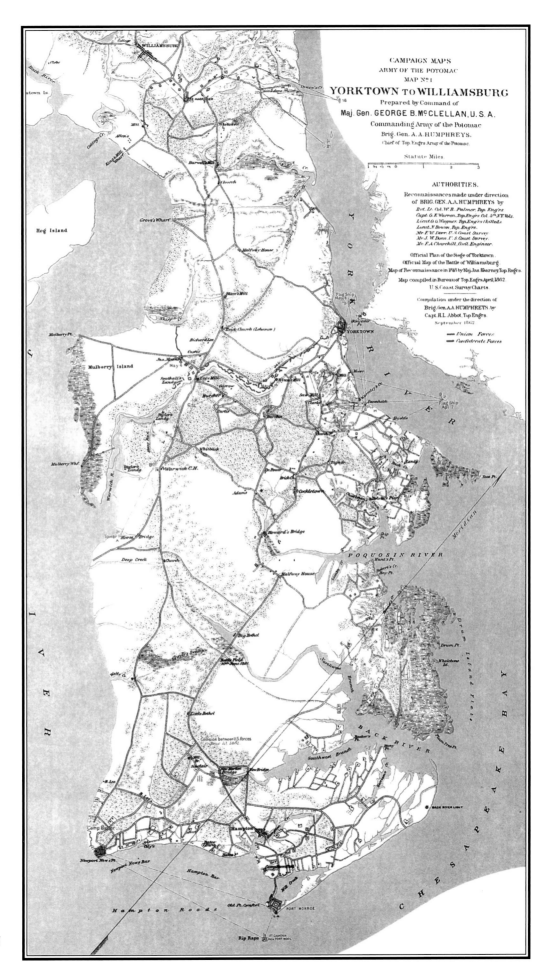

**Virginia Peninsula from
Old Point Comfort to Williamsburg**

Atlas, Official Records

of agricultural states by seizing its singularly important city. McClellan's civilian superiors were certainly confident that the impending campaign would mark the beginning of the end to the war. President Lincoln decided to visit with McClellan at Fortress Monroe, and while President Lincoln was there, Buildings Commissioner B. B. French wrote that: "The rebellion is on its last legs." With things already going well elsewhere, Lincoln's Secretary of War Edwin Stanton confidently closed his recruiting offices in early April, a move that one historian described as "the ultimate statement of his [Stanton] confidence in the Confederacy's early doom."[23]

Indeed, the way misfortunes kept piling up for the Confederacy, Stanton had every reason to be confident that the war

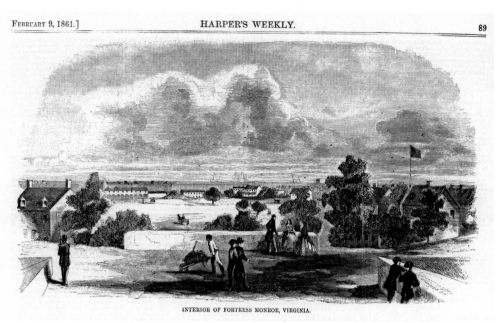

INTERIOR OF FORTRESS MONROE, VIRGINIA.

Courtesy Harpers Weekly

Fortress Monroe

would soon be over. In the West, the Confederates suffered the defeat at Shiloh on April 6th and 7th, along with the mortal wounding of Sidney Johnston on the first day of the battle. Meanwhile, further defeats ensued; another Confederate army was beaten at Pea Ridge, Arkansas, followed by the fall of Island No. 10 on the Mississippi. With its surrender, nothing, it appeared, could save Memphis from capture. Later in the month on the Gulf end of the Mississippi, a powerful Yankee fleet under Admiral David Farragut daringly ran past the river forts guarding New Orleans. This bold move led to the abandonment of the great Crescent City to the consternation of Davis, who had conveniently chosen to believe that the Federals would only approach New Orleans from the other direction, downriver over several hundreds miles, rather than steam upriver a mere 90 miles. Emerging from that Federal victory was Benjamin Butler, commander in New Orleans, yet another marginally competent military man foisted to Federal glory via a flawed defensive concept. As New Orleans stood so far away from the war's epicenter, events in Virginia soon swept Davis' culpability in losing the South's largest port from the papers. Along the Atlantic coast on April

PANORAMIC VIEW OF NEW ORLEANS—THE FEDERAL FLEET AT ANCHOR IN THE RIVER, APRIL 25th, 1862.

Courtesy Library of Congress

New Orleans Battle

---

[23] *Official Records*, Series I, vol. 11, part 3, Robert E. Lee to J. B. Magruder, March 26, 1862, pp. 398-399, and Robert E. Lee to Joseph E. Johnston, March 28, 1862, pp. 408-409; Benjamin Brown French, *Witness to the Young Republic: A Yankee's Journal 1828-1870* (Hanover, 1989 reprint), p. 397; (Emory Thomas, *The Confederate Nation: 1861-1865* (New York, 1979), p. 145. Also see: *Official Records*, Series 3, vol. 2, "General Orders, No. 33," also known as "Stanton's Act," pp. 2-3. Catton, *Terrible Swift Sword*, p. 264.

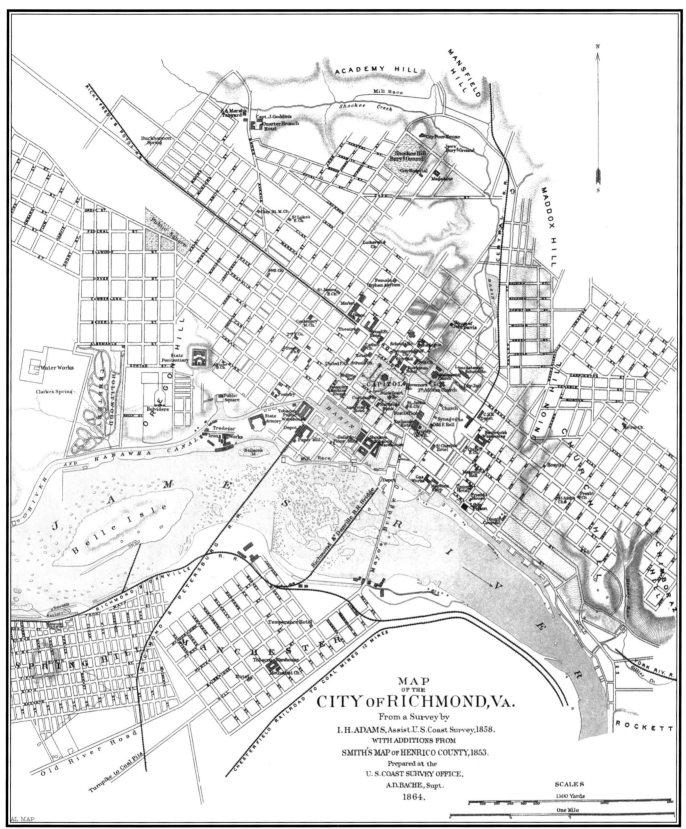

MAP
OF THE
CITY OF RICHMOND, VA.
From a Survey by
I. H. ADAMS, Assist. U. S. Coast Survey, 1858.
WITH ADDITIONS FROM
SMITH'S MAP OF HENRICO COUNTY, 1853.
Prepared at the
U. S. COAST SURVEY OFFICE,
A. D. BACHE, Supt.
1864.

Detailed Map of the City of Richmond

Atlas, Official Records

11th, the Federal blockade tightened when combined forces pulverized and captured Fort Pulaski near Savannah, thus sealing the Savannah River and closing one of the south's most vital ports. Certainly, the litany of Southern reverses ominously pointed to the Confederacy fast approaching its end.[24]

By mid-April, 1862, Richmond remained as the most valuable city in the South, its strategic importance incalculable. Like Paris and London, Richmond was a capital in every sense. Originally a fort, the river town had been built at the fall line of the James River more than two centuries earlier to protect the Jamestown colony downstream against Indians. After it became the capital of Virginia in 1780, the city grew out from the river, spreading across seven hills and beyond,

Courtesy Harpers Weekly

Richmond Armory

prompting citizens to liken the place to Rome. To a pseudo-feudal society rooted in an agrarian economy fighting for its independence, Richmond was the South's heart. In addition to being the political center of the Confederacy, Charles Marshall wrote that, "Richmond had a value from a military point of view that far exceeded its political importance." Richmond was indeed the South's industrial center, described by historian Robert G. Tanner as "virtually the Ruhr of the Confederacy." Factories in and around the city exceeded the total factory capacity of half of the 11 Confederate states combined. Richmond's importance to the food-producing region that ran from that Atlantic Ocean to the mountains west of the fertile Shenandoah Valley was evidenced by its 12 meal and flour mills and included the world's largest, Gallego, noted for its superb quality. The city also boasted the world's largest tobacco market, consisting of 60 factories and related firms. Joseph R. Anderson's Tredegar Iron Works, North America's second largest foundry, employed 20-percent of the city's labor force. The Richmond Armory under the superintendence of the innovative James H. Burton was utterly essential to the Confederate war effort. Richmond also ranked as Virginia's largest port and vital transportation hub. Ocean and coastal ships docked at the Rockett's wharf, and four railroads connected the city to points in all directions, making it the most important rail center in the upper South. In addition, Richmond was one of the most populous and economically advanced regions in the South, an important center of Southern finance, publishing and Tidewater society.[25]

Courtesy Library of Congress

Rockett's Wharf

---

[24] William C. Davis, *Jefferson Davis*, pp. 407-408.

[25] Furgurson, *Ashes of Glory*, p. 4; *Encyclopedia of the Confederacy*, vol. 3, pp. 1329-1330;

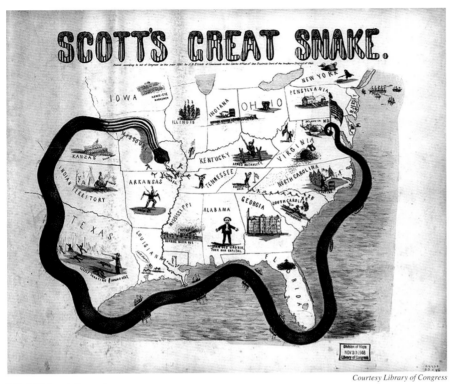

Courtesy Library of Congress

Winfield Scott's Legendary Anaconda Plan

Students of the Great Captains will recall that during the Second Punic War the Carthaginian general, Hannibal Barca, facing daunting odds, boldly defended Carthage by invading the Italian peninsula and menacing Rome, thereby engaging the enemy as far away from his capital as possible. Two millennia later, the Confederacy could ill-afford to have Richmond isolated or besieged, much less fall into enemy hands to suffer Carthage's fate, and Lee grasped that the Federals needed to be kept clear of the gates. Thus, McClellan had to be bottled up on the Peninsula's tip as long as possible, and reinforcing Magruder's command to the hilt represented the urgent priority. In turn, confronted by growing numbers, McClellan would spend more time in preparing his methodical advance and inexorable attack. Merely stalling McClellan would not be enough to alter the outcome, as the Federal Anaconda Plan, with the Army of the Potomac as a dagger keeping pressure on Richmond, would inevitably strangle Davis' cordon "defense by dispersal" approach combined with Johnston's method of warfare. This is why Lee believed that other measures designed to impact McClellan's campaign needed to be put into motion. Working against him, however, were Northern victories on every front that resulted in calls for reinforcements throughout the Confederacy. These appeals swamped the War Department, and when combined with Johnston's constant objections about willingly transferring his army onto the Peninsula, Davis' attention completely diverted from the most important message of Lee's counsel. "It is impossible," Lee wrote Magruder on March 29th, "to place at every point which is threatened a force which shall prove equal to every emergency." When Davis finally came to the realization that more troops than what could be wrangled from other Virginia commands were going to be required in front of Richmond, the President called for a council of war.[26]

Beginning late in the morning of April 14th, the meeting took place between Davis, Lee, Secretary of War Randolph, Johnston, and two of his senior subordinates, Gustavus Woodson Smith and James Longstreet. The council of war turned into a grueling, 14-hour marathon that extended into

Courtesy Harpers Weekly

The abandoning of Norfolk

The Official Military Atlas of the Civil War, also known as the *Atlas to Accompany the Official Records of the Union and Confederate Armies, 1861-1865* (Washington, 1891-1895), Plate XX, "Map of the Battle-Grounds in the Vicinity of Richmond, Va.," signed by Robert E. Lee, 4 April 1863; Dowdey, *The Land They Fought For*, p. 185; Marshall, *Lee's Aide de Camp*, p. 70; Charles Marshall, "Address on the Strategic Value of Richmond," October 29, 1874, *Army of Northern Virginia Memorial Volume*, complied by Rev. J. William Jones, D. D. (Richmond, 1880), p. 77; Robert G. Tanner, *Retreat to Victory? Confederate Strategy Reconsidered* (Wilmington, 2001), p. 18. James H. Burton was the former Acting Master Armorer of the United States Armory and Arsenal at Harpers Ferry and Chief Engineer of the Royal Small Arms Manufactory in Enfield, England, whose modified design for the *Minié* bullet was adopted by the U. S. Army before the war.

[26] Dowdey and Manarin, *The Wartime Papers of R. E. Lee*, number 136, "To General John B. Magruder," March 29, 1862, p. 140.

the early morning hours of the next day. Describing the central points of the meeting in briefest terms, Johnston opposed sending his army to reinforce Magruder at Yorktown. Johnston instead preferred a plan that drew McClellan to advance to the gates of Richmond, where he would be met by large numbers of Confederates that included those stripped from other areas and railed in for the massive confrontation. War Secretary Randolph was opposed to quickly withdrawing so close to Richmond, as it unnecessarily broke the uneasy stalemate on the lower Peninsula, gave up Norfolk and with it the loss of the *Virginia*, and surrendered the control of the James River to the Federal navy before additional river defensive measures closer to Richmond could be effected. Lee advised of the benefits of keeping the enemy as far away from Richmond as possible for as long as possible in order to better prepare defenses along the upper Peninsula, as well as open the door for other opportunities. Furthermore, Lee believed that given the present strategic policy of the President and the different concerns on other fronts, large numbers of reinforcements would not be forthcoming from the Atlantic coast, and that recalling troops operating in the Shenandoah would only free up the Federals around Washington, allowing them the freedom to move south to join with McClellan in his advance.

After everyone had staked their position, a process that occupied the men until the dawn hours, Davis finally made the call. It's doubtful that the President considered the subtlety of Lee's argument to engage as far away from the shadows Richmond for as long as possible in order to buy time so that defenses could be better prepared and other opportunities could develop. Instead, consistent with his philosophy of defending every inch of Southern soil, Davis ordered Johnston to reinforce Magruder by marching his army to the Peninsula and into the defensive line at Yorktown. Yet, Johnston felt that the President's directive meant that he would have to confront the enemy too far from his railroads in Richmond; for the hero of Manassas, this smacked of too much risk. Johnston later wrote: "The belief that events on the Peninsula would compel the government to adopt my method of opposing the Federal army, reconciled me somewhat to the necessity of obeying the President's order." The sullen Johnston would go to the Peninsula with no intent of carrying out the spirit of his orders, a passive but not uncommon form of insubordination. In his mind he had already decided that he would soon fall back on the capital; unlike McClellan and Lee, Johnston did not grasp the implications of siege warfare, nor, in the critical time since Manassas, did he seem to understand that the Federal Army of the Potomac marked a much more dangerous foe than McDowell's forces the previous year. Instead, Johnston had been mostly complacent in his preparations for the upcoming campaign, essentially resting on his victor's laurels. At the same time, without Davis flinching from his strategic course, Lee was reduced to urging local commanders in other departments to consider sending some troops to the mobile army. All the while the Federal pressure mounted, and with it the corresponding dangers that prompted Lee to admit to his wife on April 22nd, "the enemy is pressing us on all sides."[27]

Courtesy Harpers Weekly

The Virginia Peninsula looking from east to west

---

[27] For some details concerning the council of war, see Freeman, *R. E. Lee*, vol. 2, pp. 20-23.

* * *

With the decision to try and contain the Federals for as long as possible along the Yorktown line, Lee turned his attention to northern Virginia and the Shenandoah Valley. When Johnston withdrew from Northern Virginia and moved to the Peninsula, he left only a small force of observation consisting of a 2,500-man brigade under Brigadier General Charles William Field between Washington City and Richmond. Meanwhile, Johnston ordered two of his division generals, "Stonewall" Jackson and Major General Richard S. Ewell, then stationed significantly west of the army, to communicate with him through the adjutant general's office in Richmond. Without any formal orders forthcoming from President Davis, and although Jackson and Ewell were under the nominal command of Johnston, Lee's proximity required that he supervise the movements of these two officers detached from Johnston. Once again the baffling chain-of-command left Lee in a nebulous and needlessly complicated position. In order to exercise some operational direction of these divisions, Lee had to first defer to the chief executive and acquire permission for such movements, while, after having done so, try with great tact to avoid offending the touchy Johnston. Despite the bizarre arrangement, Lee persevered.[28]

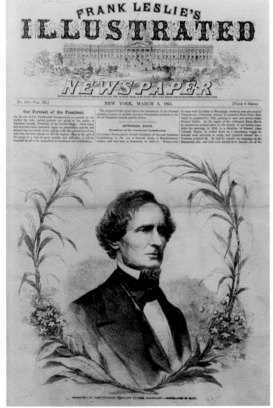

Courtesy Library of Congress

Jeff Davis' image in Leslie's Illustrated

Lee's challenges mounted far beyond the personality flaws of Davis and his main army commander. Nonetheless, bereft of real authority, the "advisor" hoped to negotiate an operational plan through Jackson that could hopefully offset Davis' defective strategy and Johnston's timidity—Lee advocated a scheme intended to impose Confederate will on the enemy. At its core was Lee's desire to save the Confederate capital. In order to accomplish that, the first order of business was that McClellan had to be denied further reinforcements. Furthermore, McDowell had to be somehow prevented from moving overland to Richmond to effect a concentration with McClellan. To those familiar with Frederick the Great's and Napoleon's operational art of war, the Confederacy possessed a key advantage that formed the genesis of Lee's version of the "strategy of the central position." In simple terms, both Frederick and Napoleon had utilized interior lines, and shorter distances, to mount a series of aggressive counter-attacks whereby an outnumbered nation could, through hard-marching and audacious generalship, achieve battlefield superiority again and again. Clearly, Lee understood this theory of warfare, and knew it to be the antidote for Davis' poisonous recipe for endless defeat.[29]

Thus, to accomplish his immediate goals and to begin to change the tenor of the war, Lee conceived a diversionary offensive whereby Jackson, cooperating with Ewell and able to draw on other formations such as the division under Edward Johnson, would, as Lee urged, "strike a successful blow at the enemy" in the Shenandoah Valley. Since the geography of the Shenandoah made it, in essence, a dagger aimed at Washington City, Lee reasoned that a successful

Dowdey and Manarin, *The Wartime Papers of R. E. Lee*, number 142, telegram "To General John C. Pemberton," April 10, 1862, p. 145; number 150, "To General John C. Pemberton," April 20, 1862, p. 150; number 155, "To His Wife," April 22, 1862, pp. 153-154. After Pemberton did not forward any troops, Lee wrote again on April 22nd. See: *Official Records*, Series I, vol. 11, part 3, Robert E. Lee to John C. Pemberton, April 22, 1862, p. 455. In addition to these duties, Lee was given many other correspondence duties. For a summary of the tasks hoisted on Lee's shoulders, refer to Freeman, *R. E. Lee*, vol. 2, pp. 30-31.

[28] Freeman, *R. E. Lee*, vol. 2, p. 31; Johnston, *Narrative of Military Operations*, pp. 128-129.

[29] A complete discussion of Lee's art of war is presented in Volume Four of this study.

Confederate offensive down the Valley (towards Washington) would yield incalculable benefits. Lee had not forgotten Jackson's hard work at Harpers Ferry the previous summer, and knew that he could "communicate with him soldier to soldier and not deferential diplomat to sensitive individualist." Whenever Jackson was ready to attack, Lee advised him on April 25th that, "The blow, wherever struck, must, to be successful, be sudden and heavy. The troops used must be efficient and [their movements] light." Writing to Ewell the same day, Lee expressed his burning desire to get at the enemy: "I hope a blow from the combined forces of yourself and General Jackson can destroy [General Bank's column]." Jackson subsequently submitted three possible plans of operation, and on May 1st, Lee sanctioned Jackson to commence the gambit.[30]

Courtesy Harpers Weekly

Washington City 1861

One week later, the campaign's fighting opened at the village of McDowell, forcing the Federals back. The action was by no means decisive, but it did create doubt in the minds of the Federals as to the strength and intentions of the Confederates in the Valley. Lee hoped to capitalize on that fear, and in a May 16th letter to Jackson, encouraged Jackson to concentrate his forces and to be as swift and aggressive as possible. "Whatever movements you make against [Federal forces under Nathaniel P.] Banks do it speedily, and if successful, drive him back towards the Potomac, and create the impression as far as practicable that you design threatening that line." Jackson embraced Lee's offensive plan and attacked Banks on three consecutive days at Front Royal on May 23th, Newtown on May 24th and Winchester on May 25th. In assuming the offensive during those days, Jackson lost only 400 killed and wounded, while inflicting more than 3,500 losses on the enemy, including capturing 3,000 prisoners, two pieces of ordnance, 9,000 small arms and droves of cattle and sheep, along with tons of food and other stores. Battered and badly beaten, Banks fled down the Valley towards the Potomac, with Jackson nipping at his heels. Alarmed by the flight of Banks and the Confederate advance towards Washington City, President Lincoln wanted McDowell's 45,000-man command repositioned from its current staging area preparatory to a move towards Richmond, choosing instead to insure the security of the Federal capital. If the Confederates ever took Washington City, reasoned Lincoln, the war would quickly collapse, and with it, the political

---

[30] McCaslin, *Lee in the Shadow of Washington*, p. 98; *Official Records*, Series I, vol. 12, part 3, Robert E. Lee to Thomas J. Jackson, April 25, 1862, pp. 865-866; Robert E. Lee to Richard S. Ewell, April 25, 1862, pp. 866-867; Robert E. Lee to Thomas J. Jackson, May 1, 1862, p. 878. In the meanwhile, Lee was looking everywhere for reinforcements for the Virginia theater. While he understood that the coastal departments could not be stripped of all its troops as proposed by Johnston, Lee did look for reinforcements for Virginia by procuring arms that would go to new troops who could then take up static positions of observation and thereby releasing to Virginia mobile regiments and brigades. For example, see: Dowdey and Manarin, *The Wartime Papers of R. E. Lee*, number 162, "To General Theophilus H. Holmes," April 28, 1862, p. 159. An example of Lee's preparations for troops arriving in the theater of operations can be seen in: *Official Records*, Series I, vol. 12, part 3, Robert E. Lee to L. B. Northrup, April 28, 1862, p. 871. Lee also considered pulling troops from western Virginia to reinforce the Valley Army. See: *Official Records*, Series I, vol. 12, part 3, Walter H. Taylor to Henry Heth, April 27, 1862, pp. 869-870.

stock of his administration and the Republican Party. In cowing Lincoln with an aggressive diversion, Lee and Jackson attained operational and strategic results from a series of tactical victories, freezing out most of the men under McDowell from moving on the Federals' main objective of Richmond.[31]

Despite McDowell being temporarily unavailable to move south to effect a junction with McClellan, and even though there were alarms being sounded in Washington as Jackson pursued the remnants of Banks' army, the operational situation east of Richmond was bleak for the Confederates. On May 1st, the day that Lee was sanctioning Jackson to begin the Valley campaign, Joe Johnston announced his plans to retreat from the Yorktown lines. He had taken command on the Peninsula only two weeks earlier. "The determination of General Johnston to fall back on the Peninsula," as described by Secretary of War Randolph, created the domino effect feared by General Lee, including the necessity as described by Randolph of "a speedy evacuation of Norfolk."[32]

When Johnston left the Yorktown lines on May 3th-4th, he acted in the same manner that he had displayed at Harpers Ferry the previous June and again at Centreville only a few weeks before. Johnston withdrew his troops without first taking proper steps to remove valuable artillery and ammunition. To be sure, some of the ordnance was antiquated, being naval smoothbores that weighed so much that their being moved would have required more forethought and effort than Johnston was willing to expend. Nevertheless, guns were still at a premium in the South, and Johnston was becoming used to abandoning them. Once Johnston pulled back, Benjamin Huger and his 10,000 man force at Norfolk became isolated. Huger withdrew and Norfolk and its naval base were evacuated. With Norfolk lost, the *Virginia*, with its 22-foot draft, was unable to navigate shallow river waters. Without a port, the crew scuttled her on May 11th. Absent the *Virginia* at the mouth of the James, "which some citizens believed was worth 50,000 troops in the field," Federal gunboats could move all the way to Richmond. And they tried. Four days after the *Virginia* settled to the bottom off Norfolk, Federal gunboats steamed up the broad, winding James. Moving past the ruins of the original Virginia settlement at Jamestown, past many historic and picturesque river plantations, silencing batteries and smothering small vessels on their way, the small, but powerful Federal squadron led by the ironclad *Monitor*, approached the Confederate capital. "The proximity of the gunboats of the enemy to this city places it in very great danger," began one article in *The Richmond Dispatch* on May 15th. That day the gunboats traded shots with Confederate guns of Fort Darling on the 80-foot high bank

Courtesy Library of Congress

The *U.S.S. Monitor* shortly after its battle with the Virginia

---

[31] *Official Records*, Series I, vol. 11, see various communiqués between Abraham Lincoln and George B. McClellan, May 24, 1862, p. 30; multiple ones on May 25, 1862, pp. 31-32; and May 26, 1862, p. 32; also, see vol. 11, part 3, Edwin M. Stanton to George B. McClellan, May 27, 1862, p. 194; Dowdey and Manarin, *The Wartime Papers of R. E. Lee*, number 180, "To General Thomas J. Jackson," May 16, 1862, pp. 174-175; Robert G. Tanner, *Stonewall in the Valley: Thomas J. "Stonewall" Jackson's Shenandoah Valley Campaign, Spring 1862* (New York, 1976) pp. 162-169 and pp. 193-259.

[32] *Official Records*, Series I, vol. 11, part 3, George W. Randolph to Benjamin Huger, May 3, 1862, p. 490.

at Drewry's Bluff, only seven miles from Richmond.   Fortunately for the Confederates, Robert E. Lee had understood the domino effect from Johnston's retreat from Yorktown, and exerted considerable efforts in superintending the construction of defenses of Drewry's Bluff. These measures stopped the Federal gunboats.[33]

It was now Richmond's turn to panic. With Johnston not ending his retreat until he was within the shadows of the capital city, untold numbers of rural Virginians swarmed into the city ahead of McClellan's slogging advance through the mud of a wet spring season. They called it "refugeeing" in Richmond, and the influx of the displaced souls caused many citizens in the capital to flee in turn. The panic gripped politicians as well. Without the slightest attack of conscience, with their territory being gobbled up, key cities occupied, powerful Federal armies poised to conquer all, and "in the very crisis of the country's agony, when the existence of the nation which it pretends to represent is trembling in the balance of fate," the Confederate Congress shamelessly voted itself a pay raise and then fled the capital in haste. Without shame, some members cowardly vied with other citizens for seats on southbound trains. There were so many people looking to get out of the Confederacy altogether that the passport office in the War Department was overwhelmed. Outside government offices, packing cases of vital archives, addressed to Columbia, South Carolina, were being stacked for railroad cars preparatory to evacuation. *The Richmond Examiner* reported that some people "are selling all they have" before they skedaddled. Davis did not want the city to suffer siege and ruin, and after evacuating his family, along with his most cherished books and the Mexican War pistols he had used at Buena Vista, the President declared that he would never allow Johnston to be "penned up" in the city. Nevertheless, in case of disaster, members of Davis'

Courtesy Library of Congress

Courtesy Library of Congress

Top: Inside view of the fort at Drewry's Bluff
Bottom: View from Drewry's Bluff

cabinet wanted Lee's advice as to where Johnston's army might draw a defensive line if Richmond had to be abandoned. Lee stated at the Staunton River, nearly 100 miles to the southwest. However, Lee understood that the loss of Richmond would mean the loss of Virginia, and the loss of Virginia would in turn mean the loss of the war. In this crisis, and seeing the moves preparatory to evacuating the capital, Lee's temper reached boiling point. He blurted out to Davis: *"Richmond must not be given up; it shall not be given up!"* As he passionately cried out, Postmaster John H. Reagan saw tears in Lee's eyes, and later maintained that "the very fate of the Confederacy hung in the balance; but I never saw him [Lee] show" greater emotion. The editors

---

[33] *Official Records*, Series I, vol. 11, part 3, Robert E. Lee to Joseph E. Johnston, May 1, 1862, p. 485; George W. Randolph to Benjamin Huger, May 3, 1862, p. 490; Robert E. Lee to Joseph E. Johnston, May 16, 1862, p. 520; Furgurson, *Ashes of Glory*, p. 130-131. *The Richmond Dispatch*, article entitled "The Peril of Richmond," May 15, 1862; Long, *Memoirs of Robert E. Lee*, pp. 155-156 and 161.

Courtesy Harpers Weekly

Refugees

"There were alarm and excitement in the mixed and restless population of Richmond; and the popular feeling found but little assurance in the visible tremor of the authorities. The Confederate Congress had adjourned in such haste as to show that the members were anxious to provide for their own personal safety. President Davis sent his family to North Carolina ... At the railroad depots were piles of baggage awaiting transportation, and the trains were crowed with women and children going to distant points in the country..."

—Edward A. Pollard

of *The Richmond Dispatch* joined Lee with their appeal to hold Richmond. In the May 16th edition, under the headline "VIRGINIA NOT TO BE SURRENDERED," the editors believed what Robert E. Lee understood. "[Everyone] should resolve to the uttermost to defend Richmond...[because should Richmond fall] it would be giving up much more. The Cause would be, indeed, itself well nigh surrendered in that event."[34]

However, the man currently in command of the army wasn't so boisterous. As the Yankee flotillas worked their way up the James and York rivers, between the two flowing waters Johnston was leading his army's retreat on Richmond, and did so without providing details to President Davis. With no news about what the army was up to, Davis decided to go see Johnston. They met on May 12th after the latter had pulled back to the Chickahominy River on the south, extending northward through New Kent Court House to the York River. That put Johnston's army only 30 miles east of Richmond, with only the Chickahominy River between the enemy and the capital city. As the President mingled among the troops, he happily noted that the soldiers were in good spirits. At the same time, Davis registered shock at how much of their artillery and ammunition had been abandoned along the Yorktown lines, and he wrote his wife, blaming Johnston for not thinking ahead before implementing the retreat, a pattern of error now painfully evident in Johnson's generalship. Further proof of Johnston retreating without preparation could be seen in his thoughtlessly leaving the vital York River Railroad intact. This baffling act of careless ineptitude should have led to Johnston's immediate removal. A potentially fatal blunder, Johnston had granted McClellan access to the only practicable rail line over which the Federal siege guns could be moved to the very gates of Richmond. Insofar as telling the President exactly what he was going to do, Johnston was deliberately vague, as if he was, in the words of Clifford Dowdey, "an important personage dismissing an unwanted newspaper reporter."[35]

Over the next several days, Lee repeatedly wrote Johnston, only to get silence in return. In retrospect, Johnston's actions revealed that he had just

[34] Dowdey, *The Land They Fought For*, p. 183; Furgurson, *Ashes of Glory*, pp. 131 and 134; William C. Davis, *Jefferson Davis*, p. 421; Dowdey, *The Land They Fought For*, p. 183; John H. Reagan, *Memoirs: With Special Reference to Secession and the Civil War* (New York, 1906), p. 139; *The Richmond Dispatch*, article entitled "Virginia Not To Be Surrendered," May 16, 1862.

[35] William C. Davis, *Jefferson Davis*, p. 420; Symonds, *Joseph E. Johnston*, p. 158. Davis places the meeting on May 12, 1862, with the President venting his frustrations to his wife the next day. Symonds places the meeting two days later, and that Davis had barely left on the morning of the May 15, 1862, when news was received about the Federal ironclads engaging the Confederate works at Drewry's Bluff. Furgurson, *Ashes of Glory*, p. 133, places the meeting "two days before the fight at Drewry's Bluff," which would be May 13, 1862. Stephen W. Sears, *To The Gates of Richmond: The Peninsula Campaign* (New York, 1992), pp. 105-106; Dowdey, *Lee*, p. 203.

a dawning grasp of the dire results of continual retreat, and certainly no understanding of McClellan's strength in contemporary siege warfare. From the army's recent position, part of which was already behind the Chickahominy that was the last natural obstacle between McClellan's army and Richmond, another retreat was ordered. This time, the army did not stop until it reached the outskirts of Richmond itself. In response to Johnston's alarming silence, Davis again went to see the general and to ask why the Confederate army was tented within five miles of the Capitol. Johnston explained that he thought the muddy water of the Chickahominy unhealthy for his army, and decided to retreat to Richmond's doorstep. Obviously, this is exactly what Johnston had proposed in the April 14th council of war. By ignoring President Davis' order to defend the Peninsula— always pleading that circumstances left him with no choice but to retreat, he tacitly achieved his design on how to engage McClellan. Thus, Johnston had carried out his original insubordinate intentions with seeming malice. Now, with no more room to retreat this side of Richmond, Davis asked Johnston what offensive plan he had in mind: Johnston equivocated.

Courtesy Library of Congress

Bridge over the Chickahominy River built by the Federals in May, 1862

With Johnston not committing to an attack, he found time to restart his communications with his detached divisions in the Valley, and in doing so, minimized "the value of Lee's simple plan to drive Banks from the Valley." During his correspondence with his Valley generals, Johnston again indicated that the Confederates must concentrate around Richmond, because Johnston believed that nothing could prevent the junction of McClellan and McDowell, and admonished them not to attack if the Federals were behind any fortifications, and instead to bring troops "here." When Jackson received orders from Johnston that conflicted with those previously given by Lee, he asked Lee what to do. While there is no record of the details surrounding how Lee handled Jackson's May 20th appeal, what is known is that the answer was quickly returned, and the result of that answer was that at dawn on May 21st, Jackson set his troops in motion down the Valley to affect a junction with Ewell for an attack on Banks. For Lee—and for Jackson—it was a calculated risk. Finally, two men in gray were meant to impose Confederate will on the adversary.[36]

Courtesy Harpers Weekly

Major General McClellan

While Jackson was marching and fighting, Johnston retreated some more. He ordered a covering brigade to pull back from the line of the Rappahannock. At the same time, Johnston prepared to abandon the indispensable Virginia Central Railroad west of Hanover Junction. Due to these moves, almost all of Northern Virginia, with the most notable exception being the Shenandoah Valley where Jackson was operating, stood virtually defenseless. By May 24th, McClellan's Federals had occupied Mechanicsville, only five miles from

---

[36] *Official Records*, Series I, vol. 12, part 3, J. E. Johnston to R. S. Ewell, May 17, 1862, pp. 896-897; T. J. Jackson to R. S. Ewell, May 18, 1862, p. 897; T. J. Jackson to Robert E. Lee, May 20, 1862, p. 898; Tanner, *Stonewall in the Valley*, pp. 199-202; Freeman, *R. E. Lee*, vol. 2, pp. 52-57.

Richmond. That position marked a perfect place from which "Little Mac" could form a junction with McDowell when the latter resumed his movement southward. Whenever McDowell joined McClellan's forces (and Johnston believed that nothing could prevent that from happening), the combined Federal host on the Peninsula would number more than 140,000. With an army less than half that size, Johnston had done everything in his power to get his battle of concentration.[37]

"A phenomenally mismanaged battle"— Johnston's Abortive Offensive at Seven Pines and its Aftermath

Following his May 20th answer to Jackson's appeal to resume the Valley offensive, thus seriously opening up a second front in the Virginia theater of operations, Robert E. Lee spent the rest of May relegated to mundane chores of expediting his Excellency's orders or providing consultations on points far distant from the war's epicenter. As Lee toiled uselessly in his backroom office on Ninth Street, Johnston was giving orders to almost all troops in Virginia. Having backed his army into the environs of the Confederate capital, Johnston waited there incommunicado for McClellan to methodically prepare for the inevitable siege. The combination of circumstances inside and outside Lee's office must have chipped away at his formidable patience. Finally, unable any longer to sit behind a desk whose paperwork flow any of his staff members could have handled, Lee rode out on May 30th to do what he had always done with consummate skill—reconnaissance.[38]

What Lee saw up close the citizens of Richmond had been observing from a distance. McClellan's great host was so close to Richmond that the glow of its campfires could be seen against the night sky. For those wanting to get a distant glimpse of the enemy, the Jewish cemetery on Shockoe Hill at Fourth and Hospital streets provided the necessary elevation, and people would gather there at dusk every night. For more than a week in late May, citizens watched flashes of gunfire up to six miles from the city as the Army of the Potomac methodically extended its reach northward past Mechanicsville in anticipation of McDowell's arrival. That command, however, had been recalled by Lincoln in the wake of Jackson's Valley successes—one of the things Lee had hoped would happen—and on the afternoon of May 28th, new intelligence reports from "Jeb" Stuart's active cavalry patrols confirmed that McDowell had turned around to head north. For the time being, McClellan knew that he would have to confront the Confederates in front of Richmond without the help of all of First Corps.[39]

1862 photo of a farm at near the Chickahominy River

Courtesy Library of Congress

---

[37] *Official Records*, Series I, vol. 11, part 1, George B. McClellan to E. M. Stanton, May 24, 1862, p. 651; *Official Records*, Series I, vol. 11, part 3, J. E. Johnston to L. O'B. Branch, May 23, 1862, p. 537.

[38] *Official Records*, Series I, vol. 11, part 3, Robert E. Lee to Joseph E. Johnston, May 30, 1862, p. 560. For Johnston's correspondence with subordinates during this time, consult *Official Records*, Series I, part 3, vol. 11, pp. 541-559.

[39] Johnston, *Narrative of Military Operations*, pp. 131-132; Dowdey, *The Land They Fought*

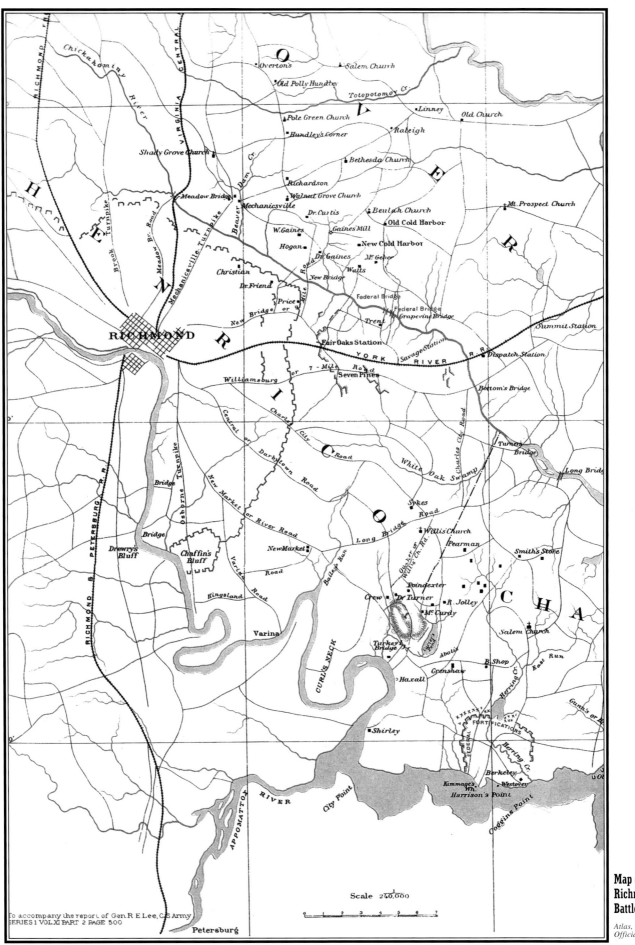

Map of
Richmond
Battleground

Atlas,
Official Records

McClellan had divided his approximately 100,000 men before Richmond into two broad arrows separated by the Chickahominy River. Two corps—two-fifths of the Federal army then in front of the Confederate capital—were south of the Chickahominy River, stretching across flat farmland and large belts of knotted timber that pointed straight at the eastern part of the city. Three corps advanced north of the Chickahominy. Historian Clifford Dowdey, whose familiarity with Richmond's battlefields and terrain was equaled by few, described what Lee knew about the Chickahominy: "This swampy stream, after coursing southward about fifteen miles to the northeast of Richmond, at five miles to the northeast of the city swung on a relatively straight course eastward for about ten miles. There it curved in an arc to the south and crossed the Williamsburg Road at Bottom's Bridge, twelve miles from Richmond. On its eastward course the sluggish river, swollen by recent rains, spread to from one-half mile to one mile of swamp inhabited only by moccasins."[40]

Days prior to news reaching those in and around Richmond about McDowell being recalled closer to Washington City, and with so many pressing him to do something other than retreat, Johnston finally admitted on May 29th that "it may become proper to attack." However, no attack took place that day, and Johnston, with his continued silence, gave cause for many to believe that he would uncoil the counterattack the following day. The air thickened with anticipation for battle on the 30th as Lee sent a staff officer to Johnston offering his services. When Johnston turned down that gesture, Lee could not simply remain in his office. He decided to go reconnoiter. If Johnston refused to tell him anything, then Lee would personally find out where or when the battle would be joined. Lee didn't discover anything, and the 30th passed

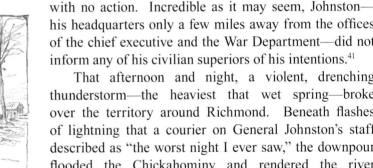

The area of Fair Oaks

Courtesy Harpers Weekly

with no action. Incredible as it may seem, Johnston—his headquarters only a few miles away from the offices of the chief executive and the War Department—did not inform any of his civilian superiors of his intentions.[41]

That afternoon and night, a violent, drenching thunderstorm—the heaviest that wet spring—broke over the territory around Richmond. Beneath flashes of lightning that a courier on General Johnston's staff described as "the worst night I ever saw," the downpour flooded the Chickahominy and rendered the river impassable except over the threatened bridges that linked McClellan's divided army. The circumstances for the Confederates to strike were perfect. "Seldom," wrote one biographer, "was a general presented with the opportunity Johnston had now to bring military destruction on a part of the enemy's army."[42]

No longer able to resist taking offensive action, Johnston intended to strike toward the road junction of Seven Pines and the rail station at Fair Oaks, barely seven miles east of the Capitol. There, the Federal forces south of the Chickahominy—namely the Third and Fourth Corps—stood isolated. Lee's old acquaintance, Erasmus Keyes, commanding the Federal Fourth Corps, was the most exposed. Keyes' troops occupied a mile-wide front from the station of Fair Oaks, on the York River Railroad, to the crossroads of Seven Pines,

For, p. 183; Symonds, *Joseph E. Johnston*, p. 162.
[40] Dowdey, *Lee*, pp. 205-206.
[41] *Official Records*, Series I., vol. 11, part 3, J. E. Johnston to D. H. Hill, May 29, 1862, p. 559; Long, *Memoirs of Robert E. Lee*, p. 158; Freeman, *R. E. Lee*, vol. 2, pp. 64-66.
[42] Long, *Memoirs of Robert E. Lee*, p. 157; Furgurson, *Ashes of Glory*, p. 136; Dowdey, *Lee*, p. 208.

southeast of Fair Oaks. Separated by six miles from Samuel Heintzelman's Third Corps, Keyes' position invited attack. Johnston's secretive battle plans aimed for a concentration against Keyes' isolated command, and although the design was straightforward, it required orders that were clear, an efficient staff to implement the plan, and capable subordinates to execute it. However, what became known as the Battle of Seven Pines, or Fair Oaks, fought on May 31st, 1862, demonstrated that Joe Johnston failed to make proper reconnaissance, did not issue clear orders and had not developed a staff that knew how to properly communicate his intentions. As a result, poor intelligence, bad

Courtesy Harpers Weekly

The fighting at Seven Pines

timing and even worse coordination resulted in a very poorly managed battle that bore little resemblance to the original idea. Of the approximately 54,000 men Johnston had available to descend upon two isolated Federal corps, each with an "average over 15,000 men each," he could never get more than 14,000 Confederates into the fighting. As a result, of the 23 Confederate brigades intended to be in action that Saturday, only nine became heavily engaged. Edward Porter Alexander, chief of ordnance for Johnston, later claimed that "nowhere were ever over four brigades in action at one time."[43]

Meanwhile, Lee could not remain inactive in his Ninth Street office with a battle supposedly so close at hand. With no word from Johnston, Lee summoned staffer Charles Marshall, and together, the general and the aide again rode out of Richmond shortly after noon to find the fighting. Dampness still hung in the air as Lee and Marshall approached the front, finding numerous brigades of Confederate troops idle along the road. The pair occasionally heard faint sounds of firing coming over the wet, thick timber, and it was sometime after 2:00 P.M. that they found General Johnston and his staff in a farmhouse along Nine Mile Road. Even though Johnston did not welcome the curious outriders, Lee took a seat in a chair to find out what was afoot. Over the next one and one-half hours, it became painfully obvious to the observing Lee that the strained atmosphere at headquarters that included the commanding general's inactivity and continued secrecy to discuss the situation "indicated that something was going very wrong with Johnston's battle."[44]

Finally, after 4:00 P.M., word arrived from a divisional staff officer

"McClellan's men were slowly being pressed back into and through the Chickahominy swamp...but at almost every step they were pouring terrific volleys into my lines...My field officers and adjutants were all dead. Every horse ridden into the fight, my own among them, was dead. Fully one-half of my line officers and half my men were dead or wounded."

—John B. Gordon, colonel of the 6th Alabama, describing the fighting at Seven Pines

[43] Symonds, *Joseph E. Johnston*, pp. 163-165. Symonds states that only 21 brigades were intended by Johnston to be in action. Also, Symonds is of the opinion that Johnston's orders "were not a model of clarity." Edward Porter Alexander, *Military Memoirs of a Confederate* (New York, 1907) pp. 90 and 93. Alexander claims that Johnston wished to concentrate "23 of our 27 brigades against McClellan's left wing."

[44] Dowdey, *Lee*, pp. 208-210; Symonds, *Joseph E. Johnston*, pp. 167-170.

Courtesy Harpers Weekly

View from behind Federal lines of the fighting at Seven Pines near Fair Oaks

concerning the progress of the fighting, and Johnston decided then to go see what was developing. As he and others moved outside, seen coming up the road was President Davis and his entourage. The last thing Johnston wanted was to spend time explaining himself to his civilian chief. Consequently, Johnston sprang to his horse and, together with the staff officer who had brought him the news of the confused fighting, churned mud as they cantered off towards Fair Oaks.[45]

Lee then greeted Davis, and each questioned the other about what they knew, and neither had much to share. After all, Johnston had not disclosed any information to either, and the noise of gun fire represented the scant extent of what Lee and Davis knew: the sound of battle emanated from the direction of Fair Oaks and further off, Seven Pines. Both men wanted to know more, and together, Lee and the President decided to ride towards the firing. After guiding their horses for more than a mile between heavily foliaged woods, Lee and Davis found the confused rear areas that were steadily becoming more chaotic in the fading light of the late afternoon. As historian Ernest B. Furgurson described it, Davis "was where a president had no business being, amid artillery fire just behind the attacking waves, acting as a staff officer, trying to shuffle brigades about."

Sometime after 6:00 P.M. events assumed an ominous feel. Lee and Davis sat on their horses in a clearing, staring into smoke-covered woods while

---

[45] Alexander, *Military Memoirs of a Confederate*, p. 92; Dowdey, *Lee*, p. 210; Symonds, *Joseph E. Johnston*, p. 170.

trying to ascertain the course of events that involved more and more retreating Southerners. Escaping the maelstrom of battle, bewildered Confederate soldiers—including whole regiments—came stumbling back, harbingers of what felt like yet another unfolding disaster. Suddenly, someone ran past yelling that General Johnston was down.[46]

With the shadows of dusk gathering, Davis and Lee spurred their mounts closer to the fighting. Amidst the sounds of crackling gunfire and the dangers of overshot artillery bursts, Davis and Lee saw two staff officers carrying a stretcher on which there was a familiar uniform and the slight figure of Joseph E. Johnston. Quickly dismounting, the President and Lee hurried towards the fallen general. The litter bearers struggled to carry their wounded chief, slipping often in the mud. When Davis and Lee reached him, Johnston was conscious and his wounds obviously painful. Although Davis and Lee did not know the specifics of his injuries, Johnston had multiple wounds with his shoulder blade and two ribs also broken. It was later determined that he had been hit twice, one in the right shoulder by a musket ball and a second in the chest by a fragment of an exploding artillery shell that also knocked him from his horse. As Lee stood silently by, the President temporarily suppressed his accumulated resentments towards Johnston and offered his genuine concern for the suffering man. Johnston opened his eyes and extended his hand before being quickly borne away and loaded into an ambulance.[47]

Courtesy Library of Congress

Joseph E. Johnston

Johnston's departure did not alter the tenure of the fighting; the battle continued to sputter on until nightfall. The command of the Confederate forces devolved to Gustavus Woodson Smith, the senior Confederate major general on the field. When President Davis asked Smith what his plans were, the general mentally froze and could not answer. The next day, Smith tried to renew the attack, but his attempt was more feeble than Johnston's. When the Battle of Seven Pines (or Fair Oaks) sputtered to an end by midday on June 1st, 1862, the Confederates had suffered in excess of 6,100 casualties. Instead of annihilating Keyes' and Heintzelman's isolated corps, the Confederates had only accomplished pushing back the Federals about one mile, capturing in the process 10 pieces of ordnance and 5,000 small arms while inflicting just over 5,000 casualties.[48]

While it is often easy to criticize battle plans gone wrong, Porter Alexander probably summed things up accurately when he called Seven Pines "a phenomenally mismanaged battle" where Joe Johnston fumbled "an opportunity for one of the most brilliant strokes in the war was here overlooked and lost." Following General Smith's failure to tell Davis anything, the President decided that Smith—whose undiagnosed mental anxieties and resulting partial physical paralysis were apparently well known—would not command the army. On his way back to Richmond late in the evening of May 31st, Davis came to the conclusion that the handsome and highly-regarded Smith "suffered from too big a reputation based on little or no justification,

---

[46] Furgurson, *Ashes of Glory*, p. 136.

[47] *Southern Historical Society Papers*, vol. 18, "The Battle in Which General Johnston Was Wounded," described by his courier, Drury L. Armistead, p. 187; Jack D. Welsh, *Medical Histories of Confederate Generals* (Kent, 1999), p. 120; Dowdey, *Lee*, pp. 211-212; Symonds, *Joseph E. Johnston*, p. 172; William C. Davis, *Jefferson Davis*, pp. 423-424.

[48] Alexander, *Military Memoirs of a Confederate*, pp. 83 and 89.

"No, sir. The shot that struck me down is the very best that has been fired for the Southern cause yet."

—Joseph E. Johnston

and the closer he came to having it put on the line by action, the more terrified he became."[49]

In the aftermath of the action, Joe Johnston lay recovering at a friend's house on Church Hill in Richmond. Physicians that removed the Federal bullet and shrapnel from the general seemed to have had the effect of also extracting some of Johnston's petulance. When a well-wisher dropped by the house to give Johnston his sympathy and commented that his wounding was a calamity to the Confederacy, Johnston confessed in a moment of total candor, "No, sir. The shot that struck me down is the very best that has been fired for the Southern cause yet."[50]

With no other realistic choice, the President informed Robert E. Lee in the night of May 31st—June 1st that he would command the army. It was a decision long overdue, and even at this late hour was made begrudgingly. Robert E. Lee was finally going to get his chance.[51]

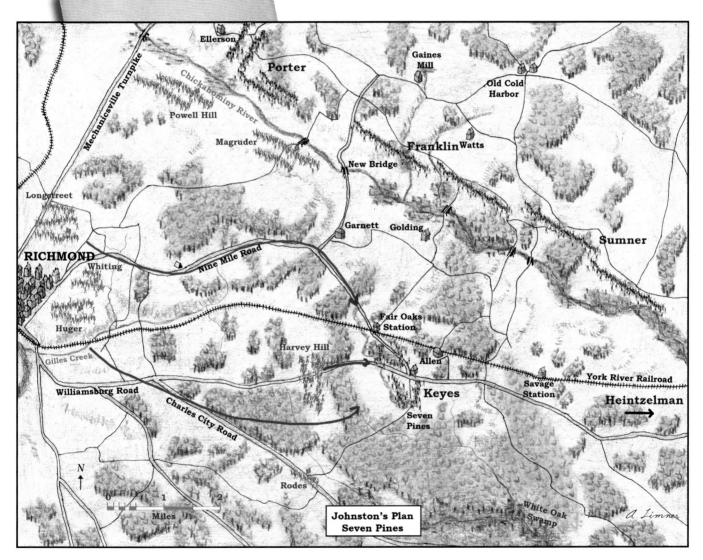

Johnston's Plan Seven Pines

---

[49] Alexander, *Military Memoirs of a Confederate*, pp. 77-93; Dowdey, *Lee*, p. 212. William C. Davis, *Jefferson Davis*, p. 425; *The Confederate General*, edited by William C. Davis, 6 volumes (National Historical Society, 1991), "Gustavus Woodson Smith," by William C. Davis, vol. 5, pp. 173-175.

[50] Dabney H. Maury, *Recollections of a Virginian in the Mexican, Indian, and Civil Wars* (New York, 1894), p. 161.

[51] William C. Davis, *Jefferson Davis*, p. 425; *The Confederate General*, edited by William C. Davis, 5 volumes (National Historical Society, 1991), "Gustavus Woodson Smith," by William C. Davis, vol. 5, pp. 173-175.

APPENDICES
★ ★ ★ ★ ★

Appendix A: Lee's Military Timeline

LAFAYETTE.

January 19, 1807

Robert Edward Lee is born at Stratford Hall mansion, Westmoreland County, Virginia, the fifth child of Colonel Henry (aka "Light Horse Harry") Lee (1756-1818) and Anne Hill Carter Lee (1773-1829), prominent members of the Virginia Tidewater aristocracy. His mother descends from one of the wealthiest and oldest families in Virginia, while his father had served prominently during the American Revolutionary War, during which time earned the respect and friendship of George Washington.

1812-1813

"Light Horse Harry" is severely injured in a riot in Baltimore. With a combination of lasting internal injuries and deep financial troubles, he ignominiously flees his creditors and leaves the country for the West Indies. As a result, Robert is raised by his mother.

1819-1825

Guided by his mother's steady hand, Robert's schooling continues well, and one of his teachers finds him to be "a most exemplary student in every respect." In 1824, the Marquis de Lafayette visits Alexandria and calls on the Lee household. The visit makes a great impression on Robert, for it is about this time that he decides to be a soldier.

1829-1831

Lee receives his first assignment, and reports to Cockspur Island, Georgia, to begin a 17-month long engineering assignment to supervise what would become Fort Pulaski. During this time, Lee vigorously continues his study of military history and theory. During the summer of 1830, while on leave, Lee meets Mary Randolph Custis (1807-1873), whose family's estate, "Arlington," offers a majestic overlook of Washington City and the Potomac. Returning to the southeast coast, Lee continues his work until ordered to Fortress Monroe at Old Point Comfort, Virginia. Beginning his duties there in early May, 1831, Lee helps supervise the construction of approaches and outworks on the fortress. Less than two months later, Lee and Mary wed at "Arlington."

1846-1848

As war comes between Mexico and the United States, Lee serves for three months as engineer on the staff of Brigadier General John E. Wool, before joining the staff of Major General Winfield Scott in January, 1847. During the campaign from Vera Cruz to Mexico City, Lee impresses all with his keen eye for terrain, extraordinary stamina and heroic actions. Brevetted three times for his bravery and conspicuous service, Robert E. Lee is declared by Winfield Scott to be "the very best soldier I ever saw in the field," and, more than any other man in uniform, responsible for the successful campaign.

1810 1815 1820 1825 1830 THRU 1845 18

1809-1810

Despite his father's status as a graduate of New Jersey College (now Princeton), Revolutionary War hero and deep political connections as a former Virginia governor, "Light Horse Harry" lands in debtors prison, the result of a series of bad financial investments. While in prison, the elder Lee writes his Memoirs of the War in the Southern Department of the United States concerning the Southern campaigns of the Revolutionary War. No longer able to afford Stratford Hall, the family moves into a small house in Alexandria.

1816-1818

Robert's much older brother, Charles Carter Lee, goes to Harvard. Meanwhile, Lee's father, dying from his injuries, decides to return to his family. He expired at "Dungeness," the plantation home of American Revolutionary War commander Nathanael Greene, Cumberland Island, Georgia.

1825-1829

Lee's diligent school work leads to an appointment to the United States Military Academy at West Point, becoming a cadet on July 1, 1825. At the time, West Point curriculum included mathematics, engineering, French, tactics, artillery, chemistry, natural philosophy, mineralogy, rhetoric, drawing and moral philosophy. By the time of his senior year, Lee attains the coveted rank of Corps Adjutant. Although he finishes at the top of his class in tactics and artillery, Lee graduates 2nd overall among 46 cadets in the West Point Class of 1829. Even more impressive than his academic record is that during his four years at West Point, he does not earn a single demerit for misconduct. He applies for and is accepted into the Corps of Engineers on July 1, 1829, as a 2nd Lieutenant. Later that month, Robert's mother dies

1831-1846

During his duty stops, among which are Virginia, the Great Lakes, Missouri, Iowa, North Carolina and New York, Lee continues his self-taught study of military history's greatest generals, their campaigns and battles, and all the while gaining a sterling reputation as a remarkably gifted officer and engineer. On September 21, 1836, Lee is promoted the 1st Lieutenant; two summers later, on July 7, 1838, he is promoted to Captain. During this time, Lee accomplishes his greatest engineer feat, "moving" the Mississippi River. and saving the port of Saint Louis. In 1844, Lee is named to serve on the prestigious Board of Visitors for the United States Military Academy at West Point, during which time he works with America's most-famous and influential soldier, Winfield Scott.

1855-1860

Lack of security in the territories and Texas prompts Federal authorities to raise four new regiments for service on the frontier. On March 3, 1855, Lee is promoted to Lieutenant Colonel and second in command of the new 2nd Cavalry. With the promotion, Lee transfers from the staff to the line. Lee arrives at his Camp Cooper, Texas, frontier post in April, 1856. Lee demonstrates many leadership qualities to go with his already famed horsemanship, leading the 2nd Cavalry against hostile American Indians and performing other duties. While on leave in 1859, Lee is called upon to command the troops dispatched to Harpers Ferry to suppress John Brown and his raiders. Lee admirably accomplishes his mission and returns to Texas in 1860 where he leads another expedition to quell Mexican banditos along the Rio Grande. Meanwhile, the sectional crisis intensifies; Lincoln is elected and South Carolina secedes from the Union.

1861

As more states pass ordinances for secession, Lee is ordered to Washington City for a new assignment. Lee arrives in Virginia on March 1st; Lincoln takes office March 4th, and on March 16th, the new President sends through Lee's commission as Colonel in command of the 1st Cavalry. Within a month, Southern guns fire on Fort Sumter, prompting Lincoln to call for 75,000 volunteers to invade the "Cotton States." On April 18th, Lee is offered command of the soon-to-be-forming Federal army around the capital; he declines. The following day, Virginia delegates vote to leave the Union. Lee resigns his commission 15 hours later. Traveling to Richmond on April 22nd, Lee accepts the offer to become Commander-in-Chief of Virginia's military forces. Once these pass into the service of the central government in June, Lee sits idle for the next six weeks. Finally, President Davis sends Lee to western Virginia to coordinate three Confederate "armies" in the area, but does not empower Lee with command authority, a mission that Lee describes as "insane." Confederate defeat at Cheat Mountain, followed by stalemate at Sewell Mountain virtually ends the campaign. While on this assignment, Lee is named as one of five full generals of the Confederacy. Returning to Richmond on October 31st, Lee is soon dispatched by Davis to the southeastern coast, a mission is described by Lee as "another forlorn hope expedition. Worse than West Virginia."

1864-1865

Robert E. Lee and the Army of Northern Virginia are tendered the "Thanks of Congress" on January 8, 1864, "for the great and signal victory they have won over the vast hosts of the enemy and for the inestimable services they have rendered in defense of liberty and independence of our country." Beginning in May, Lee leads the army during the Overland campaign, followed by the Petersburg campaign. On January 31, 1865, Lee is made General-in-Chief of the Confederate armies. In April, the Federals break the siege lines and capture Petersburg and Richmond. Heading westward, Lee is cornered at Appomattox Court House and surrenders the Army of Northern Virginia on April 9th. An oath of amnesty is sworn on October 2nd (the day Lee took office at Washington College) but not acted upon until it was discovered in the National Archives in 1970. A joint resolution by both houses of Congress, dated August 5, 1975, was signed into law by President Gerald R. Ford, Jr., officially granting amnesty for Robert E. Lee 110 years after the end of the war.

0   **1855**   **1860**   **1865**

1848-1855

Returning from the war with Mexico, Lee is assigned to engineering duty in Washington City, and then to Baltimore. While Lee works on the construction of Fort Carroll, he conducts inspection tours from Florida to Rhode Island. In 1852, over his objection, Lee is named Superintendent at West Point, a post he assumes on September 1st. For the next two and one-half years, Lee serves as the Academy's ninth superintendent; it is a confining, sedentary and administratively-laden job in which he finds little pleasure. During this time, Lee intensifies his study of military history and the Great Captains, becoming a member of the "Napoleon Club."

1862

Rapidly deteriorating Confederate fortunes prompt Congress to force President Davis to summon Lee back to Richmond. Lee returns on March 7th, and the House introduces "a bill to create the office of commanding general of the armies of the Confederate States" which Lee is believed to be named. Davis, however, outmaneuvers the Congress and Lee is named as an advisor without authority. For the next two months, Lee works in a Richmond office. On May 31st, army commander Joe Johnston is seriously wounded at Seven Pines. Lee is named the replacement, and on June 1st, assumes command, renaming it The Army of Northern Virginia. Lee begins a reorganization while also formulating a plan to save Richmond from the closeby Federal army. Within a month, Lee launches his Seven Days counter offensive, drives back the Federals and saves Richmond. Further reorganization takes place, after which Lee leads the army to victory at Second Manassas, then crosses the Potomac and conducts the Maryland campaign. Following the capture of Harpers Ferry and the tactical draw at Sharpsburg, Lee returns to Virginia. Needing to complete the restructuring of his inherited army, Lee oversees the "October reorganization." The year closes with Lee repulsing the latest Federal incursion in the Fredericksburg campaign.

1863

Supplies, food and fodder—always lacking in Confederate service—becomes so acute during the early weeks of 1863 that Lee must disperse significant portions of his army just so that the men and animals can survive. Before Lee has the opportunity to reunite his command, the Federals open their spring offensive. Lee recovers from the blue army's opening moves and triumphs at Chancellorsville. The mortal wounding of "Stonewall" Jackson at Chancellorsville prompts Lee to conduct another army reorganization. Shortly thereafter, Lee again transfers the defense of Richmond north of the Potomac which ends with his repulse at Gettysburg. Lee offers to resign army command; Davis refuses to accept. Following a brief maneuver in the fall at Mine Run, the remainder of 1863 is spent in preparing for the inevitable reopening of the campaigning season the following spring.

GENEALOGY,
LEE FAMILY
OF VIRGINIA AND MARYLAND.

COL. RICHARD LEE
1st
Emigrated to Va.
1641
married
ANNA
died
1663

1st Generation

This tree, with its 403 limbs, contains the Genealogy of the Lee Family—
descended from Col. Richard Lee, of Virginia.
Each generation is represented by a distinct branch, and its descendants
by smaller off-shoots.
Where one has died, a broken limb remains as a memento.
The roots represent these antique progenitors, who, being far remote, have
long since passed from memory's page; while the twining vine, in each cir-
cuit around the trunk, marks the time when each generation gave place to
its successor.—An Original Drawing by Mrs. Hattie Mann Marshall, of Amelia County, Virginia.

WASHINGTON AND LEE UNIVERSITY.

"LEE CHAPEL," BENEATH WHICH HE IS BURIED.

COPYRIGHT 1886 BY MRS. H. A. MARSHALL.

"STRATFORD HOUSE," BIRTHPLACE OF GENERAL R. E. LEE.

Selected, Notable Military and Political Relatives of Robert E. Lee

"I do not mean to say that he is not competent, but from what I have seen of him I do not know that he is."
—Robert E. Lee of his distant relative, artillery chief and President Davis confidant, William Nelson Pendleton

Francis Preston Blair, Sr. (1791-1876) US politician, third cousin-in-law, once removed
Francis Preston Blair, Jr. (1821-1875) USA, Major General, third cousin-in-law
Montgomery Blair (1813-1883) US, Postmaster General, third cousin-in-law
John Cabell Breckinridge (1821-1875) US Vice President, CSA, Major General and Secretary of War, grandnephew of Robert Carter Harrison, a granduncle of Lee
Stephen Grover Cleveland (1837-1908) US 22nd and 24th President, third cousin-in-law
Samuel Cooper (1798-1876) CSA ranking General, Adjutant and Inspector General, brother-in-law
George Davis (1820-1896) CS Attorney General, part of the Fitzhugh family relatives
Jefferson Finis Davis (1808-1889) CS President, fourth cousin-in-law
John Buchanan Floyd (1806-1863) US Secretary of War, CSA Brigadier General, first cousin-in law of John C. Breckinridge and part of the Harrison and Lee families
John Brown Gordon (1832-1904) CSA Major General, fifth cousin-in-law
Wade Hampton III (1818-1902) CSA Lieutenant general, first cousin, once removed of John C. Breckinridge and part of the Harrison and Lee families
Benjamin Harrison IV (1833-1901) US 23rd President and USA brevet Brigadier General, first cousin-in-law, four times removed of Lee's great-granduncle
William Henry Harrison (1773-1841) US 9th President, first cousin-in-law, twice removed of Lee's great-granduncle
Patrick Henry (1736-1799) Virginia colonial orator and politician, later Virginia governor, cousin-in-law of the Harrison and Lee families
Eppa Hunton, Sr. (1822-1908) CSA Brig. General, third cousin-in-law, once removed
Thomas Jonathan Jackson (1824-1863) CSA Lieutenant General, distant relative, as he was brother-in-law of Anne Aylett Anderson, a fourth cousin-in-law, once removed, of Lee
Thomas Jefferson (1743-1826) US 3rd President, second cousin-in-law, twice removed
Albert Sidney Johnston (1802-1862) CSA General, first cousin-in-law of John C. Breckinridge and part of the Harrison and Lee families
Joseph Eggleston Johnston (1807-1891) CSA General, first cousin, once removed of Francis Preston, first cousin-in-law of John C. Breckinridge, and therefore part of the Harrison and Lee families
Robert Garlick Hill Kean (1828-1898) CS War Bureau, fourth cousin-in-law, once removed
Fitzhugh Lee, Sr. (1835-1905) CSA Major General, nephew
Henry Lee III (1756-1818) "Light Horse Harry," Revolutionary war officer, later Virginia governor, father
Samuel Philips Lee (1812-1887) USN acting Rear Admiral, third cousin
James Madison, Jr. (1751-1836) US 4th President, first cousin-in-law, twice removed

Opposite: Lee Geneaology Tree
Courtesy Library of Congress

John Marshall (1735-1835)	US Chief Justice, third cousin-in-law, once removed
James Monroe (1758-1831)	US 5th President, second cousin, once removed, of Arthur Alexander Moragn Payne, a third cousin-in-law
Richard Lucien Page (1807-1901)	CSA Brigadier General and CSN Captain, first cousin
William Henry Fitzhugh Payne (1830-1904)	CSA Brigadier General, third cousin-in-law, once removed
William Nelson Pendleton (1809-1883)	CSA Brigadier General, father of a first cousin-in-law
James Knox Polk (1795-1849)	US 11th President, third cousin-in-law of Mary Townsend Polk, and hence part of the Fitzhugh family relatives
Leonidas Polk (1806-1864)	CSA Lieutenant General, fourth cousin of Mary Townsend Polk, and hence part of the Fitzhugh family relatives
George Wythe Randolph (1813-1867)	CS Secretary of War and Brigadier General, further cousin-in-law
Franklin Delano Roosevelt (1858-1919)	US 32nd President, part of the Fitzhugh family relatives
Theodore Roosevelt, Jr. (1858-1919)	US 26th President, part of the Fitzhugh family relatives
Edmund Kirby Smith (1824-1883)	CSA General, fourth cousin-in-law, three times removed
James Ewell Brown Stuart (1833-1864)	CSA Major General, third cousin-in-law, once removed
Richard Taylor II (1826-1879)	CSA Lieutenant General, fourth cousin
Zachary Taylor, Jr. (1784-1850)	US 12th President, third cousin, once removed
Martin Van Buren (1782-1862)	US 8th President, part of the Fitzhugh family relatives
George Washington (1732-1799)	US 1st President, great grandfather-in-law
Frank Wheaton (1833-1903)	USA Brigadier General, nephew-in-law

Additional Lee relatives include five more signers of the Declaration of Independence, several kinsmen who had been Virginia governors or acting governors, plus many ancestors and immediate family who were former members of the House of Burgesses and Virginia state legislators.

Order of Battle:
Confederate Forces in Northwest Virginia,
Late Summer and Fall, 1862

*"If any one had told me that the next time I traveled that road would have been on my present errand,
I should have supposed him insane."*—Robert E. Lee to his wife, describing his mission to northwestern Virginia[1]

On September 8, 1861, General Loring issued General Orders, No. 10 (included in its entirety in Chapter Two of this volume). Within those orders was the long overdue brigading of the Army of the Northwest. The fact that Lee had no official command authority probably explains why it was that the regiments were not sensibly organized as much as a month earlier. Nevertheless, it was probably through Lee's cordial persuasion that Loring finally moved to make the assembled regiments resemble something more like an army.[2]

General Robert E. Lee, advising general
Lieutenant Colonel John Augustine Washington, Aide-de-camp
Captain Walter Herron Taylor, Aide-de-camp

Army of the Northwest
Brigadier General William Wing Loring, commanding
Colonel Cater Stevenson, Assistant Adjutant Ceneral
Major Armistead Lindsay Long, Chief of Artillery
Captain James L. Corley, Chief Quartermaster
Captain R. G. Cole, Chief Commissary
Lieutenant H. M. Mathews, Aide-de-camp
September 8, 1861

FIRST BRIGADE—Brigadier General Henry Rootes Jackson
      12th Georgia Infantry Regiment—Colonel Edward Johnson
      3rd Arkansas Infantry Regiment—Colonel Albert Rust
      31st Virginia Infantry Regiment—Colonel William L. Jackson
      52nd Virginia Infantry Regiment—Colonel John B. Baldwin
      9th Virginia Infantry Battalion—Major George W. Hansborough
      Danville Virginia Artillery—Captain L. M. Shumaker
      Jackson Virginia Cavalry—Major George Jackson

---

[1] Robert E. Lee, Jr., *Recollections and Letters*, Robert E. Lee to His Wife, August 4, 1861, pp. 32-33.
[2] *Official Records*, Series I, vol. 51, part 2 Supplement, "General Orders, No. 10," September 8, 1861, pp. 283-284.

SECOND BRIGADE—Brigadier General Samuel Read Anderson
> 8th Tennessee Infantry Regiment—Colonel A. S. Fulton
> 16th Tennessee Infantry Regiment—Colonel John S. Savage
> 1st Georgia Infantry Regiment—Colonel J. N. Ramsey
> 14th Georgia Infantry Regiment—Colonel A. V. Brumby
> Hampden Virginia Artillery, less one section
> Alexander's Company of Cavalry

THIRD BRIGADE—Brigadier General Daniel Smith Donelson
> 1st Tennessee Infantry Regiment—Colonel George Maney
> 7th Tennessee Infantry Regiment—Colonel Robert Hatton
> 14th Tennessee Infantry Regiment—Colonel W. A. Forbes
> One section, Hampden Virginia Artillery
> Greenbrier Virginia Cavalry

FOURTH BRIGADE—Colonel William Gilham
> 21st Virginia Infantry Regiment—Colonel William Gilham
> 6th North Carolina Infantry Regiment—Colonel Stephen Dill Lee[3]
> 1st Battalion, Confederate States Provisional Army—Major John D. Munford
> Georgia Troup Artillery, less one section

FIFTH BRIGADE—Colonel William B. Taliaferro
> 23rd Virginia Infantry Regiment—Colonel William B. Taliaferro
> 25th Virginia Infantry Regiment—Major A. G. Reger
> 37th Virginia Infantry Regiment—Colonel S. V. Fulkerson
> 44th Virginia Infantry Regiment—Colonel W. C. Scott
> Lee Virginia Artillery
> Rice's Virginia Artillery

SIXTH BRIGADE—Colonel Jesse S. Burks
> 42nd Virginia Infantry Regiment—Colonel Jesse S. Burks
> 48th Virginia Infantry Regiment—Colonel J. A. Campbell
> One squadron of the 9th Virginia Cavalry—Major W. H. F. "Rooney" Lee
> One section, Georgia Troup Artillery

The six brigades were further organized into two *ad-hoc* divisions, with W. W. Loring commanding the so-called "Huntersville Division," and H. R. Jackson commanding the smaller "Montery Division."

"Huntersville Division"—Brigadier General William Wing Loring
> Second Brigade—Brigadier General S. R. Anderson
> Third Brigade—Brigadier General D. S. Donelson
> Fourth Brigade—Colonel William Gilham
> Sixth Brigade—Colonel Jesse S. Burks

"Montery Division"—Brigadier General Henry Rootes Jackson
> First Brigade—Colonel Rust to command Jackson's First Brigade
> Fifth Brigade—Colonel William B. Taliaferro

There seem to be no surviving "parade-states" for these six brigades as of early September, 1861. However, Lindsay Long, the army's chief of artillery, states that Loring's division numbered 6,000 and Jackson's division numbered 5,000.[4]

---

[3] Later the 16th North Carolina Infantry.
[4] Long, *Memoirs of Robert E. Lee,* p. 123.

Army of the Kanahwa
Brigadier General John B. Floyd
Strength as of September 1, 1861
3,500 officers and men present and under arms

Wise's Division
Brigadier General Henry A. Wise
Unknown Strength

Wise Legion
State Volunteers
Militia

Prior to General Lee returning to Richmond, parade-states were taken for Loring's command. Although the editors of the *Official Records* did not indicate the date(s) of the parade-states, the strength returns are described as "for the month of October."

General Robert E. Lee, advising general
Captain Walter Herron Taylor, Aide-de-camp

Army of the Northwest[5]
Brigadier General William Wing Loring, commanding
Parade States "for the month of October, 1861"

	Infantry	Cavalry	Artillery
Anderson's Brigade	1,932	103	63
Donelson's Brigade	2,123	37	---
Gilham's Brigade	1,036	---	65
Jackson's Brigade	1,290	---	74
Taliaferro's Brigade	1,262	---	112
Other commands	1,303	138	---
Total	**8,937**	**278**	**314**

Aggregate officers and other ranks, present and under arms: 9,529

---

[5] *Official Records,* Series I, vol. 5, "Abstract From Returns of the Army of the Northwest...for the month of October, 1861," p. 933.

Fort Pulaski

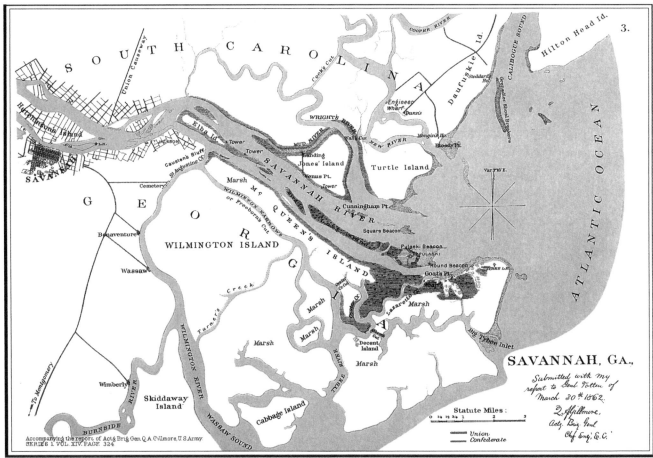

Order of Battle:
Confederate Forces on the Southeastern Coast
under command of General Robert E. Lee
Late 1861-Early 1862

"...Another forlorn hope expedition. Worse than West Virginia."—Robert E. Lee to his daughter, Mildred, describing his assignment from President Jefferson Davis to go to the Southeastern Coast[6]

Department of South Carolina, Georgia and East Florida
General Robert E. Lee, commanding,
from November 5, 1861 to March 5, 1862

Department of Georgia[7]
Brigadier General Alexander Robert Lawton
October, 1861

Stations	Strength Present & Under Arms	Pieces of Ordnance Heavy	Field
South and Big Cumberland Island	122	4	
Fort Pulaski	307	36	
Brunswick, Georgia	138		5
Oglethorpe Barracks	69		6
Genesis Point	41	5	
Great Warsaw Battery	126	5	
Thunderbolt Battery	103	4	
Saint Simon's Island	736	8	
Sapello Island	279	5	
Isle of Hope	52		6
Jekyl Island	382	6	
Sunbury, Georgia	46		
South Newport	73		
Near Darien	72		
Carteret's Point	56		
Camp Lawton (Savannah)	415		
Camp Cumming (Savannah)	69		
Skidaway Island	526		
Tybee Island	950	2	
Camp Wayne, Waynesville	172	8	
Other points	71		
Total	**4,805**	**83**	**17**

---

[6] Robert E. Lee, Jr., *Recollections and Letters*, Robert E. Lee to Mildred, November 15, 1861, p. 47.
[7] *Official Records*, Series I, vol. 6, "Abstract from monthly returns of the Department of Georgia…for October, 1861," pp. 304-305.

State of South Carolina[8]
Governor Francis W. Pickens
November 19, 1861

Command (in alphabetical order)	*Stations*	*Strength*
Boyce's Artillery		124
Citadel Cadets		128
Claremont troops		65
Clingman's Regiment	Grahamville	1,100
Coit's Artillery		132
de Saussure's Brigade	Charleston	2,750
de Saussure's Regiment	Hardeeville	800
Dunovant's Regiment	Pocotalige and Hardeeville	800
Edwards' Regiment	Coosawhatchie	600
Gonzales' Siege Train (four guns)	Haguenin's Neck	80
Hagood's Regiment	Cole's Island	750
Hatch's Battalion	James Island and Bull's Bay	500
Hayward's Regiment	Hardeeville	1,000
Jones' Regiment	Garden's Corner	800
Lafayette Artillery	Fort Pickens (Stone)	60
Lamar's Artillery	Fort Johnson	131
Lucas' Battalion	Fort Pickens (Stone)	70
Martin's Regiment (mounted)	---	650
McCord's Zouaves		92
Moore's Artillery (six guns)	Grahamville	110
Radcliffe's Regiment	Huguenin's Neck	1,000
Regular Artillery	Fort Sumter	500
Regular Infantry	To be kept in Fort Moultrie	420
Vigilant Rifles	Fort Palmetto (Stone)	80
White's Battalion	---	240
State Total		**13,109**

---

[8] *Official Records*, Series I, vol. 6, Francis W. Pickens to Robert E. Lee, November 19, 1861, p. 326.

Department of Middle and Eastern Florida[9]
Brigadier General James Heyward Trapier
December, 1861

Commands	Strength Present and Under Arms		
	Infantry	Cavalry	Artillery
3rd Florida Volunteer Regiment	844		
4th Florida Volunteer Regiment	703		
24th Mississippi Volunteers Regiment	449		
1st Florida Special Battalion	414		
Simmons' Coast guard onboard steamer Gen. Grayson	45		
1st Florida Cavalry		656	
Hopkins' Independent Troop		65	
Owens' Independent Troop		96	
Pickett's Independent Troop		73	
Turner's Independent Troop		94	
Baya's Artillery Company			66
Martin's Light Artillery Battery			63
Totals:	2,455	984	129
Department Total			**3,568**

Department of Middle and Eastern Florida[10]
Brigadier General James Heyward Trapier
January, 1862

Commands	Strength Present and Under Arms		
	Infantry	Cavalry	Artillery
4th Florida Volunteer Regiment	511		
3rd Georgia Volunteers Regiment	579		
24th Mississippi Volunteers Regiment	482		
Bailey's Infantry Company	78		
Evans' Infantry Company	83		
Simmons' Coast guard	45		
1st Florida Special Battalion	349		
1st Florida Cavalry		796	
Hopkins' Independent Troop		79	
Owens' Independent Troop		77	
Pickett's Independent Troop		70	
Turner's Independent Troop		104	
Baya's Artillery Company			32
Martin's Light Artillery Battery			63
Totals:	2,127	1,126	95
Department Total			**3,348**

---

[9] *Official Records*, Series I, vol. 6, "Abstract from monthly report of the Department of Middle and East Florida… for December, 1861," p. 364.

[10] *Official Records*, Series I, vol. 6, "Abstract from monthly report of the Department of Middle and East Florida… for January, 1862," p. 371.

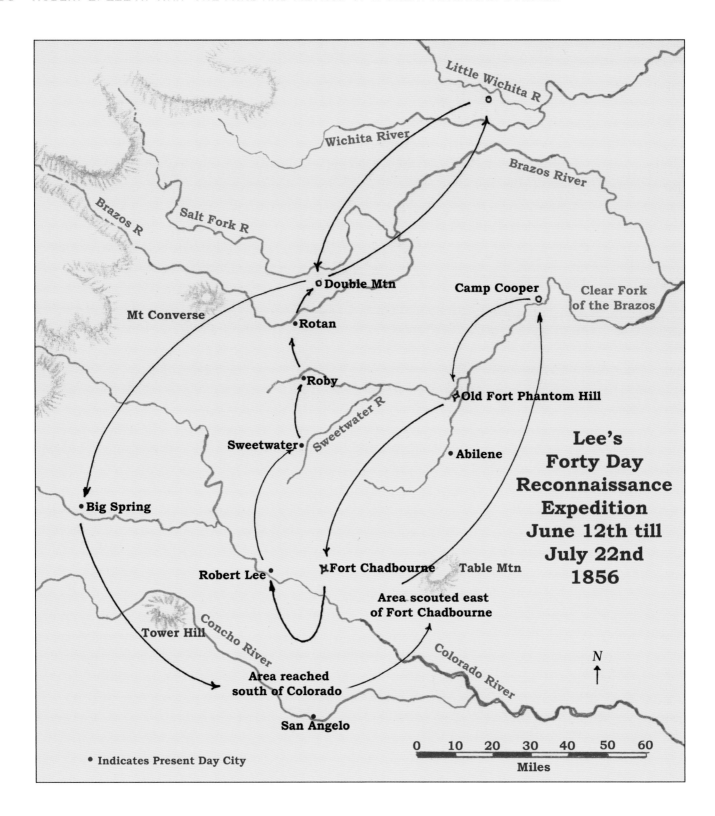

Lee's
Forty Day
Reconnaissance
Expedition
June 12th till
July 22nd
1856

Further Comments on Robert E. Lee, the 2nd Cavalry, Camp Cooper and the 40-Day Reconnaissance Through West Texas

"The sun was fiery hot, the atmosphere here like a blast from a hot air furnace, the water salt. Still my feeling for my country were as ardent, my faith in her future as true, and my hopes for her advancement as under better circumstances."—Robert E. Lee to his wife, describing his thoughts on July 4th, 1856, while leading an expedition against the Indians on the plains of Texas.[1]

On September 27th, 1855, General Orders, No. 5, issued from the Headquarters of the Army in New York referenced the movement of the newly-formed 2nd Cavalry to the state of Texas. Two weeks later, Captain W. B. Blair at department headquarters in San Antonio issued a call for four months of supplies to be dispatched from New Orleans in anticipation of the arrival of the new regiment. The creation and deployment of the new cavalry regiment had begun with a request by Secretary of War Jefferson Davis for additional troops to better protect America's frontier and borders.

About six months earlier, on March 3rd, 1855, Congress had passed a bill creating four new regiments—two cavalry and two infantry. There was no doubt that one regiment of cavalry and at least part of one regiment of infantry would be earmarked for duty in Texas. Backed by friends in the Texas legislature and aided by War Secretary Davis who was an admiring friend, Albert Sidney Johnston (who was a native Kentuckian but considered Texas his home) was appointed commander of the new 2nd Cavalry with the rank of colonel. Robert E. Lee was appointed as second in command with the rank of lieutenant colonel, and William J. Hardee and George H. Thomas were appointed majors. Captains for the new regiment included Earl Van Dorn, Edmund Kirby Smith, George Stoneman and Nathanial G. ("Shanks") Evans.[2]

Special Orders, No. 126, issued on December 4th, 1855, by General Perisfor F. Smith at department headquarters directed that four companies (two squadrons) of the 2nd Cavalry would "take post at or near the Indian Agency in the Comanche reservation" west of the vicinity of Fort Belknap. That fort was the northern-most of those that anchored the Texas frontier, and was located three miles south of present day Newcastle, in Young County, Texas.[3]

Led by its commander, Sidney Johnston, the 2nd Cavalry moved overland from Louisville, Kentucky, to Jefferson Barracks, Missouri, through the Ozarks of southwestern Missouri to Fort Gibson and Fort Washita in the Indian Territory, across the Red River to Fort Belknap, where they arrived two days after Christmas, 1855. Following a few days of rest, the regiment left Belknap and headed west/southwest. Following a march of about 41 miles, four companies under Major William Hardee were detached once they reached "the Clear Fork of the Brazos River." Below a ridge that provided some shelter from the howling northern wind that days later would bring driving sleet and snow, Hardee established Camp Cooper on January 2nd, 1856.[4]

While the remainder of the regiment under Johnston continued moving southward via Fort Chadbourne to Fort Mason, reaching the later destination on January 14th, 1856, the four companies of troopers left at Camp Cooper tried to make the best of a miserable winter. The new camp was across the river from the Indian reservation, and the newly-arrived troopers had only

---

[1] Fitzhugh Lee, *General Lee: A Biography of Robert E. Lee* (New York, 1994 reprint of 1894 original), Robert E. Lee to Mary Custis Lee, Camp Cooper, August 4, 1856, pp. 59-60.

[2] *Documents, 1st Session, 34th Congress,* vol. 1, part 2, p. 3, as cited in Freeman, *R. E. Lee,* vol. 1, p. 349; W. B. Blair to George Gibson, San Antonio, April 5, 1856. Box 406, RG92, *National Archives*; William Preston Johnston, *The Life of General Albert Sidney Johnston: Embracing His Services in the Armies of the Unites States, the Republic of Texas and the Confederate States* (New York, 1878), pp. 183-185.

[3] "Special Orders, No. 126," December 4, 1855, issued by Brevet Major General Persifor F. Smith, Box 406, RG92, *National Archives.*

[4] W. B. Blair to George Gibson, San Antonio, April 5, 1856. Box 406, RG92, *National Archives*; Rister, *Robert E. Lee in Texas,* pp. 14 and 16; Camp Cooper Post returns, January, 1856, Microcopy No. 617, Roll 233, *National Archives.* Colonel Sidney Johnston recorded that prior to the regiment arriving at Belknap, the regiment was overtaken by a "Norther" and suffered winds of "sixty miles an hour, unceasing, unrelenting (the mercury below zero, ice six inches thick), coming suddenly down on the highest tableland of Texas, 2,000 feet above the sea." *Carl Coke Rister Papers,* Research Files, Box 11, Southwest Collection, Texas Tech University, Lubbock, Texas.

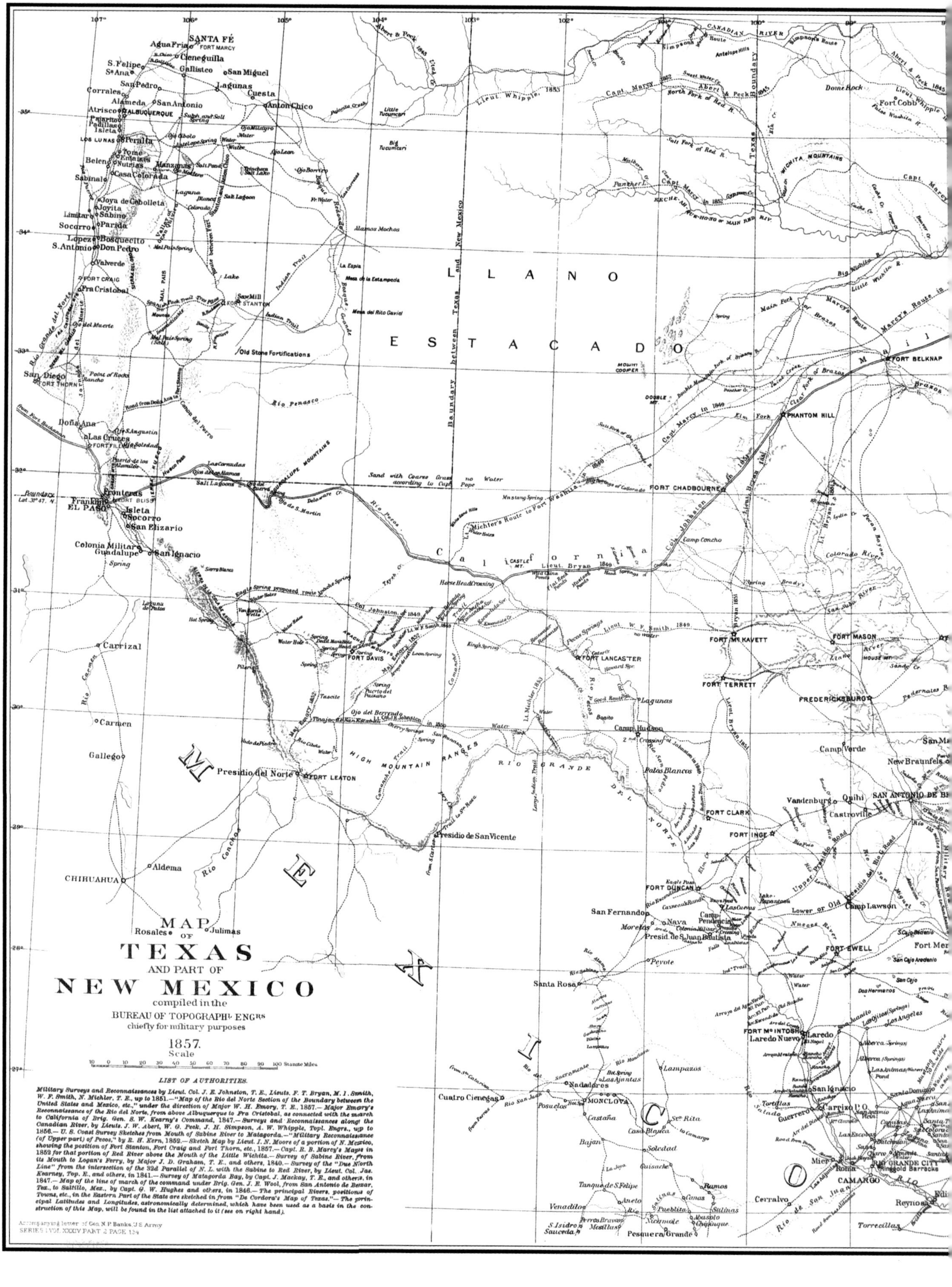

MAP OF TEXAS AND PART OF NEW MEXICO
compiled in the
BUREAU OF TOPOGRAPHL. ENGRS
chiefly for military purposes
1857.
Scale
10 0 10 20 30 40 50 60 70 80 90 100 Statute Miles
LIST OF AUTHORITIES.
Military Surveys and Reconnaissances by Lieut. Col. J. E. Johnston, T. E., Lieuts. F. T. Bryan, M. L. Smith, W. F. Smith, N. Michler, T. E., up to 1851.—"Map of the Rio del Norte Section of the Boundary between the United States and Mexico, etc.," under the direction of Major W. H. Emory, T. E., 1857.— Major Emory's Reconnaissance of the Rio del Norte, from above Albuquerque to Fra Cristobal, as connected with the march to California of Brig. Gen. S. W. Kearny's Command, 1847.— Surveys and Reconnaissances along the Canadian River, by Lieuts. J. W. Abert, W. G. Peck, J. H. Simpson, A. W. Whipple, Topl. Engrs., up to 1856.— U. S. Coast Survey Sketches from Mouth of Sabine River to Matagorda.—"Military Reconnaissance (of Upper part) of Pecos," by R. H. Kern, 1852.— Sketch Map by Lieut. I. N. Moore of a portion of N. Mexico, showing the position of Fort Stanton, Fort Craig and Fort Thorn, etc., 1857.— Capt. R. B. Marcy's Maps in 1852 for that portion of Red River above the Mouth of the Little Wichita.— Survey of Sabine River, from its Mouth to Logan's Ferry, by Major J. D. Graham, T. E., and others, 1840.— Survey of the "Due North Line" from the intersection of the 32d Parallel of N. L. with the Sabine to Red River, by Lieut. Col. Jas. Kearney, Top. E., and others, in 1841.— Survey of Matagorda Bay, by Capt. J. Mackay, T. E., and others, in 1847.— Map of the line of march of the command under Brig. Gen. J. E. Wool, from San Antonio de Bexar, Tex., to Saltillo, Mex., by Capt. G. W. Hughes and others, in 1846.— The principal Rivers, positions of Towns, etc., in the Eastern Part of the State are sketched in from "De Cordova's Map of Texas."— The principal Latitudes and Longitudes, astronomically determined, which have been used as a basis in the construction of this Map, will be found in the list attached to it (see on right hand).
Accompanying letter of Gen N.P. Banks U.S. Army
SERIES I VOL XXXIV PART 2 PAGE 134
LLANO ESTACADO
MEXICO
SANTA FÉ
ALBUQUERQUE
EL PASO
CHIHUAHUA
SAN ANTONIO DE BEXAR
FORT DAVIS
FORT BELKNAP
FORT CHADBOURNE
FREDERICKSBURG
Boundary between Texas and New Mexico
RIO GRANDE DEL NORTE

Far Left: Map of Texas, 1857
Atlas, Official Records

Top: Modern-day image, grounds of
Camp Cooper, looking northward
Middle: Modern-day image, Building at
Camp Cooper
Bottom: Camp Cooper Historical Marker
Author's Collection

tents for shelter while the horses suffered from a lack of any protection from the elements. Exposed for weeks, the splendid mounts were by late March described by Indian agent John R. Baylor as too "poor condition to do anything." Finally, warmer weather arrived in April, and with it, Lieutenant Colonel Robert E. Lee.[5]

Lee had been with the 2nd Cavalry during its initial forming stages, and was at Jefferson Barracks when he received orders for court-martial duty beginning in September, 1855. First traveling to Fort Leavenworth, Kansas for a hearing, then farther west in the same state to Fort Riley, Lee was then directed in January, 1856, to journey to Carlisle Barracks, Pennsylvania. From there he was ordered back to West Point where he had been commandant. After finishing his business along the Hudson, Lee journeyed to Virginia to see his family before starting for Texas. Leaving the Arlington estate on February 12th, 1856, Lee took ship to Indianola on the Texas coast. From there he traveled over roads that were quagmires to San Antonio where he checked into the Plaza Hotel; it had taken Lee 24 days to journey from Arlington to San Antonio. After spending a few days in Bexar where he renewed acquaintances with several officers, Lee purchased some camp chairs, tables and cooking-related items. Striking out for Fort Mason, Lee reached the headquarters of the 2nd Cavalry on March 25th, 1856. After spending a few days with Sidney Johnston and the most of the regiment, Lee departed for Camp Cooper. "Before leaving," wrote historian Carl Coke Rister, "[Lee] nailed to the end-gate of one of his wagons a coop of seven hens, which furnished him eggs for the trip."[6]

* * *

Lee arrived at Camp Cooper on April 9th. Four days later, after meetings with his officers, the local Indian agent and visiting the nearby Comanche reservation across the river, Lee held an inspection of his new command.[7] Like all companies of the 2nd Cavalry, the four stationed at Camp Cooper were recruited from specific geographical areas, and mounted horses selected from the best blooded stock available in Kentucky, Indiana and Ohio. For the purposes of smart appearance and to engender *éspirt de corps*, each company rode horses of a designated color. Company A, recruited from Alabama, was called the "Alabama Grays" since the company horses were gray; Company E was from Missouri and rode sorrels; Company F was recruited from Kentucky and rode bays; and Company K was from Ohio and mounted roans.[8]

Looking over the men, Lee saw that each trooper, as described by Rister:

> was furnished a brass-mounted Campbell saddle with wooden stirrups, or Grimbsby equipment; a spring, moveable stock, or Perry carbine; a Colt navy revolver and dragoon saber, carried by a saber belt and carbine sling; a gutta-percha cartridge box; and a cape or talma, with loose sleeves extending to the knees. He wore pale blue trousers, a close-fitting dark blue jacket trimmed with yellow braid, a silken sash, a black hat with looped "eagle at the right side" with trailing ostrich plumes on the left. On his shoulders he had brass scales to turn saber strokes of the enemy. He wore no boots or gauntlets.[9]

The four company captains at Camp Cooper were all experienced soldiers. Three were West Pointers—Charles J. Whiting (Class of 1835), Earl Van Dorn (Class of 1842) and George Stoneman (Class of 1846)—and the fourth, Theodore O'Hara, while not a West Pointer, was a Mexican War veteran.

Lee immediately set the 2nd Cavalry to task in helping defend the frontier. Texas' vast 237,000 square miles presented an immense challenge to defend, especially the seemingly endless desert plains of West Texas. From the Red River to the Rio Grande there stretched a irregular line of settlements that were "protected" by isolated army posts. At points, the distance between posts was 200 miles. Even with cavalry patrols vigilantly on reconnaissance, such distances, especially when combined with topography of waterless badlands, numerous buttes, hills and canyons, explain why it was likely that Comanche and Kiowa raiding parties could slip undetected past United States troops to raid the settlements.

From his meetings with his superiors prior to arriving at Camp Cooper, as well as with Indian agents and the settled Comanches at the nearby reservation just across the Clear Fork of the Brazos River, Lee gained a grasp of the issues involving and his role within the Federal government's attempt at solving the long-standing Comanche and Kiowa raiding problem on the Texas frontier. The late winter and early spring had brought an increase in Indian activity that had plundered border settlements. As a result, cries for help had poured into the office of Department Commander, Brigadier General Persifor Smith in San Antonio. On May 27th Lee received Special Orders, No. 64 from Don Carlos Buell, Adjutant General of the department. Lee was directed to lead an expedition against the hostiles with two companies (one squadron) from his own

---

[5] John R. Baylor to Mrs. F. N. Belger, March 30, 1856, John R. Baylor Family Papers, Box 2E95, Center for American History, University of Texas, Austin.

[6] Robert E. Lee to Mrs Lee, San Antonio, March 17, 1856. Robert E. Lee Papers, Debutts-Ely Collection, *Library of Congress*; Rister, *Robert E. Lee in Texas*, pp. 16-17 and 38.

[7] Mansfield, in his inspection report of the department, states that Lee's starting date of command was April 15th. See Crimmins, *The Southwestern Historical Quarterly*, "Colonel J. K. F. Mansfield's Report of the Inspection of the Department of Texas in 1856," p. 373.

[8] Simpson, *Simpson Speaks on History* (Hillsboro, 1986), "Thunder on the Frontier: The 2nd U. S. Cavalry in Texas, 1855-1861," p. 104.

[9] Rister, *Robert E. Lee in Texas*, p. 23.

camp, along with two companies (another squadron) detached from Fort Mason. Lee was instructed to rendezvous at or near Fort Chadbourne, about 100 miles distant, then undertake "vigorous operations against certain bands of Indians that have failed to settle upon Reservations provided for them under the control and protection of the government, and are still engaged in depredations upon the settlements."[10]

Consulting with the local Special Agent Robert S. Neighbors about including in the expedition the best guides available— Jim Shaw and his Delaware trailers—Lee made thorough preparations for the reconnaissance. It is not clear if Robert Neighbors, Jim Shaw, or superiors Sidney Johnston of Persifor Smith ever told Lee that at this time of year the tribes of Southern Comanches—that included the Penatekas, the Tanimas, and the Naconies—generally migrated north to join their kinsmen in the usually cooler climate of Kansas, Colorado and Oklahoma for buffalo hunts in the Arkansas River watershed. However, one or more bands often lingered in the Texas badlands to continue marauding, and that tendency, combined with recent Indian raids, demanded that the army put forth some sort of forceful presence.

There was already a prolonged drought and the late spring had proven to be very hot as Lee departed Camp Cooper on June 12th (see Chapter Two for additional details on this reconnaissance). The unusually dry weather had already taken its toll on nature, and as Rister described it, "during better seasons these prairies were covered with grass and flowers, and the whir of wings and the call of quail, plover, curlew, and prairie chicken could be heard; but now, all life stood in silence." Against this backdrop of sun, heat and dryness, the usual springs that in other seasons would offer refreshing water were already dry. After passing west of the vicinity believed to be the 1541 camp made by Spanish explorer Coronado while en route from modern-day New Mexico to find the fabled Indian villages of "Quivira," Lee effected the rendezvous at Fort Chadbourne with the two companies coming from Fort Mason. Heading the united column southward towards the Colorado River, Lee soon received word from his scouts that the prairies beyond the Colorado to be on fire. Once Lee arrived at the river, he crossed over to the south bank and continued his march southward another 20 miles in order to give the Delaware trackers time to reconnoiter to the south/southwest. They returned with word that they had "found several camp sites and trails, evidently made the previous spring by parties of Yamparikas (Northern Comanches) on their way southward to raid Mexican settlements. But there were no signs of recent occupation."[11]

With no hostiles in the vicinity, Lee decided to head to the region of the upper Colorado, an area long controlled by the Comanche and Kiowa warriors. Redirecting his command, Lee led the expedition back towards the Colorado River, camping one night at the confluence of Mountain Creek and the Colorado near present day Robert Lee. Following the Colorado northwestward into present-day Mitchell County, crossing the ground now covered by Lake Champion that was once the site of "seven wells" where normally free-flowing, converging creeks came from the artesian wells. Certainly, there was plenty of evidence that great herds of Buffalo had been attracted to the springs, as at least four trails crisscrossed the area, cutting deep tracks into the soft sandstone. Lee had heard the Delaware scouts tell tales of how, for hundreds of years, Indians had camped in the area of the "seven wells" while hunting bison. However, the season was too hot and the area too dry for buffalo, and they had already migrated north.

With the vicinity clear of hostiles, Lee led the column northeastward, then north, passing west of present day Sweetwater, Roby and Rotan. By the time the command crossed the Double Mountain Fork of the Brazos River, many of the troopers were suffering from diarrhea and dysentery—the consequences of having to drink brackish or bitter water from stagnant pools. The country was so dry that most of the game had abandoned the eroded hills and gulleys, with only the night bringing forth any evidence of wildlife. Making camp at the southern base of the flat-top buttes known as Double Mountain in present-day Stonewall County, Lee spent the next three nights and two days thoroughly exploring what Rister described as "the breaks, draws and canyons, for twenty to thirty miles north, south, and west of the twin peaks."

When scouts reported that "they had discovered a fresh trail of a small Indian band," Lee decided to split his command. Dispatching Earl Van Dorn with two companies (one squadron) on a southward trek to investigate, Van Dorn encountered a small group of Yamparika Comanches, killed two warriors, captured a woman and 12 horses. Meanwhile, Lee had led the other two companies (one squadron) northward until they reached the Little Wichita River, where plenty of fresh water was found but no hostiles. Retracing steps to Double Mountain, then to the Clear Fork of the Brazos, Lee and his command rendezvoused with Van Dorn and his troopers. The news of Van Dorn's success served to revive spirits that had been beaten down by a combination of the Texas heat and no meaningful action. The expedition camped somewhere east of present-day Roby on July 4th, and later, back at Camp Cooper, Lee recalled in a letter to his wife the challenges of the expedition. Despite tiring weeks in the saddle while trying to find the Indians, and despite the rainless days of 100+ degree temperatures in which the air coming off the plains like a blast from a hot-air furnace, Lee wrote that his "feelings for my country were as ardent, my faith in her future as true, and my hopes for her advancement as unabated as if felt under more propitious circumstances."[12]

With many troopers still sick and a number of horses in poor condition, Lee decided to send the weak home. Selecting

---

[10] "Special Orders, No. 64," May 27, 1856, issued to Robert E. Lee, Camp Cooper, Texas. Adjutant General's Office, Orders and Special Orders, Department of Texas, 1856, Volume 517, RG94, *National Archives*. Persifor Smith held the rank of brigadier general, and was a brevet major general.

[11] Rister, *Robert E. Lee in Texas*, p. 44.

[12] Rister, *Robert E. Lee in Texas*, p. 47; Fitzhugh Lee, *General Lee,* Robert E. Lee to Mary Custis Lee, Camp Cooper, August 4, 1856, pp. 59-60.

Lieutenant Walter H. Jenifer and 27 troopers, plus the sick able to ride, and placing them on the feebler horses, Lee had these act as escort for the wagons and directed them to move down the Concho River. With the rest of the men, Lee rode south as well. Passing Big Spring, Lee then directed his troopers to work their way down the Concho and the Colorado, Lee leading the company that scouted the right bank of the latter river. Seven days later, only abandoned camp sites had been found and Lee decided that the hostiles had indeed migrated northward and that it was time to head home. After giving instructions to the two companies from Fort Mason on the march routes each was to take in searching for hostiles on their return trip and to pursue them if they were found, Lee crossed the Colorado below Valley Creek, passed east of Fort Chadbourne, made for the headwaters of Pecan Bayou, and then northward to home.[13]

On July 22nd, Robert E. Lee and his column arrived back at Camp Cooper; the grueling 40-day odyssey was over. When Lee found out that the father and mother of the woman taken captive by Van Dorn lived in the Comanche reservation just across the Brazos, he reunited the family "without delay."[14]

---

[13] Rister, *Robert E. Lee in Texas*, pp. 50-52.

[14] Rister, *Robert E. Lee in Texas*, p. 52. For additional details concerning Camp Cooper, the 2nd Cavalry, and Lee's expedition against the Comanche, please see: Freeman, *R. E. Lee*, vol. 1, pp. 363-364; Thomas, *Robert E. Lee: A Biography*, pp. 165-166; Dowdey, *Lee*, p. 107; Maurine Whorton Redway, *Marks of Lee on Our Land* (San Antonio, 1972), p. 54; Carl Coke Rister, *Robert E. Lee in Texas*, pp. 19-52; James R. Arnold, *Jeff Davis' Own*, pp. 78-91; Colonel M. L. Crimmins, "Colonel Robert E. Lee's Report on Indian Combat in Texas," *Southwestern Historical Quarterly*, vol. 39, no. 1 (July 1935), pp. 23-24 and 54-55; Harold B. Simpson, "Lee West of the River," and "Thunder on the Frontier: The 2nd U. S. Cavalry in Texas, 1855-1861," *Simpson Speaks on History*, pp. 94 and 104; Frances Mayhugh Holden, *Lambshead Before Interwoven*, pp. 50-54; Joan Farmer and Lawrence Clayton, *Tracks Along the Clear Fork*, pp. 82-90; Herbert M. Hart, *Old Forts of the Southwest*, pp. 41-44; unpublished article titled "Camp Cooper: 1856-1861," by Martha Doty Freeman; unpublished manuscript titled "A History of Camp Cooper, Throckmorton County, Texas," by Martha Doty Freeman, for Aztec of Albany Foundation, Inc., Albany, Texas, October, 1996.

As mentioned previously, each company of the 2nd Cavalry was raised from a specific geographic area and rode specific colored horses. The four companies under Lee's command at Camp Cooper were: Company A, consisting of troopers from the state of Alabama and rode grays; Company E, made up of troopers raised from Missouri and rode sorrels; Company F, comprised of troopers raised from Kentucky and rode bays; and Company K, consisting of troopers raised from Ohio, and rode roans. The two companies from Fort Mason that joined Lee for the 40-day reconnaissance mission were Company B, consisting of troopers from Virginia and rode sorrels, along with Company G, recruited nation-wide and rode browns.

In the Comanche country expedition that began on June 12th, 1856, Lee pushed his command an average of more than 27 miles a day—a total of 1,100 miles, which was a remarkable achievement given the barren nature of the Texas terrain combined with the brutally-hot weather. Some accounts state that all the columns comprising this expedition collectively traveled an astounding 1,600 miles during this grueling 40-day expedition, and all done under conditions described by Robert E. Lee as: "The weather was intensely hot, and as we had no tents we had the full benefit of the sun…the water was scarce and bad, salt, bitter and brackish."

The horses of the 2nd Cavalry were known to have been superior animals, selectively purchased by a special team of officers "authorized to buy the best blooded stock available" from Kentucky, Indiana and Ohio. During the six years that the 2nd Cavalry was on the Texas frontier, "most of these horses were still serviceable" when the regiment was ordered to the East for the beginning of the Civil War. The animals that had not been able to stand the Texas climate had been replaced with Texas stock. Even with this impressive service record by the four-legged warriors of the regiment, the claim by some that Lee pushed his men and horses during the Comanche country expedition across West Texas a total of 1,600 miles over a consecutive 40-day period of time during the summer where "the water was scarce and bad," can only be described as a feat bordering on the near-unbelievable.

J. K. F. Mansfield's Inspection Report of Camp Cooper, Texas, July 31st through August 3rd, 1856

"The post is very well commanded by Col. Lee & in good discipline."
—Colonel J. K. F. Mansfield[1]

This post was under the command of Lieutenant Colonel Robert Edward Lee of the 2nd Cavalry with two companies of the 2nd Cavalry [then present] and two companies of 1st Infantry, as follows:

Field & Staff. Lt. Colonel Robert E. Lee with a citizen physician Dr. John G. Gaenslen.

Company E, 2nd Cavalry. Captain George Stoneman; 1st Lt. Robert N. Eagle; 2nd Lt. J. F. Minton absent with leave for 30 days from 17th July 1856—two Sergeants, three Corporals, one bugler, one farrier, 24 privates for duty—eight on extra duty—eight sick—two confined—two absent sick. Total at command: two officers, 49 men and 59 horses.

Company K, 2nd Cavalry. Captain Charles J. Whiting; 1st Lt. Charles Radzminski; 2nd Lt. William W. Lowe acting Adjutant Post and Quartermaster and Commissary—four Sergeants, three Corporals, one bugler, 30 privates for duty—eight on extra duty—six sick—two confined—two absent sick. Total at command: three officers, 54 men and 50 horses.

Company A, 1st Infantry. Captain J. N. Caldwell; 1st Lt. E. D. Stockton on duty at Military Academy since 7 January 1852; 2nd Lt. George McGaw Dick died on 31st July—three Sergeants, one Corporal, two musicians, 20 privates for duty—four on extra duty—three sick—one detached—one absent with leave. Total at command: one officer and 34 men.

Company I, 1st Infantry. Captain J. H. King on leave for eight months, since 14th January, 1856; 1st Lt. S. B. Holabird detached at headquarters, 1st Infantry, since 1st July 1852 as Regimental Quartermaster; 2nd Lt. E. D. Phillips in command of company—three Sergeants, four Corporals, two musicians, 20 privates for duty—three on extra duty—four sick—one detached—one absent sick. Total at command: one officer and 37 men.

Aggregate at Camp Cooper: eight officers and 174 men [and 109 horses].

Company E, 2nd Cavalry, was in tents, both officers and men, and horses at picket rope, no stables for them—a good farrier and [black]smith, caps of different patterns and some with plumes—deficiency of canteens, haversacks, and sword knots. The curb straps to the bridle inefficient and unequal to the object of them.—Wipers of the rifled musketoon can not be used on the swivel ramrods for want of space and evidently an oversight in the manufacture by the Ordnance Department.—The ages of the horses are from four to six years; should be from six to eight years for service—only two sizes of saddles and the girths not considered as safe as the Mexican style without buckles.—Curry combs with whole iron backs considered the best—horses grazed and well groomed—one laundress—books in good order—37 desertions at Jefferson Barracks in 1855 and three in 1856—deficient in clothing of all kinds, and the size of boots and shoes most wanted are 7, 8, 9, and 10.—Company property and ordnance in tents—discipline good. Attached to this company are 48 rifled musketoons, five rifles, five pistols, 85 Colt pistols, 79 sabers, with ample ammunition and a wagon and a four-mule team in good order. I condemned to be dropped three canteens and seven haversacks.

Company K, 2nd Cavalry, like Company E, in tents, both officers and men, and in all respects especially like Company E, except desertions 37 at Jefferson Barracks in 1855 and none in 1856. Attached to this company are 84 sabers, 80 Colt revolvers, five rifles, 42 rifled carbines, and ample ammunition, and a wagon and four-mule team.

Company A, 1st Infantry. In tents, both officers and men—in excellent order—no non-commissioned officer swords—books in order, company property and ordnance in tents—three laundresses—12 desertions in 1855, and five in 1856—discipline good. Attached to this company are 66 muskets with Maynard primer which do not always discharge the gun at the first blow

---

[1] Crimmins, *The Southwestern Historical Quarterly*, "Colonel J. K. F. Mansfield's Report of the Inspection of the Department of Texas in 1856," p. 373.

POST RETURN of a Detachment of the 2d Cavalry Stationed at Camp Cooper, Texas, &command

[In filling up the return the mode observed in the Model

ENLISTED MEN, reported on the line "Temporarily at the Post," (see the *Model Post Return*) accounted for by NAME.

NOTE.—The *Ordnance Sergeant* will be also accounted for by name, and be placed at the head of the list.—See G. O. No. 47, (A. G. O.) of 1849.

No.	NAMES.	Rank.	Regiment.	Letter of Company.	When received at the Post.	Transferred, Discharged, Died or Deserted. When.	To what station, and how.	REMARKS.
1	Jacob Miller	Private	2d Cav.	"H"	Apl. 14/56			Left sick at Post, awaiting opportunity to join Co
2	Henry Johnson			"C"	May 5/56			

Top and Right: Post Returns from May, 1856
Courtesy National Archives

Left: Modern-day image, Camp Cooper Grounds
Author's Collection

by _____ *Bvt. Colo: & Lieut Colo R. E. Lee* _____ for the month of _____ *May* _____, 185*6*.

[*return distributed in April, 1850, will be strictly followed.*]

		PRESENT AND ABSENT. (See note 5 of "Remarks.")			ALTERATIONS SINCE LAST RETURN.					MEMORANDA.				
					JOINED.	DETACHED Discharg'd	DIED.				HORSES.				
Commissioned Officers	Enlisted Men.	Aggregate.	Aggregate, last month (at the post.)	Commissioned Officers.	Enlisted Men.	Commissioned Officers.	Enlisted Men.	Killed in action, or from wounds rec'd in action.	From disease, &c.	Deserted.	No. of recruits required.	Wounded in action.	Serviceable.	Unserviceable.	No. of blank return on hand.
1		1	1				1								
3	54	57	60		1		1			3	31		56	3	
3	53	56	57								32		58	5	
3	65	68	71				3				20		63	32	
3	56	59	59								29		27 26	28	
13	228	241	248		1		4		1	3	112				

OFFICIAL COMMUNICATIONS RECEIVED DURING THE MONTH.

[See the Regulations (paragraph 905) as to the mode of obtaining missing orders.]

Description of communication.	No. of order.	Date

of the hammer.—Ample ammunition—brass scales of the men decidedly objectionable.

Company I, 1st Infantry, in tents, both officers and men.—Caps old.—Company property and ammunition in tents but in good order—three laundresses—books in good order—discipline good—eight desertions in 1855, and one in 1856. Attached to this company are 64 muskets, 11 rifles, 12 Colt pistols, and ample ammunition.

Drills. The cavalry companies had not yet completed the platoon drill, and no squadron drill was had. But both companies drilled at the platoon extremely well as far as they had progressed.—Company E [from Missouri] was a little in advance of Company K [from Ohio]. The officers of both companies were ambitious to advance their companies.

The infantry companies were too small for a battalion drill, and the two made one company and went through the heavy infantry company drill very well, first by Captain Caldwell, and afterward by Lieutenant Phillips.

Quarter Master. And here I must remark again on the brass scales, that in going through the motions of firing 30 out of 36 were displaced. Three companies did not know the new drill as skirmishers.

Target firing was at a target at 100 yards.—Cavalry Company E made one-quarter and K made one-third; and infantry Company A made one-sixth and Company I made one-third—each man firing independently at will twice.

Hospital and supplies were in tents.—Dr. Gaenslen in charge.—He was sent to this department by the Surgeon General. Much sickness of scurvy and dysentery; nine in hospital, and Lieutenant Dick just dead.—Supplies good and ample.

Guard in tents 13 strong; six prisoners.

Bakery a tent and good bread.

Quartermasters Department is managed temporarily by Lieutenant Lowe in place of Lieutenant Minton. All returns and accounts forwarded to the close of June, 1856, and correctly kept. There was on hand 30th June $2,178.44; dispersed since $189.90; balance on hand $2,010.40, of which $2,000 is in Assistant Treasury at New Orleans. He employs one citizen as guide at $40, and a ration and forage for a horse.—And as extra duty men, one clerk, six teamsters, four express men—six wagons, 60 mules, one spring wagon. Hay is had at $20 the ton; but this year it is doubtful if it can be obtained at all, on account of the dry season. Corn at $2.50 the bushel—a very high price, but none is raised in this quarter this year. Grazing not very good in consequence of the vicinity of the Comanches who keep a great many ponies and mules. Wood at hand but a deficiency of boards for coffins and clothing for men.

Commissary Department is also in the hands of Lieutenant Lowe, and well conducted. Accounts and returns to the 30th June properly forwarded. On hand 30th June $1,137.88, expended since $275.54—balance on hand $862.34 in cash. Supplies all good and ample, and come generally from San Antonio—fresh beef is had at 06.7 cents the pound, and flour comes from Texas via Fort Belknap, and is excellent. He keeps in his employ as extra duty men one Commissary Sergeant and an assistant and supplies are all in store houses of canvas.

This post was established 2nd January 1856 by [Major] Hardee, 2nd Cavalry, and [Lieutenant] Colonel R. E. Lee from the 15th April to 13th June 1856. Captain Stoneman, 2nd Cavalry, in command from 13th June to 12th July 1856.—Captain Caldwell from 12th July to 23rd July, and [Lt.] Col. Lee again from 23rd July to date.

The post is very well commanded by [Lt.] Colonel Lee, and in good discipline. It labors under the disadvantages of being in an open camp in winter, and poor water in summer and dry seasons which cut off crops of summer vegetables. It is 40 miles from Fort Belknap on the Comanche reservation. As soon as these Indians get settled down in houses and permanently established, these troops might be better located, say at Fort Belknap, where there are accommodations.

There are at this post 900 Sharps carbines, 1,000 Halls carbines, 8,150 rifled musketoons, 1,160 rifles, 18,970 Colt pistol cartridges, etc., etc.

Indians. The Indians in this region are the Wild Comanches, but recently brought by the Agent onto this reservation on the Clear Fork of the Brazos. They number 500 souls, and at present friendly and promise to remain under the Agent, Captain John R. Baylor, who resides among them.

Colonel James K. F. Mansfield,[2]
Inspector General

---

[2] Crimmins, *The Southwestern Historical Quarterly*, "Colonel J. K. F. Mansfield's Report of the Inspection of the Department of Texas in 1856," pp. 369-373.

APPENDIX G
★ ★ ★ ★ ★

1860 Population Distribution of the Eleven Future Confederate States

	WHITE	SLAVE	FREE BLACK*	TOTAL
ALABAMA	526,271 (54.6%)	435,080 (45.1%)	2,690 (0.3%)	964,041
ARKANSAS	324,143 (74.4%)	111,115 (25.5%)	144 (0.1%)	435,402
FLORIDA	77,747 (55.4%)	61,745 (44.0%)	932 (0.7%)	140,424
GEORGIA	591,550 (56.0%)	462,198 (43.7%)	3,500 (0.3%)	1,057,248
LOUISIANA	357,456 (50.5%)	331,726 (46.9%)	18,647 (2.6%)	707,829
MISSISSIPPI	353,899 (44.7%)	436,631 (55.2%)	773 (0.1%)	791,303
NORTH CAROLINA	629,942 (63.5%)	331,059 (33.4%)	30,463 (3.1%)	991,464
SOUTH CAROLINA	291,300 (41.4%)	402,406 (57.2%)	9,914 (1.4%)	703,620
TENNESSEE	826,722 (74.5%)	275,719 (24.9%)	7,300 (0.7%)	1,109,741
TEXAS	420,891 (69.7%)	182,566 (30.2%)	355 (0.1%)	603,812
VIRGINIA	1,047,299 (65.6%)	490,865 (30.8%)	58,042 (3.6%)	1,596,206
TOTAL	5,447,220 (59.9%)	3,521,110 (38.7%)	132,760 (1.5%)	9,101,090

*Includes all free persons of African descent.

SOURCE: U.S. Census Office, Eighth Census (1860), *Population*, Washington, D.C., 1864

Summit Fort

Kimball

Red Run

Cheat River

APPENDIX H
★ ★ ★ ★ ★

Cheat Mountain Map Study

6:00 A.M.	Initial Positions
7:00 A.M.	Rust Captures Wagon Train
8:00 A.M.	Rust Skirmishes with Brooks
8:30 A.M	Brooks Pursues Rust; Jackson Advances Forward
9:00 A.M.	Anderson Maneuvers Across Turnpike
10:00 A.M.	Higgins Approaches Anderson
10:15 A.M.	Higgins Skirmishes with 1TN; Coons Returns
10:30 A.M.	Coons and Higgins Attack Anderson
11:00 A.M.	Anderson in Trouble
12:00 P.M.	Anderson Withdraws

12th September Camp Elkwater
10:30 A.M.   Donelson Moves on Camp Elkwater

13th September Camp Elkwater
Morning of September 13th   Colonel Washington Killed

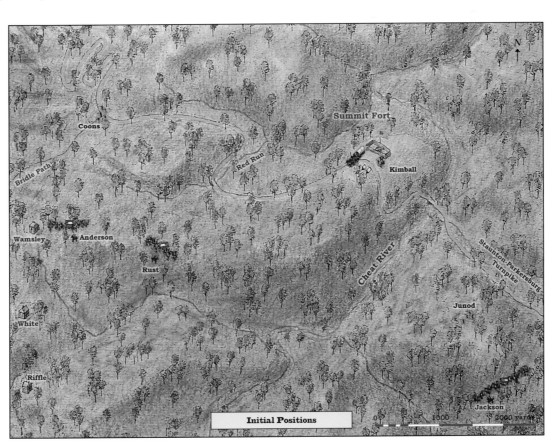

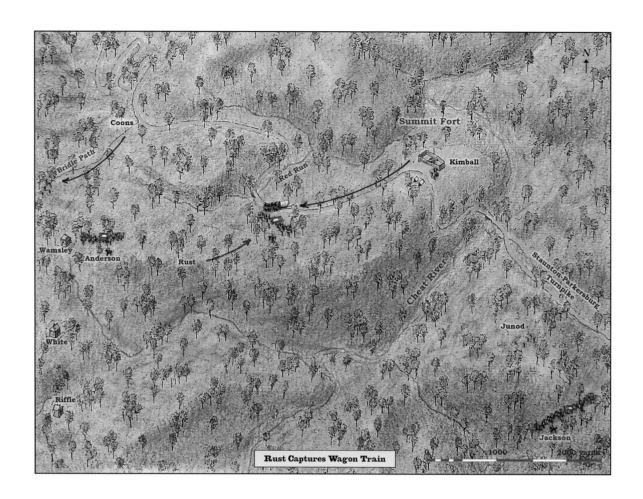

Rust Captures Wagon Train

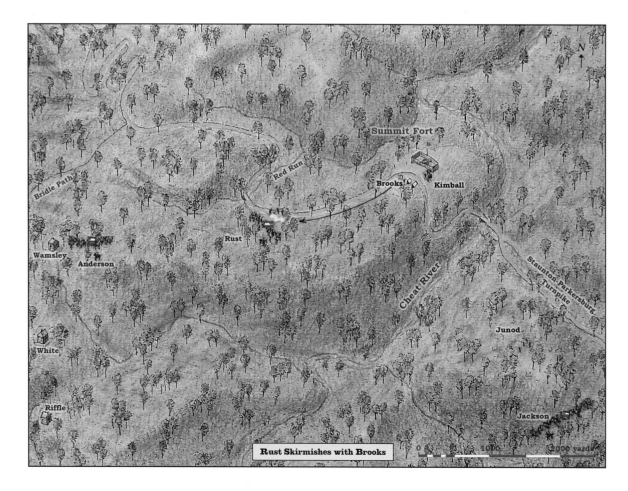

Rust Skirmishes with Brooks

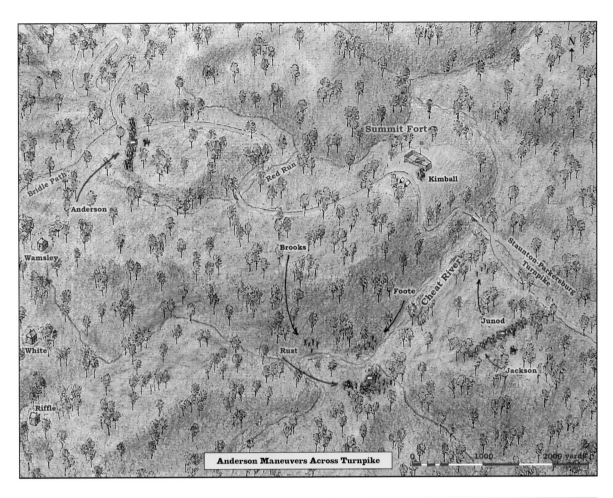

Anderson Maneuvers Across Turnpike

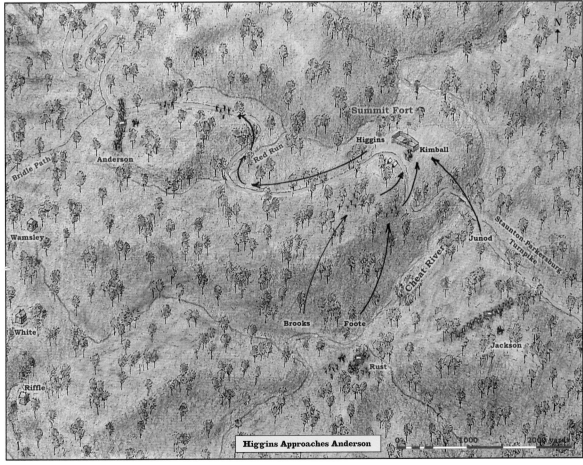

Higgins Approaches Anderson

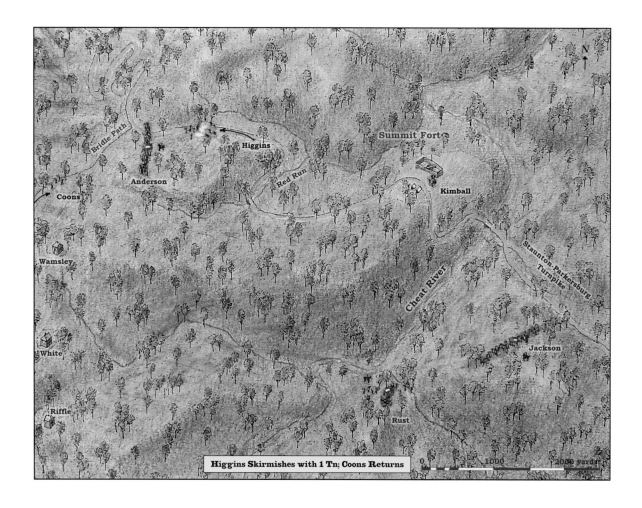

Higgins Skirmishes with 1 Tn; Coons Returns

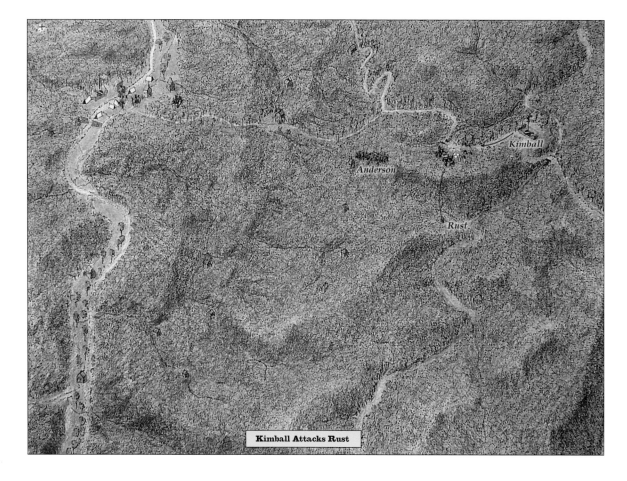

Kimball Attacks Rust

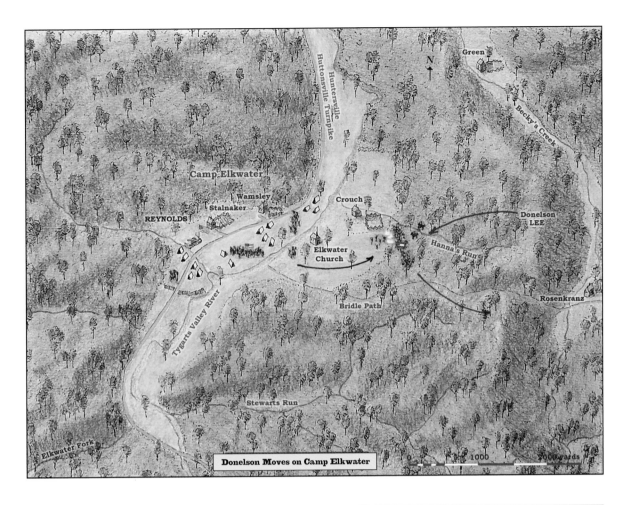

Donelson Moves on Camp Elkwater

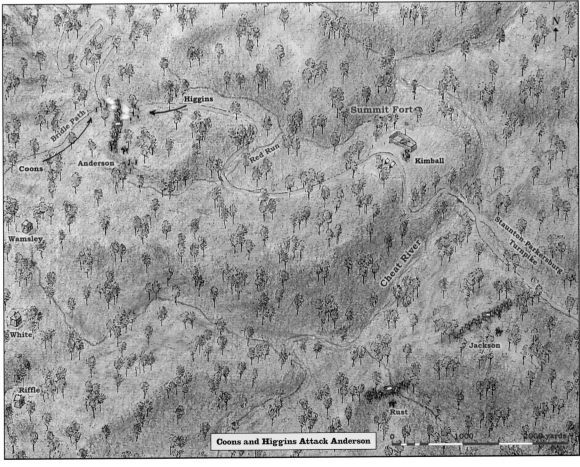

Coons and Higgins Attack Anderson

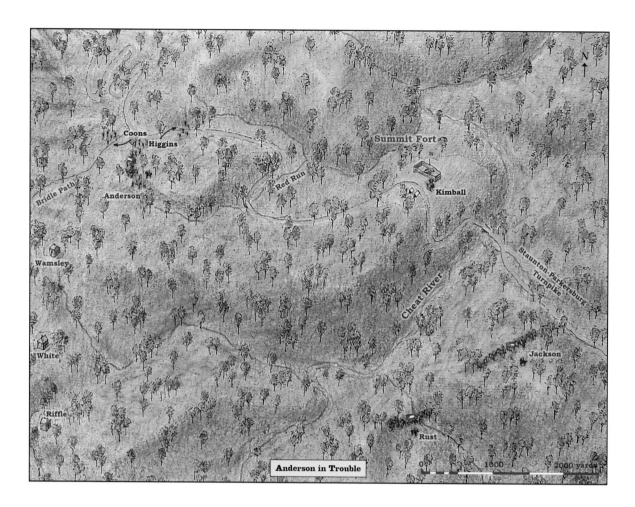

Anderson in Trouble

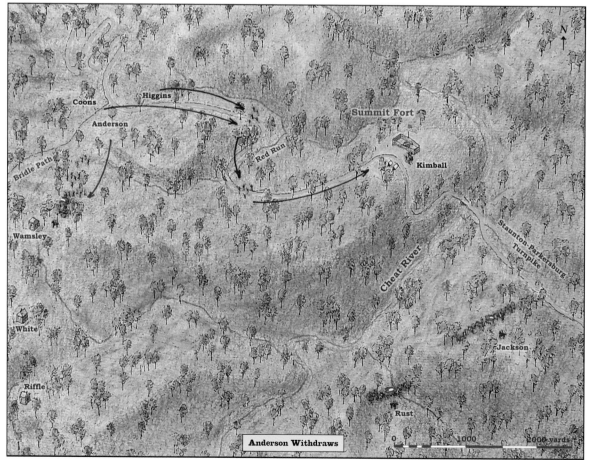

Anderson Withdraws

Area in Which Colonel Washington Meets his Fate